Internet of Things from Scratch

Build IoT solutions for Industry 4.0 with ESP32, Raspberry Pi, and AWS

Renaldi Gondosubroto

Internet of Things from Scratch

Copyright © 2024 Packt Publishing

Group Product Manager: Preet Ahuja

Publishing Product Manager: Surbhi Suman

Book Project Manager: Ashwin Dinesh Kharwa

Senior Editor: Mohd Hammad

Technical Editor: Irfa Ansari

Copy Editor: Safis Editing

Proofreader: Safis Editing

Indexer: Subalakshmi Govindhan

Production Designer: Vijay Kamble

DevRel Marketing Coordinator: Rohan Dobhal

First published: February 2024

Production reference: 1190124

Published by Packt Publishing Ltd.

Grosvenor House

11 St Paul's Square

Birmingham

B3 1RB, UK

ISBN 978-1-83763-854-3

www.packtpub.com

Contributors

About the author

Renaldi Gondosubroto is an accomplished software engineer and developer advocate in the tech community. With a wealth of experience in developing proprietary and open-source solutions, he has made significant contributions to numerous organizations and communities. Currently, he holds all 12 AWS certifications, along with 20 Microsoft Azure certifications. He has a Bachelor of Science in Computing and Software Systems from the University of Melbourne and a Master of Science in Computer Science from Columbia University. Outside of the industry, he is active in the academic community, with his research focused on IoT and Artificial Intelligence. Having spoken at over 40 events, conferences, and workshops, he has been an international speaker for the past six years, sharing his experiences and projects. He aims to build open-source solutions and deliver content that can help people achieve more value in what they do and promote best practices for practitioners.

About the reviewers

Jun Wen, the founder of *AI Discovery Academy*, is a highly accomplished expert in the wireless, IoT, and AI domains. He has had a successful career spanning over 20 years in the fields of 4G/LTE, 5G, Wi-Fi, LoRaWAN, industrial IoT, and robotics. Jun has held senior product lead positions at Fortune 500 companies such as Amazon, Cisco, and Motorola. He holds a master of science degree from Brown University and is an AWS Certified Solutions Architect – Professional. Jun is passionate about crafting IoT innovations using Arduino, Raspberry Pi, RISC-V, and the AWS cloud. In his new career chapter at AI Discovery Academy, he is dedicated to course instruction for students, allowing them to learn and practice AI through a series of interesting engineering projects.

Dheerendra Panwar is a seasoned professional in the field of IoT, with over 10 years of experience. He earned his master's degree in embedded electrical and computer systems from San Francisco State University, further fortifying his expertise in the domain. Throughout his career, he has contributed significantly to various IoT projects, ranging from manufacturing and smart cities to the retail and energy sectors. Having worked at both large organizations and start-ups, he possesses a comprehensive understanding of the intricacies of IoT/edge technologies and their practical applications.

Table of Contents

2

Understanding and Designing IoT Networks   39

3

Integrating Application Protocols   69

4

Examining Communication and Connectivity Technologies   99

Part 2: Developing and Optimizing IoT Systems for Smart Environments

5

Realizing Wireless Sensor Networks within Smart Spaces   125

6

Creating Applications on the Edge   147

7

Working with Cloud Computing to Power IoT Solutions   171

8

Designing for Interoperability   199

Part 3: Operating, Maintaining, and Securing IoT Networks

9

Operating and Monitoring IoT Networks   227

10

Working with Data and Analytics   249

11

Examining Security and Privacy in IoT   269

12

Exploring and Innovating with Open Source IoT   297

xii Table of Contents

Part 4: Delving into Complex Systems and the Future of IoT

13

Developing IoT Solutions for Digital Transformation within Industry 4.0   315

14

Architecting Complex, Holistic IoT Environments   357

15

Looking Ahead into the Future of IoT   379

Preface

Greetings, fellow tech enthusiast! The **Internet of Things (IoT)** is rapidly reshaping the way we perceive and interact with our environment. From the convenience of our homes to the hustle of modern industries, the convergence of the physical and digital is bringing forth innovations that seemed futuristic not so long ago. This book is your comprehensive guide to navigating this dynamic landscape, broken down into four pivotal sections.

In *Part One*, we embark on an introductory journey, covering the foundational aspects of IoT. We explore the core architecture and real-life applications, delve deep into designing IoT networks, and study communication and connectivity technologies.

Part Two thrusts us into the world of smart environments. Here, we dissect wireless sensor networks, the marvels of edge computing, cloud-integrated IoT solutions, and the quintessential aspect of system interoperability.

In *Part Three*, the spotlight turns to the operational heart of IoT. From the meticulous nuances of monitoring IoT networks to harnessing data analytics, ensuring robust security and privacy, and pushing the boundaries with open source IoT, this section prepares you for the challenges and solutions to maintain and safeguard IoT networks.

Finally, *Part Four* catapults us toward the future, discussing the role of IoT in the digital transformation of Industry 4.0 and the intricacies of architecting complex IoT environments, and offering a contemplative look into what the future holds.

Drawing from my extensive experience, including innovative projects such as the GReS Envimo and the wireless, image machine-learning remote-controlled car, as well as insights from industry stalwarts, this book is packed with practical knowledge. It combines my hands-on projects with insights from current IoT deployments in the industry.

Who this book is for

This book caters to a broad spectrum, from beginner-level electronics engineers to seasoned IoT developers eager to deepen their insights. If you're an embedded systems engineer, student, cloud enthusiast, or application developer aspiring to foray into the world of industry-based IoT applications, you're in for a treat. While no prior knowledge of IoT is necessary, a basic familiarity with one or two programming languages will be advantageous. Throughout these pages, you'll gain the knowledge, tools, and confidence to innovate and lead in the IoT domain. Dive in and let the journey begin!

What this book covers

Chapter 1, An Introduction to IoT Architecture, Hardware, and Real-Life Applications, introduces you to the big picture of IoT, discussing everyday use cases of it and the mindset that is needed to grasp the topics fully and effectively in the book.

Chapter 2, Understanding and Designing IoT Networks, discusses the common network technologies that have been used to deploy IoT networks, including 3G, 4G, LoRa, and WAN, and how to optimize network architecture based on them.

Chapter 3, Integrating Application Protocols, discusses the common application protocols for IoT, such as HTTP, MQTT, and CoAP, while exploring the benefits of each one, choosing between them, and integrating them into our network design based on the use case.

Chapter 4, Examining Communication and Connectivity Technologies, discusses common communication protocols and technologies for short- and long-range networks, while exploring the considerations of using each one depending on the needs of the user and how each network serves as a base guideline for them.

Chapter 5, Realizing Wireless Sensor Networks within Smart Spaces, introduces you to sensors, exploring how they fit within the architecture of wireless sensor network setups and how choosing the appropriate ones is done for specific contexts to monitor the system, physical, or environmental conditions.

Chapter 6, Creating Applications on the Edge, introduces building on edge network architecture and the theory related to how data travels within a network, as well as factors relevant to latency and costs, such as volume, traffic, and the distance that is traveled.

Chapter 7, Working with Cloud Computing to Power IoT Solutions, introduces you to a high-level overview of the capabilities of cloud computing to build your IoT network – in this case, utilizing AWS as the main cloud provider.

Chapter 8, Designing for Interoperability, discusses how interoperability has been an issue for some time in many IoT networks and explores the considerations of how interoperable design can be done efficiently, ensuring as many smart devices can interact with one another, thus furthering the concept of the smart home.

Chapter 9, Operating and Monitoring IoT Networks, discusses how IoT systems and networks are operated and maintained once put in place, and it looks at the tools that are used both on-premises and in the cloud as part of this.

Chapter 10, Working with Data and Analytics, discusses the analytics tools that can be used as part of managing current IoT network deployments and extracting data from them, such as Amazon CloudWatch. The chapter also explores how queries can also be built and set up to be run smartly, allowing you to analyze data on the go automatically instead of having to rely on manual analysis to do so.

Chapter 11, Examining Security and Privacy in IoT, discusses the security landscape for IoT, the currently emerging threats that many users will need to consider within the landscape, the privacy concerns for IoT, and how to build around these challenges to stay compliant with regulations.

Chapter 12, Exploring and Innovating with Open Source IoT, introduces open source work that has been done with the IoT and recommends work that you can build on for your own projects.

Chapter 13, Developing IoT Solutions for Digital Transformation within Industry 4.0, discusses how IoT can be brought into organizations that are not familiar with the concept and how to build around a smart ecosystem within the workplace as part of Industry 4.0, leveraging frameworks and standards from best practices within the industry.

Chapter 14, Architecting Complex, Holistic IoT Environments, looks at more complex IoT environments and the considerations that go into architecting and building them, allowing you to explore the threats and risks within such environments. The chapter also explores how factors such as multi-cloud deployments based on hybrid models can create many attack surfaces that have to be considered.

Chapter 15, Looking Ahead into the Future of IoT, discusses the future of IoT five years from now and how sustainable it can be, analyzing trends that have been popular so far and the challenges that come along with them, alongside the author's own perspectives on the do's and don'ts, based on best practices.

To get the most out of this book

No prior knowledge is assumed of this book, but familiarity with one or two programming languages will help you get through more of the practical exercises in this book faster.

Software/hardware covered in the book	Operating system requirements
Amazon Web Services (AWS)	Windows, macOS, or Linux
Raspberry Pi 3	Linux
Arduino	Windows, macOS, or Linux

If you are using the digital version of this book, we advise you to type the code yourself or access the code from the book's GitHub repository (a link is available in the next section). Doing so will help you avoid any potential errors related to the copying and pasting of code.

Download the example code files

You can download the example code files for this book from GitHub at `https://github.com/PacktPublishing/IoT-Made-Easy-for-Beginners`. If there's an update to the code, it will be updated in the GitHub repository.

Conventions used

There are a number of text conventions used throughout this book.

`Code in text`: Indicates code words in text, database table names, folder names, filenames, file extensions, pathnames, dummy URLs, user input, and Twitter handles. Here is an example: "The `payload[length] = '\0';` line adds a null character (0) at the end of the payload data to indicate the end of the string."

A block of code is set as follows:

```
const byte led_gpio = 32;
void setup() {
    pinMode(led_gpio, OUTPUT);
}
```

Any command-line input or output is written as follows:

```
$ git config –global user.name "{firstname} {lastname}"
```

Bold: Indicates a new term, an important word, or words that you see on screen. For instance, words in menus or dialog boxes appear in **bold**. Here is an example: "You should see the **Status** change to **Connected**. Click on the **Raw data** tab; you can see the data with the latest data model uploaded from the device."

> **Tips or important notes**
> Appear like this.

Get in touch

Feedback from our readers is always welcome.

General feedback: If you have questions about any aspect of this book, email us at `customercare@packtpub.com` and mention the book title in the subject of your message.

Errata: Although we have taken every care to ensure the accuracy of our content, mistakes do happen. If you have found a mistake in this book, we would be grateful if you would report this to us. Please visit `www.packtpub.com/support/errata` and fill in the form.

Piracy: If you come across any illegal copies of our works in any form on the internet, we would be grateful if you would provide us with the location address or website name. Please contact us at `copyright@packt.com` with a link to the material.

If you are interested in becoming an author: If there is a topic that you have expertise in and you are interested in either writing or contributing to a book, please visit `authors.packtpub.com`.

Share Your Thoughts

Once you've read *Internet of Things from Scratch*, we'd love to hear your thoughts! Scan the QR code below to go straight to the Amazon review page for this book and share your feedback.

https://packt.link/r/1837638543

Your review is important to us and the tech community and will help us make sure we're delivering excellent quality content.

Download a free PDF copy of this book

Thanks for purchasing this book!

Do you like to read on the go but are unable to carry your print books everywhere?

Is your eBook purchase not compatible with the device of your choice?

Don't worry, now with every Packt book you get a DRM-free PDF version of that book at no cost.

Read anywhere, any place, on any device. Search, copy, and paste code from your favorite technical books directly into your application.

The perks don't stop there, you can get exclusive access to discounts, newsletters, and great free content in your inbox daily

Follow these simple steps to get the benefits:

1. Scan the QR code or visit the link below

https://packt.link/free-ebook/9781837638543

2. Submit your proof of purchase
3. That's it! We'll send your free PDF and other benefits to your email directly

Part 1: Getting Started with the Internet of Things

In this part, we embark on a journey to explore the realm of the **Internet of Things** (**IoT**). Starting with an in-depth understanding of the IoT architecture, its hardware components, and real-world applications, we transition into the intricacies of designing robust IoT networks. Our focus will then shift to the application protocols that empower these devices, followed by a deep dive into the communication and connectivity technologies that bind them together. Throughout these chapters, you'll be guided by practical examples using the ESP32 and its associated kit, offering a hands-on approach to grasp the foundational knowledge and lay the groundwork for more extensive IoT projects.

This part has the following chapters:

- *Chapter 1, An Introduction to IoT Architecture, Hardware, and Real-Life Applications*

- *Chapter 2, Understanding and Designing IoT Networks*

- *Chapter 3, Integrating Application Protocols*

- *Chapter 4, Examining Communication and Connectivity Technologies*

1

An Introduction to IoT Architecture, Hardware, and Real-Life Applications

If you are a practitioner within the tech industry, the term **Internet of Things (IoT)** should not sound foreign to you. With the growing reliance of industries on the power of the internet, the web of IoT continues to expand. We now see it everywhere around us, even if we sometimes do not realize it.

IoT, through its various implementations such as real-time sensor data retrieval and automated task execution based on this data, plays a pivotal role in the development of smart cities. These systems, equipped with numerous sensors, take action when specific thresholds are exceeded, demonstrating IoT's profound impact on our urban landscape, which is increasingly evident all around us.

In this chapter, we will explore IoT in your everyday life, how it contributes to the bigger picture of its ever-expanding ecosystem, and how to understand the architecture and hardware that make it up. As part of this, you will learn how to create simple systems diagrams for designing IoT architecture, build your own repository to store these solutions, and write code for a temperature sensor practical exercise. You will also be seeing the big picture of how component-based IoT is; that is, how small subsets of the architecture make up the larger implementations of it. These will be the foundational building blocks of designing industry-grade, complex systems, which we will build up in the later chapters of the book.

In this chapter, we will look to discuss the following main topics:

- What is IoT?
- Setting up the development environment of the book
- Choosing between IoT hardware
- Designing a simple IoT system diagram

- Defining systems and processes for smart objects
- Practical – creating a mini weather station

Technical requirements

Despite there being no technical requirements in particular, general knowledge of microcontrollers and networking technology would be helpful. As we will be working with microcontrollers, it would also be great to know some foundational C++. C++ is a powerful language that is used in many low-level environments, and it is an especially powerful language for building IoT systems. Because of this, the book's hardware-based exercises are all based on C++. If you are not familiar with ++C, that's alright, as we will explain what is happening in every part of the code and allow you to get familiarized with this language.

For this chapter, you can obtain all the code that will be used at `https://github.com/PacktPublishing/IoT-Made-Easy-for-Beginners/tree/main/Chapter01`. All code that is used throughout this book will be in their corresponding chapters within the `IoT-Made-Easy-for-Beginners` repository.

We recommend looking up any technical concepts that you do not understand, though we will keep it as foundational as possible to allow you to build up on the foundations from here.

What is IoT?

IoT, coined by computer scientist *Kevin Ashton* in 1999, is the term used to refer to the continuously growing network of physical objects that are connected to the internet, having them send and receive data. These objects vary from objects you find in your everyday life, such as smart fridges and mobile phones, to objects spanning entire industries or even cities, such as smart agriculture and smart cities.

Starting from just within your home, IoT has revolutionized how we live and interact with our environment. Some benefits of IoT within the household include the following:

- **Increased convenience**: Devices can be programmed and controlled remotely. For example, imagine adjusting your home's lighting or heating using just your smartphone even when you're miles away.
- **Energy efficiency**: Smart thermostats or lighting systems can optimize their operations based on your usage patterns, saving energy and cutting down on utility bills.
- **Safety and security**: IoT-enabled security systems and cameras can notify homeowners of potential breaches, and smart locks can grant or deny entry based on recognized users.
- **Health monitoring**: Smart wearables and devices can track health metrics and provide real-time feedback, potentially notifying users or medical professionals of concerning changes.
- **Enhanced user experience**: Devices can learn and adapt to users' preferences, ensuring tailored and improved interactions over time.

Including the smart home, some vastly popular areas IoT has been implemented in can be seen in the following figure:

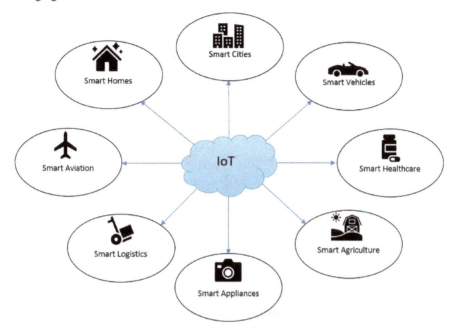

Figure 1.1 – Areas of use for IoT

As can be seen, the applications of IoT reach beyond just smart homes; they also assist with smart vehicles by facilitating GPS tracking and allowing you to upload images online from your smart camera. What makes this extremely powerful is that many actions that are put through this system can be automated through **actuators**. Actuators convert a control signal sent from the internet to perform certain motions, such as locking doors, turning off lights, and many more. These actions can be set to take place based on thresholds that are exceeded. For example, if the temperature of a room dips below 15°C, a user can use a smart thermostat and remotely schedule it to turn off the air conditioning until it reaches a temperature of at least 25°C, at which point it will turn on again.

The vision of the IoT

The original vision of the internet since the era of the **World Wide Web** (**WWW**) intends to focus on providing the convenience of searching for information and communicating with others. The widely held vision of the IoT, on the other hand, built up further from there and aims to be able to create a world where convenience of life can be granted in the form of having everyday things that are connected to the internet that in turn can communicate between themselves and with people, allowing for a vast number of capabilities. We have already seen this in a myriad of industries, particularly how it has helped reduce the manual labor that is needed to perform certain tasks.

IoT is often seen as a convergence of three different visions: the **Internet Vision**, the **Things Vision**, and the **Semantic Vision**. Each of these visions has its own part to play within the dynamic picture of the IoT.

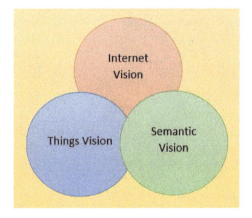

Figure 1.2 – Visions of IoT

Things Vision

The Things Vision focuses on the technologies that are related to *making things smarter*; that is, those that can add capabilities to devices that allow them to communicated with the internet and with each other, alongside the data that they generate. The key aim here is to be able to gather and analyze data from a myriad of devices to gain insights and make better decisions. This is what has resulted in its evolution into smart sensor networks today.

Internet Vision

The Internet Vision focuses on the connectivity of the things that are connected to the internet and each other. The key aim of this vision is to be able to accelerate the ability and performance of the connectivity aspect as part of the IoT. As part of this, the storage and management of the data that has been gathered or generated is a key consideration, as it is important to understand the constraints, challenges, and opportunities of creating such solutions for the communication of the things. This was what led to the creation of many standards and communities, such as the open source **Internet Protocol for Smart Object** (**IPSO**) communities, which focus on finding solutions for smart sensor communication.

Semantic Vision

The Semantic Vision of IoT focuses on understanding the meaning of the data that is generated as part of the connected devices. It focuses on the challenge of interoperability; that is, how we can work with devices from different manufacturers and allow them to communicate with one another despite the different standards they may abide by. Interoperability is a big challenge within the industry, particularly with the different standards that many **smart objects** follow, and we are going to cover it in more depth in *Chapter 8, Designing for Interoperability*.

The evolution of the IoT

The concept of the IoT started with a lesser-known story based at Carnegie Mellon University in the 1980s, where a group of researchers developed a soda machine. The researchers wanted to track the content of the machine remotely, which led to them modifying the machine by installing a board that was able to obtain the status of indicator lights that show whether the sodas were currently stocked or empty. The status of each column within the soda machine was checked a few times per second. If a light went from off to on to off again in a matter of seconds, they would know that a Coke had been purchased. If the light stayed on for more than five seconds, it was assumed that the column was empty. With this kind of logic, alongside other indicators, they were able to create what the world regards as the first IoT-based machine.

Despite this, it was not until the 21st century that IoT really took off, powered by the development of low-cost and low-power consumption **microelectromechanical systems** (**MEMS**) sensors. This trend toward energy efficiency was crucial, especially as many IoT devices are battery-powered and need to operate efficiently for extended periods, so more hardware and software optimizations were made to conserve more energy. Another significant push came from the widespread adoption of internet-connected smartphones. The popularity of IoT further skyrocketed with the launch of the Raspberry Pi and the release of the IPv6 protocol, and now we have billions of IoT devices around the world. With technologies such as 5G and edge computing, it is only expected to grow further, as we can see how the performance capabilities of IoT networks only increase further with the new additions that are put forward by innovations.

Over time, there have been evolutions of concepts that have overlaps and may have been thought to be the same as IoT but are different. The next section presents comparisons to three main concepts: the web of things, machine-to-machine, and cyber-physical systems.

IoT versus the Web of Things

The **Web of Things** (**WoT**) is based on the connection and interoperability of smart devices through utilizing web standards and protocols. It aims to enable seamless communication and integration between a myriad of devices and systems without differentiating their underlying platforms. This usually uses web APIs to allow access for devices to interact with each other. IoT is about the connected devices themselves, but WoT is about the web infrastructure that allows the devices to interact and interoperate with each other over the web.

IoT versus machine-to-machine

Machine-to-machine (**M2M**) is based on the communication between two machines without the need for human intervention, which can be achieved through several technologies such as RFID or Bluetooth. IoT has a much wider range of applications compared to M2M, given that it is about the connection of an ecosystem of devices and systems, compared to the communication method of M2M, which is based on a closed system.

IoT versus cyber–physical systems

Cyber-physical systems (**CPSs**) are based on systems that integrate computational elements with physical components to allow for the capability of sensing, analyzing, and controlling physical processes. Such systems are intended to work in real time and are used in critical infrastructure such as emergency services, power grids, and transportation systems. Although they share common elements in the sense that they both use sensors and integrate computational and physical elements in powering actions to be taken, CPSs are usually more complex and pose more requirements based on the need for real-time performance and reliability.

The four pillars of IoT

There are four pillars of IoT that together form the IoT ecosystem, which ensures that devices can communicate with each other and other systems, enabling the generation of valuable data and insights.

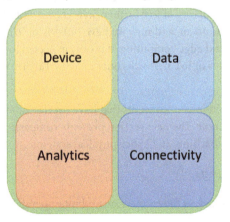

Figure 1.3 – Four pillars of IoT

Let's understand these pillars.

Device

The first pillar of IoT is **device**, which refers to anything around you, including phones, cars, and other electronic appliances, that can connect to the internet. With its dependence on the internet, it requires a wireless network or other connectivity solutions to allow it to continually transmit data to the internet and support the other pillars of IoT. Because of this, the question of where the data is to be stored temporarily if the device cannot connect to the internet should be considered when picking the appropriate devices.

Data

The second pillar of IoT is **data**, which is all about the information that is obtained by the connected devices as part of the IoT network. This data is then further analyzed and used for various purposes, including improving the deployed network, making decisions, and more. This is a pillar we will be seeing clearly throughout the exercises that we do in this book, as we will be referring to it to improve our data-gathering systems and make better decisions based on them.

Connectivity

The third pillar of IoT is **connectivity**, which is about the transmission of data and ensuring that all the pillars are connected. The importance of this pillar increases with the need for real-time data processing where no interruption to the connection to the internet is imperative, as missing data points could alter the interpretation of a system. For example, there could be data points that are gathered from a smart fire alarm system that signals that there is a fire, but if it is not connected to the internet, this may not go through and the actuators that would have been put in motion to alert the fire emergency services and sprinklers would not work, putting lives in danger. Because of this, considering the environment of your use case and the different edge cases that you may need for your deployment to work effectively is paramount to any IoT system that we are looking to build.

Analytics

The final pillar of IoT is **analytics**, which is all about analyzing the collected data, whether it be directly on the device, on an edge location such as a gateway, or on the cloud. It is a powerful step in the data collection process, as it is all about interpreting the data that we have obtained and understanding how it will impact our decisions. Some workloads may have simple analytical processes, such as simply generating charts based on the data that is obtained to summarize important insights, while others may go through more strenuous workloads, such as letting machine learning models analyze them on the cloud to derive more insights from them.

> **Important note**
>
> It is important to note that other books or standards may propose other pillars of IoT, though, in reality, most of them abide by the principles of the four pillars just mentioned, as it really is the functionality that is communicated by the pillars. In this book, we intend to provide the principles that are most universal around the IoT community, as just seen.

Now that you have a good idea of what IoT is about, we can move ahead and explore how we can set up the development environment for this book.

Setting up the development environment of the book

In this section, we will walk you through setting up the foundational development environment for the book. There may be additional configurations that will need to be done for specific chapters, but the setup here will be enough for you to make those additional ones with ease. The two main components that need to be set up here are the **Arduino IDE** for uploading code to your **ESP32 microcontroller** and your **GitHub environment** for source control. Note that ESP-32 is not part of the Arduino family hardware; we are simply using it as it is an editor that supports the development of ESP-32. We will also set up your AWS environment, but we will explore that in *Chapter 7, Working with Cloud Computing to Power IoT Solutions* where working with your workloads on AWS will be discussed further.

Setting up your Arduino IDE environment

Your Arduino IDE environment is where you will be working with your code and uploading that code onto your ESP32. Note that you are not limited to only using the Arduino IDE environment for doing this, so if you are familiar with other environments, feel free to use them. For the purposes of this book, we will be working with this IDE.

Arduino IDE environment

The Arduino **integrated development environment** (IDE) is a powerful, user-friendly software platform designed for programming and interacting with Arduino microcontroller boards. The IDE makes it easy for beginners to get started with microcontroller programming while also offering advanced features for experienced developers. In this section, we will guide you through the process of setting it up on your computer, enabling you to bring projects described in this book and beyond to life:

1. Download the Arduino IDE environment at https://www.arduino.cc/en/software. Go through the installation process and accept the defaults, ensuring that you know where the program will be installed.

2. Open your newly installed Arduino IDE. By default, we will not be able to find ESP32 as a supported board unless we specify it within our preferences. Go to **File | Preferences**. On the window that is opened, you should see a space for additional boards manager URLs. Enter the

URL `https://raw.githubusercontent.com/espressif/arduino-esp32/gh-pages/package_esp32_index.json`. Click **OK**.

3. Go to **Tools | Board | Boards Manager** and enter `esp32` into the search bar. Click **Install** on the latest ESP32 version that pops up:

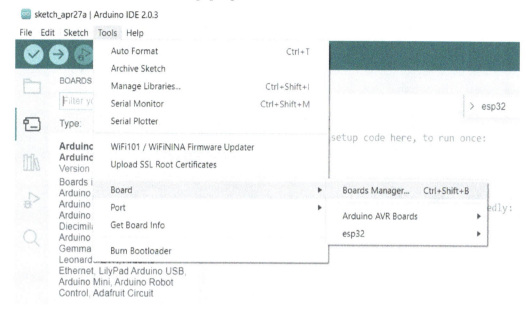

Figure 1.4 – Accessing Boards Manager on the Arduino IDE

4. After installation, navigate to **Tools | Board | esp32** and select **NodeMCU-32S**.

5. We then need to install the driver for the ESP32. To check which type you are using, navigate to **Device Manager** on your device by searching it up on the Windows Start menu and expanding the **Ports (COM & LPT)** dropdown. Take note of the COM port that is being used; we will also need to set our Arduino accordingly to that later. If the same type is used, which will require the CP210x driver, you will be able to download it at `https://www.silabs.com/developers/usb-to-uart-bridge-vcp-drivers?tab=downloads`.

6. On the Arduino IDE, navigate to **Tools | Port** and select the COM port that is being used.

7. Attach your ESP32 to your laptop using a mini USB.

8. Click **File | New Sketch** in the top-left corner of the program.

9. You will see the following code in your environment:

```
void setup() {
  // put your setup code here, to run once:
}
void loop() {
  // put your main code here, to run repeatedly:
}
```

To see whether your IDE is working correctly, click on **Verify**, which is the button in the top-left corner of the screen.

10. To see whether your device is configured correctly, click on **Upload**, which is the second button from the left. While the upload is, hold down the **Boot** button, which is the button in the bottom right.

Check your IDE's terminal to see whether the code has been uploaded successfully.

With this, your Arduino IDE should be set up and ready to be used. We can now proceed to try it out with our inaugural *Hello World* exercise.

Red LED Lighting Hello World exercise

To test the functionality of the ESP32 and to give you a taste of working with your new development kit, we are going to create the equivalent of a *Hello World* exercise—a practical exercise to light up a red LED bulb.

Components you'll need

For this, you will need the following components:

- An ESP32 microcontroller
- A red LED (or any other color you would like to use)
- An 830-hole breadboard
- Two jumper wires
- A 1k Ohm resistor

As you go along, you can refer to the upcoming assembly diagram to see the placement of the components on the board and get an overall idea of what we are trying to create to follow the instructions more easily.

Setting up the required hardware

Now, we will proceed to set up the hardware accordingly. The following figure shows the breadboard diagram that can be used as a reference while you follow the instructions to wire up the board, breadboard, LED, and resistor:

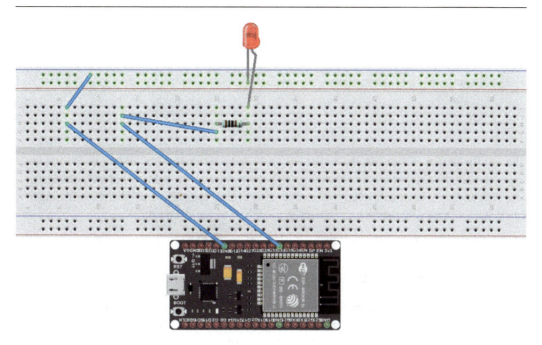

Figure 1.5 – Breadboard diagram for connecting the LED

1. The long leg of the LED is the anode and the shorter leg is the cathode. Attach the anode to hole 30j and the cathode to hole 30- on the breadboard.

2. We now will attach the ESP32 to the board. Attach the **ground** pin (**GND** on the board) as shown in the figure to hole 6h and 3g to hole 13h. You can either do this with a jumper cable or just directly put it down with the corresponding legs of the microcontroller as such.

3. Attach the 1k Ohm resistor with one leg on hole 30h and the other on hole 25h.

4. Attach a wire from hole 25g to hole 13i.

5. Attach a wire from hole 6j to 9-.

    Now we have successfully set up the hardware that is needed for this practical exercise. We can now move on to producing the necessary code on our Arduino IDE.

Coding it up on the Arduino IDE

Now, we will upload the code for running the LED experiment to the ESP32. Use the following code for this purpose:

```
const byte led_gpio = 32;
void setup() {
  pinMode(led_gpio, OUTPUT);
}
```

```
void loop() {
  digitalWrite(led_gpio, HIGH);
  delay(1000);
  digitalWrite(led_gpio, LOW);
  delay(1000);
}
```

In the `setup` section of the code, the digital pin `led_gpio` is initialized as an output. Within the `loop` section of the code, we are simply alternating between turning the light on and off (as indicated by the high and low). Each wait 1,000 milliseconds—equivalent to one second—before switching to the next state, as seen with the `delay` statement.

And with that, you've just created your first IoT program on the ESP32!

Setting up your GitHub repository

GitHub is a code repository platform that is used for version control and collaboration on your code. With it, developers can track changes to code and collaborate on a project, while also setting extra restrictions for changes as part of best practices such as letting developers review each other's code and merge changes from anywhere. We will be using GitHub throughout this book for you to both use the platform to pull the code that we use throughout our chapters and put in your code.

Setting up your GitHub account

To start, we will create our GitHub account to use to set up our repository:

1. Navigate to `https://github.com/` and click on the **Sign Up** button in the top right.
2. Enter your email, password, and username as prompted. Check your email for verification and log in to GitHub.

You now have a GitHub account, which is the first step for setting up our version control environment and for making optimum use of the resources of this book that are ready for you to pull onto your local environment.

Setting up your GitHub CLI

When you pull code or create local repositories to push up to GitHub, it is much easier if you use the **command-line interface** (**CLI**). The following are the steps that you need to take to install the CLI on your laptop:

1. Assuming you are on Windows, you will need to go to `https://github.com/cli/cli/releases`. Navigate to the latest release (at the time of the writing of the book, it is `2.21.1`, but this may change, so navigate accordingly) and download the file that ends with `windows_amd64.msi`.

2. Follow through with the default installation prompt and install the CLI in a location of your choice.

3. In the case that it is not done by default, open your Windows Start Menu, go to **Control Panel | System | Advanced System Settings | Environmental Variables**, and click **Edit** on the `Path` variable within the user variables for your account. Click **New** and add the path of the folder that contains your GitHub installation.

4. Check whether your CLI has been installed successfully by opening your command prompt and typing `git -version`. If the output returns the version, that confirms that Git is already installed.

5. You will now have to set your GitHub credentials. Configure your username to record changes you make to your local repository with the command as follows:

    ```
    $ git config -global user.name "{firstname} {lastname}"
    ```

6. Configure an email address that will be associated with each of your history markers:

    ```
    $ git config -global user.email "{youremail}"
    ```

7. You now need to authorize your device to modify repositories that are owned by your GitHub account. As part of this, we need to register an SSH key. Start by generating an SSH key via the command prompt with the following command:

    ```
    $ ssh-keygen -t ed25519 -C "{youremailhere}"
    ```

8. When prompted, specify the folder to generate the SSH key to; otherwise, let the default be and change the directory into the folder that it is generated in.

9. Open the `id_ed25519` file that is generated in a text editor of your choice and copy the contents of the file.

10. In GitHub, in the top-right corner, click your profile photo and click **Settings**.

11. In the `Access` section, click on the **SSH** and **GPG** keys.

12. Click **New SSH Key** or **Add SSH Key**.

13. In the `Title` field, add a label that describes the purpose of your key, such as an identifying name for the device you are linking it with. Select the type of key, which in this case is **Authentication Key**. Paste the key that you have copied into the **Key** field and click the **SSH** key.

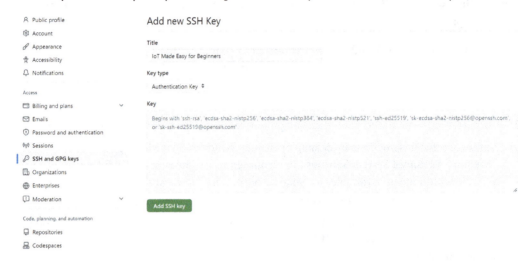

Figure 1.6 – GitHub page to add a new SSH key

You should now have authorized your device to modify repositories on GitHub, so we will now be able to push code from our local development environment onto the GitHub repositories.

Pulling your code from a repository

If your CLI is configured properly, you should be able to pull the code from the repository straight to your local development environment:

1. Navigate to the repository from which you would like to pull your code.

2. Click on **Code** and click **SSH**.

3. Copy the SSH line that is noted there. Ensure that your command line is currently open in the folder that you want the repository to be cloned into. Run the following command on it:

```
$ git clone {SSHLine}
```

4. Your repository should now be in the form of a folder; you just need to change the directory into that new folder.

Creating a GitHub repository for your code

Your GitHub repository is where you will be storing, committing, and pushing your code. You will need to create one via GitHub to then push and pull to and from your local development environment:

1. On your GitHub home page, click on **New repository**.

2. Type a name for your repository and add a description of it.

3. Choose the visibility of your repository. Unless you want to prevent your repository from being accessed publicly, select **Private**.

4. Select **Initialize this repository with a README** to continually update your repository with a summary.

5. Select **Create Repository**.

You should now be able to push to the repository as part of the next section.

Initializing, committing, staging, and pushing – oh my!

These four steps are a crucial part of any GitHub experience, as you want to store the code and continually update the repository based on the changes you have done to collaborate with others or simply just to track the changes that you have made as part of the version control process.

To understand how these four steps work for your projects, let's go through them:

1. To initialize a folder as a Git development folder, type in the following and a `.git` folder should be initialized in your folder:

   ```
   $ git init
   ```

2. You next need to add the files in your local repository to be staged. We use a dot to add all files; otherwise, we specify which file(s) we would like to add:

   ```
   $ git add .
   ```

3. We then commit the files that have been staged in the local repository, adding a commit message:

   ```
   $ git commit -m "{Your commit message here}"
   ```

4. We then specify the URL for the remote repository that we intend to push the code toward:

   ```
   $ git remote add origin {remoteURL}
   ```

5. We then verify that it was successfully added by running the verify command:

   ```
   $ git remote -v
   ```

6. We then push the changes we have already staged to our repository:

```
$ git push origin main
```

Note that if the folder is already initialized as a local repository and the remote URL is already set, we will only have to repeat *steps 2, 3,* and *6* for every consecutive push.

Testing it for your newly created Hello World LED project

Now that we have the skills for GitHub, let's use it to push your newly created *Hello World* LED project's code into GitHub:

1. Create a repository on GitHub as per the instructions just given for creating a new repository.

2. On your command prompt, navigate to the folder containing your project code. Run `git init` to initialize the folder as a repository:

```
$ git init
```

3. Add all files in the folder to be staged:

```
$ git add .
```

4. Enter a commit message that makes sense for adding this deployment. In this case, it might be something as simple as this:

```
$ git commit -m "Created Hello World LED IoT Project"
```

5. Navigate to your repository page on GitHub and copy the HTTPS URL on the project. Paste it within the command to add the origin for the project:

```
git remote add origin https://github.com/renaldig/
firstledproject.git
```

6. Push the changes you already have staged to the repository:

```
$ git push origin main
```

And with that, you have your first repository good to go! Try to practice making a few changes to your code and repeating the process. See whether you can answer the following questions:

-   How can I revert to a previous version of my code?

-   What types of branches would I need to create for an industry-based IoT project?

With this, you should now be able to use the Arduino IDE, try out a practical exercise that demonstrates the capabilities of Arduino at a high level, and create and use GitHub in your local environment for version control. In the next section, we will explore how we can choose between IoT hardware, considering the unique set of requirements that projects need.

Choosing between IoT hardware

Choosing optimal hardware for an IoT project is imperative, especially when it comes to creating industry-grade implementations. Related hardware and software for IoT go through a standardized design process: requirements specification, conceptual design, prototyping, testing, and finally the rollout of the hardware and software that are part of the system. Some platforms, such as ESP8266 microcontrollers, facilitate easy prototyping and deployment, but this convenience often comes at the expense of lower processing power when compared to other options.

There are many factors to consider, but they can be categorized into four different factors: **data acquisition**, **data processing**, **connectivity**, and **power management**.

Data acquisition

Data acquisition is a major part of IoT systems, as many components of a system, in the form of sensors, function to collect data in the environment to provide real-time results and/or feedback. This data is often obtained at a fixed rate within a time known as the data sample rate and transmitted to a remote output device to be read in and sent for further processing.

Sensors are devices within an IoT network that are used to detect and measure physical quantities such as humidity, pressure, speed, light, and temperature. This data is obtained from the environment and sent through to the IoT platform either wired or wirelessly.

The way we interact with sensors also differs from use case to use case. As an example, instead of monitoring the environment, some sensors may instead monitor its internal state; these are known as proprioceptive sensors. There can also be sensors that allow personnel to interact directly with them via buttons or touchscreens while recording the actions that are done; these are known as-machine interfaces.

When evaluating which sensor to use, multiple factors come into play. The first and most obvious one is functionality. What are you going to use the sensor for? If you are going to measure changes in the environment for temperature and humidity, for example, you would consider the DHT11, which is a temperature and humidity sensor developed by Adafruit. It comes standardized in many development kits, including the one that this book uses. However, just because you have obtained a sensor that does what you need it to do does not mean that you have found the optimal sensor.

There are many options that need to be considered that are offered by sensors, which is why comparing sensors by their specifications is very important. The condition in which the sensor can operate is another important consideration. Where will you use it? Will it be used at room temperature or in extremely hot or cold environments?

The next consideration is the accuracy and precision of the sensor. Precision is the repeatability or consistency of the measurement. With high precision, a sensor will be able to produce results that deviate very slightly from one another when the same measurement is taken multiple times with the same conditions put on it. On the other hand, with low precision, a sensor would produce results that would deviate more from each other despite the same conditions put on it. This often comes as a trade-off with accuracy, which is how close the measured value is to the actual value of the physical quantity that is being measured. High accuracy for a sensor can produce results that are very close to the actual value, while low accuracy for sensors outputs results that deviate further from the true value. It is important to understand that a sensor can be precise but not accurate and vice versa. Optimally, we would like the sensor to be both precise and accurate, but there are often trade-offs between the two.

Finally, we must consider the resolution of the sensors. The resolution determines the smallest change within the physical quantity that the sensor is capable of detecting. For example, if a temperature sensor has a resolution of 0.1°C, this means that the sensor can detect changes in temperature as granular as 0.1°C. Hence, higher resolutions for sensors allow them to detect smaller changes within the physical quantity, while lower resolutions are only able to detect larger changes. It is also important to note that other factors aside from the sensor may also affect the resolution, such as the accuracy of the **analog-to-digital converter** (**ADC**), which converts the sensor's output to digital form, and the accuracy of the software that processes the data sent by the sensor, which affects the overall resolution of the measurement system.

For example, we can compare the DHT11 and DHT22 sensors that are both developed by Adafruit. The following are the specifications for them from the Adafruit website:

DHT11

- Ultra-low cost
- 3 to 5V power and I/O
- 2.5mA max current use during conversion (while requesting data)
- Good for 20-80% humidity readings with 5% accuracy
- Good for 0-50°C temperature readings ±2°C accuracy
- No more than 1 Hz sampling rate (once every second)
- Body size 15.5mm x 12mm x 5.5mm
- 4 pins with 0.1" spacing

VS

DHT22

- Low cost
- 3 to 5V power and I/O
- 2.5mA max current use during conversion (while requesting data)
- Good for 0-100% humidity readings with 2-5% accuracy
- Good for -40 to 80°C temperature readings ±0.5°C accuracy
- No more than 0.5 Hz sampling rate (once every 2 seconds)
- Body size 15.1mm x 25mm x 7.7mm
- 4 pins with 0.1" spacing

Figure 1.7 – Comparison of DHT11 and DHT22 sensors from Adafruit

At first glance, they both provide the functionality of being able to measure temperature and humidity, but they both have different specifications that can meet your deployments' needs differently. When comparing the specifications, we can see that despite there being many factors that are the same between them, each has its own set of advantages. The DHT11 has a lower cost and a better resolution compared to the DHT22, while the latter has higher accuracy and works over a larger temperature range than the former. Depending on our priorities, this will affect how we choose one sensor over another with these specifications.

These sensors then lead to the next part of the consideration of hardware for the architecture, which is within data processing.

Data processing and storage

Data processing and storage is a crucial part of working with data as part of the IoT. Once we have obtained the data, we must determine how we can analyze, interpret, and work with the data. In different use cases, data is processed in different places of the architecture; the device obtaining the data may process the data itself while in other use cases, it may transmit the data to other places first, such as gateway devices or cloud applications, for the purpose of conducting further analysis.

The processing power and storage size that an IoT application needs rely on the performance needed by the consumers of the data; consumers may use different services of applications that utilize the data either for further processing or as an end goal. These may include factors such as memory, number of cores, clock speed, or processor specifications; all determine the device's capability for data processing.

Two distinct scenarios arise when considering where to process and store the data:

- **Battery-powered devices**: Consider a simple device such as a temperature sensor powered by batteries. Such *dummy devices* aren't typically designed for local data processing and storage. The simpler the design, the lower the power consumption and, subsequently, costs.

- **Externally powered devices**: Devices with an external power source, such as machines or electricity meters, can afford to have local data processing and storage. This arrangement not only reduces service latency but also conserves wireless backhaul bandwidth, enhancing the overall efficiency.

On the capacity side, this is what makes the consideration of non-volatile memory—the temporary data storage before data is transmitted upstream—imperative; we want to account for being able to hold data while considering the different environments that the device may be in. Is the data in environments of intermittent internet connectivity meaning there may be a chance of data loss if it relies fully on the internet to continuously store data in an upstream provider? Do we do data processing within the device itself? These are all questions that we need to consider when carefully choosing the hardware we need.

Connectivity

Connectivity to networks is a crucial element of IoT devices. There are different types of connectivity to consider. It may be wired or wireless, depending on its use case. Wired communication is usually used for stationary devices and connected via the Ethernet, such as with smart buildings or home automation. On the other hand, wireless communication includes technologies such as Wi-Fi, Bluetooth, WAN technologies (such as LoRa), NB-IoT, and cellular networks. Don't worry if you don't know these terms; we'll talk more about them in the upcoming chapters and ensure that you have a thorough understanding of them and how to make the best use of them depending on your individual use case!

In connecting such devices together over a network, there are two main methods of communication: serial and parallel. With serial communication, data is transmitted one bit at a time over a singular communication line. Serial communication is usually used when the distance that the communication must be based on is relatively long or when the data rate is relatively low. Furthermore, it is used when there are a limited number of available communication lines or when the complexity of the system needs to be minimized. It uses protocols such as the RS-232 or the RS-422 protocols. Some examples of when serial communication would be used are as follows:

- Communication between a microcontroller and a sensor

- When two computers are located at a long distance from one another

In parallel communication, multiple bits are transmitted at the same time through multiple communication lines. It is normally used when the communication distance is short and the data rate is high. Furthermore, it is often seen in systems where the number of bits that are transmitted simultaneously is huge. It includes protocols such as IEEE, 1284, and PCI. Some examples of parallel communication's uses are as follows:

- Communication between two computers that need to exchange large amounts of data quickly

- Communication between a computer and a printer

We will cover connectivity in more detail in *Chapter 4, Examining Communication and Connectivity Technologies*, when we talk about connectivity and communication solutions.

Power management

Power management is a critical consideration within any IoT network. This is particularly true for devices that rely on a wireless power source, which usually depends on batteries or solar cells. There are mainly three main power consumption factors: the sensor, the microcontroller unit, and the wireless backhaul. Aspects that we need to consider include the cost, performance, and battery life of a device. There are multiple approaches that are often used to manage this effectively:

- **Cloud computing**: Letting the cloud handle processing and storage is often a great solution for reducing the power consumption of the device, as it will allow it to process data minimally when communicating with the cloud or to simply just perform its data collection when needed and sleep when it is not required for usage at a particular moment.

- **Sleep modes**: Microcontrollers and other types of hardware can often enter a sleep mode when there's low power consumption. It often is up to the user to configure the device to sleep and wake at certain times, which necessitates them to know the periods of high consumption and low consumption or simply to set a threshold and let the device detect on its own. This often reduces power consumption significantly.

- **Power-efficient hardware**: Using power-efficient hardware is a very important consideration and may be why some pick one microcontroller over another. This factor is listed on the specifications of the microcontroller, sensor, or other peripherals, as choosing such efficient devices would minimize costs, especially when working with a network filled with them. However, this may come with performance trade-offs, which is why it is important to look at all the specifications carefully to see whether the trade-offs are ones you can afford to make and consider what you really would like to prioritize.

- **Power management integrated circuits (PMICs)**: PMICs are chips that are used to manage the power consumption of a device. They are used to regulate the power supply to various components within the system, ensuring that only the portion that is allocated to the components gets through. This can be a powerful tool to regulate your system.

- **Energy harvesting**: Some energy harvesting methods, such as solar panels, are also effective ways of making use of power in a natural and cost-effective way. This would help you extend the device's battery life while also reducing the need to purchase batteries. However, this would depend on the environment of the device, as not all environments are conducive to this practice. For instance, not all areas have constant sunlight; solar panels would not work in these cases, and alternative means must be considered.

As can be seen from this section, all of the outlined factors depend on one another. This also leads to certain trade-offs, as it is often not possible to find the ideal device that can satisfy all four factors perfectly while still saving costs. It all depends on what your use case is and to what extent you would like your IoT system to meet it.

With this, you will have understood much more about selecting IoT hardware. As can be seen, sometimes some decisions are not as easily made when there are important trade-offs to consider, but it is often important to prioritize what you want to get out of it instead of trying to achieve the best of everything. In the next section, we will discuss how we can start designing simple IoT system diagrams.

Designing a simple IoT system diagram

Designing an IoT diagram is a skill that you will need to pick up and get familiar with when working with system/network deployments, especially in designing and presenting industry-grade solutions within the industry, as you will be architecting solutions and showing your thought processes behind certain design choices. The technical depth of your design will also differ from user to user. For example, a CIO might not care that much about the full list of services that you use on AWS to ingest, process, and analyze data that you have obtained on your sensor and have sent to be processed; rather, they would just like to see how it works overall. The technical depth may be more suited for an engineering manager or another developer on the team to help them better understand the design choices that are being proposed and why certain choices have been made. This will also serve as a reference for you to go back to when considering which parts of the architecture you can revise in the future.

In this section, we will start by looking at two high-level design flows: one for the flow of a smart lightbulb's communication with a user interface and one for a design flow that is based on AWS. In the following chapters, we will be discussing how to create more complex diagrams, so this will help you get used to how these flows can be represented and what the best practices are to make them presentable to your target audience.

A high-level design flow for a smart lightbulb

In this diagram, we can see the design flow of how a smart lightbulb communicates to reach the user interface:

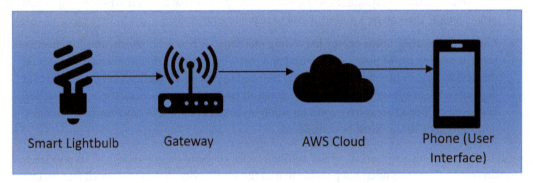

Figure 1.8 – Communication flow diagram of a smart lightbulb

To start off with, we can assume that we have a smart lightbulb that is able to detect a change to its state; that is, when it is turned on and off. The smart lightbulb—fitted with a sensor—communicates its ON status to the gateway. This gateway can be a Wi-Fi router, which then transmits the status to the AWS cloud. The AWS cloud then uses a service such as Amazon **Simple Notification Service (SNS)**, which sends a notification to the user's phone stating the lightbulb has been turned on.

This simple flow illustrates at a high level the communication flow. As you can already tell by seeing the picture and reading the description (or if you are already familiar with AWS), we have omitted illustrating the services that oversee receiving and delivering the communication from the gateway and to the phone. As mentioned, we have intended this to be a high-level overview of the process. In the next chapters, you will see more of the inner workings of the infrastructure and learn about how the message gets passed through more deeply.

Now, here are a couple of exercises for you to try out yourself:

- Draw a diagram that illustrates the flow of a smart fridge alerting a user's laptop that it is currently empty

- Draw a diagram that illustrates a user's phone alerting another phone through AWS that it is lost

For your drawings, you can find a lot of tools either offline or online that can help you draw properly. Some tools that you can use for this may be the following:

- **Draw.io and Lucidchart**: Both are great free online tools that you can use to create different types of diagrams.

- **Draw by hand**: You can create drawings by hand, although it is best to do so digitally to make them easily editable and presentable later. In industry-based settings, drawings are almost always done digitally.

- **Microsoft Word and PowerPoint**: These are great and convenient to make diagrams and sketches on due to the availability of different shapes and icons that you can search for, although it's hard to make them scalable later.

Note that there are no correct or wrong answers here; simply design sample diagrams based on the technologies and flows that you have learned within this chapter!

A high-level design flow for AWS

Now, we will look at a sample of a design flow based on AWS; a zoom-into-the-cloud icon from the previous example, if you will. AWS diagrams can be created via AWS' Workload Discovery tool or using other tools that were mentioned in the last subsection. If you do use other tools, AWS also provides a set of architecture icons to make illustrating your workloads much simpler, which can be found at `https://aws.amazon.com/architecture/icons/`.

In this example, we see the communication of a smart device storing data be processed further in a downstream application:

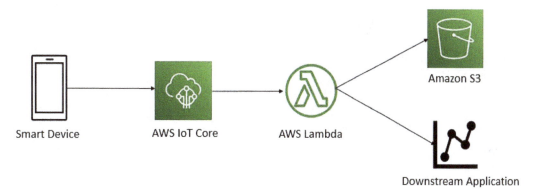

Figure 1.9 – Communication flow diagram of a smart device via the cloud

In this flow, we can see a smart device sending data to AWS IoT Core, which is a service that allows multiple IoT devices to connect at one time and route the messages accordingly, which, in this case, is to a lambda function. The lambda function then runs analytical workloads before storing the data in Amazon S3 and sends some that require further processing to a downstream application to be reported on.

As can be seen, these diagrams show in detail how communication occurs from a device to its endpoint. It is because of this that creating effective diagrams is key to communicating design decisions within architecting IoT solutions. It is also useful for your own documentation purposes to help you keep track of changes that you make to the solution.

We will discuss more about AWS, its cloud computing offerings, and its capabilities in helping us work with our IoT solutions in *Chapter 7, Working with Cloud Computing to Power IoT Solutions.*

With this, we have been able to get a high-level understanding of developing simple IoT system diagrams based on both smart objects and AWS, the latter of which will be imperative in our discussion in *Chapter 7, Working with Cloud Computing to Power IoT Solutions* as it plays a crucial role within the world of IoT. In the next section, we will discuss how we can dig deeper into the overview and how we can define the flows of processes and data of smart objects through further understanding how they move from source to destination.

Defining systems and processes for smart objects

As stated many times within the chapter, devices and sensors must be connected to the internet to be able to efficiently perform their tasks and utilize their data. By definition, a smart object is an object that needs to be able to communicate and interact with other devices and systems, making them a key component of IoT, as we want them to perform without the need for human intervention. As part of this, we need to understand the why, what, and how of every system and process that we define as part of the interaction of smart objects. In this section, we will define these systems and processes and show how we can properly define flows to transfer information from one part of the system to another, ensuring that our use case's goals are met. We will then delve deeper into this in the next chapter.

Defining a problem

Throughout this book, you will encounter different kinds of problems that require you to understand your environment and make appropriate decisions. As part of this, you need to consider what your intended goal is. It could be something as simple as the following:

I want to automate my home's lighting system to turn on from 9:00 to 18:00 and turn off/on every other hour when I am not at home.

This is a broad goal, but it certainly is the start of being able to narrow down what kind of system we intend to build. Next, we will look at a three-step model for realizing that goal, allowing us to further build on the picture that we have put forward and consider what types of components we will need.

The three-step model for working on IoT systems

In this section, we can model the actions that we will take to reach our goal through three key activities:

Sense

In this activity, we define what we want to measure and how we look toward measuring it. Understanding the parameters specifically is important. Are we measuring temperature? Humidity? We need to have this understanding and list them before considering options for sensors that we can use to measure these parameters.

Configure

Based on the data obtained, we then must continually use it to determine which data is relevant and which is not while iteratively building on the system based on what is being sensed. This is where we convert data into information and manage it according to what we obtain.

Actuate

After configuration, we set rules to ensure that we are notified if any thresholds are crossed and send a signal to the actuator to act. Actions can include turning off lights when we need to or turning up the thermostat when the temperature gets too cold. This is where information is then converted into action.

Creating the flow

Defining a flow diagram of the path that your data will take from its acquisition to the action that will be triggered as part of readings is crucial to starting any IoT network. This is also part of understanding what outcomes we would like to get out of the network design, which are most notably increasing the quality of life based on the automation that can be done and ensuring we save costs in the process.

The following figure is a sample design flow of how data is transmitted, from data acquisition to triggering an actuator to take action and generate reports based on analysis results:

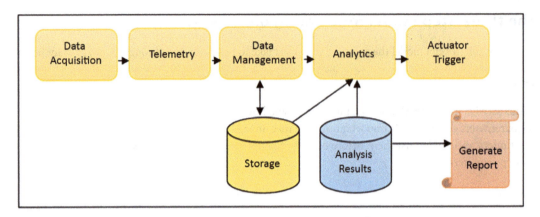

Figure 1.10 – Sample design data flow diagram

In this diagram, data is acquired as part of data acquisition and is accordingly converted into telemetry data within the smart object it is based in, which then transmits this to a data management service. This data management service may accordingly store data within a storage service. This is then forwarded on to analytics, where the data is further analyzed and the results are stored accordingly. From here, it may go on further to trigger an action to be done by an actuator and a report may be generated, allowing for further interpretation of the results to be done. This flow is common in most systems, as they most likely contain a large portion of these components, if not all of them, particularly if they are industry-standard ones. This flow will be something that you can refer to when you work on the IoT weather station exercise in the next section.

With this, we have built on our high-level overview of the simple IoT diagrams we looked at in the last section and now understand how simple flow diagrams for transmitting data from source to destination for smart objects are created. We will dive more into the specifics in the next chapters and explore how we can further build on these diagrams to account for many other factors. Next, we will see how we can use our knowledge so far to build a mini weather station.

Practical exercise – creating a mini weather station

For our first project of this book, we will be creating a mini weather station that will be based on getting readings from the BME680 air quality sensor, which takes pressure, humidity, and temperature readings. We will be using the ESP32 as the microcontroller and a breadboard to connect the circuits.

The following section contains the instructions for this practical exercise.

Hardware

In this book, we use **Arduino IDE** as our IDE, as it is one of the most popular options for makers and has a large community support. Arduino is an open source piece of software that offers a wide variety of libraries for different types of sensors, devices, and IoT platforms.

For the microcontroller used in our experiments, we use the ESP32 from Espressif. The ESP32 is a powerful microcontroller that comes with integrated Wi-Fi and Bluetooth connectivity and has a strong support base within the IoT community. The board type we use is the NodeMCU ESP32S, which can easily be found on Amazon. There are many different ESP32 boards available, but please note that the pin position can vary between boards, so pay attention to this when using different boards.

It is important that we familiarize ourselves with the layout of the NodeMCU ESP32S. In *Figure 1.11*, we provide a pin layout diagram of the NodeMCU ESP32S. You can use this alongside your own direct observations to complete this exercise and gain a better understanding of how the pins interact with the other components that will be used in this chapter and throughout the book.

Do not worry if it looks complicated at first; you'll get used to it with the practicals that you will undertake along the way!

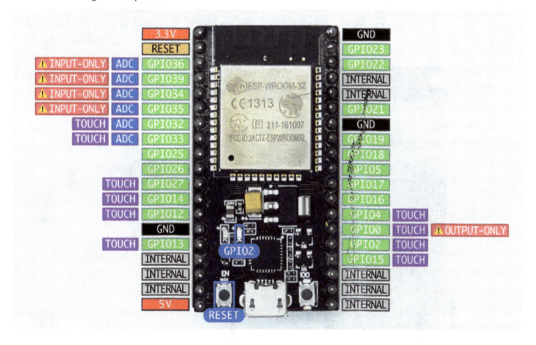

Figure 1.11 – NodeMCU ESP32S pinout diagram

We can now move forward and read from a sensor. The first sensor we will be working with is the BME680 sensor from Bosch Sensortech. This sensor can be easily found on Amazon, and it can measure relative humidity, barometric pressure, ambient temperature, and gas or **volatile organic compounds (VOCs)**. You can find detailed information about this sensor at `https://www.bosch-sensortec.com/products/environmental-sensors/gas-sensors/bme680/`.

There are two ways to read the data produced by the sensor: through I2C or SPI. In this experiment, we will be communicating with the BME680 sensor through an I2C connection.

I2C, short for **inter-integrated circuit**, represents a connection method utilized in serial communication as a bus interface protocol. Commonly referred to as the **Two-Wire Interface (TWI)**, it is a popular choice for short-range communication. This protocol relies on two bi-directional open-drain lines named SDA and SCL. The **Serial Data (SDA)** line facilitates data transmission, while the **Serial Clock (SCL)** line conveys the clock signal.

Since the I2C bus can be used to connect multiple devices, each device connected to the bus should have a different address to distinguish it from others.

We need to connect the SCL pin of the BME680 board to D22 on the ESP32 board (or IO22 on other ESP32 board), the SDA pin of BME680 to D21 on the ESP32, the VCC of BME680 to the 3V3 pin of the ESP32, and the GND pin on BME680 to the GND pin on ESP32. We can use the protoboard or direct jumper cable between those boards. The connection should look like that in the following figure:

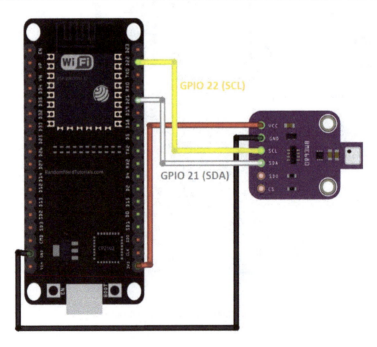

Figure 1.12 – Pinout diagram for attaching BME680 to ESP32

Working with the BME680

Due to the different addresses used by different BME680 board manufacturers, we need to verify the I2C address of the BME680 board we use (we also need to do this for every I2C device unless we already have the address from the manufacturer). To get the I2C address of the BME680 board, we need to use an **I2C Scanner** library:

1. In Arduino IDE, we can easily find code for our requirements by using the Library Manager. To access it, click on **Sketch | Include Library | Manage Libraries**.

2. Next, type I2C scanner in the search bar. Several I2C scanner libraries will appear. The one we will be using is from **Luis Llamas**, but you can try other libraries as well. To install the library, click on the **Install** button.

3. Once the library is installed, go to Arduino, click on **File**, then **Example**. Scroll through the examples until you find **I2C Scanner** under **Examples** from **Custom Libraries**. Point to **I2C Scanner** and click on **Scanner** to open the example code. The **Scanner** sketch will appear in the Arduino window, and you can upload the code to your ESP32 board by clicking the button.

```
Scanner | Arduino IDE 2.0.3
File Edit Sketch Tools Help

NodeMCU-32S

Scanner.ino   debug_custom.json
1   /******************************************************
2   Copyright (c) 2018 Luis Llamas
3   (www.luisllamas.es)
4   Licensed under the Apache License, Version 2.0 (the "License"); you may not use this file except i
5   Unless required by applicable law or agreed to in writing, software distributed under the License
6   ******************************************************/
7
8   #include "I2CScanner.h"
9
10  I2CScanner scanner;
11
12  void setup()
13  {
14    Serial.begin(9600);
15    while (!Serial) {};
16
17    scanner.Init();
18  }
19
20  void loop()
21  {
22    scanner.Scan();
23    delay(5000);
24  }
```

Figure 1.13 – Expected display for the IC2 Library in Arduino IDE

After finishing the upload, click on **Tools | Serial Monitor** to see the Arduino console (the older version will open a new window while the newer version will split the Serial Monitor under the **Sketch** window). You need to adjust the Serial Monitor baud rate to match the baud rate set in the program by finding the command in the void setup() function:

```
Serial.begin(9600);
```

This code sets the serial communication baud rate of the ESP32 board to 9600 baud, so we need to set the Arduino Serial Monitor window baud rate to 9600 to match the board. After this, we need to reset the ESP32 board by pressing the **Reset** button (marked **EN**) on the board.

If everything is set up properly, you will see the result in the Arduino window like in *Figure 1.14*:

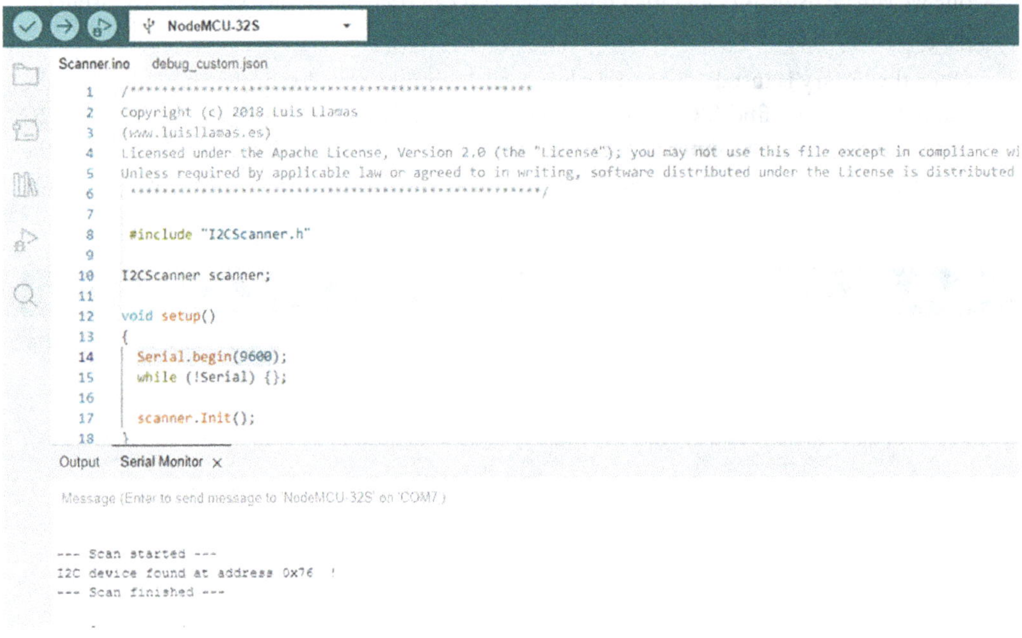

Figure 1.14 – Expected display for serial communication setup in Arduino IDE

Now we know that the BME680 board is using I2C address 0x76H.

4. Click on **Sketch | Include Library | Manage Libraries** and search for bme680. Choose BSEC Software Library by Bosch Sensortec. Click on the **Install** button. After installing, click on **File | Examples**, scroll down through the examples until you find BSEC Software Library, and click on the basic sketch. It will open the sketch. You can find this sketch also in the i2csample.c file in the Practical folder within the Chapter01 folder in the GitHub repository.

Verify the sketch by clicking on the ✓ button, and if there's no error, upload it to ESP32 by clicking the → button.

5. Open the Serial Monitor, set the baud rate to `115200` to match the sketch setting, and reset the board by pressing the **EN** button.

ESP32 Wi-Fi auto-configuration

The ESP32 has a built-in Wi-Fi functionality and can be set as an access point or a station. If it is set as an access point, you can connect your devices (mobile, other Wi-Fi devices, or computer) to it. If it is set as a station, you need to connect the ESP32 to an access point before you can read its data or it can send data to a remote server over the wireless network or internet (if the connected access point is connected to the internet). The ESP32 can also be set up as both an access point and station concurrently. This function is normally used to enable connecting the ESP32 to the available access point without having to manually configure the Wi-Fi setup and download it through a USB connection to the ESP32, which is difficult for common users.

There are two common methods of connecting the ESP32 to the Wi-Fi access point: **manual** and **auto-configuration**.

Manual configuration

The basic configuration of setting up an ESP32 connection to the access point involves manually entering the Wi-Fi SSID and password to the Arduino sketch and uploading it to the server using a serial USB cable. This manual Wi-Fi setup is very difficult to implement in real-life applications since many device users cannot do programming and Arduino IDE setup. Due to that issue, there is another way of setting up the Wi-Fi SSID and password—auto-connect configuration—which we will outline and use.

Auto-connect configuration

Another way to connect the ESP32 to the access point without having to hardcode the Wi-Fi SSID and password in the sketch and upload it to the ESP32 using a USB cable is by using auto-connect configuration. In this way, the ESP32 will be in the access point first, and if we connect to it using other devices (mobile phone or computer), it will display menus to guide us to connect to an available access point it can find by providing Wi-Fi credentials (i.e. SSID and password). Once we confirm, it will store the credentials in its memory, and then it will restart in Wi-Fi station mode and use the stored credentials to connect to the targeted access point. When we reset the ESP32, it will still be in station mode and will keep trying to connect to the designated access point.

One of the Arduino libraries that support auto-connect configuration is `ESPAsync_WiFiManager`, built by Khoi Hoang. The benefit of using asynchronous **Transmission Control Protocol/User Datagram Protocol (TCP/UDP)** connection is that the processor does not have to wait for each connection to finish before it can serve other requests, so multiple connections can occur concurrently. This will also enable faster responses.

ESPAsync_WiFiManager installation

Next, we will need to set up the `ESPAsync_WifiManager` library to configure the Wi-Fi connection for the ESP32 and proceed with our next steps:

1. Search from `Manage Libraries` to find `ESPAsync_WiFiManager` and install it. We also need to download the dependency library `ESPAsyncDNSServer`, which, unfortunately, cannot be found via the `Manage Libraries` search. For libraries that cannot be found in the Library Manager search results, we can download them by searching for them on the internet and downloading the library as a `.zip` file. We can download the `ESPAsyncDNSServer` library at `https://github.com/devyte/ESPAsyncDNSServer` and save the code as a `.zip` file.

2. To install the `.zip` file library we just downloaded, click on **Sketch | Include Library | Add Zip Library** and select that file.

3. In a new Arduino sketch screen, click on **File | Examples |** `ESPAsync_WiFiManager` and open the `Async_AutoConnect` sketch. Verify the sketch by clicking on the ☑ button, and if there are no errors, upload it to ESP32 by clicking the ➔ button. Reset the ESP32 board by pressing the **Reset** (marked **EN**) button.

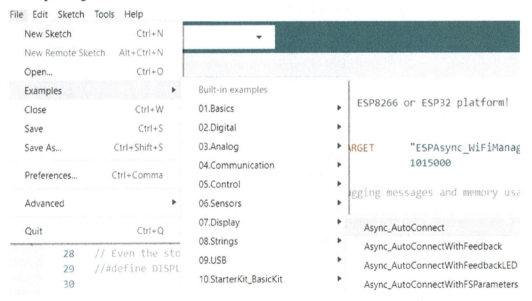

Figure 1.15 – Opening the Async_AutoConnect sketch on Arduino IDE

4. From a mobile phone or computer, search for a Wi-Fi access point to find `ESP_******_AutoConnectAP`, where `******` is the six digits of the hex number related to the ID of the ESP32. Connect to this access point with a password in the format `MyESP_******`, where the `******` should be the same six-digit hex number as the ESP32 ID. After connecting to the ESP32 access point, a browser window will open. Follow the guidance from the menu to enter the targeted access point SSID that the ESP32 should connect to and enter the password for the Wi-Fi connection. Once set, and once the ESP32 connects to that access point, the ESP32 will reset, change the mode to station mode, and automatically connect to the access point.

With this, we have successfully prepared the ESP32 to be able to communicate over Wi-Fi. We can now move on to setting up programming **over the air** (**OTA**) to be able to create and publish our code directly to the ESP-32 instead of having to connect it to our laptop.

ESP32 programming OTA with a web server and mDNS

Programming OTA allows updates to the code or configurations to be pushed over Wi-Fi so that we do not have to continually connect the ESP32 to the Wi-Fi when we push out updates to it. We will explore how we can set up the ESP32 for this so that the process of pushing out updates can go much more smoothly.

Copy the sketch on the repo named `programmingOTA.c` in the `Practical` folder within the `Chapter01` folder in the GitHub repository to the Arduino sketch window and save it as `ESP32_ElegantOTA_mDNS`.

Verify the code using the ⊘ button and upload to ESP32 using the ⊙ button. Press the **Reset (EN)** You should get a welcome message in your browser.

ESP32 reading the BME680 sensor

Now, we can begin configuring the parameters that we want to have measured from the environment. To do this, we need to code up the necessary code for the sensors so that they can connect to the ESP32 and read in accordingly.

As part of this, we can configure the libraries and the code for the BME680 sensor, which allows us to measure gas, pressure, temperature, and humidity:

1. You need to install additional libraries:

   - The Adafruit `BME680` library together with its dependencies, i.e., `Adafruit Unified Sensor Library`.

   - The `ESPAsyncWebServer` library from `https://github.com/me-no-dev/ESPAsyncWebServer/archive/master.zip`. Install this library by navigating to **Sketch | Include Library | Add .ZIP Library** and choose the downloaded file.

- The `AsyncEleganOTA` library from `https://github.com/ayushsharma82/AsyncElegantOTA`. Install this library using the method in *step B*.

- The `ESPmDNS` library from `https://github.com/espressif/arduino-esp32`. Install this library using the method in *step B*.

- The `ESPAsync` library from `https://github.com/me-no-dev/ESPAsyncTCP/archive/master.zip`. Install this library using the method in *step B*.

2. Copy the sketch in the `ESP32_BME680_OTA_mDNS.c` file in the `Practical` folder within the `Chapter01` folder in the GitHub repository to a new Arduino sketch and save it as `ESP32_BME680_OTA_mDNS`. Please do not forget to change the Wi-Fi SSID and password according to your Wi-Fi access point setup.

3. Verify the sketch by clicking on the ⊘ button, and if there are no errors, upload it to ESP32 by clicking the ⊙ button. Open the Serial Monitor and set the baud rate to **115200** to match the sketch setting and reset the board by pressing the **EN** button. Your Serial Monitor window should look like this:

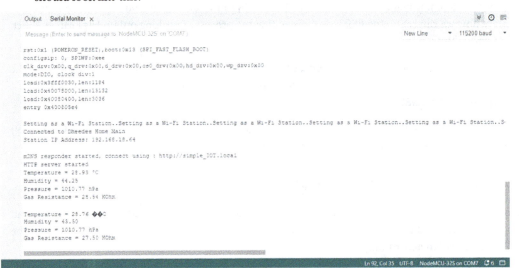

Figure 1.16 – Expected output from the Arduino IDE Serial Monitor

4. As the code also creates a web server, you can see it being visualized by opening your web browser and typing the address `http://simple_IOT.local`.

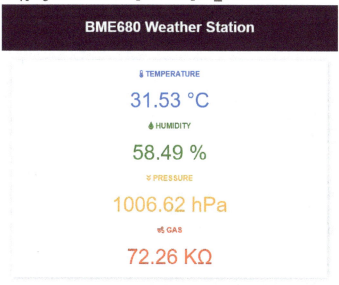

Figure 1.17 – Display on the local web server

And that's it; you've made your first IoT-based project! Now upload the code to GitHub and see whether you can also make these modifications to your hardware/code to further understand and practice the concepts that you have learned through this practical exercise:

- Can you switch the BME680 sensor with a soil humidity sensor in your kit? Which modifications do you need to make to your circuit and software for that?

- Can you modify the sample rate of the data so that it samples two times in one second?

Feel free to use the documentation from the **Keyestudio Super Starter Kit** to help you navigate the use cases of each sensor and how to properly use them. Throughout this book, the internet is going to be an effective helper for you; particularly as there may be some concepts that you may not know. However, we always intend to explain each one as thoroughly as possible so that you do not need to do so.

> **Important note**
>
> When making changes to your code such as with these experimental problems, always make sure to commit your progress so that you can revert to previous versions when your current code does not work. This is important to remember, as you will certainly run into some dead ends in a project such as this and will need to backtrack to a working version to keep things on pace.

In this practical, you have learned how to create a mini weather station that can measure three different parameters. This will serve as a building block toward understanding the potential of IoT and for us to build on the concepts that have been learned here further in other practical exercises.

Summary

In this chapter, we learned what IoT is, how we utilize it in our everyday lives despite it not being the massive presence it is in large industries, and what the four pillars that constitute it are. We then set up our development environment, laying the foundation for the rest of the book. This involved configuring the ESP32 development and GitHub environments and introducing a simple IoT demo to familiarize you with the hardware and workflows we'll be using throughout the book.

This chapter focused on selecting IoT hardware, covering considerations for different types and the trade-offs involved to ensure you choose the best option for your specific use case. We then discussed how to design a simple IoT system diagram, which will be the foundation for our more complex designs in the coming chapters, and how to connect smart objects to create the smart ecosystem that constitutes the IoT.

The hands-on experience was further enhanced by building a mini weather station in this chapter, allowing you to put the theory and skills you picked up thus far into practice and getting you more comfortable with working with IoT projects.

In the next chapter, we will be looking at the fundamentals of designing IoT networks and what to consider when doing so. This will build further on our skills for designing diagrams and making appropriate design factor decisions based on our use case.

Further reading

For more information about what was covered in this chapter, please refer to the following links:

- Learn more on getting started with GitHub: `https://docs.github.com/en/get-started`
- Understand more on what the Arduino IDE offers: `https://docs.arduino.cc/learn/starting-guide/the-arduino-software-ide`
- Learn more about the DHT module from Adafruit: `https://learn.adafruit.com/dht`
- Understand more about the concept of IoT: `https://www2.deloitte.com/ch/en/pages/innovation/articles/iot-explained.html`
- Get a better understanding of IoT microcontrollers: `https://www.nabto.com/iot-microcontroller-guide/`

2

Understanding and Designing IoT Networks

Understanding and designing IoT networks is a critical part of the work that needs to be done in establishing and deploying such systems within your smart environments. In this chapter, we will discuss the types of networks that are commonly designed, including wired and short-range wireless networks, **machine-to-machine** (**M2M**) networks, and long-range wireless networks, and discuss the use cases of each of these types of networks. We will investigate the key considerations of what to choose as part of the design, including the range, power consumption, cost, and security. We will also discuss the trade-offs to make when designing the infrastructure of the system, and the challenges and opportunities in utilizing the emerging technologies that come with these choices.

You will learn about common design patterns in how these networks are formed, how the topologies discussed in the previous chapter come into play as part of these best practices, and the types of technologies used in each scenario. As part of this, you will also apply your learnings by carrying out a practical that tasks you with creating a router from a Raspberry Pi, which involves creating your own design diagram for a household-based router and attempting to connect multiple devices to it to route them to their destination. By the end of the chapter, you will have gained an understanding of wireless technologies that are commonly part of IoT infrastructure setups, created simple network architecture for deploying IoT networks, and understand more about the potential of 5G technology for the future of IoT infrastructure and how to further optimize based on its offerings.

In this chapter, we're going to cover the following main topics:

- Understanding the fundamentals of network design
- Defining the design of an IoT network
- Designing wired and wireless IoT networks
- Practical – creating a Raspberry Pi Wi-Fi extender

Technical requirements

This chapter requires you to have the following hardware and software ready, grouped into two parts – Raspberry Pi hardware and software requirements for the practical:

- Hardware:

    - Raspberry Pi 4

    - Power supply for Raspberry Pi 4

    - MicroSD card

    - Keyboard and mouse (external)

    - Computer screen

    - HDMI/DVI/VGA cable

    - Ethernet cable (optional)

- Software:

    - Diagram design software of your choice (e.g., Draw.io)

    - Arduino IDE

The Raspberry Pi computer is a cheap, credit-card-sized but powerful computer that runs the Linux environment, while providing you with the ability to do everything a desktop computer can do, such as playing high-definition video, word processing, and making spreadsheets. It can interact with the environment around it through its **input/output (IO)** pins and can be used to control hardware projects through this. It is compatible with several programming languages such as Python, C, and C++.

We will be running our programs on the Raspberry Pi with C again, and again, don't worry if you don't understand some of the code; we will walk you through it and get you understanding the foundations of the Raspberry Pi in no time.

You can access the GitHub folder for the code that is used in this chapter at `https://github.com/PacktPublishing/IoT-Made-Easy-for-Beginners/tree/main/Chapter02`.

Understanding the fundamentals of network design

Before we head into seeing some best practices for designing networks, it is imperative that we have a good grasp of the networking concepts that go into designing them. So far, we have been looking at devices individually but not at the linking factor that brings them together: the connectivity that helps them communicate with one another as well as with the internet itself, hence the term **smart objects**. Here, we will illustrate some high-level concepts of how this is done in terms of the communication technologies needed and the seven layers of interaction that IoT goes through.

Ranges

Ranges determine the maximum distance at which devices can communicate with one another. They affect the area of coverage that the network can provide and the number of devices that can be connected. There is a vast variety of networking technologies, each with its own advantages and disadvantages on factors such as its range, its impedance by obstacles, and more. Some of the commonly used ones are as follows:

- **Bluetooth**: Bluetooth is a short-range wireless technology that is commonly used for IoT in deployments over short distances. You may have already used this several times on your phone when you wanted to pair it with another phone or were doing a data transfer. It has a range of up to 30 meters in open space, though this can be impeded by obstacles.

- **Wi-Fi**: Wi-Fi is another popular networking technology used for IoT, and certainly not a stranger to most readers, given its prevalence in our lives when we connect to the internet. Its range reaches up to 100 meters in open space, though it is impeded by obstacles if prevalent.

- **Zigbee**: Zigbee is a wireless networking technology that has a range of up to 20 meters in open space but may be expanded by using repeaters.

- **LoRa**: **Long range** (**LoRa**) is a wireless networking technology that works best for long-range communications, having a range of up to 15 kilometers in open space.

Let's look at the topology now.

Topology

A **topology** is how devices in a network are connected to one another. It provides the design and description of how routes are configured on a network, allowing communication to flow from one device to another. There are many topologies used for networking, but some topologies are more common than others in the use of IoT. The three most common ones for this purpose are point-to-point, mesh, and star topologies. We will describe and explain common use cases in this section for you to consider which ones would be appropriate for your own use. This will also help you to understand how they can later be used in designing the network flow diagrams that we will be discussing further in the following chapters. These topologies are depicted in the following figure.

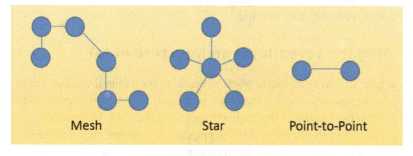

Figure 2.1 – Three network topologies used on the IoT

We will move to the first one now.

Mesh

In a **mesh topology**, devices are connected to each other in a way that creates multiple paths for data to travel from one device to another. This allows for a point of redundancy; that is, if one device fails, other networks can still communicate with each other. This is a crucial element to be used in IoT as often, high levels of reliability are required, such as in cases where production-critical workloads are being run that cannot be interrupted, or with sensors connected to patients in healthcare settings that alert providers if patients are not feeling well, given the direness of the situation.

Star

In a **star topology**, devices are connected to a central gateway that is the central point of communication within the network. Data must pass through the gateway to be transmitted from one device to another, though this makes the network more vulnerable if the gateway itself fails. It is a popular topology because it is simpler to set up. It would work well with fewer mission-critical loads, such as a leisure-based smart home network, given that although your fridge may be empty, a fault in notifying you of this would not leave you in a critical state as would some other situations that require more reliability within their networks.

Point-to-point

In a **point-to-point topology**, two devices connect directly with each other without an intermediary such as a gateway. This type of connection is often called a dedicated connection and is used for simpler applications such as connecting a sensor to a controller. Note that this is the topology that creates the least availability for your network; this would normally only be used in consumer-based deployments and those that are not running for critical purposes.

Understanding when to use which topology

To sum it up, the choice of topology depends on several factors, and it is important to consider this alongside the other considerations that you have already learned in this chapter for picking out the appropriate hardware for your use case scenario. In the next sections, we will be talking through this more and about how this all will factor into how we choose to architect our network and design it to fit the use case that we currently have in mind.

Understanding the seven-layer architecture of IoT

It is imperative to gain an understanding of where networking sits within the full spectrum of the IoT architecture. There are many models that have been proposed, but many of them mostly encompass the same processes and functionalities that each one tries to put forward. The seven-layer architecture model is a comprehensive model that reflects all the processes that go into the IoT architecture, helping us to understand what the interactions are between one layer and the next and abstracting them so that there can be visibility of how it all operates. Here, we will discuss the seven layers of the model alongside its uses, how it interacts with other layers within the model, and why it is important to the IoT architecture:

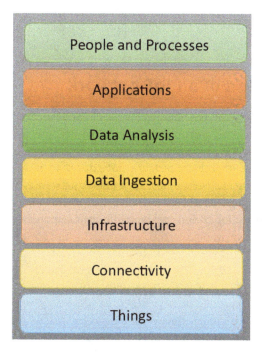

Figure 2.2 – Seven-layer architecture of IoT

- **Layer 1 – Things**: The things in this layer constitute the sensors and devices that are part of the IoT architecture that you are working with that collect data from the environment.

- **Layer 2 – Connectivity**: This layer allows devices to communicate between each other and the network. This includes protocols such as Bluetooth and Zigbee.

- **Layer 3 – Infrastructure**: This layer connects devices to the internet, enabling communication between devices, the cloud, and more. It includes networking technologies such as cellular networks, **low-power wide area networks (LPWANs)**, and more.

- **Layer 4 – Data ingestion**: This layer governs the ingestion and the solutions for storing our data. This includes storage solutions such as databases and data lakes.

- **Layer 5 – Data analysis**: This layer processes data, obtains insights, and sets actions in motion based on the data it receives. This includes workloads such as edge and cloud computing.

- **Layer 6 – Applications**: This layer provides the user interface for users to interact with. This includes mobile applications, the website interface, and voice assistants such as Amazon Alexa or Google Home.

- **Layer 7 – People and processes**: This layer constitutes the business model and strategy that is in place for the IoT solution.

With this, we have understood more about what constitutes networks and how different topologies can be used as part of forming them. Next, we will see how we can define the design of an IoT network in order to begin designing one.

Defining the design of an IoT network

It is important for us to understand the building blocks of an IoT network and how they connect with each other to form an effective, optimized network that suits our use case. In this section, we will be discussing the components of the network and how they fit together to function as we need them to. It is important to note that this is certainly not exhaustive of the components that an IoT network would have, but it contains what almost all, if not all, networks would have, and shows you how to piece the components together to be able to then apply them to the different network designs that you will see in the next section. Before we jump into the components, however, it is important we understand how we define smart objects, their components, and how they fit within the network to best utilize them in our networks.

Defining what constitutes a smart object

A smart object often has many definitions. However, it is important that we understand the fundamental building blocks of one to better envision how it fits within the network architecture. The following is an diagram of the five components that are contained within every smart object – the sensor, power source, actuator, communication device, and tiny computer:

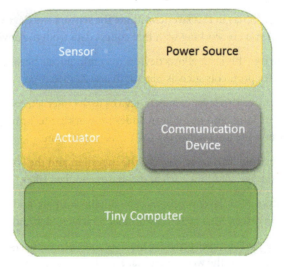

Figure 2.3 – Components of a smart object

Let's briefly define the five components:

- **Sensor**: The first component that is part of a smart object is the sensor. This is what helps detect environmental conditions such as luminosity, temperature, humidity, and many more.

- **Power source**: The second component is the power source that powers the device, allowing it to function. This may be through multiple different power sources, such as batteries, a power adapter that is simply wired to a power outlet, external power sources such as solar power, and many more.

- **Actuator**: The third component is the actuator, which acts based on the signal that is sent through to the device from the controller.

- **Communication device**: The fourth component is the communication device, which helps the device communicate with other devices and the gateways that it needs to communicate with to pass information through that it has sensed. It can be based on various communication protocols to transmit the information, which we will see more of in the following section.

- **Tiny computer**: The fifth and final component is a tiny, low-cost computer, which helps coordinate actions. This, in our use case, is the ESP32, which issues commands to the sensor and actuator while also controlling the communication device in pushing through information for our use case.

The components of a generic IoT network

There are many types of IoT networks, but many of them follow a similar pattern in terms of the main components that they must be based on. Next, we will cover three of the components that most – if not all – IoT networks have: the base station, which is derived from the fundamental requirements of a smart object, as described previously, the cloud server, and the control station.

Access point

The access point acts as the bridge between the cloud and the sensor network within the IoT network. The device generally has data processing and transmission functions while collecting data that is put through by the sensors, and can also push through updates toward them as well. It pushes data and actions that are possible to be taken to the cloud and can have different communication options, including Wi-Fi and cellular methods of communication.

An example is how a smart light bulb would have a base station that sends data toward the cloud while sending a message to the owner's phone when the light may be too dim at a certain time, informing them of which light is too dim and – if programmed to do so – triggering an action automatically based on the business intelligence rules it already is to abide by and operate with. This setup would help in multiple ways, including power consumption and automation, to make the owner's life easier.

Cloud services

Cloud services are the point where the data is received and processed and where actions are taken. As part of cloud services, cloud computing especially has become a very powerful tool that many organizations are leveraging to access massive amounts of computing power at very low costs through utilizing the concept of economies of scale. It is because of this that many companies have invested in it rather than continuing to build on their on-premises servers with the expense of setting them up and continuously maintaining them.

Cloud services are also able to continuously request that the base station send a periodic update in the form of a "heartbeat" to show that it is still functioning, and if not, alert the user in the form of a chosen notification such as a text message or an email. Users can also push through software updates to the base station, which in turn pushes it to the sensors within the network and any other hardware dependent on it. It is also able to perform analytics on the data, scale computing resources accordingly, and get the best recommendations based on its setup to both increase the effectiveness of its performance and save costs accordingly.

We will discuss this more in *Chapter 7, Working with Cloud Computing to Power IoT Solutions* where we will look at AWS's capabilities in this area.

Mobile app

The **mobile app** is where actions are taken. This could be multiple areas, such as the owner's phone, the AWS cloud console, or anything that can control the behavior of the system based on the data that is being fed in by the base station. In the example of the smart light bulb, the owner's phone might be the device used to control the mobile app where they can check the status of the light bulbs and accordingly control them based on whether they want to brighten or dim the lights, depending on the information and recommendations that the base station is providing to the network.

Putting it together

We can now put together the components and see the type of architecture that it forms. A diagram of these components put together can be seen here:

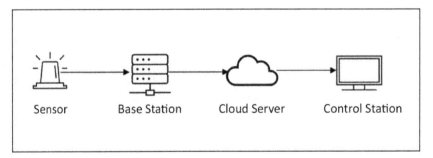

Figure 2.4 – Architecture of a simple sensor network

As can be seen, a sensor forwards its readings to a base station, which may or may not have storage or analysis capabilities within it. It then processes the findings and forwards them onto the cloud server, where the findings are then stored and further put through analysis. This all is then put through to the control station, where the data can be processed accordingly, and signals can be sent through the base station to reach the actuators in the system.

Most architectures within IoT networks will have this setup and these components under different names. As you navigate the next section filled with sample architectures, keep an eye out for equivalents to the aforementioned and see how they function within each network. Knowing these components and how they behave within the system will get you the fundamental building blocks of every IoT network, and help you to build on that knowledge and move toward the more complex systems that you will have to tackle within the later chapters of the book.

Designing wired and wireless IoT networks

When choosing the method of how you want your network to be deployed, you always have many options. In most cases, most methods of deployment would work. However, the challenge has always been finding the right type of deployment with the appropriate configurations to best ensure that the network effectively delivers and performs as it needs to, in terms of both performance and cost. In this section, we will cover the most common types of deployments for networks, including wired and short- and long-range wireless networks, as well as some other types of deployments. As part of this, the considerations behind how each network can be optimized will be discussed as well. You will also get the opportunity to design your own network deployments based on select scenarios and become more confident in your network design skills and in the choices that you make as part of the network architecture.

The following is a table of common IoT wireless standards. This is by no means an exhaustive list; this is simply a reference to look back on as you navigate this chapter and the rest of the book, as well as when making design choices between the wireless technologies that are to be used:

Technology	Frequency	Data Rate	Range	Power Usage	Cost
2G/3G	Cellular bands	10 Mb/s	A few km	High	High
802.15.4	2.4 GHz	250 kb/s	100 m	Low	Low
Bluetooth	2.4 GHz	1.2 – 1.3 Mb/s	100 m	Low	Low
LoRa	< 1 GHz	<50 kb/s	2 – 5 km	Low	Medium
LTE Cat 0/1	Cellular bands	1 – 10 Mb/s	A few km	Medium	High
NB-IoT	Cellular bands	0.1 – 1 Mb/s	A few km	Medium	High
SIGFOX	< 1 GHz	Very low	A few km	Low	Medium
Weightless	< 1 GHz	0.1 – 24 Mb/s	A few km	Low	Low
Wi-Fi (11f/h)	< 1 GHz	0.1 – 1 Mb/s	A few km	Medium	Low
WirelessHART	2.4 GHz	250 kb/s	100 m	Medium	Medium
Zigbee	2.4 GHz	250 kb/s	100 m	Low	Medium
Z-Wave	908.42 MHz	40 kb/s	30 m	Low	Medium

Figure 2.5 – Most common IoT wireless standards

As can be seen, wireless technologies certainly pose an important consideration as to which to use in what scenario.

Wired and wireless networks

In this section, we will explore wired and short-range wireless networks, seeing how they differ in functionality and understanding the scenarios of how one or the other is used.

Wired networks

The first option that many deployments have is to wire the network, having sensors, gateway, and servers wired together. This method of connecting networks fully within IoT is almost non-existent at this time; generally, only the network layer will have wired deployments. This is given that smart objects by nature are all widespread; they cannot all be connected via wires with the expectancy that they can all communicate over a long distance.

Common communication technologies as part of this are serial communication interfaces such as RS-232, which provides for single-ended signal transmission, though as expected, there are issues with ground noise being present, hence only being used for communication within 20 m, with commonly used serial lines only being 1–2 m. It is important to note that the main advantage of wired networks is that they possess incredibly fast speeds due to the highly decreased latency of communication between devices, as they do not depend on sending information wirelessly, which usually has its own challenges including impedance of obstacles, temperature-based environmental conditions, and other factors that may affect the information while it is still in transmission.

The following is an example of one such wired deployment.

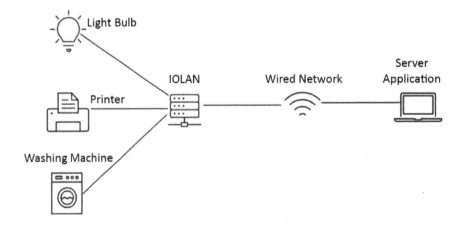

Figure 2.6 – Wired network architecture example

This wired deployment is based on RS-232. As can be seen, sensors are connected to IOLAN – servers that allow administrators to access remote serial console ports – through RS-232. From there, it connects further to the server application via RS-232 and sends the transmitted data from the sensors there. As can be seen, this architecture is very limited and needs everything to be connected by a cable to have data transmitted from one end to another. It is because of this that most IoT deployments are wireless, as we will discuss in the next few subsections as we show the capabilities of short- and long-range networks for building our own.

Scaling up wireless IoT networks

There are many types of wireless IoT networks, some spanning small scales and some going up to global ones. Here, we will look at the different types and look at building networks with technologies within them.

Home area networks

At the smallest scale, we'll explore **home area networks** (**HANs**), where IoT seamlessly blends into the fabric of daily living. Within the confines of a home, IoT devices such as smart thermostats, security cameras, and voice-activated assistants form a tightly knit network. This network, primarily aimed at enhancing comfort, security, and efficiency, transforms mundane abodes into smart homes. The simplicity and low cost of setting up HANs democratize smart living, enabling a personalized, smart living experience. Some common wireless networks include **Zigbee** and **Z-Wave**.

Local area networks

Stepping outside the home, IoT extends its reach to **local area networks** (**LANs**), commonly found in business establishments, educational institutions, and other community centers. Here, IoT devices monitor, manage, and optimize operations, fostering a conducive environment for productivity and learning. Whether it's the automated control of lighting and HVAC systems or the real-time monitoring of assets, LANs serve as the bedrock of IoT deployments at a community level. Moreover, the relatively higher data speeds and lower latencies in LANs unlock more robust and responsive IoT applications.

For the purposes of network building, we will be focusing on Zigbee, given its accessibility to build components around and its popularity among the IoT community for developing cost-effective, high-performance, short-range networks that can be used for a long period of time. Zigbee is designed to create **wireless personal area networks** (**WPANs**), utilizing the IEEE 802.15.4 standard as part of its physical and **media access control** (**MAC**) layers. The MAC layer is part of the data link layer responsible for managing device network access, addressing, and data packet control. It helps power networks at low cost, helping to monitor and take actions toward applications within the range of 10–100 m.

The Zigbee standard requires battery-powered devices to demonstrate a two-year battery life, effectively making it a suitable deployment for long periods of time. It is also starting to adopt a variety of energy-harvesting technologies, such as solar panels and even mechanical energy, with there now being light switches that are powered by the mechanical force of pressing the switch of the light itself.

The following illustrates the Zigbee architecture, which consists of four layers:

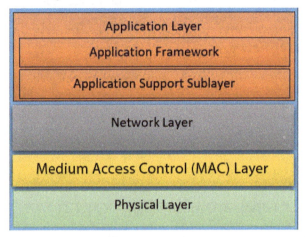

Figure 2.7 – Zigbee architecture layers

In the architecture, the physical layer transmits and receives data to and from the physical medium, defining physical characteristics of the communication such as the frequency and data rate that need to be put through. The MAC layer manages access to the wireless medium, ensuring devices can communicate with each other. It allows devices to request access to the medium and helps coordinate multiple devices that want to transmit simultaneously, while also being used for error detection and recovery. The network layer helps route data between devices, which allows the forming and maintaining of networks, as well as naming and addressing devices. The application layer is responsible for providing services to the application, including a set of standard application profiles to define the behavior and functionality of devices within different application domains.

A Zigbee network structure consists of three device types: the coordinator, router, and end device. In this deployment, each network has at least one coordinator and works as a network bridge. It helps handle data and acts as storage for the data. The routers then function as intermediate nodes that can connect multiple Zigbee devices. The end devices do not have much functionality; the interactions are mostly based on the parent nodes, allowing them to have lower power consumption, hence ensuring that they are able to operate over long periods of time.

The following is an example of this arrangement:

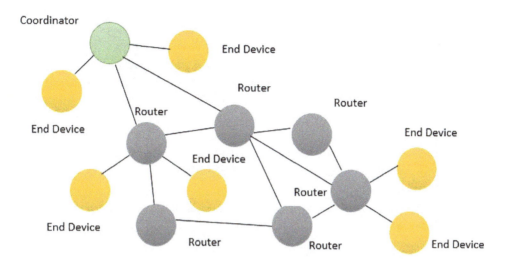

Figure 2.8 – Zigbee network structure arrangement example

As can be seen, there is only one coordinator in this diagram. The coordinator is attached to a couple of end devices: those that directly send data to it while two routers are attached to it. The routers are configured in the mesh configuration for high availability, and as we can see, one router can route to another in the event of the failure of one of them. This configuration is optimal in many use cases, especially those that are for mission-critical workloads such as within healthcare or automotive-based settings.

We can also apply this pattern to a solution within our everyday lives that we are very familiar with: a smart home. The following figure shows the network diagram of a smart home that utilizes Zigbee as its communication protocol between devices and towards the endpoint, and how it compares with a Wi-Fi network diagram:

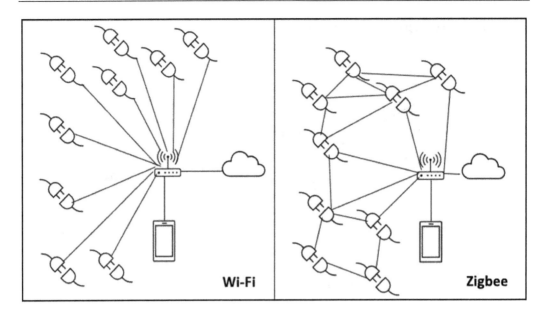

Figure 2.9 – Network diagram of Wi-Fi versus Zigbee

We can clearly see a difference between the deployment of Wi-Fi and Zigbee. While Wi-Fi uses a point-to-point deployment – having all the smart plugs connect to the same router at the same time – Zigbee forms a mesh network that then connects to a bridge before connecting to the router, allowing for higher availability due to having multiple routes where when one router goes off, another router can take charge of routing the connections through the mesh network. The bridge can act as the coordinator in this case, ensuring that connections come through it and forwarding controls toward the plug that comes from the cloud, routed by the router, with a few of the smart plugs acting as the router and the rest of the plugs acting as the end node.

Such design choices matter a lot when designing based on both use cases and protocols. We can see that Zigbee would not perform as effectively if we tried to assign it to a point-to-point network. We need to decide on the formation and pattern of the networks that we want to put through, especially when we consider issues such as reliability, availability, and security. We will see more of this in the next couple of chapters as well, but when designing networks, put these at the forefront of your mind, as networks that are optimized are different from networks that *just work*. Just like coding, you can have a solution that *just works*, but when you start deploying those solutions into industry-based settings, there will be consequences for failing to optimize.

Interactions between protocols

We can also observe the usage of multiple protocols within one environment. It is common to decide on having different devices communicate with each other within one system with multiple protocols, ensuring that the devices work well with each other. We can again return to our smart home example to see how the protocols we have discussed so far communicate within one ecosystem:

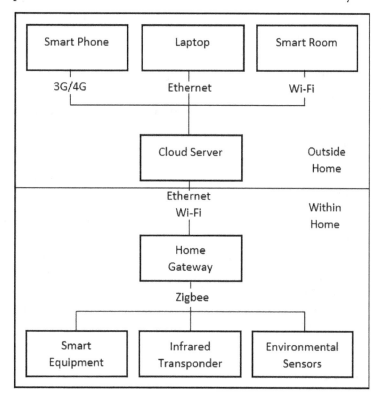

Figure 2.10 – Interaction between multiple IoT protocols

In this example, we can divide our ecosystem into two parts: the outside and the inside within the smart home ecosystem. Inside our home, we would only require short-range wireless protocols. We have three categories of smart objects that we need to connect to the cloud server: environmental sensors, infrared transponder, and other smart equipment. We can utilize Zigbee within a mesh network to connect all this to the home gateway, which then utilizes Wi-Fi to transmit the telemetry data to the cloud server to then be further analyzed and processed.

On the other hand, for the outside of the home, we have three smart devices: a smartphone, a laptop, and a smart room. These three pose more of a challenge because they are not as interoperable as the objects inside the smart home due to the differing standards that they have. In this case, we can use 3G/4G for communication between the smartphone and the cloud, use Ethernet in the form of an RG-232 cable to connect the laptop to the cloud server, and use Wi-Fi to connect the smart room to the cloud. With that, all the parts of the ecosystem are linked together toward the cloud and any of the three smart devices from the outside can control the smart home through the cloud while receiving telemetry data from the devices within the smart home.

This example shows how multiple protocols already interact with ease around us, despite us at times not being aware of it. It often is simply up to our due diligence to ascertain which protocols would work best for what device and what scenario, as we want to ensure that we get the optimal performance for our use case. In completing our discussion, we also have the option of selecting long-distance protocols, but we will cover these in depth in *Chapter 4, Examining Communication and Connectivity Technologies* where we examine more types of protocols alongside them. For the purposes of this chapter, these are the protocols that we will highlight up to this point.

Wide area networks

On a broader scale, **wide area networks** (**WANs**) lay the groundwork for large-scale IoT implementations. Covering vast geographic expanses, WANs facilitate IoT connectivity in smart cities, agricultural fields, and industrial sectors. From monitoring traffic and managing waste in urban areas to overseeing crop conditions in rural landscapes, WANs enable a myriad of IoT applications. Cellular networks, a form of WAN, are pivotal in delivering consistent and far-reaching connectivity to IoT devices, forming the backbone that supports expansive IoT ecosystems. Through WANs, the IoT narrative transcends local boundaries, ushering in a new era of connected solutions that promise to redefine the modern way of life.

Cellular networks

Cellular networks play a crucial role in the IoT ecosystem, allowing devices to communicate with each other and the internet. Unlike traditional networks that rely on wired connections, cellular networks use radio waves to transmit data wirelessly, enabling IoT devices to communicate with each other and the internet over long distances. This connectivity allows for real-time data collection, analysis, and control, enabling businesses and consumers to make more informed decisions and improve efficiency. With the proliferation of IoT devices, cellular networks will continue to play an increasingly important role in enabling seamless communication and connectivity across a wide range of applications and industries.

In this section, we will discuss three of these technologies: 3G, 4G, and LTE technologies.

3G, 4G, and LTE technologies in IoT networks

3G, 4G, and LTE cellular technologies have been widely used as a communication protocol between devices, allowing devices to transmit data and interact with each other in real time. Their main advantage is their wide availability, given that their infrastructure has already been set up in many areas of the world in the form of base stations for cellular communication. This makes it easy for IoT devices to connect to the internet even in remote or isolated locations.

We have seen these technologies be used to support a wide range of IoT applications, including asset tracking, remote monitoring, and smart home systems. They have been used to connect devices such as smart thermostats, security cameras, and other home automation devices. Despite their advantages, it is important to note that they do have some limitations, especially compared to their successor, 5G. They are, for example, slower and less reliable than 5G, and are not able to support the high-bandwidth and low-latency requirements of a select subset of IoT applications. However, due to their prevalence and ease of use, they will continue to be used in a wide range of applications over the coming years.

In *Figure 2.11*, we illustrate the different layers that make up the LTE E-UTRAN protocol stack:

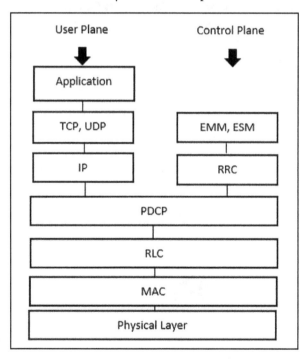

Figure 2.11 – Layers of the LTE E-UTRAN protocol stack

It is comprised of two planes and three layers. First off, we can see that the planes are comprised of the user plane and the control plane. The first layer is the physical layer, which carries the information from the MAC transport channels via the air interface. It helps facilitate link adaption, cell search, power control, and other measurements for the **Radio Resource Control** (**RRC**) layer. The RRC layer in wireless communication networks is responsible for the management and control of radio bearers, handling key functions such as connection establishment, configuration, and release. The MAC layer facilitates the connection between logical and transport channels. It aids in amalgamating MAC SDUs from logical channels into transport blocks destined for the physical layer, and also in separating them when received from the physical layer. MAC SDUs are payload data that is transmitted by the MAC layer, encapsulated within a MAC protocol data unit for network communication. Additionally, it plays a crucial role in managing scheduling data, aiding error rectification, and prioritizing data handling.

The **Radio Link Control** (**RLC**) layer helps with the transfer of upper-layer **Protocol Data Units** (**PDUs**), error correction, concatenation, segmentation, and the reassembly of RLC SDUs. PDUs are the units of data exchanged, encapsulating user data and control information for reliable and efficient communication. It also helps to re-segment, discard, and reorder RLC data PDUs, detect duplicates, re-establish RLC, and detect protocol errors. The **Packet Data Convergence Protocol** (**PDCP**) layer assists with header compression and decompression of IP data, the transfer of data between the user plane and control plane, the maintenance of PDCP sequence numbers, delivering upper-layer PDUs in-sequence, and duplicate elimination of lower-layer SDUs. The RRC helps to broadcast system information that is related to the non-access stratum, helps to broadcast system information that is related to the access stratum, and helps with the paging, establishment, maintenance, and release of a certain RRC connection.

In the following diagram, we show how a base station is deployed within a network and how it communicates with the two core mobile planes:

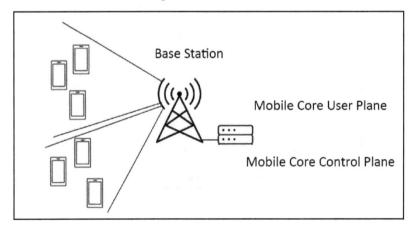

Figure 2.12 – Base station deployment within an IoT network

5G technologies in IoT networks

5G is the fifth generation of cellular technologies, designed to be faster and more reliable than its predecessors. It has the potential to revolutionize the way devices and machines interact with one another. One of its key features is that it is able to support a wide range of applications, be they in smart homes, autonomous vehicles, or industrial automation. It can also support many devices, given that it is designed for scalability and flexibility, ensuring that it is able to facilitate the connection of many smart devices without experiencing lags in performance.

Machine-to-machine IoT networks

M2M networks are a subfield of IoT that focuses on the communication between devices rather than the communication between devices and humans. It focuses on devices communicating with each other and sharing data, helping them coordinate their actions and autonomously make decisions based on the data that they have shared. Often, this leads to increased efficiency and automation in several industries and applications.

The following is a sample of how M2M nodes are structured within a network.

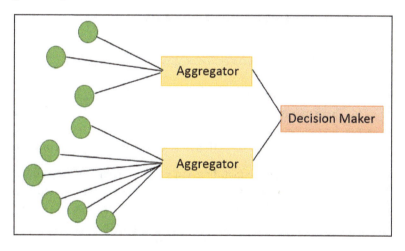

Figure 2.13 – M2M nodes within a network

As can be seen, there can be multiple nodes within one system. They are all connected to an aggregator that collects the information accordingly and then sends the information to a decision-maker within the system, which then controls the system based on the business intelligence rules that it was set with. Note that this is for a very simple system; most systems may have multiple decision-makers for a myriad of aggregators for an even larger network of sensors.

In the following, we can see how the network architecture of M2M is provisioned and the interactions within it:

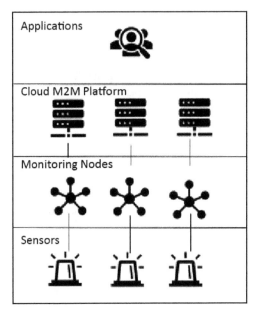

Figure 2.14 – Network architecture of M2M and its interactions

Firstly, we can see that the sensors interact with monitoring nodes that, in this case, act as the aggregators that we have discussed. These monitoring nodes then pass the data onto the cloud M2M platform, which, in this case, acts as both the analytics engine and the decision-maker. It then sends actions back to the sensors, which can also actuate and take actions based on the rules that were already formed.

As discussed in the first chapter, we can see that there is a slight difference between the focus of this type of network and IoT in general: namely, its focus on M2M interaction as opposed to machine-to-humans. By no means does this mean that it is isolated from the IoT concept; it is simply a different focus, as can be seen. It is now common to see it implemented in many industries, including smart grids, which monitor and control energy usage in buildings autonomously, transportation, which tracks the movement of goods, and healthcare, which remotely monitors patients and administers care when needed based on the condition of the patients, depending on the sensor readings that it is getting.

Other IoT networks

There are a couple of more widely known types of IoT networks, such as cellular networks, but given that we want to focus on the more consumer side of IoT, we will not be covering these.

Practicing forming your own networks

Given your understanding of the components of different types of networks and having seen examples of several of them within both everyday use and the industry, you can now form your own networks and apply them accordingly to different use cases. This subsection will allow you to practice forming such networks and get you more comfortable with different considerations. You will need this knowledge as we go deeper into the book, especially when we start to explore concepts such as wireless sensor networks and hybrid models of deployment for IoT networks.

Some IoT networks for you to think about and design a diagram for, outlining the components and flow of information through the network, are as follows:

- A network based on a hospital where sensors are in the form of heartbeat monitors, and must be controlled via a centralized computer within the hospital itself

- A network based on a smart home where sensors are everyday smart appliances, and they all need to have data put through to the cloud and be automated accordingly

For every case, ensure that you outline the components along with the protocols that you would like to be used between each component. Feel free to use any documentation online; some have been linked in the *Further reading* section that you might find useful. Don't worry if you're not sure what to use where; it takes practice to get used to these cases and you will certainly get a lot of practice throughout the book, especially since we'll move to more complex networks as we progress through further chapters.

Important note

When making changes to your code, such as with these experimental problems, always make sure to commit your progress so that you can revert to previous versions when your current code does not work. This is important to remember, as you will certainly run into some dead ends in a project such as this and will need to backtrack to a working version to keep things on pace.

In the next section, we will put all we have learned into practice by creating a Raspberry Pi Wi-Fi extender in a practical exercise.

Practical – creating a Raspberry Pi Wi-Fi extender

In this chapter's practical, we will create a Wi-Fi extender based on a Raspberry Pi. As part of this, we will be using the **dnsmasq package**, which will act as both the **Domain Name System (DNS)** and **Dynamic Host Configuration Protocol (DHCP)** server for the connections that we will need. DNS servers translate domain names into IP addresses, while DHCP servers automatically assign IP addresses and other network configuration parameters to devices on a network. We will also use the **hostapd package**, which will help set up one of the Wi-Fi modules as an access point.

Ensure that you have an active Wi-Fi router to connect to, alongside an Ethernet device we will be intending to bridge the Wi-Fi connection to.

You will be able to find any code segments used also located on GitHub, within the corresponding filename, in the `raspberry_pi_wifi_extender` subdirectory of `Chapter02` at `https://github.com/PacktPublishing/IoT-Made-Easy-for-Beginners/tree/main/Chapter02/raspberry_pi_wifi_extender`.

Hardware setup

We will start off by setting up the hardware for use as a Wi-Fi extender. In this case, most of the setup will be done on our Raspberry Pi:

1. Download Raspberry Pi Imager:

    A. Visit the official Raspberry Pi software page at `https://www.raspberrypi.org/software/`.

    B. Choose the appropriate version of Raspberry Pi Imager for your computer's operating system (Windows, macOS, or Linux) and click to download.

    C. Once the download is complete, locate the downloaded installer file on your computer.

2. Install Raspberry Pi Imager:

    A. Double-click the downloaded installer file to start the installation process.

    B. Follow the on-screen prompts to complete the installation. Raspberry Pi Imager should now be installed on your computer.

3. Insert your microSD card into the card reader on your computer. If you're using an external card reader, connect it to your computer first, then insert the microSD card.

4. Locate the Raspberry Pi Imager application on your computer and launch it. You should see a simple interface with a few buttons.

5. Choose the operating system image:

    A. Click the **Choose OS** button in Raspberry Pi Imager.

    B. A list of available operating systems will be displayed. Select the desired operating system for your Raspberry Pi – for beginners, we recommend starting with Raspberry Pi OS (32-bit):

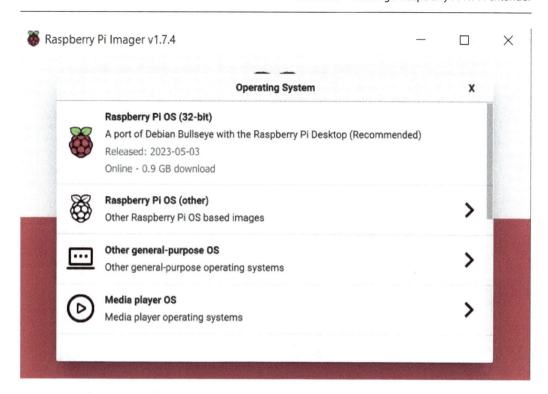

Figure 2.15 – List of available operating systems displayed after clicking Choose OS

6. Select the microSD card:

    A. Click the **Choose Storage** button in Raspberry Pi Imager.

    B. A list of available storage devices will be displayed. Select your microSD card from the list. Be careful to select the correct device, as all data on the chosen device will be erased.

7. Enable SSH, a cryptographic network protocol for secure data communication, remote command-line login, and other secure network services between two networked computers:

    A. Click on the **Advanced options** gear icon in the top-right corner of the **Raspberry Pi Imager** window.

    B. Check the **Enable SSH** box.

    C. You will be prompted to set a custom password for the **pi** user. Enter a strong password and confirm it by retyping it in the provided fields:

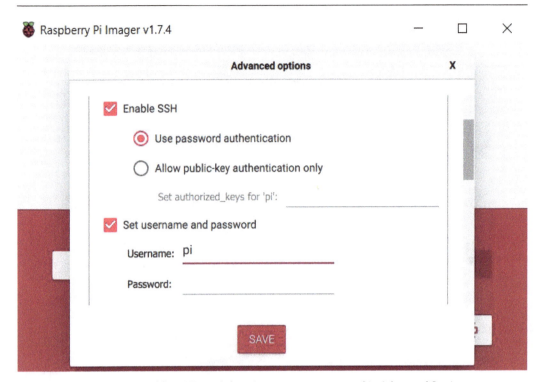

Figure 2.16 – Enabling SSH and choosing a custom password in Advanced Settings

8. Flash the image:

    A. Verify that you've selected the correct operating system and microSD card.

    B. Click the **Write** button in Raspberry Pi Imager to begin the flashing process.

    C. Raspberry Pi Imager will download the operating system image (if necessary), format the microSD card, and write the image to the card. This process may take some time, depending on the speed of your internet connection and the microSD card.

9. Safely eject the microSD card:

    A. Once the flashing process is complete, Raspberry Pi Imager will display a success message. Click the **Continue** button to close the message.

    B. Safely eject the microSD card from your computer.

10. You have successfully flashed an operating system image onto a microSD card using Raspberry Pi Imager. The SD card is now ready for use with a Raspberry Pi device. Simply insert the microSD card into your Raspberry Pi and power it up to begin using your new operating system.

11. Connect your Raspberry Pi to your local network using an Ethernet cable or by connecting to Wi-Fi.

12. SSH into the Raspberry Pi using the following command:

```
$ ssh pi@raspberrypi.local
```

```
C:¥Users>ssh pi@raspberrypi.local
pi@raspberrypi.local's password:
Linux raspberrypi 6.1.21-v8+ #1642 SMP PREEMPT Mon Apr  3 17:24:16 BST 2023 aarch64

The programs included with the Debian GNU/Linux system are free software;
the exact distribution terms for each program are described in the
individual files in /usr/share/doc/*/copyright.

Debian GNU/Linux comes with ABSOLUTELY NO WARRANTY, to the extent
permitted by applicable law.
Last login: Tue Jun 20 13:48:15 2023
pi@raspberrypi: $
```

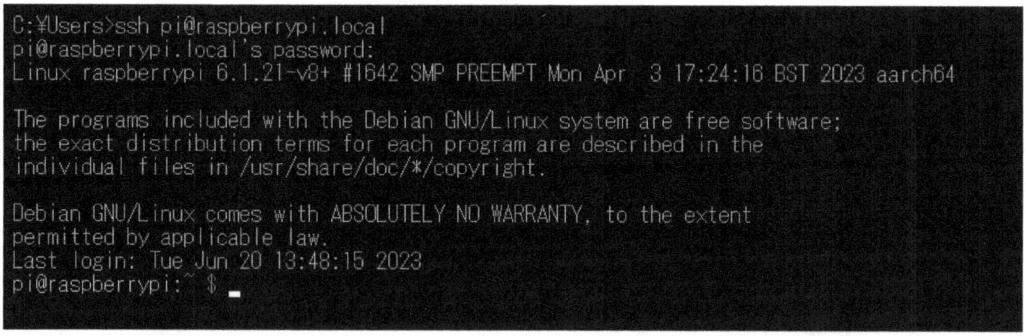

Figure 2.17 – Output from running SSH on the Raspberry Pi

Now, let's take a look at the coding part.

Coding it up

We will now create the code for running the extender:

1. Before we start installing the packages we need, we will run an update on the Raspberry Pi by running the following commands:

```
$ sudo apt update
$ sudo apt upgrade
$ sudo reboot
```

2. We will now set up systemd-networkd daemon. It serves as a system utility responsible for managing network settings. As network devices are connected or detected, it configures them accordingly. Additionally, it possesses the capability to generate virtual network devices.

To reduce the reliance on extra packages, networkd is utilized because it is integrated into the init system, eliminating the need for dhcpcd.

We first need to disable two services, networking.service and dhcpcd.service, by masking them. We use systemctl to manage the services. Masking prevents these services from being started automatically or manually, effectively disabling their functionality. Note that executing this command necessitates root privileges:

```
$ sudo systemctl mask networking.service dhcpcd.service
```

3. We then use the `sed` command, a stream editor, to modify the `/etc/resolvconf.conf` file in place (without creating a temporary file). The `-i` option tells `sed` to edit the file in place. The command inserts a new line at the beginning of the file (*line number 1*) with the content `resolvconf=NO`. This line disables the usage of the `resolvconf` program to manage the DNS resolver configuration, as indicated by the NO value:

```
$ sudo vi /etc/resolvconf.conf
```

Navigate to the first line by typing gg. Insert a new line there by typing O (the capital letter *O*).

4. Type `resolvconf=NO` and press *Enter* to start a new line below it. Press *Esc* to return to normal mode and save the changes by typing wq and pressing *Enter*.

5. Now, we can use the `systemd-networkd` daemon that is already built in. We need to enable `systemd-networkd` daemon and create a symbolic link from `/run/systemd/resolve/resolv.conf` to `/etc/resolv.conf`, using the latter as the DNS resolver configuration:

```
$ sudo systemctl enable systemd-networkd.service systemd-
resolved.service
$ sudo ln -s -f /run/systemd/resolve/resolv.conf /etc/resolv.
conf
```

6. We must now configure `wpa-supplicant`. We need to generate a new file by executing the following command:

```
$ sudo vi /etc/wpa_supplicant/wpa_supplicant-wlan0.conf
```

7. Incorporate the subsequent code and save the file by pressing *Esc* to enter normal mode, then type `:w` and hit *Enter*. The code is as follows:

```
country=AU
ctrl_interface=DIR=/var/run/wpa_supplicant GROUP=netdev
update_config=1
network={
ssid="Raspi-Extender"
mode=2
key_mgmt=WPA-PSK
psk="raspberry"
frequency=2437
}
```

Substitute `Raspi-Extender` and `raspberry` with your preferred values.

This configuration file is intended for the `wlan0` built-in Wi-Fi adapter, which will establish a wireless access point.

8. Now, we must grant the user read and write access to the file:

```
$ sudo chmod 600 /etc/wpa_supplicant/wpa_supplicant-wlan0.conf
```

We must then restart the wpa_supplicant service:

```
$ sudo systemctl disable wpa_supplicant.service
$ sudo systemctl enable wpa_supplicant@wlan0.service
```

9. We must accordingly arrange for wlan1 to act as the client. To do this, we must first generate a new file through the following command:

```
$ sudo vi /etc/wpa_supplicant/wpa_supplicant-wlan1.conf
```

10. Incorporate the given code and save the file by pressing *Esc* to enter normal mode, then type : w and hit *Enter*. The code is as follows:

```
country=AU
ctrl_interface=DIR=/var/run/wpa_supplicant GROUP=netdev
update_config=1
network={
ssid="TelstraABD215"
psk="12345678"
}
```

Substitute TelstraABD215 and 12345678 with your own router's SSID (Wi-Fi name) and password.

This configuration file is designed for the wlan01 USB Wi-Fi adapter, which will be employed to connect to a wireless router.

11. Provide the user with read and write access to the file:

```
$ sudo chmod 600 /etc/wpa_supplicant/wpa_supplicant-wlan1.conf
```

12. Now, we must restart the wpa_supplicant service:

```
$ sudo systemctl disable wpa_supplicant.service
$ sudo systemctl enable wpa_supplicant@wlan1.service
```

13. We must now configure the appropriate interfaces. First, we need to generate a new file using the following command:

```
$ sudo vi /etc/systemd/network/08-wlan0.network
```

14. Insert the provided code and save the file by pressing *Esc* to enter normal mode, then type : w and hit *Enter*. The code is as follows:

```
[Match]
Name=wlan0
```

```
[Network]
Address=192.168.9.1/24
IPForward=yes
IPMasquerade=yes
DHCPServer=yes
[DHCPServer]
DNS=1.1.1.1
```

15. Generate a fresh file by employing the following command:

```
$ sudo vi /etc/systemd/network/12-wlan1.network
```

16. Incorporate the specified code and save the file by pressing *Esc* to enter normal mode, then type : w and hit *Enter*. The specified code will look as follows:

```
[Match]
Name=wlan1
[Network]
DHCP=yes
```

17. Now restart the Raspberry Pi using the following command:

```
$ sudo reboot
```

18. Now see whether your repeater is working by checking for the Wi-Fi connection called *raspberry* on another device. If it shows up and you can connect to it with your provided password, that means everything is functioning as expected.

And that's it; you've made your first Raspberry Pi Wi-Fi extender!

Now, upload the code to GitHub and see whether you can also make the following modifications to your hardware/code for further understanding and practice on the concepts that you have learned through this practical:

- Can you also try to route the ESP32 that you have configured to connect to the router? Which modifications do you need to make to your circuit and software for that?

- Can you redirect the route of your router to another address?

Feel free to use the documentation from Raspberry Pi's official website, which is linked in the *Further reading* section at the end of the chapter. As before, the internet is going to be an effective helper for you.

Summary

In this chapter, we learned the fundamentals of IoT networks based on the components they have and how to apply different topologies as design patterns to the networks. We also gained an understanding of the design of the networks themselves. We looked at designing wired and short-range wireless networks, long-range wireless networks, and M2M networks. When factoring design considerations such as cost and environment, designing networks is not only about finding something that works but also about doing so in such a way that the flow of information from one part of the network to another can be done optimally while still meeting the requirements that are put out.

Finally, we discussed how you can use this knowledge to design the flow of a Raspberry Pi router and implement it, all while connecting objects to it that would use it as a gateway. With this practical, you should have become more confident in designing IoT networks and gained an understanding of how to apply critical knowledge within it to more use cases of your own.

In the next chapter, we will be looking at understanding the use of application protocols, learning which ones to use in what scenario, and integrating that into our IoT network design.

Further reading

For more information about what was covered in this chapter, please refer to the following links:

- Understand more on the specifications for Zigbee: `https://zigbeealliance.org/wp-content/uploads/2019/11/docs-05-3474-21-0csg-zigbee-specification.pdf`

- Explore the specifications of RS-232: `https://www.analog.com/media/en/technical-documentation/product-selector-card/rs232%20quick%20guide.pdf`

- Understand more about the Raspberry Pi's configuration: `https://www.raspberrypi.com/documentation/computers/configuration.html`

- Understand more about programming with the Raspberry Pi: `https://tutorials-raspberrypi.com/learn-how-to-program-on-the-raspberry-pi-part-1-introduction/`

- Explore more about what M2M technology entails: `https://www.ibm.com/blogs/internet-of-things/what-is-m2m-technology/`

3

Integrating Application Protocols

In the previous chapters, we learned about **IoT networks** and what constitutes them. However, to ensure that the smart devices within these networks function and communicate with each other, they rely on a diversity of **application protocols**. These come together with the **communication protocols** that we saw in the last chapter and certainly build more of a picture of the network. Integrating them further creates new challenges in terms of having trade-offs, but creates powerful opportunities to further power your solution to make use of the best communication methods.

Application protocols are the rules and standards that dictate how devices exchange information over a given network. These protocols help devices discover and connect to each other, allow them to send and receive data, and help control and manage them. This chapter will discuss why these protocols are important to the development of IoT networks and solutions and how you can design with them in consideration, given that the selection of appropriate protocols is essential to creating optimized networks for your use case. Some examples of such protocols that are used for IoT networks are **Message Queuing Telemetry Transport (MQTT)**, **Constrained Application Protocol (CoAP)**, and **Extensible Messaging and Presence Protocol (XMPP)**. Learning application protocols is crucial for IoT as they facilitate seamless communication between the vast array of interconnected devices, ensuring data is accurately exchanged in real time. Understanding these protocols is key to developing and managing efficient IoT networks, as it ensures interoperability and security and optimizes data transmission across various devices and platforms.

In this chapter, we're going to cover the following main topics:

- Application protocols and how they fit into the picture
- Requirements for application protocols
- Integrating application protocols into the design
- Creating an MQTT pub and sub communication between ESP32 and Raspberry Pi

Technical requirements

This chapter will require you to have the following hardware and software installed:

- Hardware:

  - Two laptops (if you don't have two, you can use the Raspberry Pi as one of them)

- Software:

  - Mosquitto client

  - Arduino IDE

  - Command Prompt (you already have this on Windows)

  - cURL

If you are not familiar with Mosquitto or cuRL and/or currently do not have them installed, we will guide you through installation in the following subsections. Otherwise, feel free to skip the next subsections and go to the next heading.

Installing Mosquitto

Mosquitto is an MQTT-based, open source message broker service that sends and receives messages. It is used within remote locations to power connections where the network bandwidth is limited or only a *small code footprint* is required. It is lightweight and can be used over all types of devices, from low-power microcomputers to full servers. In this chapter, we will be using it to establish MQTT connections. We will discuss more about MQTT later in this chapter, but in the meantime, we will guide you through installing Mosquitto onto your laptop.

To begin installing Mosquitto, navigate to the MQTT Mosquitto broker download from the official website. The link to the website is `https://mosquitto.org/download/`.

The following are the steps to install Mosquitto on your computer:

1. Choose either 32-bit or 64-bit for your Windows computer, depending on what you are using. If you are not sure, you can check this by going to **Start** | **Settings** | **System** | **About** and checking **System type** under **Device specifications**.

2. Execute the `.exe` file that you obtain after downloading the installer.

3. Follow the prompts, take note of the folder your Mosquitto is installed in, and install it.

4. Open your command prompt as an administrator and navigate to where your broker is installed.

5. Run the following command to finish the installation of your client:

```
$ mosquitto install
```

6. You will most likely receive a message that the Mosquitto broker is installed on your Windows machine. Run the following command to start Mosquitto to check its successful installation:

```
$ net mosquitto start
```

7. You will receive a message that the broker has started successfully; this means that you have successfully installed the Mosquitto broker onto your machine.

8. You can also check the version of Mosquitto with the following command to verify its installation:

```
$ mosquitto -V
```

And with that, you're done with the installation!

We will be running our programs on Python during this chapter, and again, don't worry if you don't understand some of the code; we will walk you through it and get you understanding how each part of the code works in no time.

You can access the GitHub folder for the code that is used in this chapter at https://github.com/PacktPublishing/IoT-Made-Easy-for-Beginners/tree/main/Chapter03/.

Installing Client for URL (cURL)

cURL is a popular command-line tool that is used to transfer data over the network using a variety of protocols, including **Hypertext Transfer Protocol (HTTP)**, **Hypertext Transfer Protocol Secure (HTTPS)**, **File Transfer Protocol (FTP)**, and **Secure File Transfer Protocol (SFTP)**. There are many requests that can be made with cURL, including **GET**, **POST**, and **HEAD** requests. This allows many functions to be done, including retrieving HTTP headers, downloading HTML pages, submitting forms, downloading and uploading files, and much more.

The following is a step-by-step guide on how to install cURL onto your machine:

1. Navigate to the cURL download wizard at the link https://curl.se/dlwiz/. Download the cURL executable.

2. Execute the cURL executable and follow through with the installation. Take note of the folder in which it is installed, as you will need to refer to it later.

3. Update your environmental variables the same way it was done in *Chapter 1, An Introduction to IoT Architecture, Hardware, and Real-Life Applications*, so that you can call cURL easily from anywhere in your environment.

4. Open your command prompt and type the following command to check the version of cURL (and that it is successfully installed):

```
$ curl --version
```

And with that, cURL is successfully installed!

Application protocols and they fit into the picture

We have discussed much about how IoT networks are formed and their considerations as part of different components, including communication protocols, components for the networks, and many more. However, we have not yet discussed one very important component that operates on the application layer: application protocols. Application protocols operate to ensure that data is sent from one device to another, and understanding which protocol to use and when is imperative for designing effective and optimized networks. In this section, we will be discussing the fundamental application protocols that are usually used within different IoT deployments, and what we should consider when we are faced with different use cases.

We will also have some practical exercises within the section to help you understand the process of how communications work between devices that use the protocol. We will then apply this understanding to the more complex use cases we will discuss in the following chapters.

The different types of application protocols

There are many different types of application protocols, but only a subset of them is normally used for IoT solutions. We will discuss four main protocols that are popular for use within IoT: MQTT, COaP, XMPP, and HTTP. We will discuss common use cases for them and help you understand when to use each one.

Message Queuing Telemetry Transport (MQTT)

MQTT is a lightweight publish-subscribe messaging protocol used mainly within IoT and M2M communication. Developed by IBM in the 1990s, it is now an ISO standard and commonly used in many industrial settings. One of its key features that sets it apart from other application protocols is its low bandwidth and resource requirements, allowing it to be suitable for devices that only have limited processing power or network connectivity. This helps it be commonly served through not only common protocols such as Wi-Fi, but also through LTE as well when used for devices that are not in fixed locations and/or do not have access to traditional Wi-Fi or wired networks.

Within its **publish-subscribe model**, clients publish messages to a topic, which subscribed clients to the topic then receive. This model makes the system very scalable, given that new clients can be added or removed without the worry of affecting other clients. Clients can publish a message to a broker, which can then distribute the message to all the subscribed clients. With this method, it helps all devices communicate with each other in a decentralized way, not necessitating a central server to mediate the communication. We will be using the terms publish-subscribe and pub/sub interchangeably throughout the book.

There are three main **quality of service (QoS)** levels – levels that determine how hard the broker and clients will attempt to deliver the message. QoS 0 is the lowest level, where the message is delivered once at most, and no confirmation will be sent. QoS 1 is a level higher than 0, where the message is delivered at least once with confirmation being sent. QoS 2 is the highest level among the levels, where the message is delivered exactly once and confirmation for it is sent.

To understand how MQTT messages are structured, let us take a look at the format of such messages:

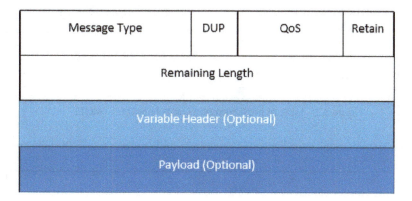

Figure 3.1 – Structure of an MQTT message

The **fixed header** is the first part of the MQTT message and is always present, regardless of the message type. It comprises the two first layers, which in turn comprise the **Message type**, **Duplicate (DUP)**, **QoS**, **Retain**, and **Remaining Length**. The message type includes information on the type of action being performed (e.g., CONNECT, PUBLISH, or SUBSCRIBE). The flags for the message simply contain additional information about the message, such as the QoS level described earlier and whether the message is retained. **Variable Header** contains additional information about the message, though this may depend on the message type. CONNECT messages, for example, have a variable header that includes the protocol name, version, keep-alive timer, and client identifier. Not all types of messages contain the same information, which is why it is mostly customized to the type of message. **Payload** contains the actual data being transmitted in the message, though it may not be present in all messages as it is deemed optional.

The following is a table of the most common control packets you will see as you use MQTT, the flow directions that each of the packets has, and the description of each of the packets. Feel free to refer to this table as you navigate through the exercises of this chapter, as it will help you better understand the outputs that you will get and, hence, the flow of the data as part of MQTT:

Control Packet	Flow Direction	Description
CONNECT	Client to server	Client request to connect to server
CONNACK	Client to server	Connect acknowledgement
PUBLISH	Client to server or server to client	Publish message
PUBACK	Client to server or server to client	Publish acknowledgement
PUBREC	Client to server or server to client	Publish received (assured delivery part 1)
PUBREL	Client to server or server to client	Publish release (assured delivery part 2)
PUBCOMP	Client to server or server to client	Publish completed (assured delivery part 3)
SUBSCRIBE	Client to server	Client subscribe request
SUBACK	Client to server	Subscribe acknowledgement
UBSUBSCRIBE	Client to server	Unsubscribe request
UNSUBACK	Server to client	Unsubscribe acknowledgement
PINGREP	Client to server	PING request
PINGRESP	Server to client	PING response
DISCONNECT	Client to server	Client is disconnecting

Figure 3.2 – Table of most common control packets in MQTT

Next, we can see how communication between a client and a broker takes place in the following diagram:

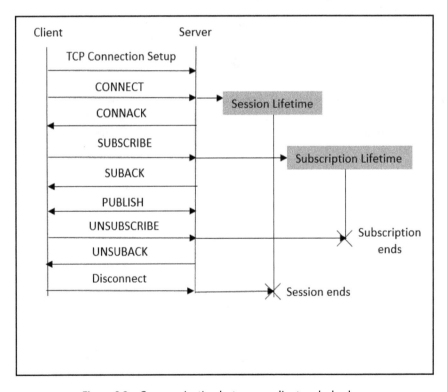

Figure 3.3 – Communication between a client and a broker

In this diagram, we can see that the first action that is taken is **TCP Connection Setup**. The client uses this to establish a connection with a server, and it will then send a CONNECT request to the server. The server then replies with a CONNACK message type, short for **connection acknowledgment**. This means that the connection is acknowledged, and established the connection session.

The client then sends a SUBSCRIBE request to subscribe to the topic, which also starts the **Subscription Lifetime**. The server then replies with a SUBACK request, short for **subscription back**, which acknowledges the subscription and allows the subscription to be done. Afterward, messages can be published between the client and the broker, opening a back-and-forth between them both to transmit messages. After the client is done, it will send an UNSUBSCRIBE message to remove its subscription from the topic, hence also ending its subscription lifetime. To confirm this request, the broker will then send through an UNSUBACK message, confirming that it is no longer subscribed to the topic. After this last message, the client can then disconnect from the broker.

As can be seen, requests between the client and the broker follow a standard process. Any steps that are not followed can result in retries being done, which may eventually lead to a timeout if too many attempts have been made. Being able to understand how the flow works is crucial to understanding the outputs that we will receive within the MQTT practical that we will attempt later in this section, so take note of the actions here. Feel free to reference the outputs that you receive as part of that section against the flow here to understand what is happening between the client and the broker.

Now we can look at the pub/sub model at a high level when one publisher is connected to three subscribers, as can be seen in the following diagram:

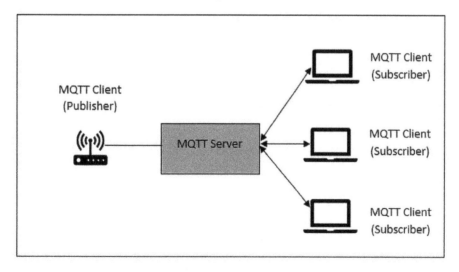

Figure 3.4 – Publish-subscribe model of one publisher to three subscribers

As can be seen, a **publisher** connects with an **MQTT Server** where it then publishes messages to the server, which in turn distributes the messages to each of the subscribers that it has. The subscribers have two-way communication with the MQTT server; they can receive the messages sent by the publisher, but also send through messages of their own as well.

Now that you have obtained a better understanding of MQTT, let's look at the other protocols that are quite popular in IoT.

Hypertext Transfer Protocol (HTTP)

You most likely are no stranger to HTTP, given that it is the most common protocol that is used in browsing the internet. It is the foundation of the **World Wide Web** and is used by millions of websites to transfer data. IoT is no stranger to it either, as HTTP is often used as a communication protocol between devices and servers. Devices have the option of using HTTP to send data to a server where it is then processed and stored. It is a reliable and well-established protocol, and given its high usage throughout the internet, it is very easy to use with a myriad of programming languages and development environments.

The widespread adoption of HTTP within IoT is one of its biggest advantages, given that nearly all devices and servers have the capability of utilizing HTTP for their own purposes, making it simple to integrate with existing systems and infrastructure. It is relatively lightweight and efficient; hence, it's also well suited to be used within resource-constrained environments. However, it does have limitations; given that it is a **connection-oriented protocol**, a dedicated connection must be established between the client and server for each given request, which can be inefficient where many requests need to be sent or received simultaneously. It is because of this that it does not perform well in real-time or low-latency scenarios.

You may already be used to browsing the internet but not be aware that you are sending GET, POST, and many other requests that are fundamental within the receiving and sending of IoT devices and services. With this in mind, let's get onto an exercise where you will use cURL for retrieving and sending messages.

We are going to start by performing a GET request with cURL. In your command prompt, type the following:

```
$ curl https://www.google.com
```

You probably will have received a huge wall of output. This output shows the contents of the Google search page we have queried. How much of the context can you make out? We will not cover understanding HTML within this book, but do have a read of the HTML documentation that is linked within the *Further reading* section of this chapter if you are interested in reading more about it.

Next, we will do a POST request. We can send the following request:

```
$ curl -X POST https://reqbin.com/echo/post/json -H "Content-Type:
application/json" -d '{"productId": 252159, "quantity": 50}'
```

In the preceding command, the -X parameter refers to the type of request, the -H parameter is the data content type, and the -d parameter is the data that we are intending to put through in the form of JSON syntax. We will then get an output indicating that the POST request that we have made was a success.

That is all we will cover up to this point for HTTP, but there are still so many more uses for it; this only scratches the surface of what it can do. We will see that many protocols have adapted HTTP's GET/MOST methodology of requesting, such as the protocol we will discuss next, CoAP. Take note of how each protocol differs from the other, despite them both using a similar methodology of handling requests; this will help you later in understanding how to choose between different protocols to handle different use cases.

Constrained Application Protocol (CoAP)

CoAP is a transfer protocol that is specialized within resource-constrained networks and devices. Like the MQTT protocol, it is designed to be simple and lightweight. It is based on the REST model and uses a **request/response design**, which is like what HTTP uses. Some methods it supports include GET, POST, PUT, and DELETE.

One of the main reasons why CoAP is popularly used as a protocol is its support for **multicast communication**, which allows for one message to be sent to multiple recipients simultaneously. As you remember from the case with HTTP, this is a big step up from how it handled multiple recipients, given that it had to only handle dedicated requests. CoAP also has support for reliability, allowing for retransmission and acknowledgment to ensure that messages that are in delivery are delivered successfully.

Extensible Messaging and Presence Protocol (XMPP)

XMPP is a decentralized protocol that is used within the open source community, and aims for communication between devices. One of the key reasons that it is popular is its ability to handle real-time messaging, a key need within many IoT environments, as many industrial settings require the fast communication of data and delays can be fatal in how the environments that they are based in are managed. XMPP is also able to track whether a device is online or offline and send messages accordingly, a feature known as presence.

XMPP is also extensible, allowing it to be customized to meet the specific use cases of various IoT applications, which is a very welcome feature for many IoT developers. Given its advantages, it is often used in home automation, industrial control systems, and some messaging and chat applications.

Other application protocols

There are certainly many more protocols that are used within IoT, such as **WebSocket**, a bi-directional communication protocol that helps to send large quantities of data within web applications, and the **Advanced Message Queuing Protocol** (**AMQP**), which helps establish communications between devices, systems, and applications from multiple vendors, but for the purposes of this book, we will just focus on the four described previously in the chapter, given their widespread use within the IoT community compared to the other protocols that are not mentioned. However, we do still encourage you to look at those protocols as well and have linked you in the *Further reading* section to a list of the main protocols that are used for IoT. As you read along, take note of why certain protocols work and why some do not for certain scenarios. Understanding this will be key to deciding which protocols to use for which use cases, which will be crucial when you begin creating solutions for critical industry-based applications.

Now, let's see an experimental practical that will help us gain a deeper understanding of one of the protocols we have discussed: MQTT.

An exercise to create a pub/sub MQTT broker

Now, let's get hands-on with some MQTT! In this exercise, we will be working with the Mosquitto MQTT broker to create a publisher/subscriber scenario between two command prompts, so download and install the broker as per the instructions in the *Technical requirements* section if you have not yet done so.

The following are the steps to get us started.

1. Ensure you already have Mosquitto started. Again, if you have not yet started Mosquitto, run the following command. Observe that the output is also given as follows to ensure that it has started successfully:

    ```
    $ net mosquitto start
    The Mosquitto Broker service was started successfully.
    ```

2. Open two command prompts on your computer as an administrator. One will function as our publisher and the other, our subscriber. If you are not sure how to run applications as an administrator, go to the Windows **Start** menu, search for command prompt, right-click on it, and select **Run as Administrator**.

3. We will now start by creating a topic to publish and subscribe to. Subscribe to a topic with the following command:

    ```
    $ mosquitto_sub -d -t MyTopic
    Client null sending CONNECT
    Client null received CONNACK (0)
    Client null sending SUBSCRIBE (Mid: 1, Topic: MyTopic, QoS: 0,
    Options: 0x00)
    Client null received SUBACK
    Subscribed (mid: 1): 0
    ```

    At first glance, this all might seem a bit hard to understand, but let's use what we've discussed about MQTT to make sense of this response:

    *   Line 1: In this response, the first line means that the client is sending a CONNECT message to the MQTT server.

- Line 2: In the second line, the client then receives a CONNACK message from the server, acknowledging the client's CONNECT message.

- Line 3: In the third line, the client then sends a SUBSCRIBE message to the server, asking to subscribe to our topic, MyTopic. Mid is a message ID that helps us track the SUBSCRIBE message, while the QoS and Options fields are simply additional information about the subscription.

- Line 4: In the fourth line, the client then receives a SUBACK message from the server, acknowledging that the client's SUBSCRIBE message has been received successfully.

- Line 5: In line 5, the client has successfully subscribed to our topic MyTopic, providing a message ID of 1. The 0 at the end of the line shows that the subscription was successful.

You may also see these lines returned periodically when you are not currently sending any further requests to the subscriber:

```
Client null sending PINGREQ
Client null received PINGRESP
```

- Line 1: The first line shows that the client is sending a PINGREQ message to the MQTT server.

- Line 2: The client then acknowledges that it has received the PINGRESP message from the server.

4. In the other terminal, publish a message to the MyTopic topic that you have just created with the following command:

```
$ mosquitto_pub -d -t MyTopic -m "Hello World"
Client null sending CONNECT
Client null received CONNACK (0)
Client null sending PUBLISH (d0, q0, r0, m1, 'MyTopic', ... (11
bytes))
Client null sending DISCONNECT
```

On the publisher side, as before, when we send the message through the broker, the CONNECT and CONNACK requests are put through. The third line is the crucial line, as it shows that the client is sending a PUBLISH message to the server, containing a payload of data that is to be published to our MyTopic topic. 11 bytes indicates the size of the payload, and the d0, q0, r0, and m1 values are flags that provide additional information about the message. We will not discuss them here, but feel free to refer to them in the MQTT documentation page linked in the *Further reading* section of this chapter.

On the subscriber side, we will see the following response:

```
Client null received PUBLISH (d0, q0, r0, m0, 'MyTopic', ... (11
bytes))
Hello World
```

It is a similar response to what we have received on the publisher side, except that we just see that the client has received the `PUBLISH` request that was sent through, and we will then be able to see the `Hello World` message printed that we have sent through the publisher successfully.

5. (Optional) If you would like to change the port where your MQTT broker is installed, you will have to change the listening port. If you'd like to do this, go to the folder that contains your Mosquitto installation, open the `mosquitto.conf` file with your preferred text editor, and add the listener port, `port 1889`. Save and close the file. By doing this, you have successfully installed the broker on a different port.

And with that, you have managed to make a simple publish/subscribe model with MQTT! This will serve as the foundation that you will build on in utilizing MQTT for more complex IoT networks that we will build in the following chapters.

> **Important note**
>
> Note that the MQTT network made here still lacks much in security compared to many industry-based implementations; many would require you to have further encryption done and to consider other standards. This will be discussed in more depth within *Chapter 7, Working with Cloud Computing to Power IoT Solutions,* when you begin to see how standards are abided by legally and the extra mile we must go to secure the MQTT protocol.

At this point, you should be able to understand common application protocols and how they are used, and to create a simple publish-subscribe model yourself. In the next section, we will look at the requirements that warrant the use of certain protocols over others.

Requirements for application protocols

Within the different protocols that we have discussed, we have been able to understand the strengths and weaknesses of each and how they have been used in various use cases. However, how can we further understand the requirements that warrant the use of certain protocols over others? This section will highlight some of the factors that come into play while optimizing networks based on protocols, and help you understand design decisions that come as part of this.

Reliability

Error handling and being able to ensure that messages are delivered are very important aspects of application protocols. Often, there may be scenarios that require much more capability of handling errors and retries than others, such as networks that are based in urban locations and may have connections that are intermittent. Factors that can affect the reliability of how data is transmitted on the application layer include network congestion, interference, and failure. Ensuring that reliability is maintained prevents scenarios such as lost data, incorrect data, and system failures. Some protocols that are able to demonstrate this include MQTT and CoAP.

Power usage

Power usage is another major consideration in selecting an application protocol because devices are often battery-powered and have resource constraints. Factors that impact the power usage of an application include the amount of data transmitted by the device, the frequency of communication, and the complexity of the protocol. The complexity of a protocol is relevant as those that are more complex may require additional processing to encode and decode data as part of transmitting it. Some examples of protocols that can minimize power usage include MQTT, due to its lightweight nature, and CoAP.

Security

Security is a very important consideration in selecting an application protocol because it helps protect the confidentiality, integrity, and availability of the data that is being transmitted. The goal of security is always to protect the data from unauthorized access or tampering, as such a breach can have dire consequences. There are many factors to consider that can impact how secure an application protocol is, such as the type of encryption used, the strength of the encryption, and the controls put in place to authenticate devices while ensuring that only authorized devices can access the network.

Aside from a personal standpoint, industry-based applications are also often legally required to ensure a minimum amount of security. This is especially true of solutions that handle sensitive data such as personal or financial information. MQTT, for example, is considered one of the more secure ones, given its use of **Transport Layer Security** (**TLS**) for encrypting data and authentication, while CoAP uses **Datagram Transport Layer Security** for encrypting data and authenticating devices. Again, regulatory standards usually require you to abide by a particular standard, and there will be times when a secure protocol does not abide by that select standard, so it is important to choose not only from a security standpoint, but from a legal standpoint as well.

We will be looking more at security within IoT networks in *Chapter 11*, *Examining Security and Privacy in IoT*. In the next section, we will look at how we can integrate application protocols into the design of IoT networks.

Integrating application protocols into the design

Now that we've seen the considerations of choosing an application protocol, let's look at integrating the protocols into the design of a network. We already have the knowledge of the components of an IoT network and have seen the interactions that take place between several protocols, so we can put that knowledge to use with the following set of use cases, and see how we can apply our understanding to building our own networks for our use cases based on best practices.

A simple integration into the smart thermostat network

Let's return to our smart home example, starting off with a simple example of a smart thermostat's communications with an MQTT broker, which we can see implemented as follows:

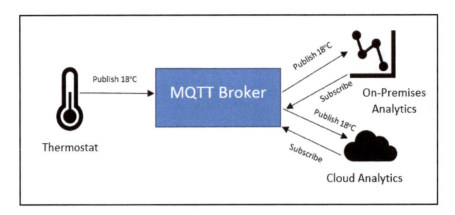

Figure 3.5 – Simple smart thermostat communication with MQTT broker

In this network, we can see that the **Thermostat** would publish its measurement of the temperature in the environment; that is, it sends its telemetry data to the **MQTT Broker** and tells it that the current reading is **18°C**. We can then have two different clients subscribe to the MQTT broker: one client on-premises and one on the cloud, to perform analytics on their own separate servers. After both have subscribed, the MQTT broker can publish to both and accordingly update the other with information that one may also post. This is a simple but powerful use case of how MQTT can be used within many environments and shows how effective it is in multi-channel communication.

A cloud scenario

Now, let's look at the same scenario, but see how it can be based on the cloud. To give some context, we will be seeing two different environments: one on our local, on-premises environment and the other based on the **AWS cloud**. The AWS cloud refers to the collection of remote computing services offered by **Amazon Web Services** (**AWS**), a subsidiary of Amazon. It provides a wide variety of services such as computing power, storage, and databases, delivered as on-demand resources over the internet and helping businesses scale and grow by building sophisticated applications with increased flexibility, scalability, and reliability. Here, we will also be encountering a service that is specialized for handling IoT devices: **AWS IoT Core**.

AWS IoT Core is a managed cloud platform that allows devices to securely connect to the cloud with simplicity. It provides a set of APIs and tools that allow devices to send and receive data while interacting with other AWS services. It also provides scalable infrastructure, allowing for the management and data processing of millions of devices.

In the following figure, we can see where AWS IoT Core is used to manage the data that is sent to the MQTT broker:

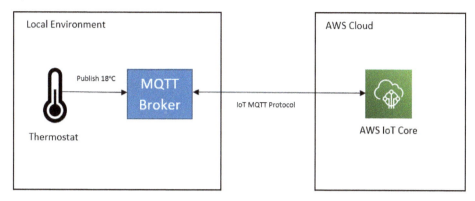

Figure 3.6 – Diagram of using AWS IoT Core to manage data sent to the MQTT broker

With the change that is made in the preceding figure, we are seeing the inside of the cloud analytics that we mentioned in the previous subsection. We can use **AWS IoT Core** to receive messages from the **MQTT Broker** and have it interact with other services to process the data further, store the data, or perform other tasks with it. We can also see that the communication between the MQTT broker and AWS IoT Core is done via the **IoT MQTT Protocol**, a protocol from AWS that is secure.

We will discuss more about the capabilities of AWS in *Chapter 7, Working with Cloud Computing to Power IoT Solutions*. Next, we will look at using multiple clients for connections through a broker.

Multiple clients

Here, we outline the connection diagram seen in the preceding example, but with multiple clients. In the following diagram, we can see that **Client 2** or **3** may want to update the temperature to the broker based on the thermostat's sensor:

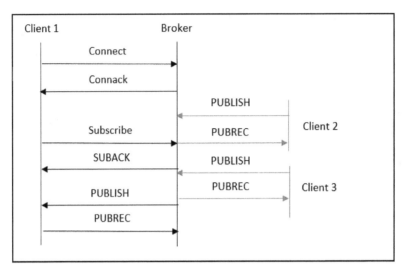

Figure 3.7 – Connection between multiple clients through a broker

Clients 2 and 3 will update the broker using the PUBLISH message. This is stored in the database and will be sent to all subscribers that have subscribed to the topics, having the information then be pushed to all the subscribed clients. If **Client 1** has already subscribed at that time, it will get the information from the **Broker**. With this method, different types of sensing information can be obtained directly and autonomously whenever there are any updates from any of the clients.

In the next section, we will explore a practical exercise of creating an MQTT publish-subscribe communication between an ESP32 and a Raspberry Pi.

Practical – creating an MQTT pub and sub communication between an ESP32 and a Raspberry Pi

One of the best ways to see MQTT in action is to create a pub/sub model based on communication between two devices. In this case, we will be using the **ESP32** and the **Raspberry Pi**, where the ESP32 will serve as the publisher and subscriber while the Pi serves as the MQTT broker. Here is a breakdown of the roles of all three in this practical:

- **Publisher**: The ESP32 publishes messages to the MQTT broker. It sends messages to the / topic/test1 topic when there is user input from the serial monitor, and it also periodically sends Hello World messages to the /topic/test3 topic every 15 seconds.

- **Subscriber**: The ESP32 is also a subscriber, as it listens for messages on the /topic/test1 and /topic/test2 topics. When it receives a message on one of these topics, it processes the message in the callback function, which in this case prints the received message to the Serial Monitor.

- **Broker**: The MQTT broker is a separate server that manages the message flow between publishers and subscribers. In this practical, the MQTT broker runs on the IP address `192.168.0.117` and listens on `port 1883`. The broker is responsible for receiving messages from the ESP32 and other publishers and then distributing those messages to the appropriate subscribers based on the topic.

Now that we have a good understanding of the processes that will be part of this practical and the roles that make them up, we can move on to the steps to achieve this.

Setting up Mosquitto as the broker on Raspberry Pi

Now, we can move ahead with setting up Mosquitto to be the broker on the Raspberry Pi:

1. Before installing Mosquitto, it's a good idea to update your Raspberry Pi to the latest packages. Open the terminal and run the following commands:

    ```
    $ sudo apt update
    $ sudo apt upgrade -y
    ```

2. Next, install Mosquitto using the following commands:

    ```
    $ sudo apt install -y mosquitto mosquitto-clients
    ```

    This will install both the Mosquitto broker and the Mosquitto clients that will allow you to interact with the broker through the terminal.

3. To enable the Mosquitto service to start automatically when the Raspberry Pi boots up, run the following:

    ```
    $ sudo systemctl enable mosquitto
    ```

4. Test that the installation has worked properly by running the following command:

    ```
    $ mosquitto -v
    ```

5. By default, Mosquitto is configured to allow only local connections. To enable non-local connections, you need to modify the configuration file. Open the configuration file for editing:

    ```
    $ sudo nano /etc/mosquitto/mosquitto.conf
    ```

6. Add the following two lines to the end of the file:

    ```
    listener 1883
    allow_anonymous true
    ```

    This line tells Mosquitto to listen on the default MQTT port (`1883`) for connections from any IP address. Save the changes by pressing *Ctrl + X*, then *Y*, and finally *Enter*.

7. Restart the Mosquitto service to apply the new configuration:

```
$ sudo systemctl restart mosquitto
```

Now, you should have the Mosquitto broker running and ready to facilitate the relationship between the publisher and subscriber.

8. Check the IP address on your Raspberry Pi and note it down, as you will need it later for the ESP32 code:

```
$ hostname -I
```

With that, we have properly set up our Mosquitto service. Now, we will start coding up the subscriber and publisher on ESP32.

Coding it up

We can now begin coding for the subscriber and publisher that are based on the ESP32:

1. We will need to start a new **sketch** in our **Arduino IDE**.

2. Include the necessary libraries by using the #include directive. WiFi.h is the library that provides functionalities to manage Wi-Fi connections on the ESP32, while PubSubClient.h is an MQTT library specifically designed for microcontrollers such as the ESP32. Both libraries need to be installed before using them in the code. If you don't have the PubSubClient library, you can download it by searching for PubSubClient by Nick O'Leary in the **Library Manager** tab and you should be able to install it from there:

```
#include <WiFi.h>
#include <PubSubClient.h>
```

3. Define constants using the #define directive for your Wi-Fi credentials (SSID and password), the MQTT server IP address, and the MQTT server port number. Replace these values with your own Wi-Fi SSID, password, and MQTT server information. The #define directive allows you to replace occurrences of the identifier with the provided value during the preprocessing phase before the program is compiled:

```
#define EXAMPLE_ESP_WIFI_SSID "YOUR_WIFI_SSID_HERE"
#define EXAMPLE_ESP_WIFI_PASS "YOUR_WIFI_PASSWORD_HERE"
#define MQTT_SERVER "YOUR_RASPBERRY_PI_IP_HERE"
#define MQTT_PORT 1883
```

4. Create a WiFiClient object named espClient. This object will act as a client for the Wi-Fi network and will be used to manage the connection with the MQTT server. Next, create a PubSubClient object named client, passing the espClient object as an argument.

This object will handle MQTT communications. Finally, declare a `lastMsg` variable, of type `unsigned long`, to store the timestamp of the last message sent. Initialize this variable to 0:

```
WiFiClient espClient;
PubSubClient client(espClient);
unsigned long lastMsg = 0;
```

5. Define a `setup_wifi` function that initializes the Wi-Fi connection using the defined credentials. First, the function calls the `delay()` function to wait for 10 milliseconds to ensure the ESP32 is ready for operation. Then, it uses the `Serial.print()` and `Serial.println()` functions to print the Wi-Fi SSID to the serial monitor.

    The `WiFi.begin()` function is called with the SSID and password as arguments, initiating the connection process. The function then enters a `while` loop, checking the Wi-Fi connection status using the `WiFi.status()` function. The loop continues until the ESP32 is connected to the Wi-Fi network (`WL_CONNECTED`). Inside the loop, the `delay()` function is called again to wait for 500 milliseconds before the next iteration, allowing the ESP32 to complete its tasks in between. Once the Wi-Fi connection is established, the function prints a confirmation message to the serial monitor using the `Serial.println()` function:

```
void connect_wifi() {
  delay(10);
  Serial.print("Connecting to ");
  Serial.println(EXAMPLE_ESP_WIFI_SSID);

  WiFi.begin(EXAMPLE_ESP_WIFI_SSID, EXAMPLE_ESP_WIFI_PASS);

  while (WiFi.status() != WL_CONNECTED) {
    delay(500);
  }

  Serial.println("WiFi connected");
}
```

6. Define the `callback` function, which is called when a subscribed MQTT topic receives a message. The function has three parameters: `char *topic`, a pointer to a character array containing the topic name; `byte *payload`, a pointer to an array of bytes containing the payload data, and `unsigned int length`, an unsigned integer representing the length of the payload data.

The `Serial.print()` and `Serial.println()` functions are used to print the topic name and the `Message arrived` message header to the serial monitor. The payload byte array needs to be converted into a null-terminated string to be properly displayed. The `payload[length] = '\0';` line adds a null character (0) at the end of the payload data to indicate the end of the string.

Next, the payload is converted into a `String` object named `message` using the `String()` constructor, which takes a character array (the `payload`) as its argument. The `Serial.println()` function is then used to print the message to the serial monitor:

```
void callback(char *topic, byte *payload, unsigned int length) {
  Serial.print("Message arrived [");
  Serial.print(topic);
  Serial.print("] ");
  payload[length] = '\0';
  String message = String((char *)payload);    Serial.
println(message);
}
```

7. Define the `reconnect` function, which attempts to connect to the MQTT server and subscribe to the desired topics. The function uses a `while` loop to check whether the MQTT client is connected to the server using the `connected()` method of the `client` object. If not connected, the loop continues.

Inside the loop, the `client.connect()` method is called with the `ESP32Client` client ID as an argument. If the connection is successful, the client subscribes to the `/topic/test1` and `/topic/test2` topics using the `client.subscribe()` method. If the connection fails, the `delay()` function is called to wait for 5,000 milliseconds before retrying the connection attempt:

```
void reconnect() {
  while (!client.connected()) {
    if (client.connect("ESP32Client")) {
      client.subscribe("/topic/test1");
      client.subscribe("/topic/test2");
    } else {
      delay(5000);
    }
  }
}
```

8. In the `setup` function, initialize the serial communication with a baud rate of `115200` using the `Serial.begin()` function. Call the `setup_wifi` function to connect the ESP32 to the Wi-Fi network. Set the MQTT server address and port using the `client.setServer()` method with the defined `MQTT_SERVER` and `MQTT_PORT` constants as arguments. Assign the `callback` function using the `client.setCallback()` method, which takes the callback function as an argument:

```
void setup() {
  Serial.begin(115200);
  connect_wifi();
  client.setServer(MQTT_SERVER, MQTT_PORT);
  client.setCallback(onMessageReceived);
}
```

9. In the `loop` function, which is the main loop of the Arduino sketch, we first check whether the MQTT client is connected to the server using the `client.connected()` method. If not connected, the `reconnect()` function is called to attempt a connection. The `client.loop()` method is called to process any incoming messages and maintain the connection with the MQTT server. This method should be called regularly. The `Serial.available()` function checks whether there is any data available in the serial buffer. If data is available, it reads the incoming message using the `Serial.readStringUntil('\n')` function, which reads the (`'\n'`) newline character. The read data is stored in a `String` object named msg. The message is then published to the `"/topic/test1"` topic using the `client.publish()` method, which takes the topic name and message as arguments. The `msg.c_str()` function is called to convert the `String` object into a character array, which is the expected data type for the `client.publish()` method.

10. Next, we check whether 15,000 milliseconds have passed since the last message was sent using the `millis()` function and the `lastMsg` variable. If the condition is met, we update the `lastMsg` variable to the current time (using `millis()` again) and publish a `"Hello World"` message to the `"/topic/test3"` topic using the `client.publish()` method.

The `loop` function will run continuously, allowing the ESP32 to maintain its connection with the MQTT server, process incoming messages, and send messages either from the serial monitor or periodically (every 15 seconds).

We can see the code needed for the following `loop` function:

```
void loop() {
  if (!client.connected()) {
    reconnect();
  }
  client.loop();

  if (Serial.available() > 0) {
    String msg = Serial.readStringUntil('\n');
```

```
        client.publish("/topic/test1", msg.c_str());
    }

    if (millis() - lastMsg > 15000) {
        lastMsg = millis();
        client.publish("/topic/test3", "Hello World");
    }
}
```

11. Upload the code to your ESP32 board.

12. We will then open the **MQTTX** application on our local desktop. Click the **+ New Connection** button:

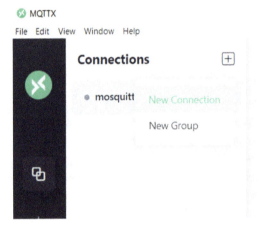

Figure 3.8 – Establishing a new connection with MQTTX

At this point, we have been able to properly configure our code and open up MQTTX on our Raspberry Pi. Now, we can use it as our publisher and subscriber.

Subscribing and publishing from MQTTX

We can now start having the MQTTX act as the subscriber and publisher:

1. Download and install MQTTX from the official website at https://mqttx.app/.

2. Open MQTTX and click the + button in the top-left corner to create a new connection, as shown in *Figure 3.9*.

3. Configure the connection with the fields as shown in *Figure 3.9*:

A. **Name**: Give your connection a name – for example, "ESP32_MQTT". For the purposes of the demo, *Figure 3.9* will use the name `mosquitto` instead.

B. Protocol (**Client ID**): Select **mqtt://** from the drop-down list.

C. **Host**: Enter the IP address of your MQTT broker (in this practical, it's `192.168.0.117`).

D. **Port**: Enter the port number of your MQTT broker (in this practical, it's `1883`).

E. **Username** and **Password**: Leave these blank unless your MQTT broker requires authentication.

F. Click **Connect** to establish a connection with the MQTT broker.

It would look like the following with these configurations:

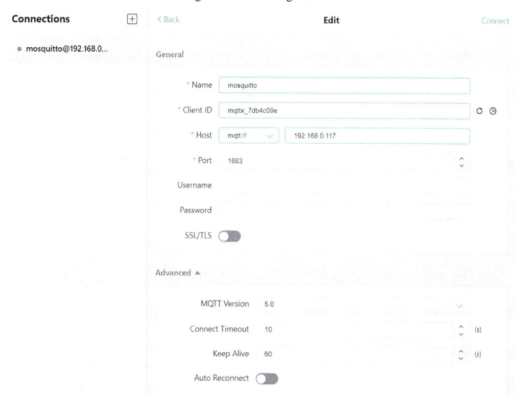

Figure 3.9 – Entering the information required for a new MQTT connection in MQTTX

4. Subscribe to topics:

   A. Click the + **New Subscription** button in the right pane:

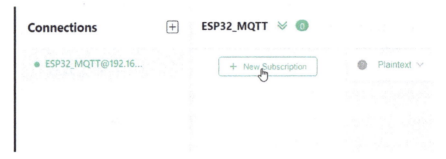

Figure 3.10 – Locating the New Subscription button in MQTTX

   B. Enter the topic you want to subscribe to (e.g., `/topic/test1` or `/topic/test2`).

   C. Click the **Confirm** button in the bottom right to subscribe to the topic:

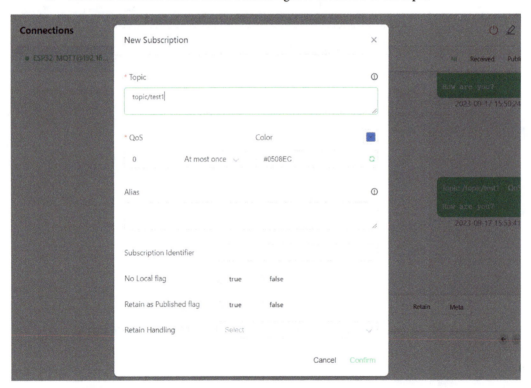

Figure 3.11 – Filling in the topic and clicking the Confirm button to subscribe to it

D. MQTTX will now listen for messages published to the subscribed topics, and they will appear in the messages panel as follows:

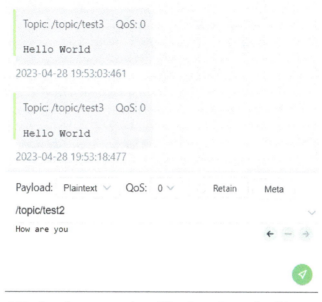

Figure 3.12 – Sample messages that will be shown from subscribing to a topic

5. Publish messages:

   A. Click the topic you want to publish to (e.g., "`/topic/test1`" or "`/topic/test2`") on your subscriptions list:

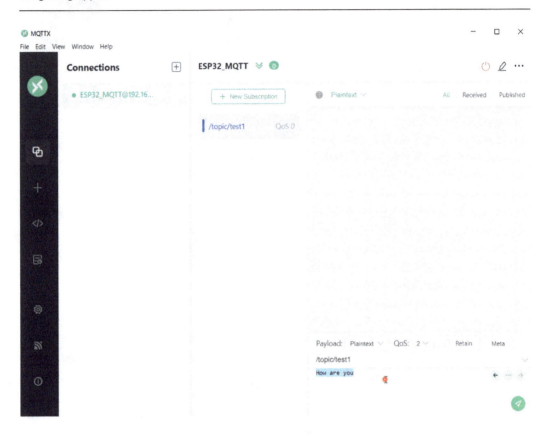

Figure 3.13 – Selecting a topic to publish to and writing a message

B. Type your message into the **Payload** input field. This can be any message, such as `Hello`.

C. Click **Publish**, in the form of a white cursor in a green button in the bottom-right corner, to send the message to the MQTT broker, which will distribute it to all subscribers (including your ESP32) listening to that topic:

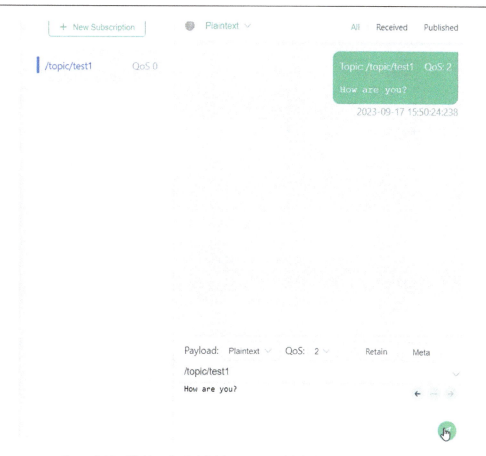

Figure 3.14 – Clicking the Publish button to publish the message to a topic

6. Open Serial Monitor from **Tools** | **Serial Monitor** and you will be able to see the output listed as follows:

```
WiFi connected
Message arrived [/topic/test1] Hello
```

7. You can also send a message from the Serial Monitor message box. You will see this on your /topic/test1 topic on MQTTX.

With these steps, you can use MQTTX to monitor messages sent by your ESP32 and send messages to your ESP32 as it subscribes to the specified topics. Additionally, you can send messages to MQTTX from your Serial Monitor.

The following is a list of MQTT events that need to be handled:

`MQTT_EVENT_CONNECTED`	This event occurs when the client successfully establishes a connection with the broker, indicating that it is now capable of exchanging data with the broker.
`MQTT_EVENT_DISCONNECTED`	When the client is unable to connect to the server, or the connection is terminated for any reason, this event is triggered. The client will not be able to communicate with the broker in this state.
`MQTT_EVENT_SUBSCRIBED`	When the client sends a subscribe request to the broker, this event is triggered if the broker accepts it. The message ID associated with the subscribe message is also included in the event data.
`MQTT_EVENT_UNSUBSCRIBED`	This event is triggered when the broker accepts the unsubscribe request from the client. The message ID linked with the unsubscribe message is included in the event data.
`MQTT_EVENT_PUBLISHED`	When the broker acknowledges the `publish` message sent by the client, this event is triggered. The message ID associated with the publish message is included in the event data, but this event is only triggered for QoS level 1 or 2, since level 0 does not involve acknowledgments.
`MQTT_EVENT_DATA`	Whenever the client receives a publish message from the broker, this event is triggered, and the event data contains the message ID, topic name, received data, and length of the data.
`MQTT_EVENT_ERROR`	When the client experiences any error, this event is triggered. The client can then use the event data to troubleshoot the issue.

Table 3.1 – Table of common MQTT events that need to be handled

And with that, you have a working ESP32-Raspberry Pi pub/sub model!

Summary

In this chapter, we have learned the fundamentals of application protocols for IoT networks, particularly those that are commonly used for IoT, including MQTT, HTTP, CoAP, and XMPP, and understood the considerations that are put in place when designing for a network. We looked at a practical use case of using an MQTT pub/sub client as part of deepening our understanding of it, and learned how to use cURL to send GET and POST requests to retrieve and send data to websites. Understanding these protocols and design considerations is paramount for anyone involved in developing or managing IoT networks as they ensure optimal communication, security, and data transmission across various devices and platforms. This knowledge is instrumental in developing efficient, secure, and scalable IoT solutions, thereby enhancing your ability to contribute effectively to IoT projects and innovations.

In the next chapter, we will be looking at understanding the use of communication and connectivity protocols, understanding which to use in what scenario, and further building that into the IoT network that we are designing, hence adding another tool to our toolkit as an IoT network developer.

Further reading

For more information about what was covered in this chapter, please refer to the following links:

- Learn more on Cloud MQTT: `https://www.cloudmqtt.com/docs/index.html`
- Understand more about XMPP: `https://docs.modernxmpp.org/`
- Learn more about what defines CoAP: `https://www.rfc-editor.org/rfc/rfc7252`
- Explore more of what Mosquitto has to offer: `https://mosquitto.org/documentation/`
- Understand more about the different protocols of IoT: `https://www.nabto.com/guide-iot-protocols-standards/`

4

Examining Communication and Connectivity Technologies

In *Chapter 3, Integrating Application Protocols* we learned how to form IoT networks, understanding the fundamental components that constitute them and how we can connect them to establish the respective networks. We also had a high-level look at a few key communication protocols that help with building the network while understanding the considerations that we take to ensure that our design choices are optimized based on our use cases. That, paired with our understanding of application protocols in *Chapter 3*, will allow us to take a deeper look at some advanced communication and connectivity protocols and understand more complex deployments in this chapter.

When navigating this chapter, ensure that you not only take in the high-level overview of the networks but understand how the protocols work and deliver the data. Understanding a low-level view of how data packets are transferred will help you think more critically about solutions and allow you to further understand the building blocks of IoT and make better decisions to optimize your network. By the end of this chapter, you will have become more confident in designing more complex networks and selecting between a bigger array of protocols. You will also have a deeper understanding of how the components work at a low level.

In this chapter, we're going to cover the following main topics:

- Choosing between short- and long-range wireless connectivity options within IoT

- Learning in more depth about mesh networking and other communication solutions, including **radio-frequency identification (RFID)**, Wi-Fi, and Bluetooth

- Examining the edge cases for protocol selection and operation

Technical requirements

This chapter will require you to have the following hardware and software installed:

- Hardware:

  - ESP32

  - A key fob

  - The RFID RC522 module

  - USB cable A male to micro B male

- Software:

  - Mosquitto client.

  - Arduino IDE.

  - Command prompt (you already have this on Windows).

  - The `SPI.h` and `MFRC522.h` libraries for Arduino. You can find these libraries at `https://www.arduino.cc/en/reference/SPI` and `https://github.com/miguelbalboa/rfid`, respectively.

  - A diagramming software such as Draw.io, as described in previous chapters

  - Fritzing.

You can access the GitHub folder that contains the code for this chapter at `https://github.com/PacktPublishing/IoT-Made-Easy-for-Beginners/tree/main/Chapter04/`.

The role of short- and long-range protocols within IoT

In designing an IoT network, deciding whether to use short- or long-range connectivity protocols is a straightforward but crucial decision. Both have their advantages and disadvantages and deciding on this will depend on your individual use case. In this section, we will highlight some factors to consider and talk about the remaining component of connectivity protocols that we have not yet discussed: long-range protocols.

Design factors

In designing networks, protocols such as Zigbee and Bluetooth are often chosen for communication within confined areas such as homes or industrial office buildings. While they excel in low power consumption and robust security features, their operational range is limited, making them unsuitable for covering large distances. However, their lower hardware costs and ability to deliver reliable services within their operational bounds make them the preferred choice for many localized applications.

Conversely, when the communication needs span broader geographies such as cities or even countries, long-range protocols such as cellular, satellite, and LoRaWAN come to the fore. These protocols can bridge vast distances, but often at the expense of higher power consumption and increased operational costs. The hardware and deployment costs associated with these long-range technologies are typically higher. Service reliability over long distances is a strong suit of these protocols, albeit the security features may vary, necessitating additional security layers in industry-based applications to ensure robust data encryption during transmission.

The trade-offs between range, data rate, power consumption, service reliability, and cost need to be meticulously weighed against the application requirements and the envisioned network performance. As we transition to discussing long-range protocols, the interplay of these factors will be further explored to provide you with a holistic understanding of protocol selection in IoT network design.

Next, we will take a look at long-range protocols to complement the short-range protocols we discussed in *Chapter 2, Understanding and Designing IoT Networks*.

Long-range communication protocols

Long-range IoT networks constitute the foundations of a **low-power wide area network (LPWAN)**. In these networks, end nodes in the form of devices that have low power consumption are connected to gateways that, in turn, transmit data to other devices and network servers. Devices on the network then analyze the data that is received and control the devices at the end nodes accordingly.

The two most popular technologies for LPWAN are Sigfox and LoRaWAN. However, for this book, we will discuss LoRa in more depth as opposed to Sigfox, given that it is based on an open standard, provides the capability of building both private and public networks – with tens of thousands of networks already established in the world – and has a lower data rate compared to Zigbee.

The following diagram shows the four different data layers of LoRa. Can you see how it differs compared to the layers that were illustrated for Zigbee? Why and how does this affect its use?

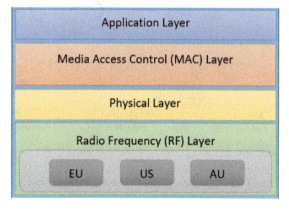

Figure 4.1 – Data layers of LoRa

The **radio frequency** (**RF**) layer works with RF assignment and helps transmit baseband information through an RF carrier through an antenna over the air. As can be seen, different frequency bands within the RF layer are allocated for the different regions of the world. For simplicity, we have omitted the numerical band identifier and instead just illustrated it with the initials of the region. The physical layer is above RF and helps with header formation, preamble, and the header's CRC. The raw data that is provided by the frame is then modulated with LoRa CSS/FSK or GFSK before RF conversion is done for uplink transmission. The layer also supports RF issues relating to interference, coverage, and optimization. The MAC layer helps assist with MAC management messages between a server and an end device. MAC takes care of functions such as energy consumption, mesh topology, and security. The application layer is the topmost layer and is designed to be used based on the specific use case of the user, such as with smart cities, smart grids, healthcare, and many more.

While both LoRaWAN and Zigbee are significant technologies within the realm of IoT networking, they cater to different use cases due to their distinct networking topologies and capabilities. LoRaWAN, with its long-range communication abilities, operates in a star-of-stars topology, making it well suited for urban and wide-area deployments. Conversely, Zigbee, with its short-range communication abilities, operates in a mesh topology, which is ideal for more compact, localized networks.

Now, let's delve into the structure of LoRaWAN while highlighting a deployment in an urban area where LoRaWAN's long-range communication capability shines. *Figure 4.2* demonstrates how such a setup might be structured:

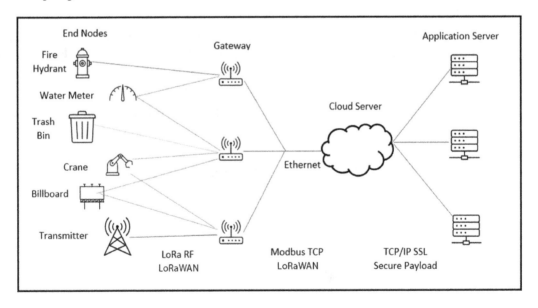

Figure 4.2 – Sample structure for the LoRa network

Within this setup, we can see that the sensors are positioned as end nodes at smart objects that are located around the urban area, including a fire hydrant, a billboard, and a transmitter. As can be surmised, these are objects that would be lying hundreds of meters – if not kilometers – from each other, making the choice of a long-distance protocol over a short-distance protocol imperative. We can see that everything connects to a specific gateway that it is assigned to, with some end node types connecting to multiple gateways while some types only connect to one. This data transmission is done through LoRa RF LoRaWAN, allowing data to be transmitted through RFs that are the defaults within LoRa networks.

The gateways are then connected to the cloud server via Ethernet, utilizing standard TCP/IP or UDP/IP protocols for the backhaul communication. This setup allows for reliable data transmission from the local network of sensors to the cloud infrastructure. Once the data reaches the cloud server, it is forwarded to the application server. This arrangement enables users to access the collected data and, if necessary, send data back to the cloud server for further processing or control operations. The communication between the cloud server and the application server, as well as between the users and the servers, can be secured using SSL/TLS protocols over TCP/IP, ensuring data integrity and confidentiality during transmission.

The network architecture, as depicted here, considers the appropriate protocols for transmitting data between devices, gateways, and servers, while also addressing the security concerns inherent in each data transmission stage. Ensuring a secure and reliable data communication framework is crucial. We'll delve into this aspect in more detail in *Chapter 11, Examining Security and Privacy in IoT*.

Allocating resources

Allocating resources effectively is an important consideration when building IoT networks because often, we will face constraints in the resources that we have to build them. In this subsection, we will explore some of the constraint types that are often encountered within IoT networks.

Constrained nodes

Constrained nodes refer to nodes that do not have features that can communicate with the internet. This is often caused by constraints such as size, weight, costs, and power to help the nodes function. Furthermore, memory may be another constraint that prevents the nodes from functioning as we would like them to. With these considerations, such nodes require a low-level understanding of how to architect networks based on them to ensure that they can still function properly within the network without any issues.

Constrained networks

Constrained networks are networks that may be limited in terms of processing power, data rates, and throughput. This may be caused by several factors, including restrictions that are imposed based on supported packet sizes. It may also lead to other limitations, including a lack of advanced Layer 3 functions, including multicasting and broadcasting, limited reachability from outside the network due to power management configurations, and packet losses that may come as part of intermittent transmissions.

Constrained devices

Constrained devices are devices that have limited resources in terms of processing power, connectivity, memory, and more. They are usually small and inexpensive and consume a low amount of power, though they come with their own set of challenges. They can be split into three different classes based on the device's functionalities, as follows:

- **Class 0**: The most constrained devices, these devices usually have very limited processing power, memory, and connectivity options. Even if connectivity was possible, the device usually has poor security capabilities due to its reduced capabilities. Usually, to make up for this, it must communicate with the internet through a gateway or proxy, where further encryption can be ensured. Some examples of devices within this class include sensors, actuators, and simple control devices.

- **Class 1**: The devices in this class have slightly more capabilities compared to the devices in Class 0, with more options in terms of processing power, memory, and connectivity. They can run more complex tasks and are designed to support more advanced protocols and applications. They cannot work with a full protocol stack such as HTTP, though some specially designed protocols such as CoAP can work with it. These devices normally do not need a gateway to access the internet. Some examples of devices in this class include smart appliances, smart meters, and devices that are within the home automation network.

- **Class 2**: Devices in this class have the same capabilities as regular portable computers such as **personal digital assistants (PDAs)** and laptops. They can work with full protocol stacks such as TLS, HTTP, and others. They can also have comparatively higher standards employed for security and also require a much higher power budget, as can be expected.

Now, we can take a look at the different infrastructure protocols that are based on IoT.

Infrastructure protocols

Many protocols usually lie on network infrastructure, but for this book, we will be covering two of the most popular communication technologies that are based on IoT: IPv6 and RPL. In contrast to IPv6 and RPL, LoRaWAN is another prevalent communication technology in IoT, albeit operating at a different layer. LoRaWAN facilitates communication from end devices to gateways using its distinct protocol, not relying on IP.

But first, we will discuss the major differences between IPv4 and IPv6, and why IoT devices have grown to use IPv6 as opposed to IPv4.

IPv4 versus IPv6

As you may already know, IPv4 is the original version of IP, which has already been in use since the internet's early days. It uses 32-bit addresses, which allows for a total of about 4.3 billion unique addresses. At the time, this seemed like a huge number, but the rapid growth of the internet has led to a shortage in the number of available IPv4 addresses. This is why IPv6 was introduced.

IPv6 was developed to address the issue of the exhaustion of addresses that was taking place with IPv4. By utilizing 128-bit addresses, it ensures that there is a virtually unlimited number of unique addresses. This makes IPv6 well suited for IoT as there are most likely many devices that need to be connected to the internet. It is this design consideration that gives it its main advantage over IPv4 since it is necessary to uniquely identify each device, which IPv4 would not have enough addresses to allocate to be able to do effectively and efficiently.

Another advantage of IPv6 is its support for a myriad of low-power networking technologies, such as 6LoWPAN. This makes it easier to connect to a large variety of devices on the internet, especially those with limited resources. It can also be seen that more devices are slowly starting to shift their support to only being for IPv6 as opposed to IPv4, such as **Narrowband Internet of Things (NB-IoT)** devices. These are devices that are based on LPWAN radio technology and utilize a subset of the LTE standard, which focuses on indoor coverage and offers low cost, high connection density, and long battery life.

Some solutions, such as utilizing a dual stack, help create a solution to support this. A dual stack is a network configuration that helps devices use both IPv4 and IPv6. This is useful to ensure that devices that use either protocol can be supported and communicated with by other devices. It is its backward compatibility with IPv4 that makes it very valuable as many devices still currently use IPv4. However, with the emergence of more IoT devices, it can still communicate with devices that are solely based on IPv6, hence allowing communication between older and newer systems. This also allows the transition to IPv6 to be smoother compared to having to directly switch everything to IPv4 all at once, especially if you are building within a production environment.

However, some disadvantages come with doing this. One disadvantage is that setting up dual stacks can be more complex and expensive. This is due to both protocols being used while having to consider all the additional resources that need to be managed. Another disadvantage is that using a dual stack would increase the size of the network, which, in turn, increases the number of addresses required, leading to additional costs for organizations. Here is an example of the difference in setup between an IPv4 stack and a dual stack:

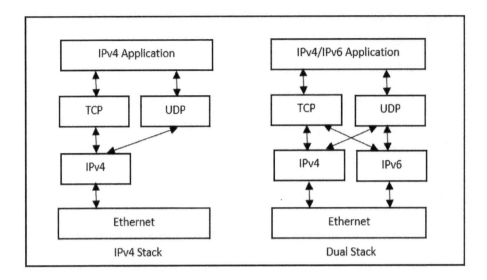

Figure 4.3 – Setup of IPv4 stack versus dual stack

As we can see, an IPv4 stack only supports IPv4 with its communications toward the TCP and UDP layers, while a dual stack can have both protocols communicate with both layers.

Next, we will look at RPL, another popular choice of IoT-based infrastructure protocol.

The IPv6 routing protocol for low-power and lossy networks (RPL)

RPL is a routing protocol that's used for powering low-power and lossy networks, such as the use cases we have highlighted for IoT networks. It is based on the IPv6 protocol and is designed to be scalable and efficient, allowing it to be used in scenarios where there are many devices with limited resources.

RPL uses a directed acyclic graph to route packets through the network, allowing it to adapt to changes in the network and maintain connectivity, even with oncoming errors or losses that may result. It can also optimize the use of energy and other resources. It can support a wide range of topologies and network configurations, some of which include a single central node or others within more distributed networks with multiple nodes. This flexibility allows it to be used within a myriad of IoT applications.

Next, we will look at some more technologies that are part of popular communication protocols: mesh networking, RFID, Wi-Fi, and Bluetooth.

Mesh networking, RFID, and Bluetooth

Many protocols are yet to be mentioned as part of IoT. Here, we'll highlight three more to add to your toolkit, with a special emphasis on RFID technologies, given their prevalence within open source and industrial communities.

RFID

RFID technologies are used to identify and track objects through radio waves, and in IoT, they are used to track a wide array of devices or sometimes people. There are two main types of RFID technologies: passive and active. Passive ones use tags that do not have power sources and instead depend on the power transmitted by the reader for them to send their data, while active systems use tags that have power sources and can transmit data over longer distances.

RFID technologies can identify and track objects without necessitating a direct line of sight, making them perfect to use within environments where objects are difficult to track, such as in manufacturing environments or within warehouses. They can provide real-time tracking and location information, which is useful for many industries, such as within supply chains or inventory management. They have the disadvantage of possibly being expensive – particularly for the active RFID systems – and that they can be disrupted by physical barriers such as metal or water, which can affect their accuracy and range.

It is simple to create IoT networks that are based on RFID; they function just as any other sensor would. The RFID reader would simply act as the sensor and pass on the information that it receives from the tag through a gateway, which, in turn, is put through the cloud for storage and further processing.

The following diagram shows one such example of how such an architecture would be positioned:

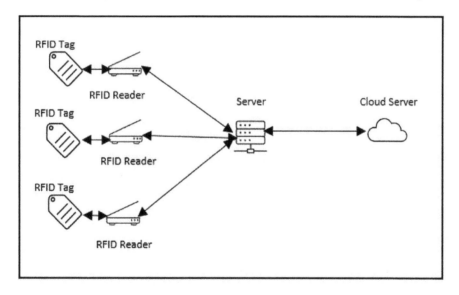

Figure 4.4 – RFID sample architecture

Now that we have a general understanding of how RFID technology works, let's consider a small practical on building a system based on RFID. We want to be able to activate a certain mechanism when the correct card is presented to the reader.

First, link your ESP32 with the hardware diagram, as shown here:

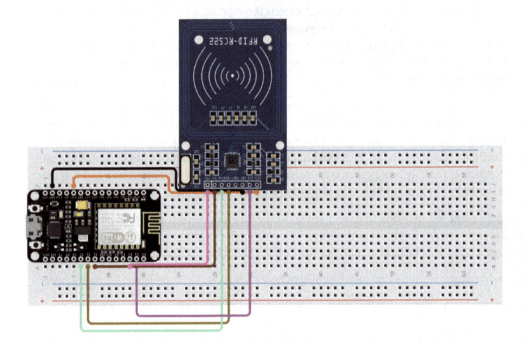

Figure 4.5 – Simple RFID wire-up diagram

Now, we want to program our ESP32 with the following code. Note that the RFID module will be using the SPI protocol to communicate with the ESP32.

First, we want to include the two libraries that we mentioned in the *Technical requirements* section. The SPI.h library will allow us to establish communication between the RFID module and the ESP32 card, while the MFRC522.h library will allow us to communicate with the module. Have a closer look at these libraries if you want to see what functions they allow us to perform:

```
#include <SPI.h>
#include <MFRC522.h>
```

Afterward, we want to declare constants in the form of SS_PIN and RST_PIN:

```
#define SS_PIN 5
#define RST_PIN 0
```

Then, we must set the parameter of the IP address, as follows:

```
const int ipaddress[4] = {103, 97, 67, 25};
```

Now, we must set the variables that are required as part of the solution. First, we want to initialize all values in nuidPICC to all zeroes. Afterward, we want to initialize a MIFARE_Key variable and create an RFID variable that corresponds to the constants that we have set:

```
byte nuidPICC[4] = {0, 0, 0, 0};
MFRC522::MIFARE_Key key;
MFRC522 rfid = MFRC522(SS_PIN, RST_PIN);
```

At this point, we can set up the system. Here, we must initialize the serial USB, where we initialize the RFID with the PCD_Init() command and print out the version of the reader:

```
void setup() {
  Serial.begin(115200);
  Serial.println(F("Initialize System"));
  SPI.begin();
  rfid.PCD_Init();

  Serial.print(F("Reader :"));
  rfid.PCD_DumpVersionToSerial();
}
```

As part of the loop section of the code, we must ask the ESP32 to continually read the RFID as we want to check whether there is a card that is being swiped to test whether it is an appropriate card:

```
void loop() {
  readRFID();
}
```

Now, we must create a new function to read the RFID card. As part of this, we'll look for a new card and verify whether the NUID has been read. Then, we can store the NUID in the nuidPICC array that has been created to track the data that has been read from it. At this point, we can print out the RFID UID and its size in decimals, then halt the PICC and stop the PCD from being encrypted:

```
void readRFID(void) {
  for (byte i = 0; i < 6; i++) {
    key.keyByte[i] = 0xFF;
  }
  if ( ! rfid.PICC_IsNewCardPresent())
    return;

  if (  !rfid.PICC_ReadCardSerial())
    return;

  for (byte i = 0; i < 4; i++) {
    nuidPICC[i] = rfid.uid.uidByte[i];
```

```
  }

  Serial.print(F("RFID In dec: "));
  printDec(rfid.uid.uidByte, rfid.uid.size);
  Serial.println();

  rfid.PICC_HaltA();

  rfid.PCD_StopCrypto1();
}
```

Afterward, we can use a helper routine to dump a byte array as a hexadecimal value:

```
void printHex(byte *buffer, byte bufferSize) {
  for (byte i = 0; i < bufferSize; i++) {
    Serial.print(buffer[i] < 0x10 ? " 0" : " ");
    Serial.print(buffer[i], HEX);
  }
}
```

For the full line of code, check out this chapter's GitHub folder in this book's GitHub repository, as mentioned in the *Technical requirements* section.

Mesh networking

Mesh networking is a network structure based on the mesh topology that we discussed in *Chapter 2, Understanding and Designing IoT Networks* where each device on the network acts as a node and relays data to other devices. Due to it having no central point of control, all devices are connected in a web-like structure, creating high resiliency in the case that one device fails.

There are three types of mesh networks: full mesh networks, partial mesh networks, and hybrid mesh networks. Full mesh networks are the networks in which every device is connected to every other device, which creates a highly resilient network. In partial mesh networks, only some devices are connected to every other device, while others are connected to only a few other devices. In hybrid mesh networks, both elements are combined.

Various mesh networking technologies exist, such as the Wi-Fi mesh, Zigbee mesh, and **Wireless Smart Ubiquitous Network (Wi-SUN)** mesh, each with its own set of characteristics and best-suited applications. Let's take a closer look:

- **Wi-Fi mesh**: These networks leverage the familiar Wi-Fi standard to create mesh links between nodes. This technology is known for its higher data rates and broader bandwidth, making it suitable for applications requiring substantial data throughput and real-time communications.

- **Zigbee mesh**: These networks are particularly known for their low power consumption and low data rate, making them a favorable choice for applications where energy efficiency and long battery life are paramount. Its self-healing mesh capability enhances network resilience, a critical trait for remote or inaccessible water utility installations.

- **Wi-SUN mesh**: These networks combine the benefits of robust wireless communication with large-scale mesh networking. They're the preferred choice for many utility applications due to their long-range communication capabilities, low power consumption, and industry-grade security features.

The choice between Wi-Fi mesh, Zigbee mesh, and Wi-SUN mesh should align with the specific requirements of the water utility IoT network, such as the geographic spread of assets, the criticality of real-time data transmission, energy efficiency considerations, and the existing network infrastructure. By assessing these factors alongside the inherent advantages and limitations of each mesh technology, network planners can better align the mesh networking solution with the overarching objectives of the water utility IoT deployment.

Bluetooth

Bluetooth is a wireless communication technology that allows devices to exchange data over short distances through radio waves. It is popular in IoT due to its low power consumption and being cost-effective, and also because it is widely supported by a wide range of devices. A smart thermostat, for example, may use Bluetooth to communicate with a smartphone app to allow the user to control the temperature remotely. It can also be used for M2M networks, with one device controlling another. The main limitation of it is its short range, which normally only reaches 9 meters, especially when there are obstacles such as walls in the way of communication.

In the next section, we will see how we can examine edge cases for selecting these protocols and understand how to operate them.

Examining edge cases for protocol selection and operation

In industry-based settings, we will often encounter scenarios where we must figure out the best solutions when it comes to edge cases. Edge cases, in this context, are cases where certain circumstances out of your control may occur, and you will need to account for this despite having no historical event of a similar occurrence which you can learn from.

In this section, we will discuss how to account for this with complex environments, understand the key factors to consider in such environments, and look at a case study to see how such factors are considered within a real industry-based scenario.

Understanding the fundamental rules of architecting for different areas

First, let's look at three key factors that often lead to uncovering edge cases when architecting within the different environments around us.

Environment

In our deployment, it is crucial to understand where we are putting the equipment with the protocol. Are we putting it in an area that may be prone to signal interference? Is it an area that experiences many floods? These are all considerations that are not part of historical data that we may have but are important to consider as they could happen. It will impact the protocols we decide to use.

Industry

When operating deployments, we also need to understand what is going on within the industry that we are in. Have there been more security breaches within our industry? How likely is it that a certain connectivity protocol that we are using will be breached over the coming months or even years? No matter the size of the company, security breaches or industry-wide issues have a fair chance of happening, and if we are to prevent issues such as those from occurring, we should always have a holistic view of what to keep on the horizon and address.

The standards

Of course, we must always consider edge cases based on the standards. What are the chances that the manufacturer's specified maximum temperature the sensor can withstand would be experienced by the device over a lengthy period? Can it withstand that continuous temperature? There are always considerations to be made regarding this, and this risk also must be accounted for.

Now that we've looked at some guidelines for identifying edge cases, let's look at a case study based on a water utility IoT network.

A look at a water utility IoT network

This is an industry-based implementation of a water utility IoT network. As you navigate the flow of the network, pay close attention to the protocols that are being used within certain areas, how different environments are handled with certain networks, and how the connections are done from one end to another:

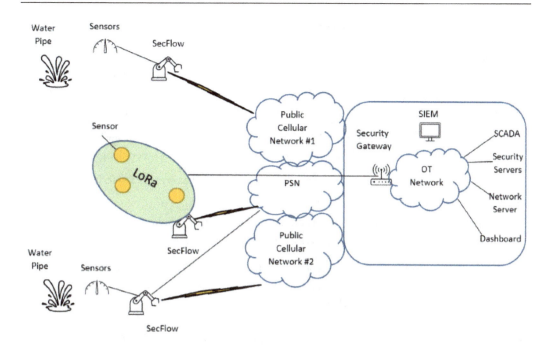

Figure 4.6 – Water utility IoT network

Here, we can see that between the sensors, the LoRaWAN network is used as the sensors are more geared toward use in long-distance scenarios. Furthermore, we can see that they have decided to use cellular networks in the form of LTE to communicate between the LoRa network and the cloud. They have done this between the three areas of sensors, although the other areas that contain the sensors use serial communication.

When planning such networks, we always need to continually ask ourselves whether the choice of protocol we have is the best choice for the given scenario. Are we optimizing the best we can and accounting for the possible edge cases based on risks that could happen? The more production-critical your workload is, the more imperative that this is considered. This will certainly be something that you will continuously have to put on the forefront of your mind as an IoT developer to prevent adverse scenarios from happening and to best support the objectives of your IoT deployment.

Practice forming more networks

Now that we have a deeper understanding of the components of various networks, let's continue to investigate forming more networks. Think how each of the following scenarios would be formed. For ease of planning for such scenarios, we recommend using diagramming software such as Draw.io to draw your sketches:

- A network based on an urban area where sensors are based on construction appliances located a kilometer from each other and they need to communicate with each other alongside the cloud

- A smart data center building that requires RFID for entry and has sensors around it to measure temperature, humidity, and air pressure

- A water treatment plant based in an urban area needs to access cellular communication based on the base stations around it to report back to the control hub

With this, you will have obtained a much deeper understanding of working with different protocols in establishing your IoT networks. Now, we can put all this into practice and work on a practical scenario where we will use multiple communication protocols with ESP32.

Practical scenario – working with multiple communication protocols with ESP32

In this hands-on project, we'll build an access control system using an MFRC522 RFID reader connected to an ESP32 microcontroller. This system will read, write, and register MIFARE 13.56 MHz RFID cards. When a scanned ID card matches any registered ID, the microcontroller will issue an MQTT publish message. This message instructs a remote MQTT subscriber, running on another ESP32 microcontroller, to activate the corresponding switch meant to enable door access. However, in this demonstration, we won't connect to an actual switch. Instead, we'll illuminate the built-in LED on the MQTT subscriber's ESP32 microcontroller to simulate the process.

You will require the following materials:

- 2x ESP32 NodeMCU microcontroller

- 1x MFRC522 RFID card reader

- 1x push button (latch) switch

- 2x MIFARE 13.56 MHz RFID cards, fobs, or NFC cards

- Jumper cables

Making the connections

Connect one of the ESP32 NodeMCUs to the MFRC522, as shown in the following diagram:

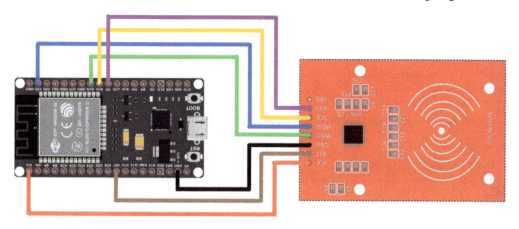

Figure 4.7 – Connection diagram for ESP32 to MFRC522

Let's take a closer look at the wiring connection between the RFID/NFC MFRC522 module and the ESP32 microcontroller:

MFRC522 Module	ESP32
SS	GPIO 5 (pin 29)
SCK	GPIO 18 (pin 30)
MOSI	GPIO 23 (pin 37)
MISO	GPIO 19 (pin 31)
IRQ	Not connected!
GND	GND (38, 32, or 14)
RST	GPIO 27 (pin 11)
VCC	3V3 (pin 1)

Table 4.1 – Connection wirings for ESP32 to MFRC522

> **Important note**
>
> As the pin placement can vary across different MFRC522 modules, please arrange them appropriately with caution. Additionally, we need to connect the push on push off switch to the ESP32 microcontroller. Connect the middle pin to the **ground** (**GND**), and the normally open pin to GPIO 32 (pin 7).

From here, we can start implementing the code. As part of this, we need to obtain the necessary MFRC522 library:

1. In the Arduino IDE, select **Sketch**, then **Include Library**, and finally **Manage Libraries…**:

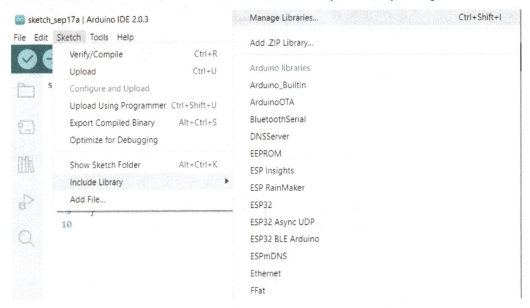

Figure 4.8 – Selecting Manage Libraries… to see the list of libraries

2. In the **LIBRARY MANAGER** area, search for mfrc522 and proceed with the installation. With this setup, we are now prepared to explore RFID cards:

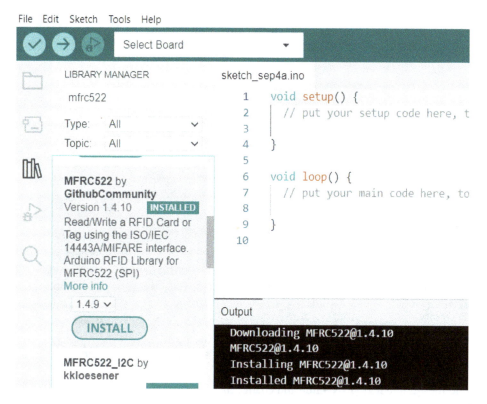

Figure 4.9 – Searching for and installing the MFRC522 library

We can now create an appropriate sketch based on the examples that are within the Arduino IDE:

1. In the Arduino IDE, click **File | Examples | MFRC522 | DumpInfo**. The sketch will appear in your Arduino window:

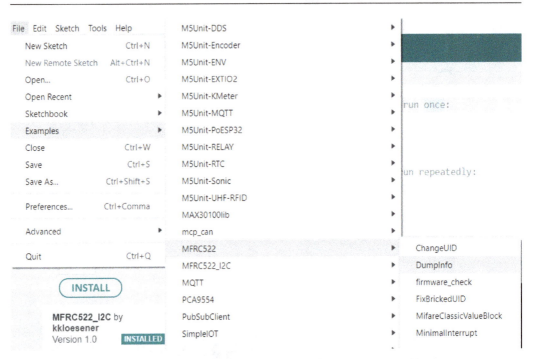

Figure 4.10 – Selecting the DumpInfo example from the MFRC522 library

2. Find the **#define RST_PIN 9** line and change the value to 27 since we're using GPIO 27 for the RST pin.

3. Find the **#define SS_PIN 10** line and change the value to 5 since we're using GPIO 5 for the SS pin:

```
DumpInfo.ino
34      *
35      * More pin layouts for other boards can be found here: https://github.com/miguel
36      */
37
38      #include <SPI.h>
39      #include <MFRC522.h>
40
41      #define RST_PIN       27        // Configurable, see typical pin layout above
42      #define SS_PIN        5         // Configurable, see typical pin layout above
43
44      MFRC522 mfrc522(SS_PIN, RST_PIN);  // Create MFRC522 instance
45
```

Figure 4.11 – Changing the code for RST_PIN and SS_PIN

4. Now, it is time to burn the code to your ESP32 microcontroller. Connect the ESP32 microcontroller to the USB port of your PC and choose the board from **Tools | Board | ESP32 | Node32S**.

5. Then, choose the port that's used by the ESP32 microcontroller by clicking **Tools | Port**; a COM port will appear. Choose the one that appears after you connect the ESP32 microcontroller. For instance, it could be port COM3.

6. After that, you can check whether the sketch is clear or contains bugs by clicking the 🔘 button, or directly upload the code to the ESP32 microcontroller by clicking the 🔘 button, as can be seen in *Figure 4.11*. Do not forget that you need to press the **EN** button to enable it in the programming mode.

Now, we can check the messages that are sent by the ESP32 to see whether the code has been uploaded successfully:

1. If uploaded successfully, click on **Tools | Serial Monitor** to see the messages sent by the ESP32 microcontroller.

2. You may press the **RST** button on the ESP32 microcontroller (the button other than the **EN** button) to force the ESP32 microcontroller to reboot so that you can see all the messages from the start.

Next, we'll learn how to grant access with the RFID tag. As part of this, we need to program the appropriate read, register, and access operations to it:

1. For this step, we will use an ESP32 microcontroller connected to the MFRC522 module as the RFID reader, register, and verify unit, while employing another ESP32 microcontroller as the remote access switch control. Begin by downloading the ESP32_MQTT_Subscriber.ino sketch from https://github.com/PacktPublishing/IoT-Made-Easy-for-Beginners/blob/main/Chapter04/mqtt_rfid_practical/ESP32_MQTT_Subscriber.ino.

2. Then, you must modify the Wi-Fi SSID and password so that they match your Wi-Fi access point credentials and choose the MQTT server you're using (you could use your Raspberry Pi MQTT server, as discussed in *Chapter 3*, *Integrating Application Protocols* or an available online MQTT server such as http://mrtg.prcn.bitcoin-analytics.com/).

3. After making these adjustments, upload the code to the ESP32 microcontroller connected to the MFRC522 module.

4. Open the **Serial Monitor** screen to observe the messages. Ensure that the system connects to both Wi-Fi and the Mosquitto server. Initially, position the switch to **OFF** and place an RFID card on the MFRC522's read area. Remember, the card must be close as the maximum reading distance (depending on the MFRC522 module) is approximately 10 cm. The RFID card ID should appear; try multiple cards to test the reader function. In read mode, the reader compares the scanned card ID with registered IDs. If the system finds a match, it will send a publish message to the Mosquitto server. However, as no card IDs are currently registered, no publish messages will be sent.

5. To register a card ID, switch to the **ON** position. Scan a card again; you should receive a message confirming the card ID registration. Register a few more cards for testing purposes.

6. Once you have registered the cards, revert the switch to the **OFF** position and scan a registered card. You should now see a message indicating that the card ID has been published.

At this point, we can work on getting the MRTG message published by the RFID reader. As part of this, we need to work on the necessary wiring:

1. Connect the ESP32 microcontroller board with the relay module, as shown here:

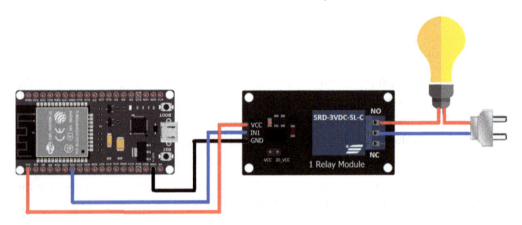

Figure 4.12 – Wire-up diagram for connecting the lamp to the relay outputs

We need to connect a load such as a lamp to the relay outputs.

2. Download the `ESP_MQTT_MFRC522.ino` sketch from `https://github.com/PacktPublishing/IoT-Made-Easy-for-Beginners/blob/main/Chapter04/mqtt_rfid_practical/ESP_MQTT_MFRC522.ino`.

3. Change the Wi-Fi SSID and password according to your Wi-Fi access point credentials and the MRTG server that you use (you can use your Raspberry Pi MRTG server, as discussed in *Chapter 3, Integrating Application Protocols*). Alternatively, you can use an available online MRTG server, as mentioned previously.

4. After changing those variables, upload the code to the ESP32 microcontroller that is connected to the relay module.

5. Go to the serial monitor and monitor the messages there. Tap an RFID card that is already registered. You should receive a message such as `S1  ON`; look at the appropriate relay that it is also switched to the **ON** position.

We can expand the project so that more relays are served. To do this, we can use a web server, where each card ID can be set to have different access to different relays. In the real world, these relays can be used to open doors and gates, switch lamps on/off, control electronic equipment, and more.

In this practical scenario, we have demonstrated how to create an access control system using RFID readers and apply concepts from the protocols we've discovered, such as employing Wi-Fi, Bluetooth, and RFID as short- and long-range communication protocols. By following the provided steps, you now understand how these protocols can work together in IoT networks and have gained hands-on experience in implementing a simple IoT communication system.

Summary

In this chapter, we learned more about communication and connectivity protocols, understanding how to apply long-range protocols to the networking knowledge that we gained in *Chapter 2*, *Understanding and Designing IoT Networks* and understanding more about how to apply the relevant protocols to our use case. We learned more about what we must consider in creating an optimal deployment that meets our needs. We also looked at edge cases in creating networks, understanding how to cater to complex needs, and considering multiple protocols to achieve the optimal design.

Then, we put what we learned into practice by completing some practical exercises, including working with an RFID module based on the ESP32 microcontroller, designing more complex networks based on select use cases, and creating a network hub model based on the ESP32 microcontroller while catering to multiple protocols that are present at the same time. With this practice, you will have become more confident in designing IoT networks and understanding more about applying the knowledge to your use cases.

In the next chapter, we will apply this knowledge to designing and implementing wireless sensor networks and build on our skills in developing networks from there.

Further reading

For more information about what was covered in this chapter, please refer to the following links:

- Learn more about the basics of RFID: https://learn.sparkfun.com/tutorials/rfid-basics/all

- Understand more about LoRa from the documentation: https://lora.readthedocs.io/en/latest/

- Understand more about the IPv6 dual stack: https://www.juniper.net/documentation/us/en/software/junos/is-is/topics/concept/ipv6-dual-stack-understanding.html

- Look more into the security interface for IPv4 and IPv6: https://www.juniper.net/documentation/us/en/software/junos/interfaces-security-devices/topics/topic-map/security-interface-ipv4-ipv6-protocol.html

- Look at an application of IPv6 for low-power networks: https://www.rfc-editor.org/rfc/rfc6550

Part 2: Developing and Optimizing IoT Systems for Smart Environments

In this part, we explore IoT further, delving into the nuanced world of developing and refining systems tailored for smart environments. Building upon the foundational concepts introduced earlier, our journey begins with understanding the intricacies of wireless sensor networks for intelligent spaces. We then transition into harnessing the power of edge computing, crafting responsive applications designed for immediate on-site data processing. Further expanding our horizons, we explore the vast potential of cloud computing in bolstering our IoT solutions, before wrapping up with essential strategies to ensure system interoperability. This section promises a holistic and profound perspective on deploying optimized IoT systems for the next generation of smart spaces.

This part has the following chapters:

- *Chapter 5, Realizing Wireless Sensor Networks within Smart Spaces*
- *Chapter 6, Creating Applications on the Edge*
- *Chapter 7, Working with Cloud Computing to Power IoT Solutions*
- *Chapter 8, Designing for Interoperability*

5

Realizing Wireless Sensor Networks within Smart Spaces

Wireless sensor networks (**WSNs**) consist of small, low-powered devices equipped with sensors, microcontrollers, and wireless communication capabilities. They consist of tiny sensor nodes that can communicate with each other and exchange data. These devices are usually deployed in large numbers to monitor a myriad of physical or environmental conditions, such as humidity, air, and sound. Once information has been obtained from the environment, the nodes then send it to a base station, which in turn sends the data to a wired network or performs an action, depending on the thresholds that have been set.

These networks use air as their transmission medium as part of wireless transmission. Compared to traditional wired sensor networks, they offer many benefits, such as cost-effectiveness and flexibility in deployment. Furthermore, they can nearly replicate the performance of wired networks, particularly with standards such as IEEE 802.11. Despite this, they have several key challenges, such as limited power, interference, and scalability. With emerging technologies such as advances in semiconductor technology, which allows for more chip capabilities, which, in turn, adds to processor capabilities, we will continue to see WSNs be formed as part of many users' IoT solutions.

In this chapter, we're going to cover the following main topics:

- Understanding the architecture, application, and challenges within WSNs
- Building APIs for WSNs
- Architecting IoT networks based on WSNs

Technical requirements

This chapter will require you to have the following hardware installed:

- ESP32-CAM
- Single channel relay
- 1 1k ohm resistor
- Push button switch
- Jumper cables
- Breadboard
- Mobile charger 5V/1A to use as a power supply
- iPhone/Android phone (to run the Blynk app)

Here's the list of software you'll need for this chapter:

- Blynk app
- Arduino IDE

The Blynk app

Blynk is a platform that allows users to build **graphical user interfaces** (**GUIs**) with ease, which allows them to monitor and control IoT devices. It provides a wide number of widgets, such as buttons, sliders, or gauges, that can be added to the GUI and have specific actions linked to them or data points on the device. It can be downloaded as an app on iOS or Android and can serve as a bridge between the GUI and the device, allowing users to remotely control and monitor the device from the convenience of their smartphone or tablet.

We will be using Blynk for our smart energy monitoring and management system practical scenario later. The steps for using it, along with how we will be building on it, will be discussed later in the practical section.

You can find the GitHub folder that contains the code for this chapter at `https://github.com/PacktPublishing/IoT-Made-Easy-for-Beginners/tree/main/Chapter05/`.

Choosing between different sensor technologies

Choosing from the numerous existing sensor technologies to build the networks we have in mind can be quite a daunting task. In this section, we will show you how to use patterns and information from different technologies to better select which ones to use, as well as how to create more effective deployments as part of the networks that you create.

Classes of sensor networks

With the continued development of WSNs, a variety of solutions have been tailored to a variety of applications. This creates many types of network designs, where there are protocols for different layers that are put in place as part of the network. Here, we'll discuss some of the main differences between various WSNs.

Data sink

One of the defining characteristics of a sensor network is how the data sink is provisioned. A data sink is a device that has the responsibility of collecting and storing the data generated by sensor nodes within a network. It is normally connected to sensor nodes through a wireless communication link and serves as a central repository for all the data collected by the sensor nodes. A data sink is also often used to perform data aggregation and processing tasks and may also have the responsibility of forwarding the data to other networks or systems for further storage or analysis.

In some WSNs, the type of data sink that's used can further be classified into two categories: fixed and mobile. Fixed data sinks are fixed devices that are located at a central location, such as a base station or gateway. Mobile WSNs, on the other hand, have the data sink based on a mobile device that may be carried by a user or vehicle. The type of data sink matters in terms of how data is collected as dispersed data storage being used as a methodology for storing data would be more effective in the latter's case.

Mobile sensors

Sensor networks may be further classified to be based on the nature of the sensor that is currently being used. Although sensors are usually stationary, some sensors have been known to also be mobile. Some examples of this include military applications such as when sensors are placed on **unmanned aerial vehicles** (**UAVs**) to communicate with an organized sensor network. Due to this, the sensors can manipulate protocols within the networking layer and do so to localize services for the use of mobility.

Resources within sensors

Nodes may differ based on the availability of resources that are provided by the computer. Memory and the conditions of how the processing is done would affect the implementation of the protocols. Thus, this is a factor that has to be considered when provisioning sensors as they have to fit the risks that are put through and ensure that they can fit the need well.

Access patterns

An especially important consideration is how traffic will be created within the network as different patterns may occur when sensors send data. Some sensors may only send data occasionally when an event is triggered and go into sleep mode to conserve energy otherwise, while others may have to continuously produce data due to continually reporting based on the readings within the environment.

Routing for WSNs

Routing is always an issue we are going to have to address within different IoT networks, and WSNs are no exception to this. With the clusters of sensors that we have within the network, we need to ensure that the best path is taken from the source node to reach the destination node. As we've discussed, some challenges come with WSNs, which consequently lead to challenges within routing. These challenges include the limited energy resources that the sensor nodes have and the dynamic nature of the WSNs in that they continually have different conditions imposed on them.

Before we dive into the more complex routing methodologies, let's introduce a simpler routing topology known as the star topology, which is often easier to grasp for those new to WSNs.

Star topology

In a star topology, all nodes communicate directly with a central node, often referred to as the gateway or hub. Each sensor node transmits its data to this central node, which then forwards the data to the respective destination or processes the data accordingly. The star topology is straightforward to manage, making it a good starting point for understanding routing in WSNs. However, its primary limitation is its range as all nodes must be within the communication range of the central node.

Now, let's explore two of the more advanced routing methodologies used in WSNs.

Multi-hop flat routing

Within multi-hop flat routing, all nodes in the network are organized into a single-layer structure, where data is then transmitted from the source node to the destination node by forwarding it by intermediate nodes, also known as *hops*. It is a simple routing approach that is used within WSNs. It is flexible to changes within the network as all the nodes within each network are equal and can act as intermediate nodes for data transmission. Despite this, there are some limitations, which include that it is not efficient for energy consumption, given that data needs to be transmitted through many hops before reaching the destination, which may, in turn, lead to congestion.

An example of how this type of routing can be implemented can be seen in the following diagram:

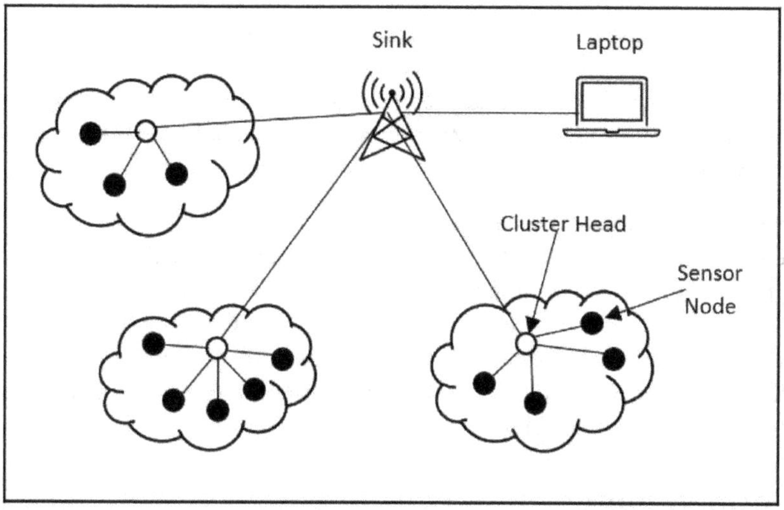

Figure 5.1 – Multi-hop flat routing network diagram

Here, we can see how different clusters of sensor nodes have a cluster head that acts as an intermediate node they forward their information to before having it sent to the data sink that is located at the center of it all.

Location-based routing

Location-based routing is an approach that depends on the location information of nodes within the network to determine the best path for data transmission. The location may be the absolute or relative location of the nodes. If the absolute location is used, the coordinates of the nodes are known – they are obtained through a method such as GPS – and routing is done based on this. If the relative location is used, the nodes measure their relative position to each other, and routing is done based on this.

This type of routing has the advantage of being able to achieve efficient and reliable data transmission through the spatial distribution of the nodes within the network. It would know to transmit data to nearby nodes to reach a destination node that is far away rather than just transmitting to any node, reducing the number of hops that would be required to reach the destination, hence saving energy. It would also help with working with the dynamic nature of WSNs, given that it can adjust to changes in the positioning of nodes or within the wireless communication conditions.

Despite this, some challenges are posed. First, it is difficult to ensure that location information is accurate and up to date, given that there may be areas, such as those within extreme temperatures or urban areas, that may not have acceptable GPS signals, which may make it difficult to achieve this. There may also be the issue of maintaining the location information and ensuring that it is updated based on changes within the location; this can increase the complexity of developing the algorithm for it. It has the potential to provide accuracy within networks but has far more potential for error compared to the other two routing approaches that we've discussed.

Choosing between routing approaches can be difficult when minimal information is known about the environment. This is why it is imperative to understand the layout and the dynamics of your IoT network. Will there be many additions and removals of nodes? Will there be bad GPS signals that may cause issues with determining location-based data later? This all needs to be considered because although many of the routing approaches create much promise, it all comes down to how you can pick the optimal algorithm for your use case, and how you can minimize the amount of complexity and errors that may result from your choice.

Design considerations

When considering the design of your WSN, there are several factors to take into account. Three of these are the connectivity that you will have at the location, the priority within the resource constraints that you have that you would like to focus on, and the proximity of the sensors to each other. These three factors will influence your design and how you will choose your hardware and software. More about this will be discussed in the next section.

Here is an example of a simple WSN setup:

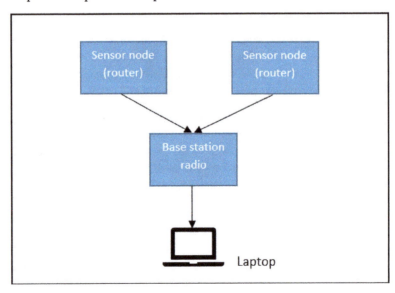

Figure 5.2 – Simple WSN setup

Here, two sensor nodes are sending data to a base station radio, where a user can then retrieve the data from their laptop.

Architecting the hardware and software

Nodes within WSNs are often packed with a small microcontroller, a radio transceiver, storage space, and a power source, usually in the form of a battery. Depending on the operations that are performed by the node, the cost may vary from mere cents to hundreds of dollars. This is why understanding how to optimize based on your use case and understanding which sensor would do the best work at the lowest possible cost is imperative to being able to appropriately get one that would satisfy the requirements that you have. In this subsection, we will talk about how each of these components is usually chosen and the characteristics of what to consider as part of them when selecting them for your use case.

Transceiver

Sensor nodes usually need to use the **industrial, scientific, and medical (ISM)** frequency band, which is available for free and doesn't require a license. Afterward, you must choose from the different types of wireless transmission media, which include radio frequency, optical fiber, and infrared. We won't dive deep into each of these; to learn more, please read the article linked in the *Further reading* section at the end of this chapter.

Microcontroller

The microcontroller performs the tasks that are needed as part of the WSN's operation. Such tasks involve processing data and taking care of the operations within the node. The bare minimum for a microcontroller is for it to have processor/CPU, I/O, and storage capabilities. There may also be substitutes such as general-purpose microprocessors, desktop computers, or laptops that are used as a replacement for it, but normally, these are not used due to their power consumption. As mentioned previously, we want to find the most optimal solution that can get the same tasks done with the least possible resources, so in this case, microcontrollers are always the preferred option.

Memory device

A node should always have the appropriate memory to be able to execute the tasks it needs to get done. This may be in the form of on-chip or external flash memory. Most of the time, flash memory is used because of its cost-effectiveness.

Power source

The power source for nodes is generally in the form of a battery or capacitor. Many sensors are designed to have energy-saving schemes, such as utilizing solar power or kinetic energy to recharge them. Nodes may also have power-saving policies such as sleep modes to conserve their power usage and use them when they are active if they do not need to be continuously active.

Sensors

As expected, sensors are a crucial part of networks. The signal that is obtained from it is converted into digital form using analog-to-digital converters; this is because microcontrollers can only process digital data. Sensors can be divided into three main categories: active sensors, passive and omnidirectional sensors, and passive and narrow-beam sensors.

Active sensors actively survey their surroundings, similar to a radar sensor. Passive and omnidirectional sensors monitor data without affecting the environment by continuously probing it. They can pick up data from all directions.

Finally, passive and narrow-beam sensors are passive but have an understanding of the direction of measurement, with this being supported by cameras. They may also be equipped with extra units such as a GPS device, along with a motor to help them move in the direction they need to:

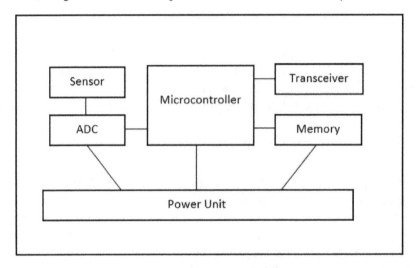

Figure 5.3 – A simple microcontroller and its associated nodes

Now, we can discuss the final important component: the operating system.

Operating system

Operating systems provide the software infrastructure for controlling the sensor nodes. The operating system is responsible for managing the node's resources and executing the tasks that it needs to. **TinyOS** is a popular operating system that is used for this purpose as it is open source and event-driven while also being designed to be lightweight, energy-efficient, and easy to program. Its architecture allows for easy extension and tailoring to fit the needs of many users' applications and provides libraries and tools that are generally needed within WSNs.

Next, we will discuss managing APIs when building solutions for WSNs.

Managing APIs

APIs are very important within WSNs as they help different components of the network communicate with each other. It operates within the application layer, allowing the layer to access the functions of the operating system, such as power management and data collection.

How they integrate within the system

APIs for WSNs can be provided at different levels, including the operating system level and the network level. An example of such an integration is how TinyOS provides an API that allows the application layer to access the functions that are provided by the operating system. At a network level, an API can provide an interface for the application layer to access the routing table, enabling it to find the best path for data transmission to be done. This can be implemented by different standard protocols such as MQTT or CoAP, two application protocols that we discussed in *Chapter 3, Integrating Application Protocols*.

APIs allow different software components to be integrated with ease and help make the services that are provided by one provider interoperable with others, such as with the cloud or other sensor networks. This, in turn, helps with developing and maintaining the applications, as well as provisioning a well-defined interface for the functionality that is provided. Despite this, there are some major challenges, two of which are complexity and security. APIs introduce another component into your architecture, so it will affect how the routing and interaction between components will work. You should understand how the API will interact with your other components and whether you truly need it for your system. Furthermore, if not implemented securely, it may pose a security risk. Often, this must be mitigated with secure communication protocols such as HTTPS and through the implementation of authentication and authorization.

Types of APIs

In this subsection, we will highlight two popular APIs that are used in developing WSNs.

REST APIs

REST is a popular architectural style of building web services and is a popular API for use within WSNs. It provides a way for the application layer to access the functions of the sensor nodes and the network, providing functions such as data collection, power management, and communication through HTTP methods such as PUT, GET, POST, and DELETE.

It is based on widely used standards, namely HTTP and URI, making them easy to implement and use. This also makes it easy to integrate with other systems. It also allows you to remotely configure and manage sensor nodes, which is useful for managing the dynamic nature of WSNs. Furthermore, it helps provide security through security mechanisms such as SSL/TLS and works when authentication and authorization must be implemented.

Despite this, it has its own set of challenges, such as the overhead that is caused by using HTTP and URI – that is, additional message headers will be introduced, which would cause various issues within WSNs, given that bandwidth is often a resource that we are trying to optimize. They are also less power-efficient compared to other APIs:

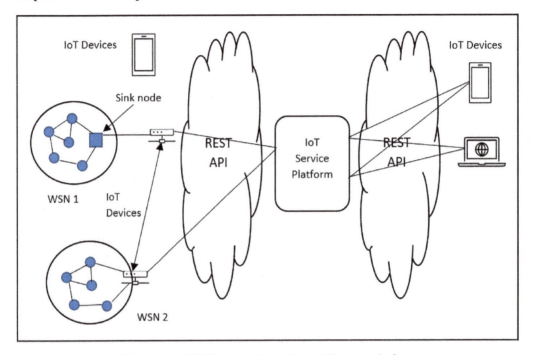

Figure 5.4 – REST API connection with an IoT service platform

An example of its implementation within one such system can be seen here:

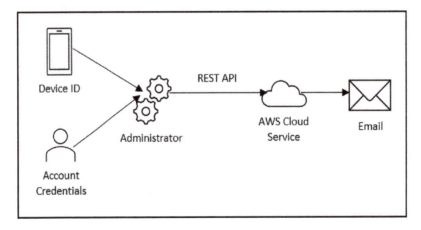

Figure 5.5 – A flow diagram showing the implementation of the REST API

As we can see, the interaction depends on a device ID and account credentials being sent through to the administrator. The administrator then sends these details through the REST API to the AWS cloud service, which, in turn, sends an email based on the information that was received. Within WSNs, we see a similar pattern with its implementation, given that we will also be forwarding the information this way.

WebSocket APIs

WebSockets are used for two-way communication over a single, long-lived connection between a client and a server. This makes them popular within WSNs as they provide low-latency communication between devices while keeping connections simple and efficient. This helps reduce the power consumption within devices as the number of transmission attempts will be reduced. However, one thing to note is that WebSockets work best when environments have reliable network connections, so the location and the circumstances of how the connection is to be established must be thought through thoroughly. It may not work when there are limitations to bandwidth or where network connections are unreliable.

With that, we have understood how to manage different kinds of APIs. Now, we can look at evaluating different kinds of WSNs and understand how to best build them depending on our use cases.

Evaluating WSNs

As mentioned multiple times in this chapter and throughout this book, one of the most imperative aspects of implementing a network is to understand how it can be best optimized. There are several key ways in which this can be done; one of them is through understanding metrics that are related to such networks and how we can apply them when we're examining networks that we encounter. We will discuss these metrics and how you can use them to evaluate your WSN deployment, as well as other deployments that you come across to better understand how to optimize your own as well.

Metrics

In this section, we'll look at different metrics that have to be considered when building WSNs:

- **Energy consumption**: This metric measures the amount of energy that is used up by the WSN and is used to assess the energy efficiency of the network.

- **Network lifetime**: This is a metric that measures the amount of time the WSN can operate before the batteries are depleted. It is closely related to the energy consumption metric and is key to understanding how efficiently your WSN is performing.

- **Packet loss rate**: This is a metric that measures the proportion of packets that are not successfully received by the recipient. This could be between nodes or from a node to the base station. This could indicate problems with the network, such as poor signal quality or congestion.

- **Latency**: This is a metric that measures the time it takes for a packet to transmit from a sender to a receiver.

- **Throughput**: This is a metric that is used to measure the amount of data that is transferred successfully across the network over a given period. It is used to assess the capacity of the network since it's responsible for large amounts of data.

- **Mobility**: This is a metric that measures how well the network can support devices being added and removed to and from a network. This makes it a very important factor in supporting IoT networks that are very dynamic.

- **Reliability**: This is a metric that measures the consistency and availability of the network over a certain period. This is especially important in workloads that have critical applications, such as within healthcare scenarios.

- **Scalability**: This is a metric that measures how well the network handles an increase in the number of devices with the amount of data being transmitted.

- **Security**: This is a metric that measures the network's protection over itself and the data it has that is being transmitted within it due to unauthorized access or tampering.

Note that all WSNs have different requirements and constraints imposed on them, so to best evaluate your use case, you should consider your own set of metrics that work best with your considerations and understand how those metrics can help you achieve success and lead you toward the road of improvement that you would like as part of your system.

Models of delivery

The second factor of evaluating networks is understanding how the data delivery process is modeled and how the interactions between the components within the nodes would affect how protocols are designed, as well as the considerations that are to be taken. There are two main models: traffic models and energy models.

Traffic models

Traffic models focus on reducing the consumption of power by the route that is taken when delivering messages within the network. An example is in querying nodes to continuously find the path that is based on nodes that are accessed the most frequently as it would consume less power this way compared to continuously establishing paths randomly. This could lead to adaptive routing protocols, which help establish a path where an event occurs most frequently as opposed to just being on demand.

Energy models

Energy models focus more on reducing how much power is consumed by sensor communications. We can achieve this by planning to save energy naturally, such as by turning off the transceiver for a certain period. We could also reduce the number of communications that are done within the network, given that it would allow the nodes to be in an idle or sleep state if they are configured with that capability.

A case study

Now, let's look at an industrial WSN to understand how it is provisioned and the considerations that are put into it. This industrial network is based on several areas, as shown in *Figure 5.6*. We can see that two main WSN clusters are connected to a sink node, where all the data from the nodes goes toward an intermediary node before being passed to a gateway at the satellite ground station. We can see that the nodes are using a location-based algorithm, which allows routing to be done based on their proximity to each other, allowing them to transmit information efficiently. This is passed through a WSN tunnel to reach the internet.

This information can then either be served directly to users or stored and processed on a cloud platform before being served to users. As we can see, this information is also passed through satellite and cellular communication directly from the base station to reach remote requesters, at which point it can be passed from satellite to satellite or base station to the base station. With this architecture, we can see how throughput, latency, and reliability are three metrics that would be very beneficial to know as part of evaluating the network, given the context of the environment and the use case. They would certainly help with understanding if the routing that's being used is efficient, and if it meets the requirements of the environment well:

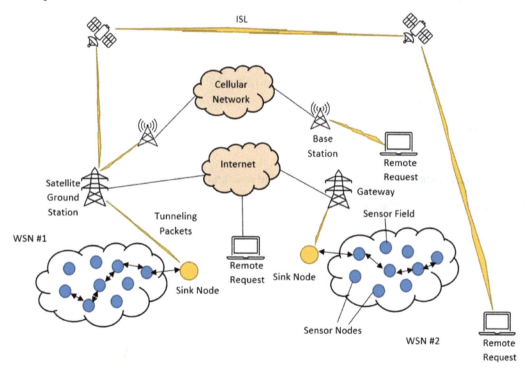

Figure 5.6 – Sample industrial WSN deployment

Now, let's move on to a practical understanding of a smart energy monitoring and management system.

Practical scenario – step-by-step smart energy monitoring and management system

In this practical project, we will build a monitoring device to monitor the electricity usage of certain electrical devices (we'll use a power distribution outlet connected to multiple electrical devices to monitor its electrical usage parameters). To monitor these electrical parameters, we will use the Peacefair PZEM-004T V3 energy monitor. The PZEM-004T module is a mains-powered module that measures the voltage, current, power, frequency, and power factor. It provides these values over a serial interface.

> **Important note**
> This project involves a direct connection to electrical lines. Please be aware that you're exposing yourself to electrical hazards that can cause fire or be fatal. If you have no experience in doing this, then you'll need to seek help from someone who has experience and understands the risks of connecting to electrical lines.

Requirements

You will require the following hardware for this practical exercise:

1. ESP32 NodeMCU
2. Peacefair PZEM-004T V3 energy monitor (including a CT transformer)
3. 4-pin 2.54mm pitch wire pin header
4. Hi-link AC 100-220VAC to DC 3.3V 3W transformer
5. Electrical wire

You will also need your Arduino IDE ready to upload code and a web browser to open the output.

Now that we have these components, we can wire up the hardware.

Connection diagram

Figure 5.7 shows how we will wire up the hardware:

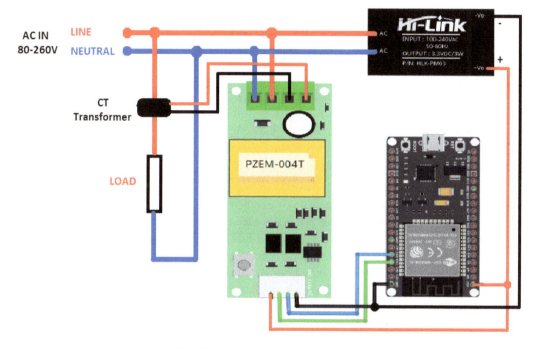

Figure 5.7 – Wiring diagram for the practical scenario

Now, we can set up the hardware.

Setting up and connecting the hardware

Follow these steps to set everything up for this practical exercise:

1.   For this sketch, you need to download and install some Arduino libraries:

   A.   PZEM-004T V3: `https://github.com/mandulaj/PZEM-004T-v30`.

   B.   ESP_ASYNC_WIFIMANAGER: `https://github.com/me-no-dev/ESPAsyncWebServer/archive/refs/heads/master.zip`.

   C.   AsyncElegantOTA: `https://github.com/ayushsharma82/AsyncElegantOTA`.

2. Connect the ESP32 NodeMCU to a USB port on your computer.

    Download the sketch from `https://github.com/PacktPublishing/IoT-Made-Easy-for-Beginners/blob/main/Chapter05/enermo/enermo.ino`. Open the code, then compile and upload it while using Node32s as the board. Select the appropriate serial port that appears when you connect the ESP32 board (you can disconnect and reconnect the board to observe the serial port used by ESP32).

3. Connect the ESP32, PZEM-004T, Hi-Link AC to DC transformer, and CT current transformer (included with PZEM-004T) according to *Figure 5.7*. Please note that only one cable of the AC that goes to the AC load (such as a lamp or electronic device) should be inserted inside the CT transformer. Be extremely careful when handling the wiring for the AC IN as it can cause electrical hazards or start a fire.

4. Since the sketch includes Wi-Fi Manager (ESP_ASYNC_WIFIMANAGER), you don't have to hardcode your Wi-Fi network credentials in the sketch. You can set your Wi-Fi network credentials during the initial stage using your mobile phone or computer. In the initial stage, the ESP32 microcontroller will act as a Wi-Fi access point. From your computer or mobile phone settings, go to your Wi-Fi settings and find the access point created by the ESP32 microcontroller; it will have the name ESP-xxxxxx, where xxxxxx represents the last six hex digits of the ESP32's microcontroller unique ID. After connecting to the ESP32 access point, you will be automatically redirected to a home screen.

With this, we can now configure the connection of the hardware for the access point.

Configuring the connection for the access point

Now, we can configure the connection to the Wi-Fi access point:

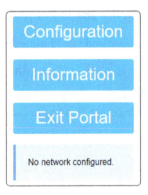

Figure 5.8 – Configuration menu for the ESP Wi-Fi access point

Follow these steps:

1. Click on the **Configuration** button; you will see the configuration menu with the available Wi-Fi access points around you:

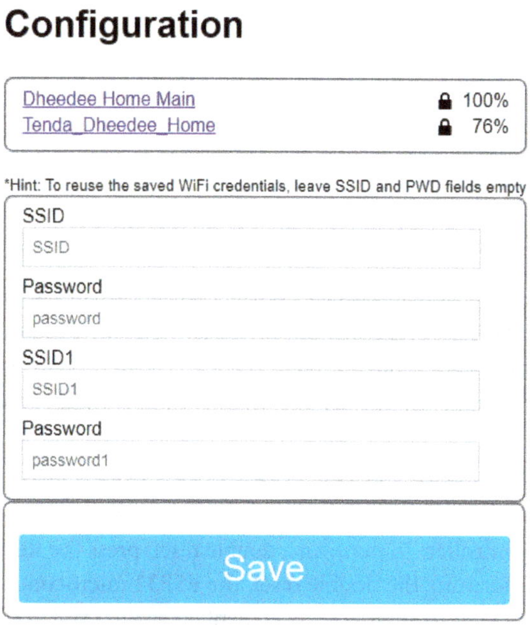

Configuration

Dheedee Home Main   🔒 100%
Tenda_Dheedee_Home   🔒 76%

*Hint: To reuse the saved WiFi credentials, leave SSID and PWD fields empty

SSID

    SSID

Password

    password

SSID1

    SSID1

Password

    password1

Save

Figure 5.9 – Configuration form for the Wi-Fi access point

2. Type in the SSID and password of your Wi-Fi access point. If you have another Wi-Fi access point, you can enter up to two SSIDs. Click the **Save** button to save the configuration.

Now, the ESP32 microcontroller will restart and switch to station mode, attempting to connect to the access point SSID that you entered and saved. In the Serial Monitor of the Arduino IDE, you will receive the following messages:

```
FS File: wifi_cred.dat, size: 334B

[WM] RFC925 Hostname = AsyncESP32-FSWebServer
[WM] Set CORS Header to :  Your Access-Control-Allow-Origin
ESP Self-Stored: SSID = Dheedee Home Main, Pass = xxxxxxxxxxxx
```

```
[WM] * Add SSID =  Dheedee Home Main , PW =  xxxxxxxxxxxx
Got ESP Self-Stored Credentials. Timeout 120s for Config Portal
[WM] LoadWiFiCfgFile
...

Custom Address:1
Voltage: 233.70V
Current: 0.56A
Power: 70.30W
Energy: 2072.798kWh
Frequency: 50.0Hz
PF: 0.62
   0203.700.5670.302072.8050.000.62
```

These messages indicate that you have successfully set up the connection between the ESP32 microcontroller and the Wi-Fi access point, as well as read data from the PZWM004T sensor. Since the configuration settings are saved in the ESP32 microcontroller's internal memory, the next time the ESP32 microcontroller boots, it will automatically connect to the configured Wi-Fi access point.

The sketch includes the ESP_Double_Reset_Detector feature within Async Wi-Fi Manager, which allows you to reset the access point connection by pressing the **Reset** button on the ESP32 microcontroller. To perform a double reset, press the **Reset** button twice within 10 seconds. After performing the double reset, the ESP32 microcontroller will return to the initial stage, allowing you to set up the Wi-Fi credentials again if you need to connect to another Wi-Fi access point.

3. Now, you can monitor the results of the energy monitoring system we just built by connecting to the local web server from the ESP32 microcontroller. To obtain the ESP32 microcontroller's IP address, check the Serial Monitor messages, as shown in the preceding code. In this case, the IP address is 192.168.18.98. Since the sketch creates a local web server to display the results, type http://192.168.18.98 in the web browser of your phone or computer, which should be connected to the same Wi-Fi network. The result will be displayed:

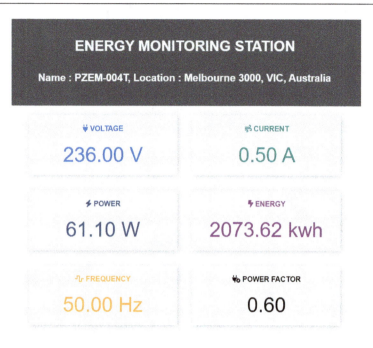

Figure 5.10 – Energy monitoring station – user interface output

4. Since the sketch also implements the mDNS library, you can use a name instead of an IP address to access the same result by typing `http://enermo.local` in your web browser.

mDNS is a protocol that enables the resolution of locally defined names to IP addresses without the need for dedicated infrastructure such as a DNS server. With mDNS, we can use a name instead of an IP in the URL to access the browser, and it will resolve the name to the corresponding IP address.

The `enermo.ino` sketch also implements `AsyncElegantOTA`, which allows you to send code updates over the air. After initially downloading the code that includes `AsyncElegantOTA`, you can send subsequent code updates through the web server by typing `http://enermo.local/update` in your browser. You will see something similar to the following:

Figure 5.11 – ElegentOTA file upload menu

5. Before we can choose the file we wish to upload, we need to generate the file from the Arduino IDE. Go to **Sketch | Export Compiled Binary**.

6. Once the process is complete, go to the Elegant OTA screen and click on the **Choose File** button. Navigate to the directory where your `enermo.ino` sketch is located.

7. Inside that directory, you will find a `build` directory. Click on the `build` directory; inside it, you will find another directory named `esp32.esp32.node32s`. Click on that directory; you will find several binary files inside.

8. Select the `Enermo.ino.bin` file and click **Open**. ElegantOTA will now upload the file and display an OTA success message. This indicates that the compiled code has been successfully uploaded to the ESP32 microcontroller via the Wi-Fi connection.

And with that, you have a working energy monitoring system! Have a look at the inputs and outputs that are involved, and play around with the parameters.

As always, feel free to look at the documentation for all the hardware and software involved in this practical.

Summary

In this chapter, we learned about the characteristics of WSNs and how we can architect them while incorporating best practices and considerations for ensuring that they can be well positioned to handle the different unique challenges that are posed by their setup compared to other networks, alongside the environment that they are deployed in. We learned more about commonly used APIs within protocol communication with IoT, such as the REST API. Then, we learned how to evaluate WSNs through metrics and understood the different models that can contribute to saving on power consumption within these systems. We took a deeper look into all this by getting hands-on and building our own WSN. We did this by creating a smart energy monitoring and management system based on what we have learned and applying Blynk as an associated IoT platform.

In the next chapter, we will further our understanding of network building by discussing building networks on the edge.

Further reading

For more information about what was covered in this chapter, please refer to the following links:

- Learn more on popular APIs to use with IoT systems: `https://dzone.com/articles/popular-apis-for-the-internet-of-things-iot-system`

- Explore more on Blynk's capabilities: `https://blynk.io/`

- Explore managing wireless sensor networks with the REST API: `https://www.worldscientific.com/doi/10.1142/9789814730464_0011`

- Gain more of an understanding on wireless sensor networks: `https://imos.org.au/facilities/wirelesssensornetworks`

- Look at an AWS case study on a sensor network: `https://aws.amazon.com/solutions/case-studies/sensornetworks/`

6
Creating Applications on the Edge

Edge computing is a nascent technology that facilitates the processing of data near or at its point of generation, rather than in a central hub such as the cloud. This will break down a centralized computing problem and instead create a decentralized, distributed way of processing data, allowing for real-time decision-making, faster response times, and a reduction in data transmission costs. This enables you to cut costs associated with traditional investments required for centralized data processing, such as setting up a data center or cloud infrastructure. Instead, you can utilize the same devices used to collect the data to perform a portion or all of the required processing work.

Often, this is a solution that many turn to when they start looking at bigger, more complex workloads. In many cases, challenges such as processing multiple streams of data that may involve hundreds or thousands of streams at the same time in a centralized system may cause bottlenecks, causing there to be delays and hence increased costs. With edge computing, you can allocate appropriate resources to each of the edge locations that are currently working on processing the data – whether it be on the device itself or nearby infrastructure – allowing for more efficient resource allocation and appropriately receiving the processed data afterward.

This chapter aims to get you oriented on how edge networks fit into the big picture of IoT and understand industry best practices for using them. You will be able to understand how to apply this to common use cases and analyze different edge computing deployments better.

In this chapter, we're going to cover the following main topics:

- Benefits edge networks provide for IoT solutions
- Designing edge networks and considerations that are made in optimizing them for different use cases
- Architecting simple edge deployments
- Smart traffic control with edge computing

Technical requirements

This chapter will require you to have the following hardware and software installed:

- Hardware:

  - ESP32 microcontroller

  - DHT11 temperature and humidity sensor

  - Keyestudio Arduino Super Starter Kit

  - Ultrasonic distance sensor (HC-SR04)

  - Servo motor (SG90)

  - Red, yellow, and green LEDs

  - 220-ohm resistors

  - Breadboard

  - Jumper wires

- Software:

  - Arduino IDE

  - TensorFlow

  - TensorFlow Lite

TensorFlow

TensorFlow is an **open source software** (**OSS**) library and platform for **machine learning** (**ML**) and **deep learning** (**DL**) that was developed by the **Google Brain** team. It is very popularly used within industry, academia, and research due to its performance, flexibility, and scalability. It allows developers to design and build ML models that are both on cloud-based platforms and edge devices. This includes a wide variety of features such as model training and deployment, data visualization, and distributed computing.

In this chapter, we will be using TensorFlow as a service to run an ML model that we will create and transfer to our ESP32 device instead of letting it run on a centralized system such as the cloud. Note that we will not be discussing ML in detail, as that is out of the scope of the book, but we will talk through the ML model that we will create and how it fits within the context of our deployment while letting you understand the concept of edge computing with this implementation.

We will be running our programs on Python in this chapter; feel free to reference the Python and TensorFlow documentation as well as necessary.

You can access the GitHub folder for the code that is used in this chapter at `https://github.com/PacktPublishing/IoT-Made-Easy-for-Beginners/tree/main/Chapter06/`.

Edge computing fundamentals and its benefits for IoT

As mentioned previously in the chapter, there are a great many benefits that are derived from edge computing. However, its nature of implementation is different than the paradigms of implementation based on the **IoT** networks we've seen thus far.

In this section, we will be examining the architecture and the benefits of edge computing, understanding more about how components within an edge network perform and where it sits within the overall picture of IoT.

Edge computing architecture

Edge computing architecture is generally composed of four different layers that play a role in the successful deployment of the network. There are two types of processing: **near edge** and **far edge**. Near edge refers to processing and data handling that occurs close to the IoT devices, often within the same local network or facility, optimizing for low latency and immediate response. Conversely, far edge involves processing done at more distant nodes, such as regional data centers, balancing the workload by handling fewer time-sensitive tasks and broader data analysis. The following diagram shows the layers in the form of models that make up how edge computing is done:

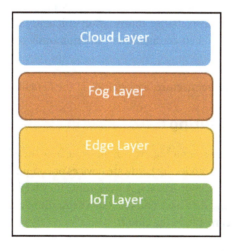

Figure 6.1 – Four layers of edge computing

We can see what each layer entails next:

- **Cloud computing**: This is based on computing resources that are connected to the end users from a **Wireless Local Area Network** (**WLAN**). It provides computing and storage to end users via the WLAN network. This is designed to be an intermediary between the processed data that is sent through and the cloud. This design has higher bandwidth, which will in turn result in lower latency for applications that we are currently running.

- **Fog computing**: Fog computing is a decentralized computing resource that can be positioned anywhere between the end users and the cloud. Based on **Fog Computing Nodes** (**FCNs**), which include routers, switches, and **access points** (**APs**), it provides an environment that is responsible for having devices within different protocol layers communicate with the FCNs.

- **Edge computing**: Edge computing is designed to operate within or near the **radio access network** (**RAN**), but with a distinct role focused on minimizing latency and optimizing data processing. Rather than managing radio resource scheduling like the RAN, which operates at the physical and **Media Access Control** (**MAC**) layers, edge computing functions at higher levels, closer to the application layer. It offers a network architecture that, while it can be integrated with RAN infrastructure such as near a **radio network controller** (**RNC**) or a similar base station, primarily serves to process data and execute applications near the IoT devices. This is achieved with the aid of an edge orchestrator, which organizes communications within the edge network. The orchestrator also provides information about the network's performance and the physical location of the computing infrastructure. This setup is crucial for IoT environments, where edge computing handles the data from various devices and sensors located at the network's periphery, enabling them to exchange information efficiently through the communication network and, depending on their configuration, autonomously control the infrastructure they are embedded in.

Now that we have an idea of the architecture, we can look at the benefits of edge computing.

Benefits of edge computing

To understand the benefits of edge computing, we can illustrate how the **edge nodes** are positioned, as within the following diagram. Edge nodes are hardware devices or computing platforms situated closer to the data source, such as IoT devices or sensors, in a network. They facilitate localized processing and storage, reducing the need to send data back and forth to a centralized cloud or data center alongside the cost of infrastructure and compute in the cloud:

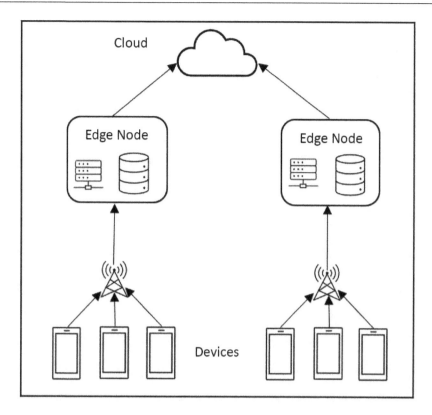

Figure 6.2 – Process of edge computing

We can see that we simplify the required processing by moving it to edge nodes, unlike a centralized system that has to handle all data processing workloads simultaneously. The devices will transmit the data to a base station, which then forwards the data for processing within an edge node. Edge nodes can have storage and processing capabilities that help them to process and store the data before accordingly transmitting it to the cloud for further analysis and storage, which ultimately also reduces latency.

Furthermore, it is easier to meet regulatory and compliance requirements with this way of working with data. For example, in healthcare and finance, there are stringent data sovereignty regulations that often require data to be stored and processed within a country's borders. By ensuring that data is both stored and processed locally, edge computing simplifies compliance with these regulations. This is especially beneficial compared to a centralized data management model, which becomes complex and challenging when dealing with data across international boundaries. In the healthcare sector, laws such as the **Health Insurance Portability and Accountability Act (HIPAA)** in the United States and the **General Data Protection Regulation (GDPR)** in Europe impose strict controls on personal data handling, making edge computing an attractive solution for maintaining compliance. Similarly, in the financial industry, regulations regarding data residency and protection are stringent, and edge computing offers a way to adhere to these rules while still leveraging the benefits of modern data processing technologies.

Additionally, security is a big advantage of this type of decentralized network, given that we are only creating, processing, and analyzing sets of data that are needed at an instance. A centralized system would let attackers access all data that is within the system, but a decentralized system would reduce the impact of this, given that they can only get what is currently being processed at an instance. This also would make customers feel better about their privacy being adhered to.

Now, let's look at a sample practical exercise where we can see the advantage of processing data at the edge.

A sample edge computing exercise

In this exercise, we would like to simulate edge computing by using an ESP32 device as the *edge device*, which will be where we both collect the data from and run processing based on an ML model at the same time.

The following is a diagram for how we will have this workload work:

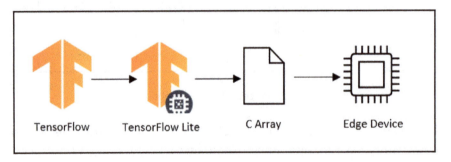

Figure 6.3 – Workflow of TensorFlow edge computing exercise

To start off, we will use a **TensorFlow Keras Sequential model**, which we will then convert into **TensorFlow Lite**, the model type that is built for use within microcontrollers. TensorFlow's Keras Sequential model is a linear stack of layers used for building **neural networks** (**NNs**) in a straightforward manner, where one can easily define and train models by adding layers in a sequential order. On the other hand, TensorFlow Lite is a lightweight solution from TensorFlow that facilitates the deployment of ML models on mobile and embedded devices, offering a smaller binary size and faster inference times, making it suitable for edge computing scenarios and on-device computations.

From TensorFlow Lite, we will then use a converter to generate a **C array**, which holds the trained model that we can then use to deploy to our ESP32 device. In this practical, we will be using the terms *TensorFlow* and *TF* – its abbreviation – interchangeably.

For the data, we will be predicting temperature and humidity, as you can tell by our usage of the DHT11 sensor.

First, we can look at getting the software requirements.

Getting the software requirements

To run the code needed for the practical, if you are running under the Windows environment, we need to install several programs, as follows:

1. **Python 3**: Download it from `https://www.python.org/ftp/python/3.9.9/python-3.9.9-amd64.exe`. Make sure your `python3` directory is already in the path environment; check this by searching `environment variables` in Windows search, clicking on **Edit the system environment variables**, and clicking on **Environment Variables** on the bottom-right window. After a new window appears, click on the **System Variables** window (bottom part), go down, and double-click on **Path**. You should find these two directories:

   - `C:\Users\User Name\AppData\Local\Programs\Python\Python311`
   - `C:\Users\Guest User\AppData\Local\Programs\Python\Python311\Scripts`

   If it does not exist, then you must add **NEW** and type in those two directories to enable the Windows program to run Python and Python script files from other directories.

2. **TensorFlow**: Install it using `pip` from the relevant terminal application (for example, Command Prompt for Windows; Terminal for Mac):

```
python3 -m pip install tensorflow
# Verify install:
python3 -c "import tensorflow as tf; print(tf.reduce_sum(tf.random.normal([1000, 1000])))"
```

3. **pandas**: Install it using `pip` from Command Prompt:

```
pip install pandas
```

   You can check whether TensorFlow and pandas are already installed by typing the following:

```
pip list
```

   You will find all the packages installed together with the version number.

With the package installed, we are ready to build our TensorFlow model.

Building the TensorFlow model

First, we need to import TensorFlow and `layers` as part of the **TensorFlow Keras library**. We also need to import pandas to run mathematical operations on our workflow:

```
import tensorflow as tf
from tensorflow.keras import layers as lyrs
import pandas as pd
```

We then need to separate the independent and dependent variables that are located within the dataset, and accordingly store them within the `inputs` and `outputs` variables.

You need to get the `humidity_data.csv` and `temperature_data.csv` files by retrieving them from your saved result history for a certain period from your sensor readings:

```
data = pd.read_csv("temperature_data.csv")
inputs = data.iloc[:, :-1].values
outputs = data.iloc[:, -1:].values
```

With Keras, we will then create an NN model that will be based on 2 layers of 16 neurons, both with the `relu` activation function. The model will then be trained using the `fit` function, with the `inputs` and `outputs` variables as the parameters to it. We then store it within the `Model_humidity_predict` file:

```
nn_model = tf.keras.Sequential([
    lyrs.Dense(16, activation='relu'),
    lyrs.Dense(16, activation='relu'),
    lyrs.Dense(1)
])
nn_model.compile(optimizer=tf.keras.optimizers.RMSprop(), loss=tf.
keras.losses.MeanSquaredError(), metrics=[tf.keras.metrics.
MeanSquaredError()])
//Fitting model to have it understand and learn from the input data
nn_model.fit(inputs, outputs, epochs=1000, batch_size=16)
nn_model.save('Model_humidity_predict')
```

With that, we have trained our NN model with TensorFlow Keras, and we can now look at converting the TensorFlow model to a TensorFlow Lite model.

Converting the TensorFlow model to a TensorFlow Lite model

Now, we need to convert the TF model that we have saved to TF Lite and save it with the `tflite` file extension. As part of optimizing the workload, we use `tf.lite.Optimize.DEFAULT` to avoid errors:

```
loaded_model = tf.keras.models.load_model('Model_humidity_predict')
lite_converter = tf.lite.TFLiteConverter.from_keras_model(loaded_model)
lite_converter.optimizations = [tf.lite.Optimize.DEFAULT]
lite_model = lite_converter.convert()
with open("predict_humidity.tflite", "wb") as file:
    file.write(lite_model)
```

With this, we now have converted the TensorFlow model to a TensorFlow Lite model by loading the model and converting and writing the model to a `lite_model` file. Now, we will convert the TF Lite model to a C array.

Converting the TF Lite model to a C array

We will then use a Linux command, xxd, to convert the TF Lite model we obtained from the previous step to a C array. This will perform a hex dump, converting the data to its hexadecimal format. We will put the `.tflite` file as the input for the xxd command, and we then specify the filename with `.h` as the file extension. We will then be able to predict both values. Thus far, we have been doing the steps for humidity, as with *Chapter 1, An Introduction to IoT Architecture, Hardware, and Real-Life Applications*, but we can repeat the same steps to get our C temperature array.

We need to convert the result to hexadecimal format by using the xxd command. As xxd is not available in the Windows environment, we need to download the xxd program for Windows from the following link: `https://sourceforge.net/projects/xxd-for-windows/files/latest/download`.

Then, put the `xxd.exe` file in the Python 3 directory, which is usually this directory: `C:\Users\User Name\AppData\Local\Programs\Python\Python311`. Here, you need to replace `User Name` with your username.

The following command runs xxd on `predict_humidity.tflite` and outputs to `predict_humidity.h`:

```
$ xxd -i predict_humidity.tflite > predict_humidity.h
```

Now, we will look at deploying to the ESP32 device.

Deploying to ESP32 (the edge device)

We can now then wire up our ESP32 device and our DHT11 sensor, as in *Figure 6.4*. Wire the 5V pin to VCC, GND to GND, and DIO4 to DATA:

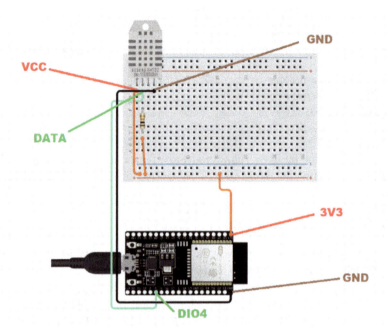

Figure 6.4 – Circuit diagram for wiring up DHT11 for exercise

We now must report the libraries that we need for running this deployment. As can be seen, we import the `TensorFlowLite.h` and `EloquentTinyML.h` libraries to run the model that we have already obtained, the `temperature_predictor.h` and `humidity_predictor.h` files as part of the predictor files we generated from the models we created as part of the C array we have generated, and use the `DHT.h` library to run the DHT11 sensor:

```
#include "EloquentTinyML.h"
#include <TensorFlowLite.h>
#include "temperature_predictor.h"
#include "humidity_predictor.h"
#include "DHT.h"
```

We will then use the `EloquentTinyML.h` library to create a `TFLite` instance, as can be seen here:

```
Eloquent::TinyML::TfLite<NUMBER_OF_INPUTS, NUMBER_OF_OUTPUTS, TENSOR_
ARENA_SIZE> temp_estimator(temperature_predictor_tflite);
```

```
Eloquent::TinyML::TfLite<NUMBER_OF_INPUTS, NUMBER_OF_OUTPUTS, 3 *
1024> humid_estimator(humidity_predictor_tflite);
```

In the case that a sensor is not able to read the values properly, we will then predict it until it is able to read the values again. We pass the previously recorded temperature and humidity values and the spliced data time values as the input to the model. As part of this, we use the **Real-Time Clock (RTC)** module to get the real date and time, store it in an array, and use that as the input. An RTC module is a supplementary component that can be interfaced with the Arduino board to provide accurate timekeeping even when the Arduino is powered off or reset. We then print out these values accordingly, ensuring that there is a delay in the capturing of the data:

```
float humid_val = dht.readHumidity();
float temp_val = dht.readTemperature(true);
delay(1000);
```

We now need to check if the humidity or temperature readings are valid numbers. If either reading is not a number (isnan() returns true), the code will print a message to the Serial Monitor indicating a failure to read from the DHT sensor:

```
if (isnan(humid_val) || isnan(temp_val)) {
Serial.println(F("Unable to read from DHT sensor; please check your
configuration."));
```

If the sensor readings are invalid, the code creates two input arrays, presumably representing a timestamp and the previously recorded temperature and humidity values. These input arrays are fed to ML models (humid_estimator and temp_estimator) to predict the current temperature and humidity based on the given input data. These estimated values are then stored for use in the next cycle:

```
float input_data[8] = {2020, 5, 26, 11, 30, 0, prev_temp_val, prev_
humid_val};
float input_data2[8] = {2020, 2, 4, 6, 40, 0, prev_humid_val, prev_
temp_val};
float humid_estimated = humid_estimator.predict(input_data2);
float temp_estimated = temp_estimator.predict(input_data);
prev_humid_val = humid_estimated;
prev_temp_val = temp_estimated;
```

Now, we want to print the estimated temperature and humidity values to the Serial Monitor for verification or debugging. The program then waits for 1 second before ending the function (via the return; statement) in case this code is part of a function:

```
Serial.print("\t predicted humidity: ");
Serial.println(humid_estimated);
Serial.print("\t predicted temp: ");
Serial.println(temp_estimated);
delay(1000);
```

```
return;
}
else {
Serial.print("\t humidity: ");
Serial.println(humid_val);
Serial.print("\t temp: ");
Serial.println(temp_val);
prev_temp_val = temp_val;
prev_humid_val = humid_val;
}
```

And that's it! Now, open the output monitor to see the output that is being put through.

As can be seen, this creates an effective system that will continually read in the temperature and humidity based on the sensor but notify you if there is a failure to read from the sensor and uses the ML model we have created to predict the humidity and temperature based on the values that we have put into it. This ensures that we do not have any holes within the collection of data, given that we fill it in with well-informed guesses in the case that we do.

Now that we've looked at how an edge computing implementation within an IoT network can have such a powerful effect on how we establish and manage our system, we will now look at the requirements that we need to consider as part of the implementation of it.

Requirements of IoT for edge computing

One of the biggest challenges of edge computing is understanding the proper allocation of resources, given its unique setup and the constraints that it provides. Having to set up resources in a decentralized way may seem simple in theory, though they pose a lot of considerations. In the following subsections, we highlight several requirements that are required as part of managing resources and understanding the laws of IoT that govern how we decide to construct our networks.

Resource management

Managing resources within IoT for edge computing is very important, as there are costs to consider as part of the requirements. The following are some common considerations:

- **Scalability**: This refers to having the network address many edge devices with differing capabilities and types, ensuring that they work and interoperate with each other well through the appropriate communication protocols.

- **Security**: Selecting a proper security mechanism is imperative for creating a functioning network that abides by regulations, given that there needs to be much concern for privacy and integrity checks to avoid any breaches that may obtain the data or have any of the data modified.

- **Heterogeneity**: There must be support for heterogeneity within the hardware or software that is deployed.

- **Volatility**: There needs to be much volatile availability that is supported.

- **Data protection**: There needs to be compliance with relevant data protection laws, depending on where you are located, as well as ensuring that data is all kept locally and encrypted both at rest and in transit.

- **Infrastructure performance**: It is important to ensure that high performance on infrastructure is available. This may be in the form of low-latency, lightweight protocols such as **Message Queuing Telemetry Transport** (**MQTT**) that are used for communication within the application layer, or using zero-touch provisioning for ease with system upgrades.

- **Application portability**: There must be a holistic architecture via enabling F**unction-as-a-Service** (**FaaS**) capabilities, given the workloads that we will be processing as we move them toward the edge.

- **Data analytics**: There must be support for data management and analytics within the workloads that are performed, given that we want to transfer those high workloads onto the edge instead of centralizing them: the whole point of edge computing within our networks.

- **Device management**: Managing a large number of devices is a significant challenge, as it involves ensuring all devices are up to date, functioning properly, and efficiently managed across different platforms and locations. This includes monitoring device health, managing software updates, and troubleshooting issues remotely.

Understanding how we can manage our resources for IoT deployments, we can now look at the three laws that govern IoT.

The three laws of IoT

With the growing number of connected devices, alongside the large amount of data that they collect, consequences are bound to result within distributed systems. It is because of this that we must be very mindful of how we design such systems, as we discussed in the earlier subsection. The consequences can be summarized into three main laws: the laws of physics, economics, and the land.

Law of physics

The law of physics is about understanding the physical limitations of data transfers that are made to the cloud. This has become more prevalent as a challenge given that more use cases have required increasingly more real-time responses to certain events, such as within healthcare or autonomous devices. In scenarios within those settings, every millisecond delay can cost lives.

Law of economics

Data that grows exponentially often causes bottlenecks within performance and overarching costs. This is what leads to edge computing in the first place, as it often is not economical for companies to transmit all IoT data to the cloud, given the costs that are associated with them, especially when it comes to transferring petabytes of data, as some large enterprises do with their line of work.

Law of the land

There are geographical and legal restrictions that often constrain the extent of how data can be gathered and transferred. Often, there are sovereignty laws that mandate data must only be kept and transmitted within the country's borders. For example, GDPR in the European Union imposes strict rules on how data is handled, including the transfer of personal data outside the EU. Similarly, China's Cybersecurity Law mandates that critical data must be stored within mainland China. Additionally, some parts of the world do not have the proper infrastructure required to support regular IoT network operations due to poor connectivity to the internet, which limits the capabilities and reliability of the cloud for that region.

Understanding the requirements, we can now look at how we can optimize our workloads.

Optimizing edge computing on networks

Optimizing edge computing on networks is a crucial step in ensuring that edge devices are utilized effectively and efficiently. In this section, we will explore various strategies for optimizing edge computing workloads, including workload distribution, resource allocation, data processing techniques, and security considerations. By understanding and applying these strategies, developers and system architects can harness the full potential of edge computing, delivering efficient, responsive, and secure IoT solutions. Additionally, we will briefly touch on optimizing the network infrastructure and communication protocols to be able to achieve this while also learning how to evaluate edge networks and will finally use all these tools to look at a *smart city case study*.

Strategies for optimizing edge computing workloads

We will discuss three main strategies to optimize edge computing workloads: load balancing, resource allocation, and data management.

Load balancing

Load balancing is a technique to distribute workloads across multiple edge devices or gateways to better the performance of each and ensure that all resources are utilized efficiently. Several algorithms can be used for edge computing for this purpose, which include round-robin and least connections. **Round-robin load balancing** is the simplest approach and operates by distributing requests to edge devices cyclically, which is best suited for applications that have relatively uniform traffic patterns.

Least connections works by distributing requests that are coming to the edge device with the fewest possible active connections, which is useful for applications that have variable traffic patterns, making it effective in preventing the overloading of specific devices.

Another great technique to test the proportion of traffic to allocate to a particular device is to perform **load testing**. Load testing is a way of simulating test loads to each of your devices to see how much they can handle for you to allocate loads appropriately to each of the devices. This is good for you to understand the behavior of your loads and the amount that can be handled by each of the devices, enabling you to configure the algorithms to allocate loads accordingly.

Resource allocation

Resource allocation is a strategy that is used to optimize edge computing workloads by assigning resources to specific tasks and applications in the most effective and efficient way possible. These resources include CPU, memory, and storage. This can be done through several resource allocation algorithms such as first-fit, best-fit, and worst-fit algorithms.

The **first-fit algorithm** allocates the first available resource that is large enough to handle the workload. The **best-fit algorithm** allocates the resource that best matches the size of the workload. The **worst-fit algorithm** allocates the resource that is the least suited for the workload. It is also possible to use a combination of the algorithms, such as having a first-fit algorithm for initial resource allocation and a best-fit algorithm for fine-tuning.

Data management

Data management is a strategy that is used to optimize edge computing workloads through techniques such as **data reduction**, **data compression**, **data caching**, or **data replication** to minimize the amount of data that is required to be transmitted over networks, along with edge computing techniques such as utilizing lightweight data processing algorithms and models within the edge devices themselves. This can help to reduce requirements for network bandwidth, promoting the efficiency and responsiveness of the edge computing workloads.

We can now complete our strategy forming with an understanding of how to evaluate edge networks.

Evaluating edge networks

There are several key metrics that we can use to evaluate the effectiveness of our deployment within an edge network. Within this subsection, we will discuss three of them.

Latency

As part of this metric, we need to measure the time that it takes for data to travel from the edge device to the centralized data center and back again. This comes hand in hand with throughput, which helps us measure the amount of data that can be transmitted over a network within a given period. We need to ensure that there is enough capacity for the edge network to handle the expected throughput of all connected devices within the network.

Resource utilization

Resource utilization is used to evaluate the effectiveness of edge computing workloads in terms of the number of resources that are being used by edge devices, ensuring that they are not overburdened. Fine-tuning them can ensure that poor performance and outages are avoided, which is why it is important to keep a close eye on this metric.

Security

As mentioned throughout the book so far, security is a very important consideration within edge computing environments. It is important that data at rest and in transit over edge networks is secure and that the devices are protected from potential attacks. It would be beneficial to have simulated attacks to see how resilient the systems are, such as through penetration testing by a third-party firm or from internal testing if you have personnel that can perform such testing.

We can now move from evaluation to look at a case study where we will see our learnings so far applied on a large scale.

Smart city case study

Now that we have looked at a holistic view of edge computing environments, we can look at a case study based on an edge computing network – a network that is based on a smart city, as can be seen in the following diagram:

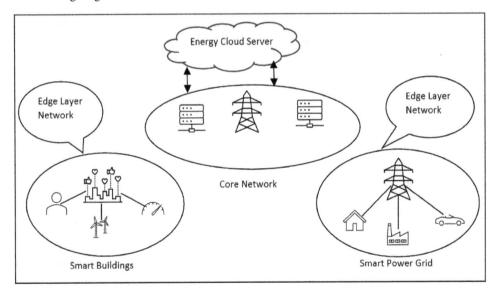

Figure 6.5 – Smart city application of edge computing

Can you identify the different layers of edge computing present in the preceding diagram? How about the edge devices that are currently present as part of the network?

Within this diagram, we can see how different types of environments are leveraging edge computing. We can see how homes, office buildings, and power grids are collecting data and passing it to the edge server.

We can also see how all the head nodes of each of the edge networks then go on to push data toward the core network, which in turn pushes it toward the cloud servers. This shows the concept of the different layers of edge computing, as we have discussed. It also shows that communications between all layers are two-way; each layer that the preceding layer sends information to can also send information back as well, hence optimizing them accordingly and updating them with the latest information. This is how certain configurations can be made to respond accordingly to changes within the environment.

To provide a clearer understanding of real-world implementations, let's consider some specific use cases of smart cities employing edge computing:

- **Traffic management**: In many cities, edge computing is utilized for intelligent traffic control systems. Sensors and cameras at intersections collect and process data locally, reducing latency and quickly adjusting traffic signals to optimize flow, improving congestion and reducing accidents.

- **Public safety**: Edge computing devices in a smart city setup can enhance public safety. For example, in cities such as Barcelona, edge-enabled surveillance cameras use AI algorithms to detect unusual activities or emergencies, promptly alerting authorities.

- **Energy efficiency**: Smart grids in cities such as Amsterdam use edge computing to monitor and manage energy consumption. By processing data locally at substations, these systems can quickly respond to changes in energy demand, improving efficiency and reducing waste.

- **Environmental monitoring**: Sensors deployed throughout a city can monitor air quality, noise levels, and other environmental factors. Edge computing allows for the rapid processing of this data, enabling immediate actions to mitigate pollution or other environmental concerns.

Edge gateways are critical in deploying these use cases. They serve as an intermediary between local IoT devices and the broader network, processing data close to the source. For instance, in a smart traffic system, the edge gateway would process data from traffic cameras and sensors before sending relevant information to the city's central traffic management system. This approach reduces the need for constant cloud connectivity, ensuring faster response times and lower bandwidth usage, essential for the seamless operation of smart city applications.

With this, you should have a good understanding of evaluating networks and will be ready for the next practical, in which you will create a simple edge network based on multiple ESP32 devices.

Practical – smart traffic control with edge computing

In this practical, we will create a simple yet effective smart traffic control system using an ESP32 microcontroller. This project will utilize edge computing to analyze and optimize traffic flow at an intersection in real time. By the end of this practical, you will understand how IoT benefits from edge networks and learn how to architect simple edge deployments.

Assembling the circuit

Now, we must wire up the circuit. Instructions for doing so and a corresponding diagram have been provided for your convenience as follows:

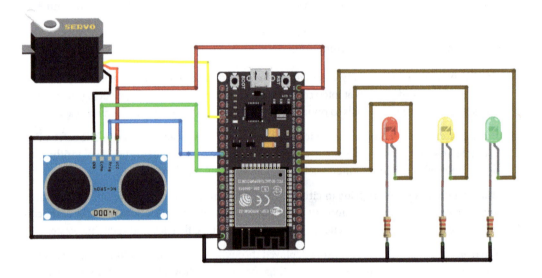

Figure 6.6 – Connection diagram for the practical

1. Connect the ultrasonic distance sensor (HC-SR04) to the ESP32 device. Connect the VCC pin to 5V, GND pin to GND, Trig pin to pin 17, and Echo pin to pin 18 of the ESP32 module.

2. Connect the servo motor's (SG90) VCC pin to 5V, GND pin to GND, and data pin to pin 16 on the ESP32 module.

3. Connect the longer leg (anode) of the red, yellow, and green LEDs to pins 25, 26, and 27, respectively, on the ESP32 module using jumper wires. Connect the shorter leg (cathode) of each LED to GND through 220-ohm resistors.

That's it for the hardware, and we can now move on to developing the software for the project.

Writing the code

Now, we can start writing the code. The code will be split into three sections: initialization, setup, and loop.

Initialization

Import the **ESP32Servo library**. You can get the library either from the **Manage Sketch Library** from the **Arduino library** or download it from this link: `https://github.com/jkb-git/ESP32Servo/archive/refs/heads/master.zip`. Define pins for the ultrasonic sensor, servo motor, and LEDs, and declare the variables for distance calculation, servo position, and LED duration::

```
#include <ESP32Servo.h>

Servo servoMotor;
int pos = 0;
int servoPin = 16;
const int sensorAlertPin = 17;
const int sensorRepeatPin = 18;
const int alertLEDRed = 25;
const int alertLEDYellow = 26;
const int alertLEDGreen = 27;
long duration;
int distance;
```

With that, we have initialized the necessary variables. Now, we can look at creating the setup segment of the code.

Setup

Set up the serial communication speed, configure the pins as INPUT or OUTPUT using the pinMode command, attach the servo motor to pin 16, and move the servo to initial position (0):

```
void setup() {
  Serial.begin(9600);
  // Allow allocation of all timers
  ESP32PWM::allocateTimer(0);
  ESP32PWM::allocateTimer(1);
  ESP32PWM::allocateTimer(2);
  ESP32PWM::allocateTimer(3);
  servoMotor.setPeriodHertz(50);  // standard 50 hz servo
  pinMode(sensorAlertPin, OUTPUT);
  pinMode(sensorRepeatPin, INPUT);
  pinMode(alertLEDRed, OUTPUT);
pinMode(alertLEDYellow, OUTPUT);
```

```
pinMode(alertLEDGreen, OUTPUT);
servoMotor.attach(servoPin);
servoMotor.write(0);  // put servo in initial position

servoMotor.attach(servoPin, 500, 2500); // attaches the servo on pin
servoPin (16) to the servo object
}
```

With that, we have created the setup segment of the code. Now, we can look at creating the loop segment of the code.

Loop

Perform the following tasks in a loop:

1. Send a trigger pulse from the ultrasonic distance sensor (by bringing it to LOW, HIGH, and LOW again with a short delay between transitions).

2. Read the duration of the echo pulse received and calculate the distance to the nearest object.

3. For monitoring purposes, print the distance result in the Serial Monitor. If the distance is greater than 100 cm, set the servo motor to 90 degrees and change the sequence of traffic light turn-on time to 0 seconds for red, 1 second for yellow, and 4 seconds for green. Otherwise, set the servo motor to 0 degrees and change the traffic light to 4 seconds for red, 1 second for yellow, and 0 seconds for green.

4. Implement the trafficLightControl function to control the LED traffic lights by specifying the duration for each LED state (red, yellow, and green):

```
void loop() {
sensorAlertPin  digitalWrite(sensorAlertPin, LOW);
  delayMicroseconds(5);
  digitalWrite(sensorAlertPin, HIGH);
  delayMicroseconds(15);
  digitalWrite(sensorAlertPin, LOW);

  duration = pulseIn(sensorRepeatPin, HIGH);
  distance = duration * 0.04 / 2;
  Serial.print("The distance is : ");
  Serial.println(distance);

  if (distance > 80) {
    servoMotor.write(95);
    trafficLightControl(4, 1, 0);
  } else {
    servoMotor.write(5);
```

```
        trafficLightControl(0, 1, 4);
    }

    delay(1000);
}

void trafficLightControl(int redDuration, int yellowDuration,
int greenDuration) {
    digitalWrite(alertLEDRed, HIGH);
    delay(redDuration * 1000);
    digitalWrite(alertLEDRed, LOW);

    digitalWrite(alertLEDYellow, HIGH);
    delay(yellowDuration * 1000);
    digitalWrite(alertLEDYellow, LOW);

    digitalWrite(alertLEDGreen, HIGH);
    delay(greenDuration * 1000);
    digitalWrite(alertLEDGreen, LOW);
}
```

Upload the code to your Arduino board.

With that, we now are ready to test the system and see it in action.

Testing the system

In testing the system, we want to test how the sensor responds to different distances of objects and how the traffic light LEDs light up accordingly. The steps are set out here:

1. Place an object in front of the ultrasonic distance sensor.
2. Observe the traffic light LEDs and the servo motor.
3. Move the object closer to the sensor (less than 100 cm). Notice the red, yellow, and green LEDs' turn-on sequence and that the servo motor moves to the 0-degree position.
4. Move the object further away from the sensor (more than 100 cm). Notice again the LEDs turn on in different sequences, and the servo motor moves to the 90-degree position.

In this practical, we have created a smart traffic control system using an ESP32 microcontroller. The ultrasonic distance sensor represents the presence of vehicles at an intersection. When the distance to the nearest vehicle is greater than 100 cm, the system optimizes the traffic flow by changing the traffic light to yellow and green in sequence and adjusting the position of the servo motor, simulating the opening of a gate. When the distance is less than 100 cm, the traffic light turns red, then yellow in sequence, and the servo motor moves to the closed position.

You can also explore the following to further build on this practical:

1. **Multiple intersections**: Extend the system to manage multiple intersections by connecting additional ultrasonic distance sensors, servo motors, and traffic light LEDs. This would allow you to explore the coordination and optimization of traffic flow across a network of intersections, simulating a more realistic traffic management system.

2. **Vehicle detection**: Replace the ultrasonic distance sensor with a camera module and integrate ML algorithms for vehicle detection and classification. This would enable the system to detect different types of vehicles (for example, cars, trucks, and bicycles) and adjust the traffic light duration accordingly, optimizing traffic flow based on vehicle type and density.

By utilizing edge computing, this system can process the sensor data locally and make decisions in real time, without the need for constant communication with a central server. This practical demonstrates how IoT benefits from edge networks, how edge networks are designed, and considerations made in optimizing them. Additionally, it shows how to architect simple edge deployments using an Arduino-based IoT device.

Summary

In this chapter, we learned the fundamentals of edge computing and discussed the benefits that can be derived from it. Although it certainly requires more understanding of its setup and has its own set of challenges based on the decentralized network it needs to abide by, it provides a cost-effective way for large workloads to be performed while ensuring that they do not get congested when they are directed toward a centralized hub, as with most solutions. We looked at an exercise where an edge device in the form of an ESP32 device was built to retrieve information from a DHT11 sensor and used for both obtaining data and running an ML model on it, seeing how powerful edge computing can be. Toward the end, we also did a practical on creating a simple network for edge computing and further learned about strategies that can be used to optimize edge networks, evaluate them, and make appropriate design decisions based on them, while also applying the knowledge that we have learned so far to a case study based on how edge computing would be set up for a smart city.

Having navigated through this chapter, readers have not only acquired foundational knowledge about edge computing but also gleaned practical insights from hands-on exercises. This understanding equips them with the skills to discern the unique advantages and potential challenges posed by decentralized networks.

In the next chapter, we will be looking at how we can utilize cloud computing based on **Amazon Web Services (AWS)** to further strengthen our workloads and make the most of the capabilities that it has to offer for building IoT networks.

Further reading

For more information about what was covered in this chapter, please refer to the following links:

- More of an understanding of fog computing: `https://www.heavy.ai/technical-glossary/fog-computing`

- Learn more about TensorFlow: `https://www.tensorflow.org/learn`

- Explore more on edge computing in smart cities: `https://stormagic.com/company/blog/edge-computing-for-iot-based-energy-management-in-smart-cities`

- Understand a case of detecting cryptocurrency mining threats with AWS: `https://aws.amazon.com/blogs/iot/detect-cryptocurrency-mining-threats-on-edge-devices-using-aws-iot/`

- Look at more case studies of edge computing solutions: `https://www.nec.com/en/global/techrep/journal/g17/n01/170106.html`

7

Working with Cloud Computing to Power IoT Solutions

IoT devices obtain and process large amounts of data that needs to be stored, analyzed, and acted upon both in real time and near real time. This is where cloud computing comes in, as it is a powerful resource for providing the necessary flexibility, scalability, and cost-effectiveness needed to handle the data that is provided by these devices. **Cloud computing** is the provision of computer system resources on demand, without manual active intervention by the user. Instead, it is mostly managed by a **cloud vendor**.

Cloud computing is especially popular because you don't have to procure and maintain hardware; instead, the cloud vendor maintains that for you. These cloud services are also distributed over multiple locations, allowing you to avoid a single point of failure and have resilience in having multiple zones that store your data, which is critical when you have production environments that require continuous access to the data. AWS is one such vendor, and we will be focusing this chapter on the services that it provides for storing, processing, and visualizing your workloads and why it is so popular for IoT solutions. Key functionalities of cloud services in IoT applications include device authentication and management, data ingestion, data processing, data storage, and the provision of data dashboards. These functions collectively contribute to the robustness and appeal of using AWS for IoT solutions.

In this chapter, we'll delve deep into AWS's vast array of services tailored for IoT solutions, offering a comprehensive understanding of how each service functions and interlinks. By the end of this chapter, you will not only have a robust grasp of the AWS ecosystem for IoT but also the know-how to design, deploy, and manage efficient IoT architectures. This knowledge will be invaluable, whether you're aiming to innovate in your current job role, launch an IoT-based venture, or simply remain at the forefront of the rapidly evolving digital landscape.

In this chapter, we're going to cover the following main topics:

- The fundamentals of cloud computing with IoT
- Services to work with for IoT

- Optimizing for resilience and low latency
- Practical: creating a cloud proximity detector

Technical requirements

This chapter will require you to have the following hardware and software installed:

- Hardware:
  - NodeMCU ESP-32S
  - IR proximity sensor
  - WS2812 RGB LED strip
  - Piezo buzzer
  - Jumper wires
- Software:
  - AWS account
  - Arduino IDE

Setting up your AWS account

To access AWS' cloud computing resources, you will first need to create an account with them on the AWS portal, which is where you can also manage the resources that you have already provisioned via their **graphical user interface** (**GUI**). The AWS Free Tier offers a variety of services at no cost for a limited amount of usage, allowing users to explore and experiment with AWS functionalities. It is advisable to utilize these free tier services whenever possible to minimize costs while running services on AWS. You will be able to set them up by reading their official documentation at `https://docs.aws.amazon.com/accounts/latest/reference/manage-acct-creating.html`.

You can access the GitHub folder for the code that is used in this chapter at `https://github.com/PacktPublishing/IoT-Made-Easy-for-Beginners/tree/main/Chapter07/`.

Fundamentals of cloud computing with IoT

In your day-to-day life, the term **cloud** may not be too alien to you. You may have already heard it being used by providers other than AWS if you haven't heard about AWS, or you may have heard about use cases. The cloud refers to a network of remote servers hosted on the internet, used for storing, managing, and processing data, as opposed to using local servers or personal computers. This technology enables on-demand access to computing resources and services, offering scalability, efficiency, and flexibility in managing IT operations. When first opening the AWS console, it can be overwhelming to see the number of different services that are available, along with the number of configurations that are associated with each service.

In this section, we will discuss the different fundamentals of cloud computing, including the different advantages of cloud computing, cloud computing models, and the deployment models that currently exist.

The main advantages of cloud computing

There are a large number of advantages that come with cloud computing. The following are seven of these advantages that you can leverage:

- **Cost savings**: One of the biggest advantages of cloud computing is that it reduces the costs associated with provisioning IT infrastructure and resources. Given that they offer a **pay-as-you-go model** that allows customers to only pay for the resources they use, alongside the fact that you do not have to provision and maintain IT hardware and software, you will be saving a lot in costs compared to a traditional deployment that you would set up.

- **Scalability**: Cloud computing allows for ease within scaling resources. They can help provide more resources according to how the business grows, such as increasing storage or computing power when working with different workloads while processing your IoT data.

- **Accessibility**: Cloud computing allows for remote access to resources and applications, allowing employees to work from anywhere as long as they have internet access. Many companies put a lot of money toward moving their workloads to the cloud after the COVID-19 pandemic due to increased amount of work being done from home.

- **Flexibility**: Cloud computing allows for the use of different types of deployment models, such as public, private, and hybrid clouds, which provides customers with the flexibility to choose the option that would best meet their needs.

- **Reliability**: Cloud providers have large, redundant data centers that employ teams of experts who ensure that their services are always available and performant. Note that much of the provisioning based on availability also depends on you, as you will be the user provisioning based on best practices to avoid a single point of failure, while they ensure that they can meet the guarantees for their reliability.

- **Security**: Cloud providers ensure that the security measures that they have protect their customers' data, applications, and infrastructure and provide them with opportunities to enforce additional services for this as well. This includes firewalls, intrusion detection and prevention, and encryption.

- **Automation**: Cloud computing allows the automation of many IT tasks that traditionally needed to be done manually, such as provisioning, scaling, and maintenance, which helps organizations save time, improve efficiency, and reduce potential human error.

We can now move ahead and look at different cloud computing models in the world of cloud computing.

Cloud computing models

There are three main cloud computing models, as follows:

- **Infrastructure as a Service (IaaS)**: The most basic type of cloud computing, IaaS, is where a provider offers virtualized computing resources such as storage, servers, and networking over the internet. This is based on a shared responsibility model; customers are responsible for managing their software and applications, while the provider manages the physical infrastructure, such as the servers and data centers. An example of this from AWS is the Amazon **Elastic Compute Cloud (EC2)** service.

- **Platform as a Service (PaaS)**: PaaS is a model that enhances the capabilities of IaaS by offering users the convenience of creating and executing their software solutions without overseeing the foundational hardware. This includes things such as databases, web servers, programming languages, and tools that are used to create, deploy, and run applications. An example of an AWS offering that provides this is **Amazon Elastic Beanstalk**.

- **Software as a Service (SaaS)**: SaaS is a model of cloud computing that provides customers access to software applications over the internet. The provider manages the underlying infrastructure and the platform, while customers simply access the software through a web browser. Examples of such providers include Salesforce and Microsoft Office 365.

Now, we can build on top of that knowledge by looking at the different deployment models for cloud computing.

Cloud computing deployment models

There are three types of cloud computing deployment models, as follows:

- **Public cloud**: A public cloud is managed by an external entity and can be accessed by users online. They are usually the most cost-effective and easy to use, as you do not have to take care of the underlying infrastructure and maintenance.

- **Private cloud**: A private cloud is owned and operated by an organization, usually used to host sensitive or proprietary data. Such clouds can be located on-premises, in a data center, or within a third-party provider's data center. They are usually more expensive than public clouds, but they offer more control over your infrastructure, given that you have direct access to all the hardware that you use.

- **Hybrid cloud**: A hybrid cloud is a combination of both public and private clouds. The model lets you leverage the cost and scalability benefits of public clouds while maintaining the control that you have over private clouds. These are usually used to host sensitive data and applications within a private cloud while using a public cloud for workloads that are less critical.

Now that we have a good understanding of the fundamentals of the cloud, we will discuss services that are part of AWS that we can highlight as part of IoT and investigate for our use cases.

Services to work with for IoT

In this section, we will look at the different services that are used within AWS for IoT and talk through a practical exercise that will show you how you can utilize some of them to make a simple IoT system.

There are a number of services in AWS that make working with IoT within it very powerful. In this chapter, we will highlight six of those services and show how you can use them within your own deployments.

Identity Access Manager (IAM)

Identity Access Manager (**IAM**) is a service that helps users/organizations control access to their AWS resources. This enables them to create and manage users and groups and define permissions for them to access AWS resources such as S3 buckets, EC2 instances, or Amazon **Relational Database Service** (**RDS**) databases. An S3 bucket is a storage solution offered by AWS, designed to hold vast amounts of data in a scalable, secure, and web-accessible environment. RDS is also an AWS offering that provides managed relational database instances, simplifying the process of setting up, operating, and scaling a database in the cloud.

IAM ensures that sensitive information is kept secure and that only the right people can access the information that they are allowed to access. Organizations can also use it to manage and audit access to AWS resources and ensure that they are compliant with regulatory requirements. Additionally, IAM can work with other AWS services and third-party identity providers to ensure that customers use single sign-on as part of enhanced security and best practices alongside other advanced identity management features.

Amazon Elastic Compute Cloud (Amazon EC2)

EC2 instances are web services that provide scalable compute capacity within the cloud, allowing users to launch virtual servers that can run a number of different operating systems and applications. These EC2 instances can be scaled up or down accordingly to meet the diversifying and changing computational needs that are part of users' applications. Users are able to configure and customize their instances with an instance type, number of CPU cores, amount of memory, storage, and more. It also offers various security features, including the requirement to configure a key pair for accessing instances. Additionally, it provides a range of other security options suitable for both internal and client-facing applications. It is often the foundation of scalable, highly available, and fault-tolerant systems within the cloud.

AWS IoT Core

AWS IoT Core is a platform that facilitates the connection, management, and communication of IoT devices with AWS services alongside other devices that may be used within the network. It connects devices securely, allowing for storage and analyzing capabilities through other services. It provides several features, including MQTT and HTTP protocols, that can communicate with devices, register devices, provide device shadows, and understand how device data is processed. It can integrate with a number of other services, such as **AWS Lambda**, **Amazon SNS**, **Amazon SQS**, and more.

AWS IoT comprises the following components: the **message broker**, the **rules engine**, the **Thing Registry**, **Thing Shadows**, and the **security and identity service**. IoT devices can access the AWS cloud through multiple approaches, including via AWS IoT Core using the MQTT protocol, via AWS API Gateway using REST/HTTP or WebSocket, or via AWS LoRaWAN. The message broker offers a secure way for IoT devices to publish and receive messages from each other using either the MQTT protocol or the HTTP REST interface. The rules engine facilitates the processing of messages and assists in integrating the workload with other AWS services. The Thing Registry helps to organize resources linked to each thing, while Thing Shadows provide persistent representations of things within the AWS cloud. Additionally, the Security and Identity Service ensures security in the AWS cloud through shared responsibility, requiring IoT devices to maintain their credentials securely to send data safely to the message broker.

The following is a diagram depicting how AWS IoT works:

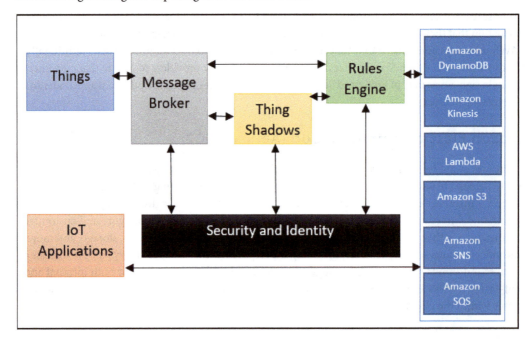

Figure 7.1 – How AWS IoT works

AWS IoT has Things within the network report their current state through JSON messages to MQTT topics. The message broker distributes incoming messages from a topic to all its subscribers. Rules can be established to determine actions based on the content of these messages. We can, for example, invoke a Lambda function or query a table within one of the storage solutions connected to our network. We can also filter the message, and when a rule matches the filtered message, it will perform the action that has been selected with the properties. The rules also have an IAM role that grants AWS IoT permission to access the AWS resources that were used to perform the action.

Each thing also has a Thing Shadow, which is able to store and retrieve the state information. Each piece of state data consists of two parts: the most recent status reported by the object and the state that an application wishes for it. An application can ask for the current status details of a specific object. In response, the shadow provides a JSON file that includes both the current and desired states, a version identifier, and additional details. Through this, an application can instruct an object to alter its state. The shadow can accept the request for the change within the state, update the state information, and send a message that shows that the information for the state has been updated. The thing then receives the message, accordingly makes the change to its state, and reports on its new state.

With that, we can look at AWS IoT Greengrass, an important complement to AWS IoT Core that we will be seeing used later in the chapter.

AWS IoT Greengrass

AWS IoT Greengrass is a service that allows you to run local compute and facilitates messaging and data caching for your connected devices. It's most notably used for edge computing. This means that even if your devices are not connected to the internet, they can still function and communicate with each other using the service. This is especially useful when internet connectivity is limited in certain environments, such as within remote locations or industrial scenarios. You can also process device data locally and send only the necessary data to the cloud for further storage and analysis. This allows your devices to be more secure and responsive while lowering costs due to less data being sent to the cloud. As you can surmise from the description of this service, this makes it an incredibly powerful tool for edge computing, and we will talk about using it to architect a deployment later in this chapter.

AWS IoT SiteWise

AWS IoT SiteWise is a service that allows companies to collect and organize data from industrial equipment and machinery, making monitoring and analyzing the performance of machines easier. Companies can track things such as temperature and humidity to identify patterns and trends. It can be set up easily without the need for complex installations or expertise.

AWS Lambda

AWS Lambda provides a platform for serverless code execution, eliminating the need for users to handle or set up servers. With Lambda, users can run code in response to specific events, including changes to data within an S3 bucket. This event-driven approach is highly scalable and can accordingly adjust the amount of computing resources required to run the code, which in turn eliminates the need for manual scaling. As part of this, Lambda also allows automatic scaling and patching for the underlying infrastructure, allowing you to focus on the code you are working on.

Amazon Simple Queue Service (SQS)

Amazon Simple Queue Service (**SQS**) is a highly scalable and secure queue service designed to manage message queues in a distributed system environment. Particularly relevant to IoT, SQS facilitates the decoupling of components in IoT architectures. It allows IoT devices and sensors to send messages to a queue, ensuring that the data is processed and consumed reliably and efficiently, even during times of high volume. This capability is essential in IoT ecosystems, where numerous devices may generate vast amounts of data, necessitating robust and flexible management to maintain system integrity and performance. SQS provides a buffered layer that absorbs data spikes and ensures smooth data processing without loss, making it a key component in scalable and resilient IoT applications.

Amazon Simple Notification Service (SNS)

Amazon Simple Notification Service (**SNS**) is a flexible, fully managed pub/sub messaging and mobile notifications service for coordinating the delivery of messages to subscribing endpoints or clients. For IoT, SNS becomes crucial for sending notifications or messages triggered by IoT devices or sensors. It enables IoT applications to push real-time alerts based on sensor data to end users or other systems, ensuring timely response to events or conditions monitored by IoT devices. This service supports a variety of communication channels, such as SMS, email, or AWS Lambda functions, making it a versatile tool for integrating IoT device activity with broader communication strategies.

Other notable AWS services for IoT

There are a number of other AWS services that are notable that we will not cover in this book, though we strongly encourage you to have a look at them to learn more about what they provide, as they are also powerful tools for managing your IoT deployments. These tools include AWS IoT Analytics, AWS IoT Button, AWS IoT Device Defender, AWS IoT Device Management, AWS IoT Events, AWS IoT Things Graph, and AWS Partner Device Catalog. These all are services that are also part of the IoT catalog offerings from AWS. We will also look at the IoT Analytics offerings in the next chapter.

With knowledge of basic AWS services, we can move on to a practical exercise to see some of these services in action.

A practical exercise utilizing the services

In this practical exercise, we will look at creating a thing and connecting it to AWS IoT Core to simulate **pub/sub communication**. In this case, we will let the thing be an EC2 instance so that you also have experience in deploying EC2 instances as well, which is a core service within AWS.

Deploying and connecting to your first EC2 instance

To start off the practical, we will deploy and connect to our EC2 instance:

1. In your EC2 console, search for EC2 to open the EC2 console or reach it at `https://console.aws.amazon.com/ec2/`.

2. Choose **Launch instances** on the console dashboard.

Figure 7.2 – The Launch instances button on the EC2 console

3. In *step 1*, you will see a list of different basic configurations, which are called **Amazon Machine Images** (**AMIs**). These act as templates to be used for your instance. Set the HVM version to Amazon Linux 2 AMI (HVM), SSD Volume Type. We are picking the free tier-eligible AMI type, as we want to keep ourselves free from costs for this exercise.

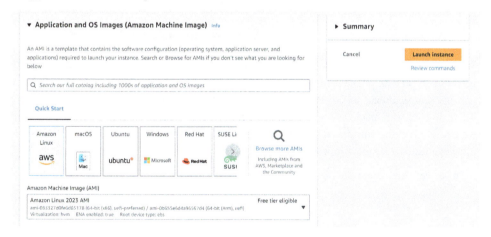

Figure 7.3 – Selecting an HVM version for EC2

4. Configure the hardware for your instance on the **Choose an Instance Type** page and select the **t2.micro** type, which is by default selected.

5. Click on **Review** and **Launch** and let the setup wizard complete the other configuration settings.

6. Within the **Review Instance Launch** page, click on **Launch**.

7. You will then be prompted for a **key pair**. A key pair allows you to connect to your instance and is provided only at the time you ask to create one, so be sure that you download it. Select **Create a new key pair**, enter an appropriate name for the key pair, and choose **Download Key Pair**. Make sure that you save your private key file in a safe place.

8. Click on **Launch instances** when you are ready to do so.

9. A confirmation page will then let you know your instance is launching. Click on **View instances** to see the instance that you have just launched. You can see the current status of the instance, which will be in **Pending** due to having been just launched. After the instance has been launched, it will have its status changed to **Running**. You can see in the information below that it receives its own public DNS name.

10. You can then connect to your EC2 instance. To make things easy for this exercise, we will connect to it through our browser. Select the instance and choose **Connect**.

11. Choose **Amazon EC2 Instance Connect** and click **Connect**. You should now have the **EC2 Instance Connect** window with your EC2 environment currently showing.

With this, we have created a new EC2 instance and will have been able to connect to it. Now, we will configure our AWS CLI so that we can perform operations to the cloud from our EC2 environment.

Configuring the AWS CLI

We now need to configure the CLI to connect to our AWS account for us to be able to perform operations with services within the cloud, as we need the proper authorization to do so. To do this, we will look at setting up our EC2 instance with the following steps:

1. We first want to install Git on our EC2 instance. But before that, we will have to update our instance for all the packages that are available. We will be using **YUM**, which is the main package management tool in Linux systems for installing, updating, removing, and accordingly managing software packages within our system. We also need to use the sudo command, as we need to run the command as a superuser or it will mention that we do not have enough privileges. Run the following command:

    ```
    $ sudo yum update -y
    ```

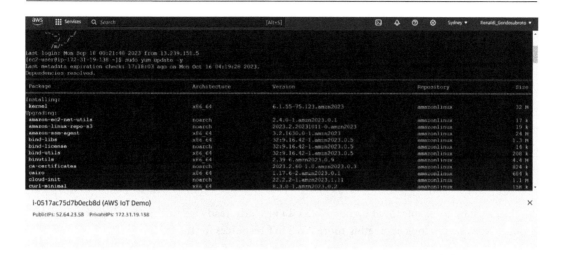

Figure 7.4 – Updating all managing software packages in EC2

2. Now, we can install Git with the following command.

    ```
    $ sudo yum install git -y
    ```

3. We now need to install **Node.js**. To do this, we need to first install **Node Version Manager** (**NVM**) using the following command. We need to use NVM so that we can install multiple versions of Node.js and switch between them when necessary:

    ```
    $ curl -o- https://raw.githubusercontent.com/nvm-sh/nvm/v0.34.0/
    install.sh | bash
    ```

4. We then need to activate NVM using this command:

    ```
    $ .~/.nvm/nvm.sh
    ```

5. We then will use NVM to install the latest version of Node.js with the following command:

    ```
    $ nvm install --lts
    ```

6. We then will test if Node.js is installed properly by running this command:

    ```
    $ node -e "console.log('Running Node.js ' + process.version)"
    ```

7. Next, we then will configure the AWS CLI. To do so, we will run the following command:

    ```
    $ aws configure
    ```

8. We will see several prompts displayed. All this information can be found under your security credentials within your **Account Info** on the AWS console. If you want the direct link to get there, you can go to `https://console.aws.amazon.com/iam/home#/security_credentials`.

9. Enter the **AWS Access Key ID**, **AWS Secret Key ID**, and **Default Region Name** of your account and enter the **Default Output Format** as `json`.

10. Test your configuration to see if you can connect to the IoT endpoint with the following command. If all is done well, you should receive an endpoint address for your AWS account:

```
$ aws iot describe-endpoint --endpoint-type iot:Data-ATS
```

With this, we have been able to set up our AWS CLI properly, ready for further development within the cloud. Now, we can look at creating more AWS IoT resources for the EC2.

Creating AWS IoT resources for the EC2

Now, we need to create the IoT resources as part of the EC2:

1. Within your **EC2 Instance Connect** window, run the following command:

    ```
    $ aws iot create-thing --thing-name "MyIotThing"
    ```

    You should receive a JSON response that looks somewhat like the following:

    ```
    {
        "thingArn": "arn:aws:iot:selected_region:select_aws_
    account:thing/TestNewThing",
        "thingName": "MyIotThing",
        "thingId": "<YOUR_THINGID_HERE>"
    }
    ```

2. You now need to create and attach AWS IoT keys and certificates. First, you will need to create a directory in which to store your certificate and key files.

    ```
    $ mkdir ~/certs
    ```

3. We now need to download a copy of the Amazon **certificate authority** (**CA**) certificate through the following command:

    ```
    $ curl -o ~/certs/Amazon-root-CA-1.pem \
    https://www.amazontrust.com/repository/AmazonRootCA1.pem
    ```

4. We then need to run the following command to create your private key, public key, and X.509 certificate files. This will also register and activate your certificate with AWS IoT:

```
$ aws iot create-keys-and-certificate \
    --set-as-active \
    --certificate-pem-outfile "~/certificates/device.pem.crt" \
    --public-key-outfile "~/certificates/public.pem.key" \
    --private-key-outfile "~/certificates/private.pem.key"
```

5. We will then receive the certificate as the response. Attach the thing object to the certificate that you have created with the `certificateArn` that was generated from the previous command with the following command:

```
$ aws iot attach-thing-principal \
    --thing-name "TestNewThing" \
    --principal "certificateArn"
```

6. Next, we'll formulate and link a policy. Set up the policy document by duplicating its content into a file named `~/policy.json`. If you're new to Linux and haven't settled on a preferred text editor, you can launch Nano with the following command.

```
$ nano ~/policy.json
```

7. Paste the policy document for `policy.json` into the file. Use *Ctrl* + *X* to exit the Nano editor and save it.

8. Create the policy by using the following command:

```
$ aws iot create-policy \
    --policy-name "MyIotThingPolicy" \
    --policy-document "file://~/policy.json"
```

9. Attach the policy to your virtual device's certificate with the following command:

```
$ aws iot attach-policy \
    --policy-name "MyIotThingPolicy" \
    --target "certificateArn"
```

With this, you will have created the thing for your virtual device to be referred to in AWS IoT, the certificate to authenticate the virtual device, and the policy document, which will be used to authorize the virtual device to connect to AWS IoT and publish, receive, and subscribe to messages.

Now, we can look at how we can work with the AWS IoT Device SDK for JavaScript to look at more functionalities we can implement.

Working with the AWS IoT device SDK for JavaScript

Now, we will install the **AWS IoT Device SDK** for JavaScript on our device:

1. To start off, we will first clone the AWS IoT Device SDK from its GitHub repository onto our local directory. To do this, run the following command:

    ```
    $ cd ~
    git clone https://github.com/aws/aws-iot-device-sdk-js-v2.git
    ```

2. We will then navigate to the aws-iot-device-sdk-js-v2 directory that was just created:

    ```
    $ cd aws-iot-device-sdk-js-v2
    ```

3. We then use npm to install the SDK:

    ```
    npm install
    ```

And with that, we have the AWS IoT Device SDK for JavaScript installed. Now, we can look at running a sample app from the AWS IoT Device SDK.

Running a sample app

We will now run the sample app, which is able to publish and subscribe to topics within IoT Core:

1. Set the directory to the aws-iot-device-sdk-js-v2/samples/node/pub_ sub directory, which was created by the SDK, and install the given sample app with the following commands:

    ```
    $ cd ~/aws-iot-device-sdk-js-v2/samples/node/pub_sub
    $ npm install
    ```

2. Get your IoT endpoint, which you need to use later, with the following command:

    ```
    $ aws iot describe-endpoint --endpoint-type iot:Data-ATS
    ```

3. Insert the endpoint that you have received within the following command and run it:

    ```
    $ node dist/index.js --topic topic_1 --ca_file ~/certs/Amazon-
    root-CA-1.pem --cert ~/certs/device.pem.crt --key ~/certs/
    private.pem.key --endpoint your-iot-endpoint
    ```

    Now, you have an app that connects to the AWS IoT service, subscribes to a message topic called topic_1, outputs the messages that it can receive on the topic, publishes 10 messages to the topic, and displays an output similar to the following:

    ```
    Publish received on topic topic_1
    {"message":"Hello world!","sequence":1}
    Publish received on topic topic_1
    ```

```
{"message":"Hello world!","sequence":2}
Publish received on topic topic_1
{"message":"Hello world!","sequence":3}
```

With this, we can also view the messages from the sample app from AWS IoT.

Viewing messages from the sample app within AWS IoT

We want to observe the messages from the sample app, as they navigate via the message broker using the MQTT client on the AWS IoT platform. To monitor the published MQTT messages, follow these instructions:

1. Access the MQTT client located within the AWS IoT dashboard.

2. Let the client connect to the `topic_1` topic previously established.

3. Once you're in the **Amazon EC2 Instance Connect** interface, initiate the sample app once more and observe the incoming messages in the MQTT client.

And with that, you've just built your first IoT system on AWS! These kinds of systems are very powerful for understanding how the benefits of IoT can permeate throughout the cloud and leverage the resources that are provided well.

Now, we can move ahead and look at how we can optimize for resilience and low latency on our deployments.

Optimizing for resilience and low latency

In this section, we will explore the different approaches to ensuring that a deployment will be resilient and have low latency when deployed. As with other IoT networks, ensuring that the configuration we have for our networks is optimal is of utmost importance. First, we will be looking at the different strategies for resilience in IoT deployments. Afterward, we will look at how we can design and architect for it and see how it's put into practice through a case study.

Strategies for resilience

For a successful IoT deployment, resilience is paramount. Ensuring that systems remain operational, even in the face of challenges, demands a multifaceted approach. The following are six pivotal strategies, each playing a unique role in fortifying the robustness and efficiency of IoT systems. These components, when implemented meticulously, not only safeguard against potential disruptions but also enhance the overall performance, scalability, and cost-effectiveness of IoT deployments.

Multi-region deployment

This strategy focuses on deploying your IoT infrastructure across multiple regions to ensure that if one region becomes unavailable, the others will continue to function and provide service. This helps ensure high availability and low latency.

Message queues and streams

Message queues and streams help ensure that data is processed in a reliable and efficient way. This is tantamount to high-throughput IoT deployments where data is sent and received in large volumes.

Edge computing

Edge computing, which you are already familiar with, allows us to process the data closer to the source of the data. This helps to reduce latency and improve the performance of our IoT deployment. Using Greengrass for this as described previously, for example, helps a lot with this.

Autoscaling

Configuring autoscaling helps with scaling the number of resources based on the amount of demand, ensuring that there is always enough capacity to handle traffic and keeping latency low, all while saving costs.

Load balancing

Load balancing distributes the incoming traffic across multiple instances to ensure that no instance is overwhelmed and availability is maintained. Therefore, load testing is often done on different instances to test the maximum capacity they can handle and assign loads based on either manual work or through load balancing algorithms accordingly.

Cloud-native services

Using services such as AWS IoT Core, AWS IoT Greengrass, or AWS IoT Analytics can help improve the efficiency, scalability, and security of your IoT deployment.

Now that we have seen the different strategies, we can look at how we can put them into practice when designing and architecting our solutions.

Designing and architecting your solutions

Now, let's discuss how you can design and architect your own use cases as part of AWS deployments for your IoT networks.

Defining the use case

You first need to define the business problem that your IoT deployment is intended to solve. Understand the type of data that will be collected, the devices that you will be using, and the outcomes that you want to achieve from this deployment.

Device connectivity

Plan how the devices will connect to the IoT platform, including through using protocols such as MQTT or HTTPS. Design the data processing pipeline alongside this, such as by using AWS IoT Core,

AWS Lambda, Amazon Kinesis, and Amazon S3. This will be imperative, as you need to understand how you can best ingest the data in your use case.

Data analysis and storage

You then need to design your data analysis solution. Understand the volume, velocity, and variety of the data that will be generated to help you design a solution that can handle the amount and complexity of the data.

Security and compliance

You need to then define the security and compliance requirements, along with the appropriate controls. Does your data need to stay within the country's borders? Do you need to restrict access to certain services? You may use different services in AWS to achieve your goals, including AWS IAM, AWS KMS, and Amazon VPC.

Testing solution

You then need to put in place and test the solution, setting up a maintenance plan that includes monitoring, updating, and continuously optimizing the deployment's performance. It is from here that you will iteratively build on the setup of the infrastructure, as there will be a continuous need for improvement within the system.

Now, let's look at the design of one such architecture.

A simple architecture

As can be seen in the following figure, this is the design of one such architecture based on AWS. What do you think its use case is?

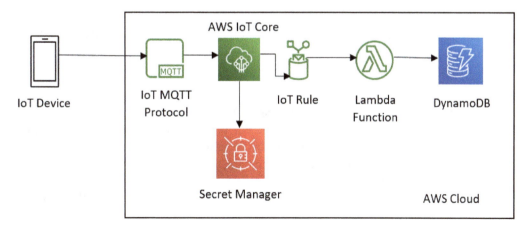

Figure 7.5 – A simple architecture that utilizes AWS IoT Core to serve an IoT device

We can see that we are obtaining data through the IoT device. We then transmit the data from the IoT device to AWS IoT Core through the IoT MQTT protocol. This is our first point of entry into the cloud. We then have AWS IoT Core reach into Secret Manager to get the appropriate authentication keys to decrypt the messages that are being transmitted. The AWS IoT Core will then read the IoT rule and act accordingly based on the filtered messages. It then sends the ones that match the rules through to the Lambda function, which will execute and store the data within DynamoDB.

Note that this solution has minimum security; most production-grade solutions have multiple layers of security. For example, they may have **virtual private clouds** (**VPCs**), which are customizable, isolated sections of the AWS cloud where users can launch and manage their own computing resources, or they may have a **web application firewall** to monitor incoming web traffic while sitting in front of the application.

Now we can look at evaluating our solution based on our deployment.

Evaluating your solution

There are many ways to evaluate an AWS IoT deployment. One of the best ways is through the **AWS Well-Architected Framework**. The AWS Well-Architected Framework is a set of best practices and guidelines that are used in designing and operating reliable, secure, efficient, and cost-effective systems within the AWS cloud. It provides a consistent approach for customers and partners to evaluate architectures and implement designs that will scale over a period. The framework consists of five pillars: security, reliability, performance, cost optimization, and operational excellence.

Security

The security pillar ensures that you keep your systems and data secure. This includes factors such as identity and access management, network security, and incident responses to threats.

Reliability

The reliability pillar ensures that your systems are highly available and can withstand failures. This includes factors such as disaster recovery, autoscaling, and Multi-AZ deployments.

Performance

The performance pillar ensures that you are optimizing your systems for performance and cost. This includes appropriately rightsizing your resources and fine-tuning your reach with services such as Amazon CloudFront and Amazon ElastiCache. Amazon CloudFront is a fast **content delivery network** (**CDN**) service that securely delivers data, videos, applications, and APIs to customers globally with low latency and high transfer speeds, all within a developer-friendly environment. Amazon ElastiCache offers a fully managed in-memory data store service, compatible with Redis or Memcached, that provides high-performance, scalable caching for applications, significantly improving their responsiveness by allowing the fast retrieval of frequently accessed data.

Cost optimization

The cost optimization pillar ensures that you have optimized your systems for cost. This includes utilizing reserved instances when you are using them for production workloads that run for a year, using the appropriate storage types, and monitoring costs to identify and eliminate unnecessary expenses.

Operational excellence

The operational excellence pillar ensures that your systems are running smoothly and that you can respond quickly to issues that pop up. This includes factors such as change management and monitoring and logging your deployments, ensuring that when an incident does occur, you can quickly and appropriately respond to it before it becomes a larger issue.

Now, we will look at a case study of a Multi-AZ active-active production environment. A Multi-AZ active-active production environment refers to a setup where resources and workloads are distributed across multiple **availability zones (AZs)** and all of these zones are actively handling traffic simultaneously. This configuration ensures high availability, fault tolerance, and seamless failover by allowing operations to continue unaffected even if one zone experiences issues, thereby maximizing uptime and resilience for applications and services.

A case study of a Multi-AZ active-active production environment

As mentioned many times throughout the book, optimization is a key feature of IoT deployments. We want to ensure that we use the resources that are most appropriate for the task. However, reliability for our services is just as important as that, given that we want to ensure that our deployment can keep functioning no matter what happens. In the following figure, we can see one such architecture that is designed for this:

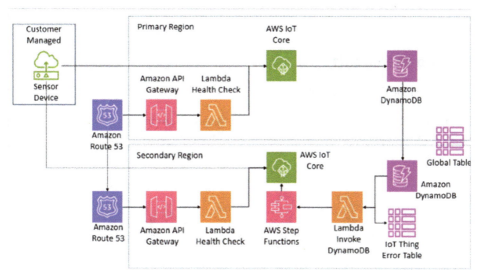

Figure 7.6 – Example of a Multi-AZ active-active production deployment on AWS

This architecture has many components, but as can be seen, it is designed for fault tolerance. First, we have two regions where our deployment is based: the primary region and the secondary region. These regions, parts of AWS's global infrastructure, are separate geographic areas that enhance reliability; if the primary region fails, the secondary region takes over to maintain service continuity and traffic will flow just as accordingly through there. Additionally, we use AWS Route 53, a scalable and highly available **domain name system** (**DNS**) web service, which directs user traffic to the infrastructure running in AWS. We can also see that we have Route 53 endpoints that perform a health check through Lambda instances, which continuously check if the services are down and take action if so. We also have our storage located within DynamoDB, a fast and flexible NoSQL database service, which is where the data that comes from the sensor device into AWS IoT Core is stored, both in terms of shadow updates and registry events. The DynamoDB table also has global table replication enabled, enabling it to continuously replicate its contents so that if one is down, the other would not be affected.

This type of deployment creates a powerful way of ensuring that the workloads will continue to operate even if one of the parts of the system were to go down. We will see more of these best practices in the next chapter, as we look to include data analytics services within the big picture of the IoT networks that we are trying to architect on AWS.

With a foundational understanding of the important AWS services and how they contribute to the IoT ecosystem, we can look at doing a practical exercise that puts our new knowledge and skills into practice.

Practical—creating a cloud proximity detector

In this practical, we will create a unique cloud proximity detector using the **Keyestudio Arduino Super Starter Kit**, which integrates with AWS IoT services. The project will use a combination of sensors, actuators, and cloud services. By the end of this practical, you will understand the benefits of utilizing AWS for IoT networks and learn how to optimize costs, resiliency, and low latency in your deployments.

Assembling the circuit

First, we will assemble the hardware of the project:

1. Connect the NodeMCU ESP-32S, IR proximity sensor, piezo buzzer, and WS2812 RGB LED strip as shown here:

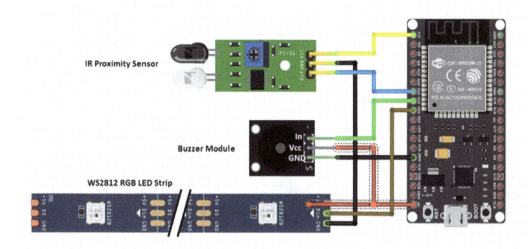

Figure 7.7 – Wire-up diagram of the hardware of the project

2. Connect the IR proximity sensor to the breadboard. Connect the VCC pin to the 3.3V output on the NodeMCU, the GND pin to GND, and the data pin to GPIO 36 (also known as VP or ADC1_CH0) on the NodeMCU.

3. Connect the RGB LED strip to the breadboard. Connect the VCC pin to the 3.3V output on the NodeMCU using a 220-ohm resistor to limit the current flow. Connect the GND pin directly to the GND and the data pin to GPIO 5 on the NodeMCU.

4. Connect the piezo buzzer to the breadboard. Connect the positive pin to GPIO 4 on the NodeMCU through a 220-ohm resistor. Connect the negative pin directly to GND on the NodeMCU.

Writing the code

Upload the following code to your Arduino board, replacing <YOUR_WIFI_SSID> and <YOUR_WIFI_PASSWORD> with appropriate values. We use a similar sketch as the previous one to publish data to AWS. We add the FastLED library to control the WS2812 LED strip and use ESP32 ADC1 (analog-to-digital converter) to control the buzzer and read the IR proximity sensor. Please note that ADC2 is used by ESP32 to accommodate Wi-Fi functions, so we cannot use it:

```
#include "secrets.h"
#include <WiFiClientSecure.h>
#include <MQTTClient.h>
#include <ArduinoJson.h>
#include <WiFi.h>
#include <FastLED.h>
#define AWS_IOT_PUBLISH_TOPIC   "esp32/topic"
#define AWS_IOT_SUBSCRIBE_TOPIC "esp32/topic"
```

```
const char WIFI_SSID[] = "YOUR_WIFI_SSID";
const char WIFI_PASSWORD[] = "YOUR_WIFI_PASSWORD";
const int irSensorPin = 32;
const int buzzerPin = 33;
int irSensorValue;
bool isObstacleDetected;
unsigned long startTime, currentTime;

// We define LED Strip pin and length (number of LEDs)
const int ledStripPin = 25;
const int ledLength = 30;
CRGB leds[ledLength];
WiFiClientSecure net = WiFiClientSecure();
MQTTClient client = MQTTClient(256);
```

First, we define the constants and import the necessary libraries. We define the LED strip pin and length and initialize an MQTT client:

```
void connectAWS()
{
  WiFi.mode(WIFI_STA);
  WiFi.begin(WIFI_SSID, WIFI_PASSWORD);

  Serial.println("Connecting to Wi-Fi");

  while (WiFi.status() != WL_CONNECTED){
    delay(500);
    Serial.print(".");
  }
```

We then make a connection to AWS through our Wi-Fi module and attempt to connect to it, printing to our Serial Monitor if it is already connected:

```
  net.setCACert(AWS_CERT_CA);
  net.setCertificate(AWS_CERT_CRT);
  net.setPrivateKey(AWS_CERT_PRIVATE);
  client.begin(AWS_IOT_ENDPOINT, 8883, net);
  client.onMessage(messageHandler);
  Serial.print("Connecting to AWS IOT");
  while (!client.connect(THINGNAME)) {
    Serial.print(".");
    delay(100);
  }
```

```
  if(!client.connected()){
    Serial.println("AWS IoT Timeout!");
    return;
  }

  client.subscribe(AWS_IOT_SUBSCRIBE_TOPIC);

  Serial.println("AWS IoT Connected!");
}
```

We then configure `WiFiClientSecure` to use the AWS IoT device credentials. We connect to the MQTT broker on the AWS endpoint we defined earlier and create a message handler. We then subscribe to a topic:

```
void publishMessage()
{
  StaticJsonDocument<200> doc;
  doc["time"] = millis();
  doc["Obstacle_detected"] = String(isObstacleDetected ? "true" :
"false");
  char jsonBuffer[512];
  serializeJson(doc, jsonBuffer); // print to client
  int publishResult = client.publish(AWS_IOT_PUBLISH_TOPIC,
jsonBuffer);
  Serial.print("A message published : Result = ");
  Serial.print(publishResult);
  Serial.print(", payload = ");
  Serial.println(jsonBuffer);
}
```

We create a function to then publish messages, which tell the client whether an obstacle is detected:

```
void messageHandler(String &topic, String &payload) {
  Serial.println("incoming: " + topic + " - " + payload);
}

void setup() {
  Serial.begin(115200);
  connectAWS();

  FastLED.addLeds<WS2812, ledStripPin, GRB>(leds, ledLength);
  FastLED.setBrightness(50);
  startTime = millis();
}
```

```
void loop() {
  client.loop();
  if (!client.connected()) {
    connectAWS();
  }

  irSensorValue = analogRead(irSensorPin);
  isObstacleDetected = irSensorValue < 500;

  Serial.print(", irSensorValue = ");
  Serial.println(irSensorValue);

  if (isObstacleDetected) {
    Serial.println("Buzzer play tone !!!");
    playTone(buzzerPin, 1000, 200);
    animateLEDs();
  } else {
    resetLEDs();
  }

  currentTime = millis();
  if(currentTime - startTime > 10000){
    publishMessage();
    startTime = currentTime;
  }

  delay(1000);
}
```

We create a loop function that continuously checks the AWS client's connection and reconnects if needed. It then reads the value from the IR sensor to detect obstacles. If an obstacle is detected (when the sensor value is below 500), it prints a message, plays a tone on a buzzer, and animates the LEDs. Otherwise, the LEDs are reset. Additionally, the program publishes a message every 10 seconds, and then it waits for a second before restarting the loop:

```
void playTone(int pin, int frequency, int duration) {
  tone(pin, frequency, duration);
  delay(duration);
}

void animateLEDs() {
  for (int i = 0; i < ledLength; i++) {
    leds[i] = CHSV(i * 10, 255, 255);
    FastLED.show();
```

```
      delay(20);
    }
}

void resetLEDs() {
  for (int i = 0; i < ledLength; i++) {
    leds[i] = CRGB::Black;
  }
  FastLED.show();
}
```

Finally, we declare some miscellaneous functions that allow us to play a tone, animate the LEDs, and reset the LEDs as per the loop.

After copying the previous sketch, we need to create a new tab in the Arduino IDE by clicking on the ... sign near the top-right window:

1. Choose **Create new tab** and give the new tab a name, such as `secrets.h`.

2. Paste the code in the following code block into the new tab that we have created and insert the AWS root CA certificate, device certificate, and device private key that we got in the *A practical exercise utilizing the services* section. Insert the certificates between the lines BEGIN CERTIFICATE and END CERTICATE for those three certificates. Change WIFI_SSID and PASSWORD according to your Wi-Fi credentials. Also, replace AWS_IOT_ENDPOINT with your own endpoint:

```
#include <pgmspace.h>
#define SECRET
#define THINGNAME "ESP32Thing"

const char WIFI_SSID[] = "YOUR_WIFI_SSID";
const char WIFI_PASSWORD[] = "YOUR_WIFI_PASSWORD";
const char AWS_IOT_ENDPOINT[] = "AWS_IOT_ENDPOINT";

// Amazon Root CA 1
static const char AWS_CERT_CA[] PROGMEM = R"EOF(
  -----BEGIN CERTIFICATE-----
  -----END CERTIFICATE-----
)EOF";

// Device Certificate
static const char AWS_CERT_CRT[] PROGMEM = R"KEY(
  -----BEGIN CERTIFICATE-----
  -----END CERTIFICATE-----
```

```
)KEY";

// Device Private Key
static const char AWS_CERT_PRIVATE[] PROGMEM = R"KEY(
  -----BEGIN RSA PRIVATE KEY-----
  -----END RSA PRIVATE KEY-----
)KEY";
```

Now that we have initialized our necessary hardware and cloud modules on AWS, we are ready to test the installation.

Testing the installation

We can now test our installation to see if it works as expected:

1. Power up the Arduino board by connecting it to your computer or a suitable power source.

2. Make sure the IR proximity sensor, RGB LED strip, and piezo buzzer are connected correctly, as described in *step 1*.

3. Verify that the ESP8266 Wi-Fi module is connected to the Wi-Fi network and can communicate with the AWS IoT Core.

4. Approach the IR proximity sensor to simulate the presence of a person. The piezo buzzer should play a tone and the RGB LED strip should animate.

5. Observe the Arduino Serial Monitor for any debugging information or error messages. Ensure that the sensor data is being sent to AWS IoT Core successfully.

```
A message published : Result = 1, payload = {"time":246701,"Obstacle_detected":"false"}
, irSensorValue = 4095
incoming: esp32/topic - {"time":246701,"Obstacle_detected":"false"}
A message published : Result = 1, payload = {"time":256709,"Obstacle_detected":"false"}
, irSensorValue = 4095
incoming: esp32/topic - {"time":256709,"Obstacle_detected":"false"}
A message published : Result = 1, payload = {"time":266716,"Obstacle_detected":"true"}
, irSensorValue = 225
Buzzer play tone !!!
E (283099) ledc: ledc_get_duty(739): LEDC is not initialized
incoming: esp32/topic - {"time":266716,"Obstacle_detected":"true"}
A message published : Result = 1, payload = {"time":277562,"Obstacle_detected":"false"}
, irSensorValue = 4095
incoming: esp32/topic - {"time":277562,"Obstacle_detected":"false"}
```

Figure 7.8 – Expected output from the Arduino Serial Monitor

6. Check the AWS IoT Core console and verify that the data is being received and processed by the Lambda function.

7. Test the installation in different environments with varying levels of light and human presence to ensure it performs well under various conditions.

Now we can move on to troubleshooting any issues and optimizing as needed.

Troubleshooting and optimization

There may be issues you encounter as you follow the instructions. If there are any, you can follow these steps and/or further optimize your deployment:

1. If the installation is not responding as expected, check the wiring and connections to ensure everything is properly connected.

2. Review the code for any syntax errors, logical issues, or incorrect configuration settings. Make sure the Wi-Fi credentials, AWS IoT endpoint, and certificate paths are correct.

3. Monitor the AWS Lambda function logs in **Amazon CloudWatch** for any errors or issues related to the processing of the IoT data.

4. If necessary, adjust the sensor thresholds and animation settings in the code to improve the installation's responsiveness and performance.

By following these steps, you can set up, test, and troubleshoot the IoT-based interactive art installation with cloud integration. This hands-on experience will provide you with a deeper understanding of how IoT devices can be integrated with cloud services and how to optimize costs, resiliency, and low latency in your deployments.

Further exploration can be done via the following avenues:

- **Multiple sensors**: Incorporate additional sensors, such as motion, temperature, or humidity sensors, to create a more dynamic and responsive installation that reacts to different environmental conditions or user interactions.

- **Advanced animations**: Develop more sophisticated LED animations and audio responses to create a more engaging and immersive experience. You can experiment with various patterns, color palettes, and audio effects to achieve the desired outcome.

- **User interaction**: Integrate input devices, such as buttons, touch sensors, or accelerometers, to allow users to interact with the installation and influence its behavior directly. This can make the experience more interactive and personalized.

With that, you've built your first cloud-based proximity detector! Now, you have learned how to apply basic skills within the cloud to IoT projects, which will serve as a foundation for the upcoming knowledge you will acquire from the book as part of your IoT learning journey.

Summary

In this chapter, we delved into the core principles of cloud computing for IoT, unpacking its myriad benefits, diverse deployment models, and the services tailored for IoT applications. Beyond the foundational knowledge, we navigated the intricacies of architecting IoT deployments within AWS. By mastering the use of a pub/sub client, we took a hands-on approach, illustrating how an EC2 instance can seamlessly interact with AWS IoT Core. As readers, internalizing this information is invaluable. It not only equips you with the tools and understanding needed to harness the full power of cloud computing in IoT but also primes you for success in the next stage of our journey: data analytics. These insights will empower you to design more robust and scalable IoT solutions, ensuring you're at the forefront of technological innovation.

In the next chapter, we will be looking at data analytics services that we can leverage with AWS that we can use to process and analyze workloads, building on our existing knowledge of cloud computing with AWS. We will also go over more best practices for architecting with those new components in mind.

Further reading

For more information about what was covered in this chapter, please refer to the following links:

- Explore more on AWS IoT with the official AWS documentation: `https://aws.amazon.com/iot/`

- Learn about the Modern XMPP project, an independent project dedicated to the improvement of messaging applications using XMPP: `https://docs.modernxmpp.org/`

- Learn more about the CoAP protocol: `https://www.rfc-editor.org/rfc/rfc7252`

- Take a look at more about Mosquitto here from its official documentation: `https://mosquitto.org/documentation/`

- Explore more on IoT protocol standards: `https://www.nabto.com/guide-iot-protocols-standards/`

8

Designing for Interoperability

Throughout the past seven chapters, the role of **IoT** in revolutionizing how we interact with technology and automate processes within the collection and analysis of data has become apparent. However, it is important to understand that for IoT to reach its full potential, devices need to communicate and work together seamlessly, without regard to the manufacturer or operating system that it works with. It is with this consideration that the imperativeness of **interoperability** comes into play, as designers of solutions for IoT need to ensure that this factor is taken into consideration.

Interoperability is the ability of different systems, devices, and software to work together with one another within data collection, exchange, and processing. This will allow users to mix and match devices and services, creating a flexible and scalable ecosystem that will be tailored toward their needs. However, it is important to note that there isn't a universal interoperability standard spanning all IoT applications. Different industrial standard groups focus on their respective domains, such as Matter, Thread, and ZigBee for smart homes or **Message Queuing Telemetry Transport (MQTT)**, **Constrained Application Protocol (CoAP)**, and **Lightweight M2M (LwM2M)** for commercial applications. Due to the many different developers of IoT solutions, interoperability has been a prevalent issue, as some may want to prevent other companies from leveraging their solutions, making them only work within their own set of solutions and partners. This challenge is one that many international standards have attempted to solve and is of great interest within the greater IoT open source community.

Building on the foundational understanding of IoT's transformative potential, this chapter delves into the crucial role of interoperability within the vast IoT landscape. We will unpack the challenges of proprietary systems, highlight global efforts pushing for standardized connectivity, and offer insights into best practices for crafting interoperable solutions. By the end of the chapter, you will not only appreciate the intricate web of device communication but also be equipped to champion or design systems that can fluidly integrate into a harmonious IoT ecosystem, driving future progress and innovation.

In this chapter, we're going to cover the following main topics:

- Understanding more about the importance of interoperability in the smart vision for many IoT devices

- Understanding the concepts, approaches, and principles within interoperability in building for IoT

- Learning to work on projects that lead toward greater interoperability and taking this into consideration when designing their architecture

- Creating a Telegram household motion detector

Technical requirements

This chapter will require you to have the following hardware and software installed:

- Hardware:

  - ESP32 microcontroller

  - **Passive Infrared (PIR)** motion detector

  - Breadboard

  - Jumper wires

  - Smartphone

- Software:

  - Telegram app

  - Arduino IDE

The Telegram app

Telegram is a cloud-based **instant messaging (IM)** platform that provides a secure and efficient way for technical users to communicate with a chatbot and receive sensor data. With its support for bots, Telegram allows for automated communication between sensors and the app. The platform's encryption and privacy features ensure that sensitive information remains secure during transmission, making it an ideal choice for technical users who need to communicate critical data from sensors. Additionally, Telegram's API and bots make it easy to integrate with other systems and automate workflows. Whether for personal or business use, Telegram provides a flexible and powerful solution for communicating sensor data.

The current state of IoT platforms and their interoperability

The current state of IoT platforms and how they interoperate with one another is a convoluted picture. The market is fragmented due to the heterogeneity that is present with controllers, device protocols, network connectivity methods, standards, data formats, and many more. This is where concepts such as data normalization come into play. Data normalization in the context of IoT involves standardizing and restructuring diverse data formats from various IoT devices and sensors into a consistent, usable format. This process is crucial for efficient data integration, analysis, and interoperability across different IoT systems and applications.

Vendors often intentionally define different IoT protocols and interfaces that are incompatible with other solutions, given their own agendas of competition. One can grasp this idea by considering smart home ecosystems: a certain smart bulb might work flawlessly with one automation platform but falter with another due to divergent communication protocols or data formats. Despite there being significant progress within the standardization of communication protocols and data formats that have increased interoperability between devices and systems, there are still many challenges that are in the way of achieving full interoperability within IoT.

However, we can see that there are many solutions that have instead looked toward standardizing their implementations to make it easier for consumers to take advantage of multiple solutions from a myriad of providers. The concept of the smart home is one such example of this, given that a consumer is able to automate their home from their smartphone, despite the products that are being controlled being from different providers. In this section, we will define what is interoperability, why it is necessary for the future of IoT, the landscape that it is based on, the costs and trade-offs involved when considering it, and finally an example of a project that takes the ESP32 microcontroller and aims to make it interoperable.

Defining interoperability in IoT

Interoperability is all about how IoT systems and components communicate and share information with each other, which is the main driving factor that will unlock all of IoT's potential. The property relies on interactions within the system, and this may involve interaction between two or more systems. An example of this is displayed in the following diagram; there can be a unified IoT platform that interoperates two objects: a sensor and a device. They may have differing communication networks and apps that are used as part of their interface, but they can interoperate and work with each other:

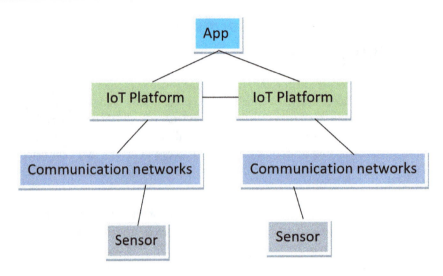

Figure 8.1 – Concept of interoperability between platforms

The diagram shows how different communication networks have different sensors attached to them but have IoT platforms that are able to interoperate and function together to be unified under one app. This allows for different platforms to be controlled centrally. Now, let's understand why we interoperate.

Why interoperate?

Interoperability on IoT is crucial because it enables different devices, systems, and applications to communicate and exchange data seamlessly. This not only improves the overall efficiency and effectiveness of the IoT system but also opens new opportunities for innovation and growth. Without interoperability, each device or system would operate in its own silo, leading to inefficiencies, redundancies, and limitations in the overall capabilities of IoT. Ensuring interoperability requires careful planning, design, and testing, as well as adherence to industry standards and protocols. This helps to ensure that the data exchanged between devices and systems is accurate, consistent, and secure.

Costs and trade-offs of interoperability

Implementing interoperability in IoT requires investments in technology, development, and testing. This includes the costs of developing and deploying standardized protocols, as well as the costs of integrating existing systems and devices to these standards. In addition, organizations may need to invest in new hardware or software to support interoperability, and there may be costs associated with retraining personnel or updating processes to accommodate changes.

While interoperability brings many benefits, it also involves trade-offs. For example, standardizing protocols may limit the ability of organizations to differentiate their products or services through proprietary technology. In addition, the process of integrating systems and devices into standardized protocols can be time-consuming and complex and may require organizations to give up control over certain aspects of their technology stack.

ESP32-H2

ESP32-H2 is a microcontroller and Bluetooth-enabled platform that demonstrates the implementation of interoperability within IoT. It is designed to work with a wide range of devices and systems, allowing for seamless communication and data exchange.

One key aspect of ESP32-H2's interoperability is its support for various communication protocols, including Bluetooth and Zigbee. This enables it to communicate with a wide range of devices, including other IoT devices, smartphones, and computers. In addition, ESP32-H2 supports several industry-standard protocols, such as MQTT and HTTP, which are commonly used for IoT communication.

Another important aspect of ESP32-H2's interoperability is its ability to connect to and interact with cloud platforms, such as **Amazon Web Services** (**AWS**) and **Google Cloud Platform** (**GCP**). This enables it to exchange data with other devices and systems, as well as to access a wide range of cloud-based services and applications.

With that, we have a good understanding of the different costs, trade-offs, and technologies involved in interoperability. Now, we can look at how we can build interoperability within IoT.

Interoperability concept, approaches, and principles for building with IoT

There are various concepts, approaches, and principles that organizations can follow to ensure interoperability in their IoT solutions. This section will not only provide an overview of these principles, patterns, and challenges but will also delve into the types of interoperability, layers of IoT, and guidelines for architecting with interoperability in focus. By understanding and applying these concepts and insights into the intricate layers of IoT, organizations can ensure that their solutions are designed and built with a cohesive vision. The goal is to create IoT solutions that are not only interoperable but also meet the needs of end users, paving the way for a more connected, scalable, and efficient IoT ecosystem.

Concepts, approaches, and principles

In this subsection, we will go through the concepts, approaches, and principles that are taken to ensure that interoperability best practices are adhered to.

Principles of interoperability

There are five key principles in interoperability that guide the best practices for designing solutions. These principles outline the strategic approaches necessary to effectively achieve interoperability.

> **Important note**
> Different sources may list these principles differently, although, by concept, they are essentially based on the same thing.

Now, we can take a look at the five main principles:

- **Open standards**: One of the biggest points about interoperability is the need for open standards. Protocols such as MQTT, CoAP (which is a lightweight web transfer protocol designed for use with constrained nodes and networks in IoT), and Zigbee are popularly used due to not only the performance and powerfulness that they offer as a solution but also because they are used by many other systems that support them. It is imperative to look to open standards when planning for a solution so that devices and systems from different manufacturers can communicate with each other seamlessly.

- **Data format consistency**: It is imperative to ensure that data is formatted and structured accordingly, regardless of source or destination, to facilitate seamless communication between devices and streams. This becomes even more important due to the possibilities of different requirements between different protocols, making consistency of protocols even more necessary and thus being a key point of interoperability.

- **Interoperable APIs**: It is crucial to implement APIs that are interoperable and can be used to seamlessly integrate devices and systems from different manufacturers.

- **Device management**: Standardizing the management of IoT devices, including firmware updates, security patches, and device configuration, will ensure that IoT devices are updated consistently, reducing the risk of security vulnerabilities and improving overall interoperability.

- **Security**: Investing in security measures to ensure that IoT devices are protected from threats such as hacking, malware, and unauthorized access will help to protect sensitive data and improve overall interoperability by reducing the risk of security breaches.

With that, we now have a grasp of the foundations that make up interoperability. Now, we can take a look at the patterns within it.

Patterns within interoperability

There are six main interoperability patterns for IoT ecosystems, which are as follows:

- **Cross-Platform Access**: Serving as the bedrock of an interoperable IoT system, this pattern aspires for a unified interface where applications or services can tap into resources from varying platforms. The challenge is in facilitating different platforms to communicate and discover necessary data coherently, irrespective of the origin.

- **Cross-Application Domain Access**: Expanding upon the Cross-Platform Access pattern, this pattern empowers applications or services to harness data not just from disparate platforms but also from those serving diverse application sectors. At this juncture, semantic interoperability—ensuring consistent meaning and interpretation of data across systems—becomes paramount. To achieve this, shared information models are essential as they provide standardized structures ensuring that data retains its meaning across varied domains.

- **Platform Independence**: Championing adaptability, this pattern emphasizes applications or services that function across a range of IoT platforms. Imagine a universal smart parking solution operating across different cities, each with its own platform but conveying parking availability seamlessly.

- **Platform-scale Independence**: Tailored to buffer applications and services from discrepancies in platform sizes, this pattern guarantees a uniform interaction experience regardless of platform magnitude.

- **Higher-level Service Facades**: This involves supplementary services that embellish the innate capabilities of the IoT platform. By standing as an intermediary layer, these services refine the foundational offerings, presenting enhanced value.

- **Platform-to-platform**: Promoting integrative capabilities, this pattern equips pre-existing applications to draw from resources across multiple platforms, creating an illusion of them operating under a singular umbrella. This consolidated approach eases user interactions and enables platforms to augment their resource suite via collaborative endeavors.

With that, we have a greater understanding of the patterns involved and can move on to seeing the challenges of interoperability.

Challenges within interoperability

There are many challenges within interoperability. They mostly converge into five different areas. Let's look at the five key challenges that are impeding the progression of interoperability within IoT and how they all fit into the big picture of the IoT solutions that we are developing, as depicted in *Figure 8.2*:

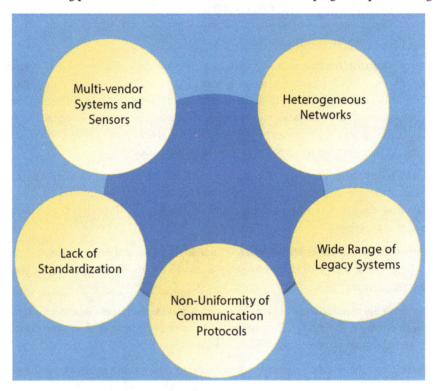

Figure 8.2 – The five key challenges of interoperability within IoT

The five key challenges can be defined as follows:

- **Multi-vendor systems and sensors**: One of the biggest challenges of interoperability for IoT is the large number of different vendors and suppliers offering IoT devices and systems. This creates a scenario where different devices have different hardware and software specifications, making it difficult for them to communicate with each other.

- **Heterogeneous networks**: Another challenge is the heterogeneous nature of IoT networks, where different devices use different communication technologies, such as Wi-Fi, Bluetooth, Zigbee, or cellular networks. This can lead to difficulties in establishing communication between devices, as they may not be compatible with each other.

- **Wide range of legacy systems**: The presence of a wide range of legacy systems, such as building automation systems and **industrial control systems (ICS)**, adds to the complexity of interoperability. These systems were not designed with IoT in mind and may use proprietary communication protocols or connectors, making it difficult to integrate them with newer IoT devices.

- **Non-uniformity of communication protocol**: The non-uniformity of communication protocols used by different IoT devices is another major challenge. This can make it difficult for devices to communicate with each other, as they may use different protocols or different versions of the same protocol.

- **Lack of standardization**: A lack of standardization in the IoT industry is a major challenge for interoperability. Without a common set of standards, it is difficult for devices from different vendors to communicate with each other, leading to fragmentation and complexity. Standardization efforts, such as the **IoT Architecture Framework**, are underway to address this issue.

With that understanding of the challenges, we can now take a look at the different types of interoperability.

Types of interoperability

There are seven levels of interoperability, each with more interoperability than the last. Next, we will discuss the different levels:

- **No interoperability**: No interoperability refers to a situation where devices or systems are completely unable to communicate with each other. In such a scenario, data or information cannot be shared or exchanged between devices, and they are completely isolated from each other.

- **Technical interoperability**: Technical interoperability refers to the ability of devices or systems to communicate with each other using common communication protocols and data exchange formats. In this case, devices can communicate with each other, but the data exchanged may not be easily understood by both parties. An example would be smart home devices such as thermostats, lighting systems, and security cameras using a common protocol such as Zigbee or Z-Wave to communicate with each other. However, the specific data each device sends might not be immediately interpretable by other devices if they are expecting data in a different format.

- **Syntactic interoperability**: Syntactic interoperability refers to the ability of devices or systems to understand and interpret the syntax or structure of data exchanged between them. In this case, data is structured and formatted in a way that both devices can understand, but the meaning or semantics of the data may not be clear.

- **Semantic interoperability**: Semantic interoperability refers to the ability of devices or systems to understand and interpret the meaning or semantics of the data exchanged between them. In this case, data is structured and formatted in a way that both devices can understand, and the semantics of the data are clear and consistent between both devices.

- **Pragmatic interoperability**: Pragmatic interoperability refers to the ability of devices or systems to interact and cooperate with each other in a practical and functional manner. In this case, devices can exchange data, understand the meaning of the data, and work together to achieve a common goal.

- **Dynamic interoperability**: Dynamic interoperability refers to the ability of devices or systems to adapt and change dynamically in response to changing requirements or conditions. In this case, devices can change their behavior, communication protocols, or data exchange formats in response to changing conditions, ensuring that they can continue to communicate and cooperate with each other.

- **Conceptual interoperability**: Conceptual interoperability refers to the ability of devices or systems to understand and work with the same concepts, models, or data representations. In this case, devices can understand and work with the same data representations and models, ensuring that they can exchange data and work together in a meaningful and consistent way.

With that understanding of the types of interoperability, we can look at the different layers of IoT involved to consider.

Layers of IoT

There are three main layers of interoperability:

- **Device layer**: At the device level, a **device-to-device (D2D)** solution will make it possible for new IoT devices to easily connect and work with existing devices. D2D refers to direct communication between two devices without the intervention or relay of a centralized control point such as a base station or a central server. It is a type of gateway that supports a variety of communication protocols and can also handle raw data transfer. It is made up of two parts—one that takes care of network access and communication, and another that handles all other gateway functions and services. If the connection is lost, the virtual part can still respond to requests from the API and middleware. This modular approach allows for the addition of extra services as needed, making it possible for the network of smart devices to grow and evolve quickly. In a smart home, various devices such as smart bulbs, smart locks, and smart thermostats can directly communicate with each other with D2D solutions, utilizing the device layer. For instance, a smart thermostat can directly communicate with smart window blinds to adjust the room temperature without needing to communicate through a central hub.

- **Middleware layer**: In the middleware layer, different types of IoT devices work together, making it easy to find and manage the resources they need. This is done by creating a pretend layer and connecting different IoT platforms to it. This pretend layer provides services that help manage the virtual representation of the devices and their information, which can be accessed through a general API. By having this layer in place, it becomes possible to use smart devices in large and complex IoT systems. For instance, in a hospital, middleware can help integrate data from various medical devices such as heart-rate monitors, oxygen-level sensors, and **electronic health records (EHRs)**, creating a unified patient monitoring system accessible via a common API.

- **Network layer**: A **node-to-node (N2N)** solution makes it so that different networks can work together easily, allowing smart devices to move around and information to be shared easily. N2N is the direct communication or interaction between two network nodes without intermediaries. It also lets different networks connect to each other using gateways and platforms. This is done by creating a pretend network using special technologies called **software-defined networking (SDN)** and **network functions virtualization (NFV)** and using the N2N API to help. SDN is an approach to networking where control functions are decoupled from the physical infrastructure, allowing for centralized and programmable network management. NFV involves the decoupling of network functions from proprietary hardware appliances, enabling these functions to run as software instances on commodity hardware. This solution will help build a system where everything works together seamlessly and will fix the problem of smart devices not being able to move around easily. Autonomous cars navigating city streets can use network-to-network solutions to communicate directly with each other for real-time traffic management and accident avoidance.

Now that we understand the different layers, we can look into architecting for interoperability.

Architecting for interoperability

When we architect for interoperability, it is important that we establish a systematic process of designing our solution. We can look into the requirements to start off with as part of architecting for it:

1. **Defining requirements**: First, it is imperative to define requirements for the IoT solution that we are to make. We need to list down the interoperability requirements; that is, address which systems our solution needs to interoperate with.

2. **Identifying standards and protocols to use**: We then will move on to researching and identifying industry standards and protocols that are commonly used in IoT solutions, such as MQTT, CoAP, and Zigbee. This is a very important step, as it will ensure that we know what the proper standards we want to use are and that it can be an appropriate fit for the use case of the systems our solution will interoperate with. It is important to ensure that the standards and protocols that are used are also widely adopted so as not to be isolated from most applications. In the industry, isolated standards often would not be appealing to the consumer, given that they will not be able to communicate with other services.

3. **Defining architecture**: Next, define the overall architecture for the IoT solution, including the communication protocols, device discovery, security, and data management.

4. **Utilizing API gateways**: API gateways can provide a common interface between different IoT devices and systems, allowing them to communicate with each other seamlessly.

5. **Implementing data management**: Data management is critical to ensuring interoperability in IoT solutions. Choose a data management system that can handle large amounts of data, is scalable, and can be integrated with other systems.

6. **Testing and validation**: Thoroughly test the IoT solution to ensure that it meets interoperability requirements, and validate the solution against industry standards.

With that understanding of architecting for interoperability, along with the other concepts that support it, we can look into what kinds of projects are working toward more interoperability, both on a local and global scale.

Projects working toward greater interoperability

Open source projects are one of the biggest contributors to the advancement of interoperability solutions. Here, we will talk about two categories within this: projects for global interoperability and projects for interoperability within the cloud. We will then see an example of such a project in a case study, which will help us look at how advancing interoperability for IoT platforms can be achieved.

Global interoperability

Many projects are currently working toward creating solutions for global interoperability; that is, solutions that allow devices and systems to universally communicate with one another seamlessly. Here, we discuss two projects that are currently working on this, which are as follows:

*   **oneM2M**: oneM2M is a global standards development organization focused on creating a standardized IoT architecture and promoting interoperability among IoT devices. The organization's goal is to provide a common platform for IoT devices to exchange data and communicate with each other, regardless of the manufacturer or communication technology. oneM2M's standardization efforts are aimed at creating a seamless and secure IoT environment where different devices can work together seamlessly.

*   **Open Interconnect Consortium (OIC)**: OIC is a non-profit organization that is working to develop open source standards and specifications for IoT interoperability. The goal of OIC is to provide a unified and standardized approach to IoT, allowing devices from different vendors to communicate and work together. OIC's efforts are aimed at creating an open and transparent IoT ecosystem where all devices can easily communicate with each other and access common services.

Now that we have seen a couple of global interoperability projects, we can now see how it is being done within the cloud.

Interoperability within the cloud

The cloud, as we have discussed, is a big community in and of itself in developing interoperability. There is much development that is made to try to utilize the cloud to create more interoperable platforms, both internally and externally. Next, we explore some open source projects that are currently prominent and looking to achieve this:

- **Eclipse Kura**: Eclipse Kura is an open source Java/**Open Service Gateway Initiative** (**OSGi**) framework for IoT gateways. It provides a modular and scalable platform for building IoT applications that can run on a range of hardware platforms, including single-board computers and gateways. Kura supports interoperability between IoT devices and the cloud by providing a range of services and APIs for connecting devices, transmitting data, and processing data in the cloud.

- **Mosquitto**: Mosquitto is an open source messaging broker that implements the MQTT protocol. MQTT is a popular communication protocol used in IoT, and Mosquitto provides a robust and scalable platform for connecting IoT devices and transmitting data to the cloud. The project provides a flexible and scalable platform for supporting interoperability between IoT devices and the cloud and is widely used in a range of IoT applications and services.

With knowledge of some popular interoperability projects, let's take a look at a case study that puts such projects into practice.

E-health platform case study

A health platform provider wants to develop a system that integrates wearable devices, such as fitness trackers and smartwatches, with a patient's EHR. The aim is to improve the accuracy and timeliness of patient health data and make it easier for healthcare providers to monitor and manage patient health. Here, we will discuss how there can be challenges and benefits and look at solutions that we can develop toward being able to appropriately handle them, as follows:

- **Challenges:**

  - **Heterogeneous devices**: The platform provider must contend with the fact that different wearable devices have different hardware and software specifications, making it difficult to integrate them with the EHR system

  - **Non-uniform communication protocols**: The wearable devices may use different communication protocols, making it difficult for the platform to receive and process the data from all devices

  - **Lack of standardization**: There is a lack of standardization in the wearable device industry, leading to fragmentation and complexity in the integration process

- **Solutions:**

  - **Device agnosticism**: The platform provider should design the system to be device agnostic, meaning it should be able to receive data from any wearable device, regardless of its hardware or software specifications

  - **Interoperable communication protocols**: The platform should use widely accepted and standardized communication protocols to receive data from wearable devices, such as **Bluetooth Low Energy (BLE)** or **Health Level Seven (HL7) International** standards

  - **Integration with EHR**: The platform should be able to seamlessly integrate the data received from wearable devices into the patient's EHR, making it easier for healthcare providers to access and use the data in their decision-making process

- **Benefits:**

  - **Improved patient outcomes**: Interoperable IoT devices in a health platform can provide more accurate and timely patient health data, leading to improved patient outcomes

  - **Better healthcare management**: With interoperable IoT devices, healthcare providers can more easily monitor and manage patient health, leading to more effective treatment plans and outcomes

  - **Increased patient engagement**: Interoperable IoT devices can also increase patient engagement by providing patients with real-time access to their health data and the ability to track their progress

And with that, we have seen such interoperability initiatives put into practice. Now, we can see how we can advance the interoperability of IoT platforms.

Advancing the interoperability of IoT platforms

There is much that can be done to advance the interoperability of IoT platforms. Five things can be done, which are as follows:

- First, there has to be more adoption of open standards. We need to encourage the adoption of open standards and protocols that are widely recognized and adopted across the industry. This will ensure that IoT devices and systems from different manufacturers can communicate with each other seamlessly.

- Second, there must be more investment in research and development for interoperability in IoT and to create new technologies and protocols that can enhance interoperability. This includes developing new standards for data format, communication protocols, and device discovery.

- Third, we need to encourage collaboration between stakeholders, including IoT device manufacturers, software providers, and end users, to identify and address interoperability challenges. By working together, stakeholders can find solutions that benefit everyone and advance the future of interoperability in IoT.

- Fourth, we need to standardize the management of IoT devices, including firmware updates, security patches, and device configuration. This will ensure that IoT devices are updated consistently, reducing the risk of security vulnerabilities and improving overall interoperability.

- Fifth, we need to invest in security measures to ensure that IoT devices are protected from threats such as hacking, malware, and unauthorized access. This will help to protect sensitive data and improve overall interoperability by reducing the risk of security breaches.

And with that, we are ready to move into a practical to put into action what we've learned to create a Telegram household motion detector.

Practical – Creating a Telegram household motion detector

In this practical, we will look into creating a Telegram bot that can pass us information regarding motion that has been detected based on a motion detector. This is a great practical to understand how to work with different APIs and how they can interoperate with one another to ensure that we can create an autonomous workload based on different components. These components are what make up the concept of smart homes and large IoT ecosystems that have them interacting with one another, and you can see these components in the *Technical requirements* section.

Creating a chatbot

To receive messages sent from the ESP32 based on the motion caught by the motion sensor, we have to first create a chatbot on the Telegram app:

1.   To start off, we need to download the **Telegram** app. We can go to Google Play or the App Store and download and install Telegram from there:

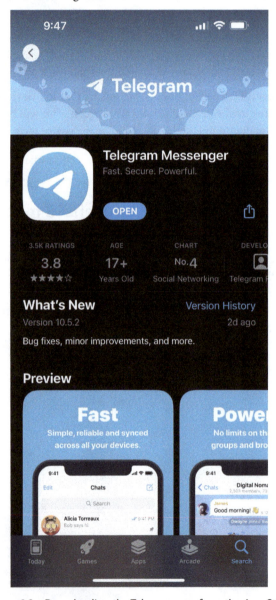

Figure 8.3 – Downloading the Telegram app from the App Store

2. Open Telegram after it has finished installing, search for Botfather, and click on it. Alternatively, you can also open the t.me/botfather link on your smartphone:

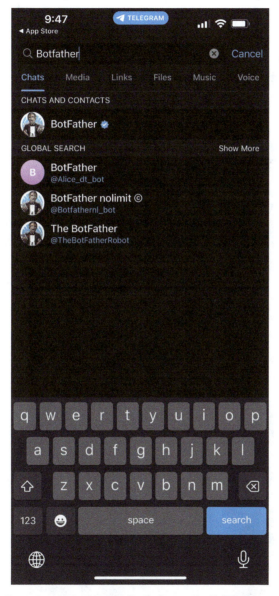

Figure 8.4 – Searching for BotFather on the Telegram app

3. You will then have a window open and be prompted to click the **Start** button. Click on it accordingly.

4. To create your bot, follow the steps by typing /newbot and then completing the required information such as the bot's name and username. Upon successful creation of your bot, a message including a link and bot token will be sent to you. It's crucial to save the bot token as it will be required for the ESP32 to communicate with the bot. Navigate to the link to get to your bot on Telegram and click **Start** to prepare to receive messages on your app:

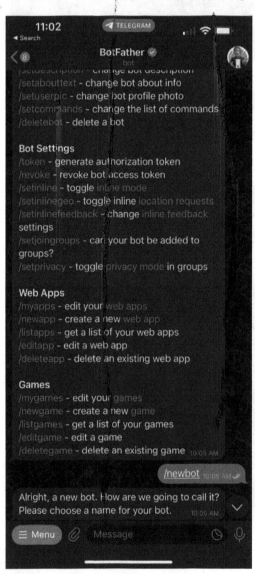

Figure 8.5 – Typing in /newbot to create a new bot

With that, we have created our bot! Now, we need to get a Telegram user ID.

Getting a Telegram user ID

By obtaining your Telegram user ID, you can ensure that your bot only interacts with authorized users. The ESP32 can compare the sender ID of incoming messages to your user ID and either process the message or disregard it, depending on the match. This way, you can filter out any messages that are not from your Telegram account or other approved sources:

1. To locate **IDBot** in your Telegram account, either conduct a search through Telegram's search bar at the top or access this link, `t.me/myidbot`, through your smartphone.

2. To obtain your user ID, initiate a conversation with **IDBot** and enter `/getid`. You will then receive a response containing your user ID, which should be saved for future reference in this tutorial:

Figure 8.6 – Entering in /getid to see your ID with IDBot

Now that we have obtained our user ID, we can start working on the Arduino segment of the practical.

Working with the Arduino IDE

Interaction with the Telegram bot will be facilitated using the **Universal Arduino Telegram Bot Library**, a tool created by Brian Lough that simplifies access to the `Telegram Bot API`. We will ensure that our Arduino IDE has these libraries and procure them if not. Proceeding from here, we can follow the following steps:

1. First, we need to download the Universal Arduino Telegram Bot library. We can find it at `https://github.com/witnessmenow/Universal-Arduino-Telegram-Bot/archive/master.zip`.

2. We then need to include the library. We need to navigate to **Sketch > Include Library > Add**. Zip the library and add the library:

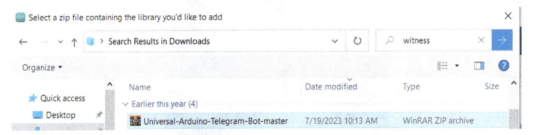

Figure 8.7 – Pop-up window to add in the Universal Arduino Telegram Bot library

> **Important note**
>
> You should not be installing the library with the Arduino Library Manager, as a deprecated version may be installed instead.

3. We then must install the `ArduinoJson` library. To do this, we navigate to **Sketch > Include Library > Manage Libraries**.

4. We then search for `arduinojson` and install its latest version:

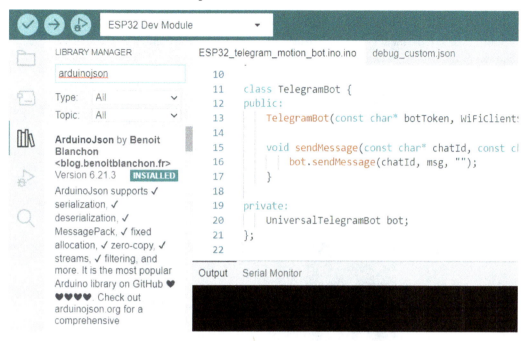

Figure 8.8 – Adding in the ArduinoJson library

With the libraries installed, we can now prepare the hardware.

Hardware setup

We will connect the ESP32 to the PIR motion sensor according to the following diagram. It is a motion sensor that detects movement by sensing changes in infrared radiation emitted by warm objects, such as humans or animals, in its field of view:

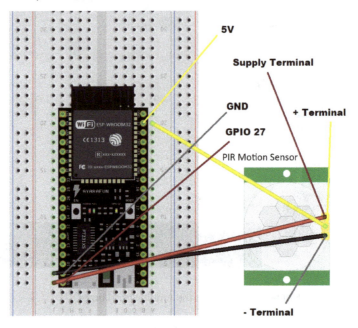

Figure 8.9 – Circuit diagram for PIR motion sensor

On the PIR to the ESP32, we will connect the negative terminal to GND, the positive terminal to 5V, and the supply terminal to GPIO 27.

Coding it up

We are now ready to start coding up the necessary code to run the program on our Arduino IDE.

We first declare the necessary libraries for the program. The WiFi.h library is used to connect to the internet over Wi-Fi. The WiFiClientSecure.h library establishes a secure client connection to ensure the data communication is encrypted. The UniversalTelegramBot.h library is for controlling the bot on Telegram, and the ArduinoJson.h library handles the JSON data format used by the Telegram bot:

```
#include <ArduinoJson.h>
#include <UniversalTelegramBot.h>
#include <WiFiClientSecure.h>
#include <WiFi.h>
```

We then create a struct to hold our network credentials (SSID and password), and you need to replace the "YOUR_SSID_HERE" and "YOUR_PASSWORD_HERE" placeholder values with your own values. Afterward, a TelegramBot class is defined that encapsulates the functionality of the UniversalTelegramBot library, simplifying our use of it later in the code. After this, we instantiate a NetworkCredentials object with bot_token and chat_id values that you need to replace with the personalized token you received for your bot and the user ID you received for your telegram account respectively, wifi_client as an instance of WiFiClientSecure to handle secure connections, and telegramBot as an instance of our TelegramBot class using the bot token and the secure client:

```
typedef struct {
    const char* network_id = "YOUR_SSID_HERE";
    const char* network_pass = "YOUR_PASSWORD_HERE";
} NetworkCredentials;

class TelegramBot {
public:
    TelegramBot(const char* botToken, WiFiClientSecure& client) :
bot(botToken, client) {}

    void sendMessage(const char* chatId, const char* msg) {
        bot.sendMessage(chatId, msg, "");
    }

private:
    UniversalTelegramBot bot;
};

NetworkCredentials networkCredentials;
const char* bot_token = "6344540752:AAHN_
xoPfRipHbAf2d5cbceWLnYvxd2uRiI";
const char* chat_id = "6394755694";

WiFiClientSecure wifi_client;
TelegramBot telegramBot(bot_token, wifi_client);
```

Following that, we set up the PIR sensor pin and a Boolean flag to track whether motion is detected. The detectMotion function will be called whenever the sensor pin detects a rising voltage (that is, motion), setting movementDetected to true:

```
constexpr int PIR_SENSOR_PIN = 27;
volatile bool movementDetected = false;

void IRAM_ATTR detectMotion() {
```

```
        movementDetected = true;
    }
}
```

We then need to create a `connectWiFi` function that sets the ESP32 to operate in Station (STA) mode and then attempts to connect it to the Wi-Fi network using the credentials we provided earlier. It also sets the certificate root on the secure client. It then waits until the ESP32 is connected before continuing the program:

```
void connectWiFi() {
    WiFi.mode(WIFI_STA);
    WiFi.begin(networkCredentials.network_id, networkCredentials.
network_pass);
    wifi_client.setCACert(TELEGRAM_CERTIFICATE_ROOT);

    while (WiFi.status() != WL_CONNECTED) {
        delay(500);
    }
}
```

Finally, we create `setup()` and `loop()` functions. The `setup()` function initializes serial communication, sets the PIR sensor pin as an input with a pull-up resistor, and attaches an interrupt to it. It then connects to the Wi-Fi and sends a message indicating that the bot is active. The `loop()` function is the main loop of the program, which constantly checks if motion has been detected. If so, it sends a message and resets the flag:

```
void setup() {
    Serial.begin(115200);
    pinMode(PIR_SENSOR_PIN, INPUT_PULLUP);
    attachInterrupt(digitalPinToInterrupt(PIR_SENSOR_PIN),
detectMotion, RISING);
    connectWiFi();
    telegramBot.sendMessage(chat_id, "Bot activated");
}

void loop() {
    if (movementDetected) {
        telegramBot.sendMessage(chat_id, "Motion detected!");
        movementDetected = false;
    }
}
```

As per usual, verify the code to ensure that you have entered everything correctly. Remember that there are four fields you must personally modify with your own information. If everything is done correctly, you should see the upload be successfully completed and your Telegram bot start churning messages after you have clicked **Start** on it.

And with that, we are ready to test our implementation.

Outcome

You should see something like the following after you have uploaded your code and start moving in front of the PIR motion sensor. When the bot is first started up, you will get the text **Bot activated**, and when you make a movement, you will get the text **Motion detected!**:

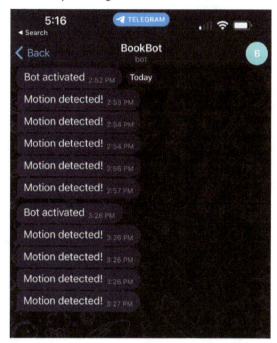

Figure 8.10 – Expected output on the Telegram bot

And that's it; you've made your interoperable solution! Now, upload the code to GitHub and see if you can also make these modifications to your hardware/code. Now, for further understanding and practice on the concepts that you have learned through this practical, you can try doing the following.

- Can you add an LED bulb to the circuit to also react when you receive a movement on the PIR motion sensor?

- Can you replace the motion sensor with a DHT11 sensor to send messages to Telegram when the temperature rises above 30°C?

Feel free to use the documentation from the Super Starter Kit to also help you navigate the use cases of each sensor and how to properly use them.

Summary

In this chapter, we learned about what interoperability is, why it is important for IoT, and how we can architect solutions for it while navigating through the challenges that are being posed. We then looked further into how it can be beneficial with our practical in building a Telegram chatbot that alerts you to motion detection based on your ESP32, showing how interoperability is imperative to functioning solutions.

Through the discussions and practical exercises in this chapter, readers have gained a comprehensive understanding of interoperability and its significance in IoT. This understanding forms a foundation for creating robust, scalable, and adaptable IoT solutions. Additionally, by exploring how to architect solutions and navigate challenges, readers have acquired valuable insights and strategies that can be applied to their own projects. This equips readers with a broader toolkit to address the complex demands of IoT environments, making them better prepared to contribute to projects in this domain, or even lead initiatives that require a deep understanding of interoperability.

In the next chapter, we will look at operating and monitoring IoT networks.

Further reading

For more information about what was covered in this chapter, please refer to the following links:

- Read more on smart home and how interoperability can support it: `https://www.iotforall.com/smart-home-interoperability-fragmented-landscape`

- Explore more insights in IoT interoperability from a governance perspective: `https://www2.gov.bc.ca/assets/gov/british-columbians-our-governments/services-policies-for-government/information-management-technology/information-security/information-security-awareness/its_7am_do_you_know_whats_on_your_network_forescout.pdf`

- Explore more on the passive infrared sensor from the Adafruit documentation: `https://cdn-learn.adafruit.com/downloads/pdf/pir-passive-infrared-proximity-motion-sensor.pdf`

- Learn more on how to use Telegram from its official website: `https://core.telegram.org/`

Part 3: Operating, Maintaining, and Securing IoT Networks

In this part, we delve deeper into the post-deployment world of IoT, ensuring that our ecosystems not only function but also thrive. Our journey commences with the ins and outs of operating and closely monitoring IoT networks, keeping them at their peak performance. We then immerse ourselves in the invaluable realm of data and analytics, understanding how to glean actionable insights from our IoT deployments. As we further our exploration, we confront the ever-evolving challenges of security and privacy, emphasizing the significance of a proactive defense mindset in today's interconnected landscapes. Concluding this section, we encourage innovation and adaptability by taking you through open source IoT, empowering you with tools and knowledge to stay at the forefront of this dynamic field. This part underscores the importance of maintaining, refining, and safeguarding our smart systems, ensuring they remain robust, secure, and poised for future advancements.

This part has the following chapters:

- *Chapter 9, Operating and Monitoring IoT Networks*

- *Chapter 10, Working with Data and Analytics*

- *Chapter 11, Examining Security and Privacy in IoT*

- *Chapter 12, Exploring and Innovating with Open Source IoT*

9

Operating and Monitoring IoT Networks

With the increasing number of connected devices and sensors, managing and monitoring IoT networks has become a critical task for organizations. Operating and monitoring IoT networks requires a comprehensive approach that includes continuous operations, setting **key performance indicators** (**KPIs**) such as the number of active users on an IoT network or the latency expected, setting/monitoring metrics to measure success, and utilizing monitoring capabilities both on-premises and on the cloud. In this chapter, we will delve into the critical aspects of operating and monitoring IoT networks. We will discuss the importance of continuous operations, exploring the challenges of keeping the system running 24/7 and techniques to ensure maximum uptime. Furthermore, we will explore the essential KPIs that organizations need to measure to ensure the success of their IoT projects, including reliability, scalability, and security.

We will examine the different monitoring capabilities available for IoT networks, including on-premises and cloud-based monitoring tools. Specifically, we will dive into the capabilities of **Amazon Web Services** (**AWS**) for monitoring IoT networks. By the end of this chapter, readers will have a comprehensive understanding of the best practices and tools for operating and monitoring IoT networks, enabling them to ensure the success of their IoT projects.

In this chapter, we're going to cover the following main topics:

- Continuous operation of IoT systems
- Setting KPIs and the metrics for success
- Monitoring capabilities on-premises and on the cloud
- Practical – operating and monitoring a joke creator with IoT Greengrass

Technical requirements

This chapter will require you to have the following software ready for the practical. The software requirements may include items that you are already familiar with, as well as new software that you may need to acquire or install.

You will need the following software:

- Diagram design software of your choice (e.g., Draw.io)
- AWS account
- OpenAI subscription (to use ChatGPT)
- Arduino IDE

ChatGPT is built on the GPT-4 architecture, presenting a big advancement in the domain of **natural language processing** (**NLP**). This model has been trained on vast swathes of data, which allows it to generate coherent and contextually relevant textual outputs, simulating human-like conversation with impressive fluency and depth.

The ChatGPT API emerges as a pivotal bridge between different key pieces of hardware and software. The API allows developers to integrate the capabilities of ChatGPT into their own applications, platforms, or services. The implications for the **Internet of Things** (**IoT**) are profound due to this. Picture a world where your smart fridge not only tells you are out of milk but also engages in a nuanced conversation about dairy alternatives, their environmental impacts, and recipes you might try. By melding the ChatGPT API with IoT devices, we can create a seamless, intelligent, and interactive ecosystem that responds and converses with us, enhancing our daily experiences and decision-making processes. In this chapter, we will look at integrating this within one such practical.

You can access the GitHub folder for the code that is used in this chapter at `https://github.com/PacktPublishing/IoT-Made-Easy-for-Beginners/tree/main/Chapter09/`.

Continuous operation of IoT systems

In today's fast-paced digital landscape, maintaining the continuous operation of IoT networks is more critical than ever. IoT networks are being used in a wide range of industries, from manufacturing and logistics to healthcare and retail, to collect and process real-time data and automate processes. As such, even a brief downtime can result in significant losses in revenue, productivity, and customer satisfaction. Therefore, it is essential to ensure that IoT networks remain operational 24/7, with little to no disruption in service.

In this section, we will explore the concept of continuous operation in IoT networks, discussing the challenges and benefits of maintaining uptime, as well as the strategies and best practices for achieving this goal. We will cover topics such as redundancy and failover mechanisms, monitoring and alerting systems, regular maintenance and updates, automation, machine learning, and KPI tracking. By the end of this section, readers will have a solid understanding of the importance of continuous operation in IoT networks and the tools and strategies needed to achieve this goal.

Challenges and benefits of maintaining continuous operation

Maintaining continuous operation of monitoring solutions can be challenging, particularly in the context of IoT networks where the volume of data being generated and transmitted can be significant. The following are key challenges that need to be looked at:

- **Managing data volumes**: The massive influx of data generated by IoT devices can be overwhelming for organizations. Managing and processing the data in real time becomes a challenge, and requires effective data management strategies to ensure that data is processed accurately and efficiently.

- **Ensuring data accuracy**: IoT monitoring data must be reliable and accurate to enable effective decision-making. Any inaccuracies or inconsistencies must be identified promptly, and mechanisms must be in place to rectify them.

- **Integrating with existing systems**: Integration of IoT monitoring solutions into the existing architecture can pose a challenge. An organization needs to ensure that IoT monitoring solutions are compatible with existing systems and that the data from different systems is integrated to provide a comprehensive view of the overall system performance.

- **Balancing monitoring with system performance**: Monitoring solutions generate huge volumes of data, which can consume resources and impact system performance. Organizations must balance monitoring requirements with system performance and implement effective resource management to avoid any adverse impact.

- **Maintaining security**: IoT monitoring systems must be safeguarded from cyberattacks, as they can become a gateway for attackers to gain access to sensitive data. Security protocols must be in place to ensure the safety of the monitoring systems and data.

- **The challenge of scalability**: IoT networks are expanding rapidly, leading to an increase in the volume of data generated. Monitoring solutions must be scalable to handle the growing data volumes, and the monitoring infrastructure must be designed to ensure effective monitoring and management of the system.

Maintaining the continuous operation of IoT monitoring solutions brings several benefits to organizations, including the following:

- **Early detection of issues**: Continuous monitoring of IoT networks enables organizations to detect issues early and resolve them before they turn into major problems. This helps prevent system downtime, reduce maintenance costs, and enhance the overall system performance.

- **Improved system performance**: Real-time monitoring of IoT networks can identify performance bottlenecks and help optimize the system for better performance. This leads to faster response times, improved system reliability, and enhanced user experience.

- **Better decision-making**: IoT monitoring solutions provide real-time data and insights that can inform effective decision-making. Organizations can use the data to make informed decisions that improve operational efficiency, reduce costs, and enhance overall business performance.

- **Enhanced security**: Continuous monitoring of IoT networks helps identify security vulnerabilities and potential threats. This enables an organization to take proactive measures to prevent attacks and protect sensitive data, ensuring the safety and security of the system.

- **Predictive maintenance**: Continuous monitoring of IoT networks can identify patterns and trends that can inform predictive maintenance. This helps an organization identify potential failures before they occur, reducing maintenance costs and increasing the overall lifespan of the system.

- **Scalability**: Continuous monitoring solutions can scale to meet the needs of expanding IoT networks. This enables an organization to handle large volumes of data and maintain a comprehensive view of the system's performance, even as the network expands.

On the other hand, it is important to understand how the monitoring framework is done over AWS and in general. In *Figure 9.1*, we can see how this framework can be visualized and stepped through for our needs:

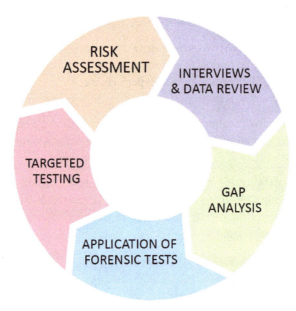

Figure 9.1 – IoT network monitoring framework

Here, we have the framework that we will walk through step by step to understand what each step encompasses:

1. **Targeted testing**: This step involves testing specific areas of the IoT network to identify potential vulnerabilities or weaknesses. Testing may involve performing a penetration test or using specialized tools to identify vulnerabilities in the network. In a smart home IoT network, targeted testing might involve using a network scanning tool such as Nmap to identify open ports on devices such as smart thermostats or security cameras.

2. **Risk assessment**: In this step, the results of the targeted testing are analyzed to identify potential risks and threats to the IoT network. A risk assessment helps to prioritize potential vulnerabilities based on their likelihood and potential impact on the network. After identifying vulnerabilities in the smart home network, a risk assessment could determine that an unpatched security camera poses a high risk due to its accessibility from the internet and the potential for it to be used as a gateway to access other devices on the network.

3. **Interviews and data review**: This step involves interviewing key stakeholders and reviewing data from various sources, such as system logs and incident reports. The goal is to gather additional information about potential vulnerabilities and risks to the IoT network. Interviews with the smart home's residents could reveal that they are unaware of the need to regularly update device firmware. Reviewing system logs might show repeated attempts to access devices from unrecognized IP addresses, indicating potential security threats.

4. **Gap analysis**: This step involves comparing the results of the previous steps to the organization's security policies and procedures. This helps to identify any gaps in the security posture of the IoT network and determine areas where improvements are needed. Comparing the current security measures of the smart home network with industry best practices might reveal gaps such as a lack of regular firmware updates, an absence of strong password policies, or a failure to segment the network to isolate critical devices from one another.

5. **Application of forensic tests**: The final step involves conducting forensic tests on the network to gather additional information about potential vulnerabilities and risks. Forensic tests may include analyzing system logs or performing a deep dive into specific areas of the network to identify potential issues. Forensic analysis of the smart home network could involve examining the security camera's logs to trace back to the origin of unauthorized access attempts. It might also include a deep dive into network traffic to identify any unusual patterns that could indicate a breach or an ongoing attack.

By following these five steps, organizations can ensure that their IoT networks are monitored effectively and continuously, helping to minimize potential risks and threats and ensuring the overall security and efficiency of their networks.

Strategies for achieving continuous operation

There are a number of key strategies that can be used to ensure that continuous operation of monitoring can be done. Ahead, we discuss some patterns that are related to monitoring IoT networks and those that are on the cloud.

Centralized versus distributed monitoring

Centralized monitoring requires the use of a single platform to monitor all IoT devices and sensors. This allows for an organization to get a holistic view of its IoT network and respond quickly to issues while also identifying trends and anomalies. Furthermore, it simplifies the management of monitoring data and ensures that there is consistency within monitoring throughout the IoT network.

On the other hand, **distributed monitoring** uses multiple monitoring tools or platforms to monitor different aspects of the IoT network. This is useful within large or complex IoT environments in which a single tool may not be sufficient for the use case. This also allows organizations to tailor their monitoring approaches to select IoT devices or use cases.

On AWS

Implementing continuous monitoring in an IoT network is crucial for ensuring its performance, reliability, and security. AWS offers a suite of tools and services to support effective continuous monitoring solutions.

Amazon CloudWatch is a monitoring and observability service that provides metrics, logs, and alarms for AWS resources and applications. It can monitor IoT devices and applications' performance and health and send alerts and notifications based on predefined thresholds or custom metrics. Another tool for continuous monitoring on AWS is **AWS IoT SiteWise**, which is a managed service that collects, structures, and searches IoT data from industrial equipment and processes. SiteWise analyzes data from multiple IoT devices and sensors to identify anomalies and trends that may indicate potential issues or opportunities for optimization.

To implement a continuous monitoring solution on AWS for IoT networks, organizations must define their monitoring requirements and establish KPIs to measure system performance. Essential KPIs might include network latency, device uptime, data throughput, and error rates, which are critical for ensuring the reliability and efficiency of IoT operations. Monitoring these KPIs helps in identifying performance bottlenecks and potential security threats. Organizations should also set up alerts and notifications to alert relevant personnel when certain KPIs or metrics fall outside predefined thresholds. Dashboards and visualization tools such as **AWS QuickSight** can provide real-time visibility into system performance and health, when customized to display relevant metrics and KPIs. These dashboards can be shared with stakeholders to ensure that everyone has a comprehensive view of system performance.

Lastly, organizations must establish processes for continuous improvement, regularly reviewing and analyzing monitoring data to identify opportunities for optimization and enhancement. By continually refining their monitoring strategies, organizations can ensure that their IoT networks remain performant, reliable, and secure over time on AWS. We can see how one such example is done on AWS in *Figure 9.2*:

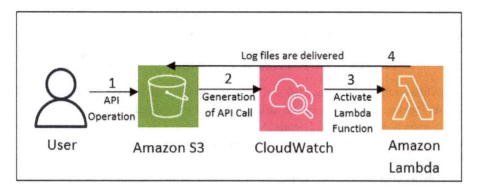

Figure 9.2 – Workflow for monitoring and logging

The example outlines how one such workflow can proceed, described as follows:

1. **User API operation**: The process begins with a user performing an API operation.

2. **Amazon S3**: The result of the API operation leads to the generation of an API call, which is then stored in Amazon S3. Amazon S3 is a scalable object storage service where users can store and retrieve data.

3. **CloudWatch**: AWS CloudWatch detects the log file or event in Amazon S3. CloudWatch is a monitoring and observability service that provides insights into resources, applications, and services running on AWS.

4. **Amazon Lambda activation**: In response to the detection of the log file by CloudWatch, an AWS Lambda function is activated. Once the Lambda function is activated, it processes the log files and carries out any defined operations, such as notifications, analysis, or other actions.

Now, we can move ahead to see how automation and machine learning can be performed as part of the monitoring that is done.

Automation and machine learning in monitoring

Automation and machine learning are important aspects of keeping IoT networks running smoothly and securely. With the help of AWS tools and services, organizations can implement these capabilities to identify and predict issues before they happen and take necessary actions automatically to prevent downtime and performance issues.

One useful tool for automation and machine learning on AWS is **Amazon SageMaker**. This is a service that allows developers and data scientists to build, train, and deploy machine learning models quickly and easily. By analyzing and predicting IoT devices and network behavior, SageMaker can automatically identify potential issues and trigger necessary actions.

AWS IoT Events is another helpful tool for automation and machine learning on AWS. It is a service that allows organizations to detect and respond to events from multiple IoT devices and applications in real time. This service can automate the detection and resolution of common IoT devices and network issues, improving the overall reliability of the system and reducing the need for manual intervention.

AWS also provides a range of data analytics and processing tools, such as **AWS Glue**, **AWS Lambda**, and **AWS Data Pipeline**. These tools can be used to automate the collection, processing, and analysis of IoT data. By identifying patterns and trends in IoT data, these tools can trigger automated responses when specific conditions are met. To implement automation and machine learning capabilities on AWS for IoT networks, organizations should first define their monitoring requirements and establish KPIs to measure system performance. They should also develop machine learning models and algorithms to analyze and predict IoT devices and network behavior and automate the detection and resolution of common issues.

Organizations can use dashboards and visualization tools, such as AWS QuickSight, to provide real-time visibility into system performance and health. These dashboards can be customized to show relevant metrics and KPIs and can be shared with relevant stakeholders to ensure everyone has a comprehensive view of system performance.

By continually reviewing and analyzing monitoring data, organizations can identify opportunities for optimization and enhancement. This process of continuous improvement ensures that their automation and machine learning strategies remain effective over time, keeping their IoT networks reliable and secure.

Exercise on simulating monitoring networks

In this exercise, we will be looking at simulating an IoT network with AWS IoT Core and monitoring it through the tools provided by the service. Here are the steps to follow along:

1. Log in to the AWS Management Console and navigate to the AWS IoT Core dashboard.
2. Click on the **Test** menu and select **Simulator** to access the AWS IoT Simulator.
3. Click on **Create a new simulation** to create a new simulation model.
4. Enter a name for the simulation model and click on **Create** to create the model.
5. Click on **Add a device** to add a new virtual device to the simulation model.
6. Enter a name for the device and select a device type from the drop-down list.
7. Enter the device's metadata, including the device ID, device attributes, and device shadow state.
8. Click on **Add a behavior** to add a behavior to the device. A behavior is a script that simulates the device's behavior and generates messages that are sent to AWS IoT Core.

9. Enter the behavior's name, type, and script code. The script can be written in JavaScript or Python.

10. Click on **Add a topic** to add a topic that the device will publish messages to.

11. Enter the topic name and click on **Add** to add the topic.

12. Click on **Run** to start the simulation.

13. Monitor the simulation metrics and logs in the **Simulation** tab. You can view the number of messages sent and received, the message throughput, and the behavior logs for each device.

14. Add additional devices, behaviors, and topics to simulate a more complex IoT network.

With the knowledge of how to simulate the monitoring of networks, we can forge ahead to understand the metrics that can affect how we configure them.

Setting KPIs and the metrics for success

It is important to understand why you are conducting the monitoring that you are doing, and the appropriate milestones for managing its progress. In this section, we will look into how we can set clear objectives and appropriately define KPIs to measure how well we are progressing.

Setting clear objectives and goals for monitoring

Setting clear objectives and goals is an important step in implementing a successful continuous monitoring strategy for IoT networks. Organizations should identify the specific metrics and KPIs they want to track and establish thresholds for acceptable performance levels. This will allow them to quickly identify any issues that may arise and take corrective action before they cause significant disruptions to their networks.

Some common objectives and goals for continuous monitoring in IoT networks include the following:

- **Improving network reliability**: Organizations may set objectives to reduce downtime and improve overall network uptime. This could include monitoring key network components and identifying potential issues before they cause disruptions.

- **Enhancing security**: Security is a critical concern for IoT networks, and organizations may set goals to ensure that their networks are protected from potential cyber threats. This could include monitoring network traffic and identifying anomalous behavior that may indicate a security breach.

- **Optimizing network performance**: Organizations may set objectives to improve the overall performance of their IoT networks, such as reducing latency or improving throughput. This could involve monitoring network traffic and identifying areas where improvements could be made.

- **Minimizing operational costs**: Organizations may set goals to reduce operational costs associated with managing their IoT networks. This could involve identifying inefficiencies in their networks and automating processes to reduce the need for manual intervention.

Once objectives and goals have been established, organizations should identify the specific metrics and KPIs that will be used to measure performance. For example, if the goal is to improve network reliability, organizations may track metrics such as network uptime, response time, and error rates. These metrics should be tracked continuously and compared against predefined thresholds to identify any potential issues.

In addition to defining metrics and KPIs, organizations should also establish processes for reviewing and analyzing monitoring data to identify opportunities for optimization and improvement. This may involve using visualization tools such as dashboards and reports to gain insights into network performance and identify areas where improvements can be made.

Different types of KPIs

There are different types of KPIs that can be used to monitor IoT networks. There are five categories of KPIs that they can fall under: device-level, network-level, user-level, security, and business-level.

Device-level KPIs

These KPIs measure the performance and health of individual IoT devices and include their availability, response time, and error rates. By monitoring these KPIs, organizations can identify devices that are not functioning properly and take corrective actions to prevent downtime.

Network-level KPIs

These KPIs measure the overall performance and health of the IoT network and include network latency, packet loss, and throughput. By monitoring these KPIs, organizations can identify potential network bottlenecks and take corrective actions to ensure smooth network operation.

User-level KPIs

These KPIs measure the user experience of IoT applications and services and include response time and availability. By monitoring these KPIs, organizations can ensure that end users are satisfied with the performance of IoT applications and services.

Security KPIs

These KPIs measure the effectiveness of security controls in place to protect IoT devices and data and include the number of security incidents, the severity of incidents, and the time to resolution. By monitoring these KPIs, organizations can identify potential security threats and take corrective actions to prevent them.

Business-level KPIs

These KPIs measure the business impact of the IoT network and include revenue generated, cost savings, and customer satisfaction. By monitoring these KPIs, organizations can understand the overall value of their IoT networks and identify opportunities for improvement.

Selecting, analyzing, and monitoring KPIs

Selecting, analyzing, and monitoring KPIs is an essential step in implementing an effective continuous monitoring strategy for IoT networks. Here are some steps to follow to ensure that KPIs are selected, analyzed, and monitored effectively:

1. **Identify your objectives**: Before selecting KPIs, it is important to identify your monitoring objectives. This involves understanding what you want to achieve with your monitoring program and what metrics will help you track progress toward those objectives.

2. **Choose relevant KPIs**: Once you have identified your objectives, choose KPIs that are relevant to your objectives. Ensure that the KPIs are **specific, measurable, achievable, relevant, and time-bound (SMART)**.

3. **Analyze the KPIs**: Analyze the selected KPIs to ensure that they provide the necessary insights into the performance and health of the IoT network. Use data analysis tools to identify trends and patterns in the KPI data and gain insights into areas that may require improvement.

4. **Monitor the KPIs**: Implement a system for monitoring the KPIs continuously. This can be achieved using tools such as AWS CloudWatch or other monitoring tools. Set up alerts and notifications to inform relevant personnel when certain KPIs or metrics fall outside predefined thresholds.

5. **Regularly review and adjust KPIs**: Regularly review and adjust your KPIs to ensure that they remain relevant and aligned with your monitoring objectives. This involves regularly analyzing KPI data and using the insights gained to refine KPIs as necessary.

Now that we've learned how to use KPIs, we can look to understand the different monitoring capabilities that are present both on-premises and on the cloud.

Monitoring capabilities on-premises and on the cloud

Monitoring capabilities are certainly an aspect that is crucial to understanding the limits of how far we can go within what we invest in our solutions. In this section, we will look at how some monitoring capabilities can be taken into consideration in designing our IoT networks.

Monitoring for security purposes

Monitoring IoT networks for security purposes is critical to ensure that the devices and data are protected from cyber threats. AWS offers a range of tools and services to help organizations monitor the security of their IoT networks.

One key tool for security monitoring on AWS is **Amazon GuardDuty**, a threat detection service that continuously monitors for malicious activity and unauthorized behavior across AWS accounts and workloads. GuardDuty can be used to detect and respond to potential security threats in real time and can alert relevant personnel when suspicious activity is detected.

Another important tool for security monitoring on AWS is **AWS IoT Device Defender**, a managed service that audits and monitors the security of IoT devices and applications. Device Defender can be used to detect and respond to security threats by monitoring device behavior, identifying anomalies, and triggering alerts when suspicious activity is detected.

AWS also offers a range of **identity and access management** (**IAM**) tools, including **AWS IAM** and **AWS Single Sign-On** (**AWS SSO**), which can be used to control and manage user access to IoT devices and data. IAM and SSO can be used to set permissions, enable multi-factor authentication, and enforce policies to ensure that only authorized personnel can access sensitive data.

To implement an effective security monitoring solution on AWS for IoT networks, organizations should first identify their security requirements and establish key security metrics to measure system performance. They should also establish security policies and procedures to govern access control, vulnerability management, incident response, and other security-related activities.

Organizations should also leverage security monitoring tools and services, such as GuardDuty and Device Defender, to continuously monitor for security threats and vulnerabilities. They should regularly review and analyze security logs and audit trails to identify potential security issues and opportunities for improvement.

Outside of AWS, there are many solutions that help with monitoring IoT deployments as well. It starts with doing an analysis of network traffic. Tools such as **Wireshark** or **tcpdump** can be employed for packet sniffing and network traffic analysis, providing insights into potential malicious activities or unauthorized data transmission. In terms of mitigating risks, endpoint security solutions such as antivirus software, **intrusion prevention systems** (**IPSs**), or **advanced threat protection** (**ATP**) services can be used to safeguard IoT devices. These solutions help in identifying and mitigating malware, ransomware, and other forms of cyberattacks targeting IoT endpoints.

Finally, organizations should establish processes for continuous improvement, regularly reviewing and updating their security monitoring strategies to ensure that they remain effective and up-to-date. By continually refining their security monitoring strategies, organizations can ensure that their IoT networks remain secure and protected from cyber threats.

Creating a unified monitoring solution

Creating a unified monitoring solution for an IoT network that includes both on-premises and cloud-based resources can be challenging, but is essential for ensuring comprehensive visibility and control over the entire network. Fortunately, AWS provides a range of tools and services that can be used to create unified monitoring solutions for IoT networks.

One key tool for creating a unified monitoring solution is AWS IoT SiteWise, which can collect, structure, and search IoT data from industrial equipment and processes across on-premises and cloud-based resources. SiteWise enables organizations to standardize and normalize data from disparate sources, making it easier to analyze and monitor the health and performance of entire networks.

Another important tool for creating a unified monitoring solution is **AWS Systems Manager**, a management service that enables an organization to automate operational tasks and manage on-premises and cloud-based resources from a single console. Systems Manager can be used to monitor system health and performance, track compliance with security and regulatory requirements, and automate responses to common issues.

To create a unified monitoring solution for IoT networks, organizations should first define their monitoring requirements and establish clear objectives and goals for the monitoring solution. They should also identify the KPIs that will be used to measure system performance and health and develop plans for monitoring those KPIs across all on-premises and cloud-based resources.

Organizations should leverage AWS CloudFormation or AWS Control Tower to automate the deployment and management of monitoring resources across both on-premises and cloud-based environments. CloudFormation enables organizations to create and manage a collection of related AWS resources, while Control Tower provides a pre-configured environment that includes best practices for security and compliance.

There are many tools that are used in conjunction with AWS to achieve such a centralized way of monitoring our resources. SIEM platforms, such as Splunk or IBM QRadar, offer this kind of integrated approach. They aggregate and analyze log data from various sources within the IoT ecosystem, helping in detecting, analyzing, and responding to security incidents and threats.

Finally, organizations should leverage dashboards and visualization tools, such as AWS QuickSight, to provide real-time visibility into system performance and health across on-premises and cloud-based resources. Dashboards can be customized to display relevant metrics and KPIs and can be shared with relevant stakeholders to ensure that everyone has a comprehensive view of system performance. By creating a unified monitoring solution for IoT networks, an organization can gain comprehensive visibility and control over its entire network, making it easier to detect and respond to potential issues before they become critical problems. An example of how such a solution has been utilized is with Philips. Philips has effectively harnessed the power of AWS to revolutionize its approach to healthcare technology. It has established a notable presence in the digital healthcare sphere with its **HealthSuite Digital Platform**, developed on AWS. This platform has been transformative in streamlining patient monitoring remotely, efficiently managing a range of devices through cloud connectivity, and unifying diverse healthcare data for more coherent analysis. This strategic move has not only sped up the introduction of new healthcare technologies but has also ensured adherence to critical security regulations.

Additionally, Philips has made significant strides in the field of medical imaging diagnostics by leveraging **artificial intelligence** (**AI**) and **machine learning** through AWS services. The HealthSuite specifically targets the complexities involved in medical imaging data analysis. It serves as a comprehensive platform that aggregates various forms of data, including patient records and readings from wearable technology. This integration, facilitated by AWS IoT Core and Amazon SageMaker, empowers Philips to handle a vast network of IoT devices and extract valuable insights for clinical use. These innovations by Philips are a testament to the importance of the power of having a unified monitoring solution in organizations and how much it contributes to growth.

Practical – operating and monitoring a joke creator with IoT Greengrass

In this exercise, we will walk through the process of creating an AWS IoT Greengrass group for edge computing. We will start by creating a new AWS IoT Greengrass group and configuring its core settings. Next, we will create a device definition and add it to the group, along with the Lambda functions and subscriptions needed for edge processing. Finally, we will deploy the AWS IoT Greengrass group to our local devices and verify that it is working as expected.

By the end of this exercise, you will have a solid understanding of how to set up an AWS IoT Greengrass group for edge computing and how to deploy it to your local devices. You will be able to leverage this knowledge to build powerful and scalable IoT applications that can process data locally and communicate with the cloud in a seamless and efficient manner.

Setting up your OpenAI account

To start off with the practical, we will need to set up our OpenAI account, which will allow us to then use ChatGPT. The following steps will guide you through doing this:

1. Sign up on OpenAI's website:

    I.   Go to OpenAI's website.

    II.   Click on the **Sign Up** or **Get Started** button.

    III. Fill out your information including your name, email, and password.

    IV.   Accept the terms and conditions and submit the form.

2. Confirm your email:

    I.   After you have signed up, OpenAI will send you a verification email.

    II. Open the email and click on the verification link. This will verify your account and allow you to continue the process.

3. Get your API key:

    I.   Navigate to the OpenAI website at `https://platform.openai.com/`.

    II. Click on your account on the top right and click on **View API Keys**.

    III. You will find the API key creation page here. Click on **Create new secret key**, copy the API key, and save it for later.

Remember to keep your API key safe and do not share it with anyone. Treat it like a password, as anyone who has it can make API requests under your account and you will be charged for them.

Finally, always make sure that the way you're using OpenAI's API follows its usage policies. If it determines that your usage is not in compliance, it may disable your API key.

Spinning up an Amazon EC2 instance

Now, we will need to create an EC2 instance to act as the intermediary of where we are going to call the ChatGPT API from:

1. Log in to the **AWS Management Console**: Access the AWS Management Console at `https://aws.amazon.com/console/` and sign in with your AWS account.

2. Go to the Amazon EC2 dashboard: Click on **Services** at the top of the page and search for EC2 under **Compute** to go to the Amazon EC2 dashboard.

3. Create a new instance: Click on the **Instances** link in the left-side menu. Then click the **Launch Instance** button.

4. Choose an **Amazon Machine Image** (**AMI**): You will see a list of available AMIs. Select the **Amazon Linux 2 AMI (HVM)** option. This is a general-purpose Linux instance that is maintained by AWS.

5. Choose an instance type: On the next page, select an instance type that fits your requirements. For this practical, you can start with a small instance type, such as `t2.micro`, which is eligible for the free tier. Click **Next: Configure Instance Details**.

6. Configure instance details: You can leave most options at their default settings. However, be sure to select the appropriate VPC and subnet, if necessary. Enable **Auto-assign Public IP** if you want AWS to assign a public IP address to your instance for remote access.

7. Add storage: Click **Next: Add Storage**. By default, Amazon Linux instances come with 8 GB of root volume. You can adjust this according to your needs.

8. Add tags: Click **Next: Add Tags**. You can assign key-value pairs as tags to your instance. This is optional but can help you manage your AWS resources.

9. Configure security group: Click **Next: Configure Security Group**. You can create a new security group or assign an existing one. At a minimum, you should allow SSH access (`port 22`) from your IP address for remote management of your instance.

10. Review and launch: Click **Next: Review and Launch**. Review your instance configuration. If everything is satisfactory, click **Launch**.

11. Key pair: A pop-up window will ask you to select an existing key pair or create a new one. This key pair is used to SSH into your instance. If you create a new one, be sure to download it and keep it secure.

12. Launch instance: Click **Launch Instance** after selecting your key pair. Your instance will now be launched.

13. Now you can SSH into your instance by clicking on the instance ID at the top of the page and clicking **Connect**. Navigate to the **EC2 Instance Connect** pane, choose **Connect Using EC2 Instance Connect**, and click on **Connect**.

With that, we have spun up the EC2 instance we need and connected to it. Now, we are ready to configure AWS Greengrass on it to simulate our IoT thing.

Configure AWS Greengrass on Amazon EC2

Now, we can set up AWS Greengrass on our Amazon EC2 to be able to simulate our IoT Thing, which will fetch the ChatGPT API along with its responses accordingly:

1. Run the following command to update the necessary dependencies:

```
$ sudo yum update
```

2. Run the following command to install Python, pip, and boto3:

```
$ sudo yum install python && sudo yum install pip && sudo yum
install boto3
```

3. Now, we will install the AWS IoT Greengrass software with automatic provisioning. First, we will need to install the Java runtime as Amazon Corretto 11:

```
$ sudo dnf install java-11-amazon-corretto -y
```

Run this command afterward to verify that Java is installed successfully:

```
$ java -version
```

4. Establish the default system user and group that operate components on the gadget. Optionally, you can delegate the task of creating this user and group to the AWS IoT Greengrass Core software installer during the installation process by utilizing the --component-default-user installer parameter. For additional details, refer to the section on installer arguments. The commands you need to run are as follows.

```
$ sudo useradd --system --create-home ggc_user
$ sudo groupadd --system ggc_group
```

5. Ensure that the user executing the AWS IoT Greengrass Core software, usually the root user, has the necessary privileges to execute sudo commands as any user and any group. Use the following command to access the /etc/sudoers file:

```
$ sudo visudo
```

Ensure that the user permission looks like the following:

```
root     ALL=(ALL:ALL) ALL
```

6. Now, you will need to provide the access key ID and secret access key for the IAM user in your AWS account to be used from the EC2 environment. Use the following commands to provide these credentials:

```
$ export AWS_ACCESS_KEY_ID={Insert your Access Key ID here}
$ export AWS_SECRET_ACCESS_KEY={Insert your secret access key here}
```

7. On your primary device, retrieve the AWS IoT Greengrass Core software and save it as a file named greengrass-nucleus-latest.zip:

```
$ curl -s https://d2s8p88vqu9w66.cloudfront.net/releases/
greengrass-nucleus-latest.zip > greengrass-nucleus-latest.zip
```

8. Decompress the AWS IoT Greengrass Core software into a directory on your device. Substitute GreengrassInstaller with the name of your desired folder:

```
$ unzip greengrass-nucleus-latest.zip -d GreengrassInstaller &&
rm greengrass-nucleus-latest.zip
```

9. We now can install the AWS IoT Greengrass Core software. Replace the values as follows:

A. /greengrass/v2 or C:\greengrass\v2: This location specifies where you plan to install the AWS IoT Greengrass Core software on your system, serving as the primary directory for the application.

B. GreengrassInstaller: This term refers to the directory where you have unpacked the installation files for the AWS IoT Greengrass Core software.

C. `region`: This is the specific geographical area within AWS where your resources will be provisioned and managed.

D. `MyGreengrassCore`: This label is used to identify your Greengrass core device as a `thing` within AWS IoT. Should this *thing* not be present already, the installation process will generate it and retrieve the necessary certificates to establish its identity.

E. `MyGreengrassCoreGroup`: This refers to the collective grouping of AWS IoT things that your Greengrass core device is part of. In the absence of this group, the installation process is designed to create it and enroll your *thing* within it. If the group is pre-existing and actively deploying, the core device will proceed to pull and initiate the deployment's software.

F. `GreengrassV2IoTThingPolicy`: This is the identifier for the AWS IoT policy that facilitates the interaction of Greengrass core devices with AWS IoT services. Lacking this policy, the installation will automatically generate one with comprehensive permissions under this name, which you can later restrict as needed.

G. `GreengrassV2TokenExchangeRole`: This is the identifier for the IAM role that allows Greengrass core devices to secure temporary AWS credentials. In the event that this role is not pre-established, the installation will create it and assign the `GreengrassV2TokenExchangeRoleAccess` policy to it.

H. `GreengrassCoreTokenExchangeRoleAlias`: This alias pertains to the IAM role that grants Greengrass core devices the ability to request temporary credentials in the future. Should this alias not be in existence, the installation process will set it up and link it to the IAM role you provide.

The following is the command you will need to run and have the values within replaced:

```
$ sudo -E java -Droot="/greengrass/v2" -Dlog.store=FILE \
-jar ./GreengrassInstaller/lib/Greengrass.jar \
--aws-region region \
--thing-name MyGreengrassCore \
--thing-group-name MyGreengrassCoreGroup \
--thing-policy-name GreengrassV2IoTThingPolicy \
--tes-role-name GreengrassV2TokenExchangeRole \
--tes-role-alias-name GreengrassCoreTokenExchangeRoleAlias \
--component-default-user ggc_user:ggc_group \
--provision true \
--setup-system-service true
```

10. Now, navigate to the root of the EC2 instance and create a file called `script.py` with the following command:

```
$ sudo vi script.py
```

11. Write the following in the script, replacing the AWS access key, secret access key, and OpenAI API key with your own values:

```python
import json
import openai
import boto3
import time
from datetime import datetime

# Initialize AWS IoT client
def create_aws_iot_client():
    iot_client = boto3.client('iot-data', region_name='{ENTER_
YOUR_AWS_REGION_HERE}', aws_access_key_id='{ENTER_YOUR_ACCESS_
KEY_HERE}', aws_secret_access_key='ENTER_YOUR_SECRET_ACCESS_KEY_
HERE')   # replace 'ap-southeast-2' with your AWS region
    return iot_client


# Initialize OpenAI client
def interact_with_chatgpt(prompt):
    openai.api_key = '{ENTER_OPENAI_API_KEY_HERE}'
    response = openai.Completion.create(
        engine="text-davinci-002",
        prompt=prompt,
        temperature=0.5,
        max_tokens=100
    )

    return response.choices[0].text.strip()


def publish_to_aws_iot_topic(iot_client, topic, message):
    # Convert the message into a JSON object
    json_message = json.dumps({"message": message})
    return iot_client.publish(
        topic=topic,
        qos=0,
        payload=json_message
    )


def main():
    prompt = "Tell a joke of the day"
    topic = "sensor/chat1"

    iot_client = create_aws_iot_client()

    while True:
```

```
        chatgpt_response = interact_with_chatgpt(prompt)
        publish_response = publish_to_aws_iot_topic(iot_client,
topic, chatgpt_response)
        print(f"{datetime.now()}: Published message to AWS IoT
topic: {topic}")
        time.sleep(300)   # pause for 5 minutes


if __name__ == "__main__":
    main()
```

Save the file and quit the vim editor.

12. Navigate to the AWS IoT page in the AWS Management Console. Go to **MQTT test client**.

13. Click on **Subscribe to a Topic** and input `sensor/chat1` into the topic filter. Click on **Subscribe**.

14. If you look in the **Subscriptions** window at the bottom of the page, you can see the topic open. Now, navigate back to the EC2 window and run the following command:

```
$ python script.py
```

15. You should now see there is a new message under the topic. You will see a joke being written there, and one being generated every five minutes (or any other duration of time, depending on what you specified).

With that, we have configured AWS Greengrass on the EC2. Now, we can look at monitoring the EC2 in terms of how it publishes messages.

Monitoring the EC2 *Thing* when publishing messages

Now, we can start monitoring how the Thing is doing in publishing messages through Amazon CloudWatch:

1. Navigate to **Services**, search for **CloudWatch**, and click on it.

2. Click on **All Metrics** under the **Metrics** menu in the left pane.

3. Navigate to **IoT** -> **Protocol Metrics** and click on the checkbox for the **PublishIn.Success** metric. You will see the metrics that have been published successfully being reflected on the graph that is shown on the page.

Hence, you've created your first Greengrass solution with monitoring based on it!

Creating an AWS IoT Greengrass group for edge computing is a useful exercise to test and validate different edge computing scenarios. By using Greengrass core components such as Lambda functions, connectors, and machine learning models, you can gain practical experience in developing and deploying edge computing solutions that process and analyze IoT data locally, without the need for cloud connectivity. You can also use the AWS IoT Greengrass dashboard to monitor and manage the Greengrass group and its components, set up alerts and notifications, and troubleshoot issues as they arise.

Now, upload the code to GitHub and see whether you can also answer the following questions, based on your hardware/code for further understanding and practice on the concepts that you have learned through this practical:

- Can you also try to connect the data to Prometheus?

- Can you recreate a similar setup but with EC2s as the devices?

> **Important note**
>
> When working with different kinds of monitoring tools, concepts will often be similar between one program and the next. This is the reason why we ask you to try out different monitoring software on your own as well. Within industrial cases, you will also find that many types of monitoring tools are used, depending on the preferences of the firm and its use cases.

Summary

In this chapter, we explored the best practices for operating and monitoring IoT networks. We discussed the importance of continuous operation, setting KPIs and metrics for success, and monitoring capabilities both on-premises and in the cloud using AWS IoT services. We also looked at several practical exercises that can be used to gain hands-on experience in operating and monitoring IoT networks. These included simulating IoT networks using virtualization, developing AWS Lambda functions to process and analyze IoT data, creating AWS CloudWatch dashboards for IoT metrics, setting up AWS IoT Greengrass groups for edge computing, and using the AWS IoT simulator to test different operating and monitoring strategies.

By learning and applying these best practices and practical exercises, students can develop the skills and knowledge necessary to design, deploy, and manage robust and reliable IoT networks. They will gain experience in using AWS IoT services and tools to monitor and analyze IoT data, set up alerts and notifications, and troubleshoot issues as they arise. Ultimately, they will be well-equipped to meet the challenges of operating and monitoring IoT networks in a variety of real-world scenarios.

In the next chapter, we will be looking at working with data and analytics within IoT with services on AWS.

Further reading

For more information about what was covered in this chapter, please refer to the following links:

- Learn more about data lakes and analytics relating to managing big data on AWS: `https://aws.amazon.com/big-data/datalakes-and-analytics/`

- Understand more on how to use Grafana through its official documentation: `https://grafana.com/docs/grafana/latest/`

- Explore further on AWS IoT Greengrass through its official documentation: `https://docs.aws.amazon.com/greengrass/index.html`

- Learn more about different analytics-based deployments through AWS' official whitepapers: `https://docs.aws.amazon.com/whitepapers/latest/aws-overview/analytics.html`

- Learn more on different analytics solutions provided by AWS: `https://aws.amazon.com/solutions/analytics/`

10
Working with Data and Analytics

Managing data and performing analytics on it is a crucial aspect of any **Internet of Things (IoT)** deployment. It allows you to gain insights based on the large amounts of data generated by IoT devices and make appropriate decisions based on data to improve operations, increase efficiency, and reduce costs. With **Amazon Web Services (AWS)** and other cloud providers, there are a variety of services that you can use to analyze and visualize data that you have obtained from your IoT devices, from simple data storage and retrieval options that you can configure without much difficulty to more complex analytics and **machine learning (ML)** tools, which you may have to learn and fine-tune, that you perform as part of the analysis.

Often, data analytics is the piece of the puzzle that completes the picture that we are trying to architect with our IoT networks, as even with edge networks in which we process data on the edge nodes to reduce costs, there is usually always further processing and storage that we want to perform when the data reaches the cloud. We want to do so while still optimizing based on the options that we have within AWS and looking further into how we can adhere to best practices within AWS' Well-Architected Framework to make the best use of our resources. The link to the framework can be found at the end of the chapter.

In this chapter, we're going to cover the following main topics:

- Introduction to data analysis at scale
- Analysis on the cloud and outside
- Practical – smart home insights with AWS IoT Analytics
- Industrial data analytics
- Practical – creating a data pipeline for end-to-end data ingestion and analysis

Technical requirements

This chapter will require you to have the following software installed

- Arduino IDE
- AWS account

We will be running our programs on Python and have a bit of **Structured Query Language** (**SQL**) syntax, a standardized programming language used for managing and manipulating relational databases, that we need to use as part of querying data in this chapter; again, don't worry if you don't understand some of the code — we will walk you through it and get you down to understanding how each part of the code works in no time.

You can access the GitHub folder for the code that is used in this chapter at `https://github.com/PacktPublishing/IoT-Made-Easy-for-Beginners/tree/main/Chapter10`.

Introduction to data analysis at scale

Data analysis is often done at scale to analyze large sets of data using the capabilities of cloud computing services such as AWS. Designing a workflow for the data analysis to follow is the pivotal starting point for this to be performed. This will follow five main categories: collection, storage, processing, visualization, and data security.

In this section, we will be introducing you to data analysis on AWS, discussing which services we can use as part of AWS to perform the data analytics workloads we need it to, and walking through the best practices that are part of this. We will understand how to design and incorporate workflows into the IoT network that we currently have and work with it to better power our capabilities.

Data analysis on AWS

Data analysis on AWS can be summarized in five main steps. These steps can be seen in the following diagram:

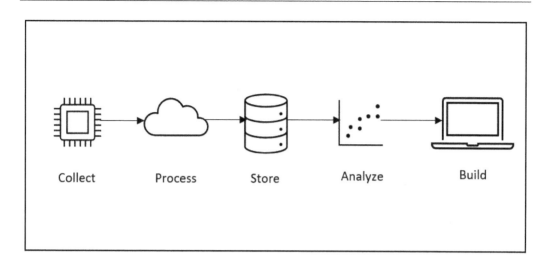

Figure 10.1 – Data analysis workflow on AWS

Let's look at the steps in more detail:

1. **Collect**: In this phase, data is collected from the devices within the environment. Services that are usually in charge of this include AWS IoT Core and AWS IoT Greengrass, which collects the data and ingests it into the cloud.

2. **Process**: Data can then be processed according to how the configuration is set up for it. Services such as AWS IoT Analytics are made for this purpose.

3. **Store**: Data can then be stored, either temporarily or for long-term storage. This can be done on services such as Amazon **Simple Storage Service** (**S3**), Amazon Redshift, and Amazon DocumentDB.

4. **Analyze**: Data will then be analyzed. Services such as AWS Glue and Amazon **Elastic MapReduce** (**EMR**) can be used for this purpose, while also potentially performing more complex analytics and ML tasks as necessary.

5. **Build**: We can then build datasets using this data, making patterns from the processed data that we have received from the workloads that are run.

With that, we have understood the different steps of how a typical data analysis workflow would go at a high level. Now, we can look at the different services in AWS that help facilitate this.

AWS services

Several important services can be used for data processing workloads. These five services are just a few of them, and there are definitely more that can be mentioned and that we encourage you to have a look at. For more information on this, you can refer to the documentation that is linked in the *Further reading* section at the end of the chapter.

AWS IoT Analytics

AWS IoT Analytics is a service that is used to collect, process, and analyze data that is obtained from IoT devices. You can process and analyze large datasets from IoT devices with the help of IoT Analytics without the need for complex infrastructure or programming. You can apply mathematical and statistical models to your data to make sense of it and make better decisions accordingly. You can also integrate it with many other services from AWS, such as Amazon S3 or Amazon QuickSight, to perform further analytical and visualization workloads.

The following are components of IoT Analytics that are crucial for you to know that we will be using as we go through our exercise within the next subsection:

- **Channel**: A channel is used to collect data from a select **Message Queuing Telemetry Transport (MQTT)** topic and archive unprocessed messages before the data is published to the pipeline. You can either use this or send messages to the channel directly through the `BatchPutMessage` API. Messages that are unprocessed will be stored within an S3 bucket that will be managed either by you or AWS IoT Analytics.

- **Pipeline**: Pipelines consume messages that come from a channel and allow you to process the messages before then storing them within a data store. The pipeline activities then perform the necessary transformations on the messages that you have, such as renaming, adding message attributes, or filtering messages based on attribute values.

- **Data store**: Pipelines then store the processed messages within a data store, which is a repository of messages that can be queried. It is important to make the distinction between this and a database as it is not a database but is more like a temporary repository. Multiple data stores can be provisioned for messages that come from different devices or locations, or you can have them filtered by their message attributes depending on how you configure your pipeline along with its requirements. The data store's processed messages will also be stored within an S3 bucket that can be managed either by you or AWS IoT Analytics.

- **Dataset**: Data is retrieved from a data store and made into a dataset. IoT Analytics allows you to create a SQL dataset or a container dataset. You can further explore insights in your dataset through integration with Amazon QuickSight or Jupyter Notebook. Jupyter Notebook is an open source web application that allows you to create and share documents containing live code, equations, visualizations, and narrative text, and is often used for data cleaning and transformation, numerical simulation, statistical modeling, data visualization, and ML. You can also send the contents of a dataset to an S3 bucket, allowing you to then enable integration with existing data lakes or in-house applications that you may have to perform further analysis and visualization. You can also send the contents to AWS IoT Events to trigger certain actions if there are failures or changes in operation.

- **SQL dataset**: An SQL dataset is like the view that would be had from a materialized view of an SQL database. You can create SQL datasets by applying an SQL action.

- **Trigger**: A trigger is a component you can specify to create a dataset automatically. It can be a time interval or based on when the content of another dataset has been created.

With an understanding of these components, we can look at other services that we will also come across in our practical exercises.

Amazon QuickSight

Amazon QuickSight is a **business intelligence** (**BI**) tool that allows you to easily create, analyze, and visualize data. You can connect to various data sources such as databases and cloud storage, and accordingly create interactive dashboards and reports to gain insights based on the data. This way, you can quickly identify patterns and trends and understand your data to make data-driven decisions. You can also integrate it with other AWS services such as IoT Analytics for more powerful data analysis.

Amazon S3

Amazon S3 is a cloud storage service that allows you to store and retrieve large amounts of data, including photos, files, videos, and more. You can integrate it with other AWS services to create powerful data management and analytics solutions, while also being affordable, providing you scalability as your data storage needs grow.

Amazon CloudWatch

Amazon CloudWatch is a service that allows you to monitor and manage your resources and applications that are based on AWS. You can collect and track metrics, monitor log files, and set alarms that trigger certain actions based on your resources to save you the time of manually doing so. You can also use it to monitor the health of your applications and receive notifications if there are any issues.

Amazon SNS

Amazon **Simple Notification Service** (**SNS**) is a messaging service that allows applications to send and receive messages and notifications, allowing a large number of recipients to send and receive messages with just a few clicks. It is widely used for sending notifications, updates, and alerts to users, customers, or other systems. These notifications can be directed to text, email, or other services that you have on AWS.

Now that we understand the various of different services that can be used as part of our data analysis workloads, let's start looking at third-party services and create data workflows within the cloud that can utilize the services that we have discussed in this section.

Analysis on the cloud and outside

When working with data, it often is necessary to visualize data to gain insights and make informed decisions. With services such as Amazon QuickSight, you are able to do this and create interactive dashboards and reports. However, some organizations' requirements may necessitate the use of third-party services alongside AWS' native tools.

Many third-party services can be used. In this section, we will discuss some of these third-party services, alongside how we can start architecting workloads within the cloud for data workflows and quickly ensure that they adhere to best practices, both when creating and evaluating them.

Third-party data services

In this section, we will talk about two different third-party data analytics and visualization services: **Datadog** and **Prometheus**.

Datadog

Datadog is a cloud-based monitoring and analytics platform that provides many features for monitoring and troubleshooting many aspects of an organization's IT infrastructure and applications. It allows for real-time data collection and monitoring from various sources, including servers, containers, and cloud services. Key features include cloud infrastructure monitoring, application performance monitoring, log management trace analysis, and its integration with many services such as AWS, Kubernetes, and Jira, allowing users to collect and analyze data within one location.

Prometheus

Prometheus is an open source monitoring and alerting system that is designed for data collection and analysis. It is appropriate to be used for monitoring and analyzing large numbers of servers alongside other types of infrastructure. It is based on a pull-based model, which means that it will periodically scrape metrics from predefined endpoints. This allows for data collection to be done accurately and efficiently and provides the ability to scale horizontally to accommodate a large number of servers.

Its data model is based on the concept of metrics and labels, allowing for powerful querying and aggregation of data. It also includes a built-in alerting system, allowing alerts to be created based on queries that are made on it. This allows for notifications to be made automatically. It can also be used in conjunction with other data visualization tools such as Grafana to create interactive dashboards that can provide real-time insights into the performance of systems and infrastructure. This is especially useful in the context of IoT deployments, where it is critical to identify and troubleshoot issues.

Designing AWS flow diagrams with data analysis

It is important to understand the steps that have to be taken to design data analysis workloads before going forward with the implementation. The following is a seven-step process for designing these data analysis workloads:

1. **Identify your data sources**: You will need to start by identifying the data sources that you will need to collect and analyze. This may include data from your IoT devices, sensor data, log files, and other data sources that may be relevant.

2. **Determine your data storage needs**: Decide on what type of data storage you will need to store the data that you have collected from your IoT devices. Services such as S3, DynamoDB, and Kinesis Data Streams can be used for this purpose.

3. **Design a data processing pipeline**: Determine how your data will be processed, cleaned, and transformed. You can utilize services such as AWS Data Pipeline or AWS Lambda for this.

4. **Choose the data analysis and visualization tools that you will need**: Select appropriate data analysis and visualization tools that best fit your use case. You can use tools such as Amazon QuickSight, AWS IoT Analytics, and Amazon ElasticSearch.

5. **Create a data security and compliance plan**: You will then need to design a security and compliance plan to protect your data and ensure that you adhere to relevant regulatory requirements. This may include steps such as data encryption and access controls.

6. **Test and optimize your deployment**: You will then need to test the design by running a small pilot and optimizing it accordingly based on the results that you receive. You must then continuously monitor the performance and make any necessary adjustments accordingly.

7. **Deploy and maintain**: Finally, you will need to deploy the design within a production environment, ensuring that you continuously monitor and maintain it to prevent any errors and ensure it runs smoothly. This is why monitoring tools such as Amazon CloudWatch are imperative for this use case, as errors in our environment can happen anytime, and we want to be ready to make any adjustments autonomously when possible.

It is important to note that this is not an exhaustive list; there can certainly be more steps based on each user's use case. However, this already encompasses most data workloads and certainly provides a guideline for how you choose to design your own flows moving forward.

Next, we will look at a practical exercise where we will create and design a data pipeline for for end-to-end data ingestion and analysis, based on the components of AWS IoT Analytics.

Practical – smart home insights with AWS IoT Analytics

In this practical exercise, we will explore IoT data analytics using AWS. Specifically, we will use AWS services such as S3, Glue, Athena, and QuickSight to analyze a dataset of IoT sensor readings collected from a smart home over a period of 1 month.

You will need the following software components as part of the practical:

- An AWS account (you can create one for free if you don't have one already)

- A dataset of IoT sensor readings (you can create a sample dataset or use a publicly available dataset)

Let's move to the various steps of the practical, as follows:

1. Download the occupancy detection dataset:

    I.   We can obtain a dataset from `https://github.com/PacktPublishing/IoT-Made-Easy-for-Beginners/tree/main/Chapter10/analyzing_smart_home_sensor_readings/datatest.csv`.

    II. Open the dataset and take note of the fields inside it.

2. To start off, we will have to load our dataset into an Amazon S3 bucket:

    I.   Sign in to your AWS Management Console.

    II.   Navigate to the Amazon S3 service.

    III. Click on the **Create bucket** button. Name the bucket and choose a region. Click **Next**.

    IV.   Keep all the default settings in the **Configure options** page and click **Next**.

    V.   Ensure public access is blocked for security reasons and click **Next**.

    VI.   Review your settings and click **Create bucket**.

    VII. Navigate inside your newly created bucket, click on **Upload**, and drag and drop (or browse to) your `datatest.csv` file. Once uploaded, click **Next**.

    VIII. Keep the default permissions and click **Next**.

    IX.   Review the properties and click **Upload**.

3. We now will look to create an AWS Glue crawler to traverse our data and create a table in the AWS Glue Data Catalog:

    I.   Navigate to the AWS Glue service.

    II.   Click on the **Crawlers** tab under **Data Catalog** and then click **Create crawler**.

    III. Name your crawler and click **Next**.

    IV.   Select **Not yet** for the question **Is your data already mapped to Glue tables.**

    V.   Click on **Add a data source** and choose **S3** as the data source. Click **Browse S3** and select the bucket you have just created. Click **Next**.

    VI.   Choose or create an **Identity and Access Management (IAM)** role that gives AWS Glue permissions to access your S3 data. Click **Next**.

VII.   For the frequency, you can choose **Run on demand**. Click **Next**.

VIII. Choose **Add database**, then name your database (for example, `SmartHomeData`). Navigate to your newly created database and click on **Add table**. Name your table (for example, `SensorReadings`) and select your database. Leave all other settings as they are. Click **Next** in the current window along with the subsequent ones, up to the window where you click **Create** to create the table.

IX.   Review the configuration and click **Create crawler**.

With that, we have created an AWS Glue crawler to traverse our data. Now, we can look at transforming our data:

1.   Use AWS Glue to transform the data and create a new table with additional columns:

I.   Navigate to **ETL Jobs** in the **AWS Glue** sidebar.

II.   Select **Visual** with a blank canvas and click on **Create**.

III.   Name your job on the top left and select or create an IAM role that has the right permissions.

IV.   An **Add nodes** window should pop up. In the **Sources** tab, click on **Amazon S3** to add an Amazon S3 node. Afterward, click on the **Transforms** tab and click on the **Select Fields** node. Finally, click on **Target** and click on **Amazon S3**.

V.   You should now have three nodes on your canvas. Connect the data source to the **Transform - SelectFields** node by dragging the black dot at the bottom of the **Data source - S3 bucket** node to the **Select Fields** node. Do the same to connect the **Select Fields** node to the **Data target - S3 bucket** node:

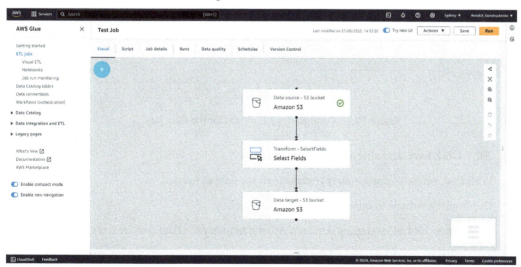

Figure 10.2 – Visualization of the three nodes on the canvas

VI.   Click on the **Data Source - S3 bucket** node. For the **S3 source** type, click on the **Data Catalog** table. Afterward, choose the database that you created. Choose the table that was created.

VII. Afterward, click on **Select Fields**. Here, choose the field's temperature and humidity.

VIII. We now need to create another S3 bucket for the output. Create a new S3 bucket with whatever name you want for it.

IX.   Click on the target S3 bucket on the canvas and select the format as **Parquet**. Specify the new Amazon S3 bucket you created (for example, s3://your_bucket_name).

X.   Go to the **Job details** tab and specify the IAM role you have been using so far. Leave everything else as it is. Rename the script filename to anything you want, as long as it ends with .py (for example, test.py):

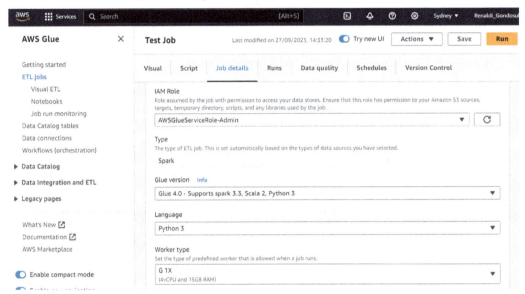

Figure 10.3 – Configuring job details for the Glue job

XI.   Click **Save**, and afterward, click **Run**.

With that, we have appropriately transformed the data as needed.

2. Use Amazon Athena to query the transformed data.

    We can now look at leveraging Amazon Athena to query the data that we have transformed:

    I.   Navigate to the Amazon Athena service.

    II. On the sidebar, click on **Query editor**.

III. There should be a prompt asking you to select an output location for your queries. Specify an S3 bucket or a folder within a bucket to do so.

IV. In the Athena dashboard, select **AWSDataCatalog** as the data source and **SmartHomeData** database (or your predefined values for them).

V. Run the following query by clicking **Run**:

```
Select * from mychannelbucket
```

VI. You should get the full table that you created before. Now, use SQL queries to answer the following questions:

  i. What is the average temperature, humidity, and light intensity for each day of the month?

  ii. What is the average temperature, humidity, and light intensity for each hour of the day?

  iii. What is the average temperature, humidity, and light intensity for each day of the week?

  iv. What is the correlation between temperature and humidity and between temperature and light intensity?

VII. View the query results and save the query results to a new S3 bucket.

In this practical exercise, we explored IoT data analytics using AWS services such as S3, Glue, and Athena. We loaded a dataset of IoT sensor readings into an S3 bucket, used Glue to transform the data and create a new table with additional columns, used Athena to query the transformed data and generate insights, and used QuickSight to visualize the insights and create a dashboard. Based on the insights generated, we provided recommendations for improving the smart home experience.

We will now move on to industrial data analytics.

Industrial data analytics

We have seen the usage of data analytics in the past two sections and how it can be beneficial for our workloads. Now, let's look at how it can benefit industry cases and how we can accordingly evaluate our deployments based on the best practices that are set out for us.

Evaluating performance

Use services such as CloudWatch metrics to monitor the performance of the IoT Analytics pipeline, such as the number of messages processed, the time it takes to process each message, and the number of errors that are encountered. This will be critical for use in further analysis and eventual optimization. The following are factors to consider in evaluating performance:

- **Analyze your data**: We can use IoT Analytics SQL or other data analytics tools to identify any patterns or issues that we may need to address if they affect system performance.

- **Optimize your pipeline**: From the analysis of the data, we can optimize the pipeline by adding data normalization, validation, and modeling to improve the performance of the data analytics workloads.

- **Use best practices**: We need to adhere to best practices for data analysis, which includes techniques such as normalization, data validation, and data modeling. For the scope of this book, we will not be covering this, but we encourage you to look up more of these techniques in the *Further reading* section and read up on the topics listed there.

- **Usage of third-party monitoring tools**: We can utilize third-party monitoring tools to collect and analyze performance metrics for our analytics workload and gain more insights into how our pipeline is performing.

- **Monitor and track usage of resources**: We need to keep an eye on resources such as CPU, memory, and storage that are used by our data analytics workloads, especially if they are consuming more resources than expected. If necessary, we should perform actions such as scaling our workloads up or optimizing the pipelines further.

Having understood how to keep track of performance, we can now review some different use cases of data analysis within industry.

Use cases within industry

Industry has many different use cases for performing data analysis on a myriad of data. Here are just a few prominent examples:

- **Predictive maintenance**: Within this use case, IoT devices are used to collect real-time sensor data that is processed and analyzed using AWS IoT Analytics to detect patterns and accordingly predict when maintenance would be required. This will help organizations schedule maintenance at the required times, reducing downtime and improving the efficiency of equipment.

- **Smart agriculture**: IoT sensors can be used to collect data on soil moisture and temperature, which is then analyzed within AWS IoT Analytics to optimize crop yields, reduce consumption of water, and improve overall farm efficiency.

- **Smart cities**: IoT devices can be used to collect data on various aspects of urban infrastructure such as traffic, air quality, and energy usage. The data can then be analyzed through AWS IoT Analytics where it can then be used to improve traffic flow, reduce pollution, and optimize energy usage to ensure that cities become more sustainable and livable for their residents.

With those use cases in mind, we can now take a look at a case study of a data analytics flow used within a production environment in an industrial setting.

A case study for data analytics

Now that we have seen use cases and have learned about how we can evaluate IoT deployments that leverage data analytics services on AWS, let's take a look at how one industrial environment can utilize the AWS environment to perform data analytics workloads and the workflow behind it. We can see this case represented in *Figure 10.4*:

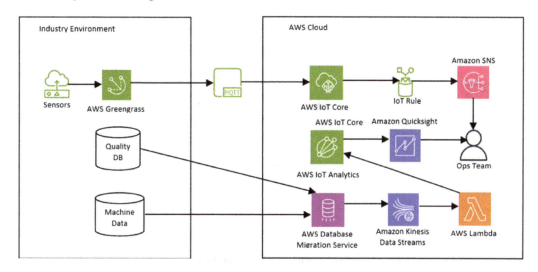

Figure 10.4 – AWS data analysis within an industrial environment

In this workflow, we can see that the industrial environment is pushing data onto AWS Greengrass, which in turn uses the IoT MQTT protocol to deliver data to AWS IoT Core. It will then in turn put through data to AWS IoT Analytics to be further visualized via QuickSight. On the other hand, if an IoT rule is triggered, it will instead feed the data to Amazon SNS, where the operations team will be notified through an alert. Additionally, data can also be fed in by moving the on-premises database onto the cloud with **Database Migration Service** (**DMS**), which is a service used for migrating databases onto AWS. It can then be ingested using Amazon Kinesis Data Streams and processed using AWS Lambda, where it then will be fed into AWS IoT Analytics.

Now that we've become more familiar with these workflows for data analytics, let's get on to our practical.

Practical – creating a data pipeline for end-to-end data ingestion and analysis

In this practical, we will look to create a data pipeline based on the AWS console. This will follow the architecture shown in the following diagram:

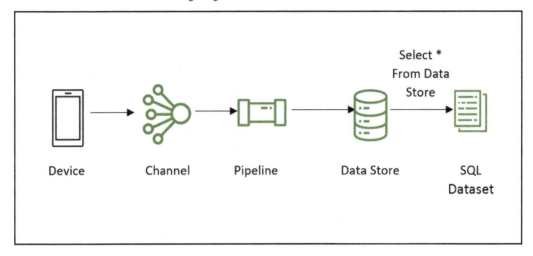

Figure 10.5 – Data pipeline workflow for data ingestion

We will have a device send data to a channel. The channel will receive the data and send it through the pipeline, which will pipe the data through to the data store. From the data store, we can then make SQL queries to create a dataset from which we will read the data.

We can now go ahead and start off by creating a channel.

Creating a channel

Let's create our channel as part of the analytics workflow:

1. If you have not already, sign in to the AWS console. Afterward, navigate to the IoT Analytics console. For your convenience, here is a link to the console: `https://console.aws.amazon.com/iotanalytics/`.

2. In the IoT Analytics dashboard, click on **Channels** on the sidebar and click the **Create channel** button.

3. Provide a name for the channel (for example, `mychannel`) and follow through with the default settings. For the storage type, pick **Service managed storage**. Click on **Create** at the bottom to finish creating the channel.

4. You can view the created channel by navigating to the **Channels** section from the sidebar:

Figure 10.6 – Channel created in the IoT Analytics list of channels

With the channel created, we can now create a data store.

Creating a data store

Creating a data store is necessary to store data that has been put through the pipeline. We will walk through its creation here:

1. We can add multiple data stores, but for the purposes of this exercise, we will use a single data store. In the IoT Analytics dashboard, click on **Data stores** on the sidebar and click the **Create data store** button.

2. Choose **Service managed storage** as the storage type:

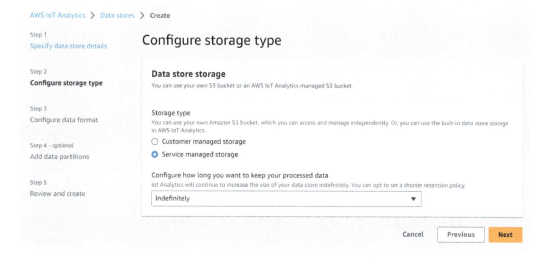

Figure 10.7 – Configuring the storage type used for the data store

3. Click **Create** to finalize the data store creation.

4. To view created data stores, go to the **Datastore** section from the sidebar.

With the data store created, we can now create a pipeline.

Creating a pipeline

A pipeline consumes messages that come from a channel and allows you to process and filter them before storing them within the data store. Here are the steps to create a pipeline:

1. In the IoT Analytics dashboard, click on **Pipelines** on the sidebar and click the **Create pipeline** button. It should then take you to the following screen:

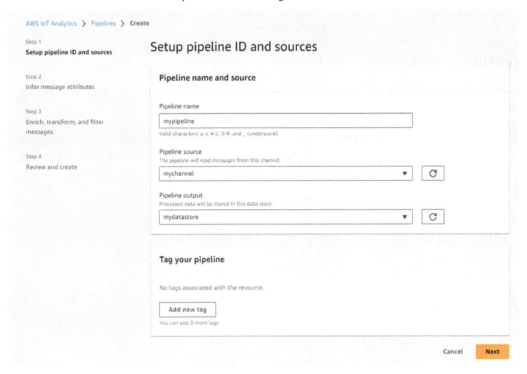

Figure 10.8 – Configuring the pipeline ID and sources for the pipeline

2. Provide a name for the pipeline (for example, `mypipeline`) and follow through with the default settings. For **Pipeline source**, pick your newly created channel, and for **Pipeline output**, pick your newly created data source.

3. For **Enrich, transform, and filter messages**, pick **Select attributes** from the message.

4. Click on **Create** at the bottom to finish creating the channel.

5. As with previous steps, we can then check whether the pipeline was created successfully by viewing it on the **Pipelines** page of the IoT Analytics dashboard.

Having created a pipeline, we can now start ingesting some data through it.

Ingesting data

We can now send some data through the pipeline. At this time, we will create some mock data to send through. To simulate data ingestion from the AWS console, you might need to utilize another AWS service such as Lambda to push data to IoT Analytics or use the AWS SDK; so, we will use the following steps:

1. Navigate to the AWS Lambda service in the AWS console.

2. Click the **Create function** button.

3. Choose **Author from scratch**. Provide a name for the Lambda function (for example, `PushTemperatureDataToIoTAnalytics`).

4. For the runtime, select a preferred language. For this walkthrough, we'll assume Python 3.8.

5. Under **Permissions**, choose or create a role that has permissions to write to IoT Analytics.

6. Click **Create function**.

7. Write the Lambda function, as shown next. This code mocks temperature data and pushes it to AWS IoT Analytics:

```
import json
import boto3
import random


client = boto3.client('iotanalytics')


def lambda_handler(event, context):

    # Mocking temperature data
    temperature_data = {
        "temperature": random.randint(15, 35)
    }

    response = client.batch_put_message(
        channelName='mychannel',
        messages=[
            {
                'messageId': str(random.randint(1, 1000000)),
```

```
                    'payload': json.dumps(temperature_data).encode()
                },
            ]
        )

        return {
            'statusCode': 200,
            'body': json.dumps('Temperature data pushed
    successfully!')
        }
```

The function creates a client to interact with AWS IoT Analytics using boto3. Inside the function, it generates mock temperature data, where the temperature value is a random integer between 15 and 35 degrees. This data is structured in a dictionary as can be seen in a snapshot of the AWS Lambda window below.

Figure 10.9 – AWS Lambda window for inserting code

Then, it sends this temperature data to a channel named mychannel in AWS IoT Analytics using the batch_put_message method. The message includes a unique ID, generated randomly, and the payload, which is the serialized temperature data. The function concludes by returning a success status code (200) and a message indicating the successful push of the temperature data.

Deploy the function after inserting the code.

8. At the top right of the Lambda function dashboard, click the **Test** button.

9. Configure a new test event. The actual event data doesn't matter in this context since our function isn't using it, so you can use the default template provided.

10. Name the test event and save it.

11. With the test event selected, click **Test**. If everything's set up correctly, you should see an execution result indicating success, and your AWS IoT Analytics channel (`mychannel` in this example) should have received a temperature data point.

Having properly ingested the data, let's now see how to monitor it.

Monitoring ingested data

Monitoring is an important component of analyzing IoT data, and we can do this as detailed next:

1. You can check messages that have been ingested into your channel through the AWS IoT Analytics console. Within the console, on the left pane, click on **Channel** and choose the name of the channel that we created.

2. On the page, scroll down to the **Monitoring** section. Adjust the time frame that you currently want to be displayed as needed by choosing one of the existing time frame indicators. You will then see a graph line that shows the number of messages that were ingested into the channel during that period.

3. You can also check for pipeline activity executions. Follow the same workflow process you went through by clicking **Pipelines**, followed by the name of the pipeline that was created on the console, and adjust the time frame indicators. You will see a graph line that shows the number of pipeline activity execution errors in that period.

Now that we can monitor the data, let's look at creating a dataset from our data.

Creating a dataset from the data

We can now look at creating a dataset from the data we have. Proceed as follows:

1. Navigate to **Datasets** from the sidebar and click on the **Create** button.

2. Name your dataset `mydataset`.

3. For the action, use a SQL expression such as `select * from mydatastore`.

4. Complete the dataset creation by clicking **Create**.

5. To generate dataset content, select the dataset and click on the **Run Now** button.

6. To view the content, click on the dataset name and navigate to its content. You should see the results and can even download them if they're available.

With that, we have been able to create an end-to-end pipeline! Note that much of this infrastructure is still based solely on AWS. In real-world deployments, we would see more interconnectivity between AWS and on-premises equipment and see real-time data analysis being performed based on the data ingested.

As always, feel free to look at the documentation for all the hardware and software involved in this practical. We encourage you to explore further data analysis options, particularly in the transformation process when creating an ETL Glue job.

Summary

In this chapter, we have covered the fundamentals of data analytics within IoT workloads, discussing how different services within AWS can handle analysis and storage loads that are required as part of our IoT cloud workflow. We then learned more about how we can design and develop the implementation of our architecture according to our use case and learned how to practically use the offerings from AWS IoT Analytics to provision an end-to-end data pipeline.

In the next chapter, we will be discussing security and privacy within IoT, which is an imperative topic to talk about, given how it has become even more prevalent as more and more people have shifted their workloads into the cloud.

Further reading

For more information on what was covered in this chapter, please refer to the following links:

- Understand more on data lakes and analytics solutions provided by AWS: `https://aws.amazon.com/big-data/datalakes-and-analytics/`

- Review more IoT Analytics success cases provided by AWS: `https://aws.amazon.com/iot-analytics/`

- Look at another reference architecture for an AWS serverless data analytics pipeline: `https://aws.amazon.com/blogs/big-data/aws-serverless-data-analytics-pipeline-reference-architecture/`

- Take a look at an implementation of real-time monitoring of industrial machines that utilizes AWS IoT: `https://ieeexplore.ieee.org/document/10016452/`

- Look at how a connected factory was able to leverage its offerings based on AWS IoT: `https://aws.amazon.com/blogs/iot/connected-factory-offering-based-on-aws-iot-for-industry-4-0-success/`

- Explore more on architecting industrial IoT workloads based on the cloud: `https://us.nttdata.com/en/blog/2022/september/architecting-cloud-industrial-iot-workloads-part-2`

11

Examining Security and Privacy in IoT

From smart homes to connected cars, IoT devices have become ubiquitous in our daily lives. However, with increased connectivity and data exchange comes the risk of security and privacy breaches. As more and more sensitive information is transmitted through these devices, it is essential to examine security and privacy measures in place to protect both the users and the devices themselves.

In this chapter, we will explore various security and privacy concerns in IoT, including risks associated with data breaches and strategies used to mitigate them. We will also discuss the importance of privacy in IoT and how it is protected, as well as the challenges of implementing security measures in a rapidly evolving technological landscape. By examining these critical issues, we can gain a better understanding of the measures needed to ensure the security and privacy of IoT devices and networks.

In this chapter, we're going to cover the following main topics:

- The current state of risk and security within IoT
- Security and privacy controls within the cloud management landscape
- Risk management within the IoT landscape
- Privacy and compliance within IoT networks
- Cryptography controls for the IoT landscape
- Practical – Creating a secure smart lock system

Technical requirements

This chapter will require you to have the following hardware and software installed:

- Hardware:
  - Raspberry Pi
  - Single-channel relay
  - 1 1k Ohm resistor
  - Push button switch
  - Jumper cables
  - Breadboard
  - Mobile charger 5V/1A to use as power supply
- Software:
  - Blynk app
  - Arduino IDE

You can access the GitHub folder for the code that is used in this chapter at `https://github.com/PacktPublishing/IoT-Made-Easy-for-Beginners/tree/main/Chapter11/`.

The current state of risk and security within IoT

As IoT technology continues to evolve and expand into new areas of our lives, it is critical that we understand the current state of risk and security within IoT networks. In this section, we will explore the current landscape of IoT security, including the most common types of IoT security threats and the current state of IoT security standards and regulations. We will also discuss best practices for securing IoT networks and devices, as well as challenges and opportunities for improving IoT security in the future. We can start off by taking a look at how security encompasses IoT in *Figure 11.1*:

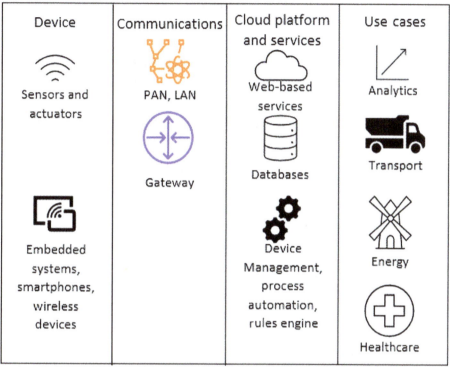

Figure 11.1 – Overview of how security encompasses IoT

Figure 11.1 presents a structured overview of the current state of risk and security within IoT. The diagram is segmented into four main columns, representing distinct aspects of IoT: **Device**, **Communications**, **Cloud platform and services**, and **Use Cases**.

The diagram emphasizes the diverse facets of IoT, spanning from device-level hardware to broad use cases. It shows expansive areas where security is paramount in the IoT ecosystem, from individual devices and their communication pathways to the cloud platforms that store and process data, and finally, the real-world applications and sectors that implement IoT solutions.

We can continue the discussion by taking a look at challenges within security on IoT networks.

Challenges within security on IoT networks

The increasing number of connected devices in IoT networks has raised several security concerns. These concerns include the following:

- **Lack of encryption**: Many IoT devices do not have proper encryption protocols in place, making them vulnerable to attacks that can compromise user data and personal information.

- **Weak authentication and authorization**: IoT devices often use weak passwords or default credentials, making them susceptible to brute-force attacks. Additionally, many IoT devices do not implement proper authentication and authorization mechanisms, allowing unauthorized access to sensitive data.

- **Inadequate software updates and patching**: IoT devices may not have proper mechanisms for software updates and patching, making them vulnerable to known vulnerabilities and exploits.

- **Lack of standardization**: There is a lack of standardization in IoT devices, making it difficult for manufacturers to provide security updates and for security researchers to identify vulnerabilities.

- **Physical security**: IoT devices may be easily physically accessible, making them vulnerable to physical attacks and tampering.

- **Malware and botnets**: IoT devices can be infected with malware and used as part of a botnet to launch **distributed denial-of-service** (**DDoS**) attacks and other malicious activities.

- **Privacy concerns**: IoT devices often collect and store sensitive data, raising privacy concerns if the data is not properly secured.

- **Lack of awareness**: Users may not be aware of the security risks associated with IoT devices and may not take appropriate measures to secure their devices and networks.

After seeing the different challenges, we can now take a look at some recommendations for remediating them properly.

Security recommendations

To enhance the security of IoT networks, it's essential to integrate both general security practices and the specific guidelines outlined by industrial standard architectures such as Matter, Thread, Zigbee, MQTT, and Wi-SUN. These standards provide well-rounded security mechanisms tailored for IoT environments. The following recommendations align with these standards:

- **Secure communication**: IoT devices must utilize secure communication protocols such as HTTPS, TLS, or SSL, which are integral to standards such as MQTT and Wi-SUN. These protocols encrypt data transmitted between devices and servers, ensuring adherence to industry benchmarks for secure communication.

- **Access control**: Strong authentication and authorization mechanisms should be implemented as per the guidelines of these standards. This ensures that only authorized devices or users gain access to the IoT network, aligning with the security protocols of Matter and Zigbee.

- **Regular software updates**: Consistent updating of IoT devices with the latest security patches and firmware is crucial. This practice aligns with the maintenance protocols recommended by these standards, ensuring devices remain safeguarded against evolving threats.

- **Data encryption**: Encryption of stored and transmitted data is a core aspect of these standards. By encrypting data, IoT devices comply with industry practices, ensuring robust protection against unauthorized access or interception.

- **Privacy protection**: Designing IoT devices to protect user privacy is a fundamental aspect of these standards. This involves limiting the collection of personal data and providing transparent privacy policies, in line with the privacy guidelines of standards such as Thread and Matter.

- **Physical security**: Implementing physical security measures such as tamper-proofing and anti-theft mechanisms is crucial. These measures are often outlined in the security protocols of these standards, ensuring a comprehensive approach to physical security in IoT environments.

- **Monitoring and analytics**: Real-time monitoring and analytics are essential for detecting and responding to security incidents. This practice is often emphasized in these standards, promoting proactive security management in IoT networks.

- **Vendor security assessment**: Conducting a thorough security assessment of IoT devices before integration is crucial. This assessment should ensure that the devices comply with the required security standards, aligning with the industry benchmarks set by these architectures.

By implementing these security recommendations, organizations can reduce the risk of security breaches and protect their IoT networks from malicious attacks. However, it is important to note that security is an ongoing process and must be regularly reviewed and updated to address emerging threats and vulnerabilities.

With that, we've gained a better understanding of the current state of security within IoT environments, including challenges and solutions for it. Now, we can take a look at how it is implemented alongside controls within the cloud environment.

Security and privacy controls within the cloud management landscape

As more and more IoT devices are connected to the internet, cloud management has become an essential component of IoT networks. The cloud provides a scalable, flexible, and cost-effective solution for storing and processing the vast amounts of data generated by IoT devices. However, with the benefits of the cloud also come security and privacy concerns.

This section will discuss security and privacy controls that are necessary within the cloud management landscape to ensure the safe and effective operation of IoT networks. We will explore key security and privacy considerations in the cloud, including data encryption, **identity and access management (IAM)**, network security, and compliance with regulatory requirements.

Types of attacks

IoT networks face numerous threats that come from various sources. Attackers could target physical devices, communication channels, or the cloud services that manage the devices. Each layer of the IoT network presents a different vulnerability, and attackers have different techniques for exploiting each layer.

Physical layer attacks

Physical attacks on IoT devices involve gaining access to the devices through direct manipulation. Attackers could physically connect to the device's ports, such as USB or Ethernet ports, and install malicious firmware or software to take control of the device. Attackers could also use side-channel attacks to obtain sensitive information from the device's hardware or firmware, such as encryption keys or other authentication data.

Data link layer attacks

Data link layer (DLL) attacks involve intercepting or manipulating communication between IoT devices and the network. Attackers could use techniques such as packet sniffing or **man-in-the-middle (MitM)** attacks to capture and modify data being transmitted between devices. Attackers could also use spoofing attacks to impersonate legitimate devices or gateways to gain access to the network.

Network layer attacks

Network layer attacks focus on disrupting the network infrastructure that connects IoT devices. Attackers could launch DDoS attacks to overload the network with traffic, causing it to become unresponsive. Attackers could also exploit vulnerabilities in the routing protocols used by IoT networks to redirect or manipulate data traffic.

Application layer attacks

Application layer attacks target the software and services that run on IoT devices or the cloud services that manage them. Attackers could exploit vulnerabilities in the software or firmware running on the device to gain control over it or access sensitive data. Attackers could also launch attacks such as SQL injection or **cross-site scripting (XSS)** attacks on the web applications used to manage the devices.

IoT networks face a wide range of attacks, and each layer of the network presents different vulnerabilities. IoT security must be implemented at each layer of the network to mitigate the risks associated with these attacks. The use of encryption, authentication, and access controls can help to secure physical devices and the data transmitted between them. Regular updates and patches should be applied to the software and firmware running on the devices to address any known vulnerabilities. Overall, a layered security approach that considers the entire IoT ecosystem can provide a more robust defense against attacks.

We can see different forms of attacks on embedded IoT systems in *Figure 11.2*:

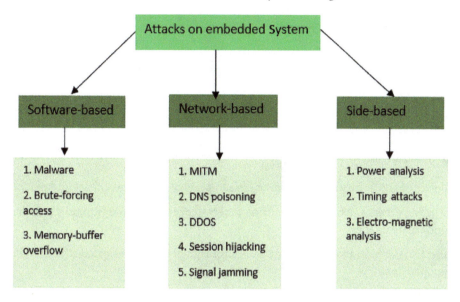

Figure 11.2 – Different attacks on embedded systems

The diagram provides a structured view of potential vulnerabilities an embedded system may face, categorizing them based on the method or perspective of the attack. It categorizes the different attacks into three main types: **Software-based**, **Network-based**, and **Side-based**, described as follows:

- **Software-based attacks**:

  - **Malware**: Malicious software intended to damage or exploit an embedded system

  - **Brute-forcing access**: A method of trial and error whereby an attacker attempts to guess the correct access credentials

  - **Memory-buffer overflow**: A situation where a program writes data outside the bounds of pre-allocated fixed-length buffers, leading to potential code execution or system crashes

- **Network-based attacks**:

  - **MITM**: An attack where the attacker secretly relays and possibly alters the communication between two parties who believe they are communicating directly with each other

  - **Domain Name System (DNS) poisoning**: An attack where the attacker redirects DNS entries to a malicious site

  - **DDOS**: An attempt to disrupt the regular functioning of a network by flooding it with excessive traffic

  - **Session hijacking**: When an attacker takes over a user's session to gain unauthorized access to a system

  - **Signal jamming**: An interference with the signal frequencies that an embedded system might use, rendering it inoperable or reducing its efficiency

- **Side-based attacks**:

  - **Power analysis**: Observing the power consumption of a device to extract information

  - **Timing attacks**: Analyzing the time taken to execute cryptographic algorithms to find vulnerabilities

  - **Electromagnetic analysis**: Using the electromagnetic emissions of a device to infer data or operations

With that understanding, we can now look at how cloud providers such as **Amazon Web Services (AWS)** provide powerful tools to manage security on the platform.

Security on AWS

Cloud providers, such as AWS, provide powerful tools and services for managing and securing IoT devices and data. One of the biggest advantages of using cloud-based IoT platforms is the built-in security features they offer. AWS, for example, provides a variety of security controls that can help you protect your IoT deployments from cyberattacks and other security threats.

One of the most important security controls provided by AWS is IAM. With IAM, you can control who has access to your IoT devices and data and what actions they can perform. You can also use AWS IAM to set up policies that define how your IoT devices should interact with each other and with other AWS services. Another key security control provided by AWS is encryption. AWS IoT supports end-to-end encryption for data transmitted between devices and the cloud, as well as encryption of data at rest. This helps ensure that your data is protected from interception and theft.

In addition to these controls, AWS also provides tools for monitoring and logging your IoT deployments. You can use AWS CloudTrail to monitor activity on your AWS account, including activity related to your IoT deployments. AWS also provides tools such as AWS IoT Device Defender and AWS IoT Device Management that help you monitor the health and security of your IoT devices and take action if any anomalies are detected. AWS IoT Device Defender is a security service that continuously monitors and audits your IoT configurations to protect against external threats and ensure compliance with best practices. AWS IoT Device Management, on the other hand, provides tools for efficiently managing, monitoring, and updating IoT devices at scale. Together, they offer a comprehensive solution for securing and managing IoT devices, addressing both security concerns and operational challenges in IoT ecosystems.

When it comes to IoT security, it is important to remember that no single control can provide complete protection. However, by using a combination of security controls and best practices, such as those provided by AWS, you can significantly reduce the risk of a security breach and ensure the safety and privacy of your IoT devices and data.

Automated security remediation with AWS IoT Device Defender

As an IoT solution involves managing a considerable number of devices, organizations need to ensure that their fleet remains secure by regularly monitoring and enforcing security best practices. However, it can be a daunting task to audit all devices and fix issues automatically, especially on a large scale.

This practical guide focuses on simplifying the process by using AWS IoT Device Defender. You will learn how to inspect and update AWS IoT policies that may be too permissive and do not follow AWS IoT best practices. The sample architecture provides an example of how to carry out these tasks effectively.

To successfully implement the practical, the following components must be created:

- A **Simple Notification Service** (**SNS**) topic that can receive notifications from AWS IoT Device Defender when an audit is completed

- A Lambda function that can parse the audit findings and resolve any identified issues

- Appropriate IAM policies and roles that enable the Lambda function to access and modify IoT policies based on the audit results

- An IAM role that permits AWS IoT Device Defender to publish to a particular SNS topic

- A Lambda permission that allows SNS to invoke the Lambda function

With that in mind, we can get started and make the necessary components, starting with AWS CloudFormation.

AWS CloudFormation

Here are the steps to create the necessary components using AWS CloudFormation:

1. Change your AWS region to `us-east-1` (North Virginia):

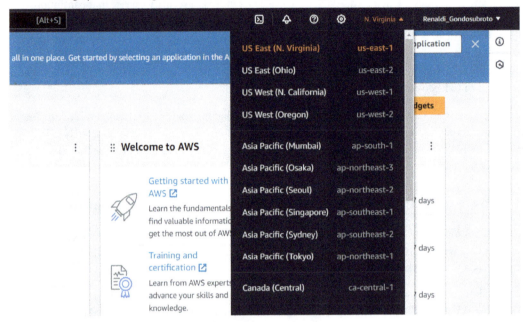

Figure 11.3 – Changing AWS region to us-east-1

2. Go to **CloudFormation** in the AWS console.

3. Click on **Stacks** on the left pane and click **Create Stack**.

4. On the Amazon S3 URL, put in `https://s3.amazonaws.com/aws-iot-blog-assets/aws-iot-device-defender-automating-actions/cloudformation.yml`:

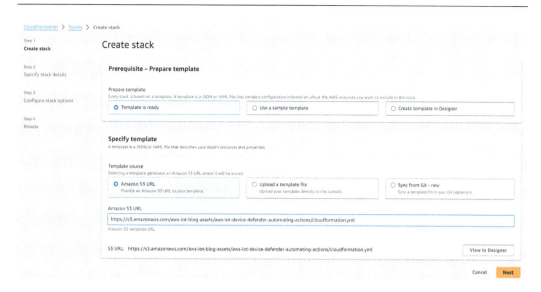

Figure 11.4 – Creating a stack on AWS CloudFormation

5. Navigate to the bottom of the **Specify stack details** section and proceed by selecting **Next**.

6. At the bottom of the **Configure stack options** page, continue by clicking **Next**.

7. Confirm that you understand AWS CloudFormation might generate IAM resources as part of the stack deployment process, that it may create those resources with custom names, and that AWS CloudFormation may require the CAPABILITY_AUTO_EXPAND capability:

Figure 11.5 – Confirmation window before creating a stack

Initiate the stack deployment by clicking on **Create Stack**.

Please allow a short duration for the stack to be fully deployed. Following the completion of the stack creation, ensure to record the SNS topic identifier and the IAM role that AWS IoT Device Defender will utilize for SNS publication.

8. Access the AWS CloudFormation console.

    Locate and click on the entry corresponding to the stack you've just set up.

9. Select the **Outputs** tab.

10. Find the `SnsTopicName` value and note the content of the **Value** column.

11. Find the `DevDefenderPublishToTopicRole` value and note the content of the **Value** column.

12. After creating the AWS CloudFormation stack, an AWS IoT policy will be generated by default, which may be too permissive and may be flagged during an audit by AWS IoT Device Defender. The following generated policy is a sample policy:

```
{
  "Version": "2012-10-17",
  "Statement": [
    {
      "Action": [
        "iot:Connect",
        "iot:Publish",
        "iot:Subscribe",
        "iot:Receive"
      ],
      "Resource": [
        "*"
      ],
      "Effect": "Allow"
    }
  ]
}
```

This policy allows devices to perform actions without resource constraints, making it non-compliant with best practices. Devices using this policy could potentially interfere with other devices by publishing messages on any topic. For more information on the analysis done by AWS IoT Device Defender, please refer to their official documentation at `https://docs.aws.amazon.com/iot/latest/developerguide/device-defender-audit.html`.

To ensure a secure production environment, it is recommended to follow the least-privilege policy by default. This means that devices should only have the permissions necessary to complete their activities. Continuous auditing can be helpful in identifying and addressing policies that do not follow the best practices.

Now, we have successfully set up the configuration for AWS CloudFormation and can move on to posting results on an SNS topic utilizing AWS IoT Device Defender.

Posting results on an SNS topic with AWS IoT Device Defender

To connect AWS IoT Device Defender to the SNS topic created by the AWS CloudFormation template, you can follow these steps:

1. Log in to the AWS IoT Core console.
2. If it's your first time, click on **Get Started** to begin.
3. On the left navigation pane, click **Defend**, then click **Settings**.
4. If you haven't completed the AWS IoT Device Defender setup wizard before, do so now to create the necessary permissions by clicking **Get started with an audit**.
5. Scroll down to the **SNS alerts** section.
6. Click **Edit**.
7. Click **Enabled**.
8. Click **Select** under **Topic** to choose an appropriate topic.
9. Select the topic that was created during the execution of AWS CloudFormation.
10. Under **Role**, click **Select**.
11. Choose the role that was created during the execution of AWS CloudFormation.
12. Click **Update** to finish the configuration.

Now that we are able to post results on the SNS topic, we can see how we can manage an on-demand audit to test the remediation strategy.

Managing an on-demand audit

Once you have completed the configuration for AWS CloudFormation and AWS IoT Device Defender as in the preceding subsections, it's time to test your remediation strategy by running an on-demand audit. Each completed audit task will trigger a Lambda function. Here's how you can run an on-demand audit:

1. Open the AWS IoT Core console.
2. From the left navigation pane, select **Defend**.
3. Click on **Audit** and then **Schedule**.
4. Click on **Create** in the upper-right corner.
5. Choose the type of check you want to perform. For example, you can select only IoT policies that are overly permissive.
6. Go to the **Set Schedule** session.
7. Choose **Run audit now** (once).
8. Click on **Create** to start the audit.

Note that you can use AWS IoT Device Defender to create separate schedules for each type of check. For instance, you can schedule a daily audit for device certificates shared and a weekly audit for CA certificates expiring.

With that, we can now manage the on-demand audit and can configure and monitor the audit progress from here.

Configuring and monitoring the audit progress

Once you have initiated an on-demand audit in AWS IoT Device Defender, the time it takes to complete the audit depends on the number of devices and checks selected. You can monitor the progress of the audit using either the console or APIs.

To check the results of the audit, follow these steps:

1. Open the AWS IoT Core console.
2. In the left navigation pane, choose **Defend**.
3. Choose **Audit** and then **Results**.
4. Locate the audit you created and click on it.
5. Review the results of the audit.
6. Click on the check named **IoT policies overly permissive** to view a detailed report.

Now, we can move ahead to understand how we can mitigate the action and validate accordingly.

Mitigating the action and validating it

To ensure the mitigation strategy has been successfully implemented, you can check the updated policy document in the AWS IoT Core console. Here are the steps to follow:

1. Open the AWS IoT Core console.
2. In the left navigation pane, select **Secure** and then select **Policies**.
3. Use the search box on the upper right to locate the policy you want to check. You can search for the policy by name; for example, `MyPermissiveIoTPolicy`.
4. Click on the policy displayed in the right panel.
5. Scroll down to the **Policy Document** section.
6. Check whether the policy document has been updated with the restrictive policy you want.

With that, we have been able to create a proper AWS IoT Device Defender flow! Now, the flow will look like something like the one shown in *Figure 11.4*:

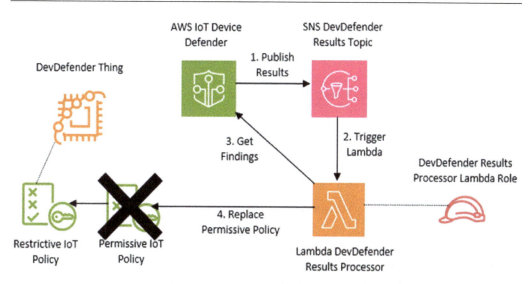

Figure 11.6 – Device Defender policy flow

At the beginning of the flow, there's **DevDefender Thing**, which is an IoT device. This device operates under two policies: **Restrictive IoT Policy** and **Permissive IoT Policy**. **Permissive IoT Policy** is marked with a cross, showing that this policy is not in use. On the other hand, **Permissive IoT Policy** is shown as the preferred or active choice.

The AWS IoT Device Defender monitors **DevDefender Thing**. The first step in the workflow involves the AWS IoT Device Defender publishing results. These results are sent to **SNS DevDefender Results Topic**, an SNS service used to relay or broadcast certain messages or findings.

Upon receiving the results from IoT Device Defender, **SNS DevDefender Results Topic** triggers a Lambda function in the second step. This function, represented as **Lambda DevDefender Results Processor**, processes the results or messages from IoT Device Defender. Notably, this Lambda function operates under a specific IAM role, labeled **DevDefender Results Processor Lambda Role**, granting it the necessary permissions to execute its tasks.

In the third step, there is a retrieval of findings, labeled **Get Findings**, which seems to imply the Lambda function or another component is fetching or analyzing the results/data that have been processed.

Lastly, in the fourth step, there's a **Replace Permissive Policy** action. This indicates that based on the findings or the processed results, the system might opt to replace or modify the active **Restrictive IoT Policy** action to enhance security or optimize operations.

With a better understanding of how these security workflows work in AWS, we can now look at how risk management is done within the IoT landscape.

Risk management within the IoT landscape

We have seen the usage of data analytics in the past two sections and how it has been beneficial for our workloads. Now, let's look at how it can benefit industry cases and how we can accordingly evaluate our deployments based on best practices that are set out for us.

Threat modeling for IoT systems

There are often many steps that can be taken for **threat modeling**, but mostly there are nine steps that generally are abided by:

1. **Identify the scope**: Identify the IoT devices, networks, applications, and data involved in the IoT network.

2. **Create an architecture diagram**: Create a diagram to map out the IoT network, including devices, sensors, gateways, networks, and cloud services. This will help in understanding the dependencies and interactions between components.

3. **Identify threats**: Identify potential threats to the IoT network, such as unauthorized access, data tampering, malware, physical theft, and data breaches. Conduct a brainstorming session with stakeholders, including IT and security personnel, to identify potential threats.

4. **Identify vulnerabilities**: Identify the vulnerabilities and weaknesses of each component, including hardware, firmware, software, and network protocols.

5. **Assess the likelihood and impact**: Evaluate the likelihood and impact of each threat based on the criticality of the component, the type of data, and the likelihood of the threat being exploited.

6. **Prioritize and rank the risks**: Prioritize and rank the risks based on the likelihood and impact, and the level of effort required to mitigate each risk.

7. **Develop risk mitigation strategies**: Develop mitigation strategies for each identified risk, including network segmentation, encryption, access control, intrusion detection and prevention, and **incident response** (IR) planning.

8. **Test the mitigation strategies**: Test the mitigation strategies to ensure they are effective in addressing the identified risks.

9. **Review and update the threat model**: Review and update the threat model regularly to ensure it remains relevant and effective in addressing new threats and vulnerabilities.

With that understanding of threat modeling, we can now take a look at different security controls that can be in use.

Security controls

Security controls are an essential aspect of risk management in IoT security. With the increasing number of IoT devices being used across various industries, it is imperative to implement security controls to minimize the risks associated with these devices. Security controls are measures put in place to manage security risks and ensure that systems and data are protected against unauthorized access, modification, or destruction. In this section, we will discuss some of the security controls that can be implemented to manage security risks in IoT networks.

One of the most important security controls in IoT security is access control. Access control is the process of limiting access to IoT devices and data to authorized personnel only. This can be done by implementing authentication mechanisms such as passwords, biometrics, or **two-factor authentication (2FA)**. Access control helps prevent unauthorized access to IoT devices and data, which can lead to data breaches or device compromise.

Another critical security control in IoT security is encryption. Encryption is the process of converting plain text data into an encoded format that can only be read by authorized personnel who have the decryption key. Encryption is essential in IoT security because it helps protect data as it is transmitted over the internet or stored in cloud-based servers. Implementing encryption mechanisms ensures that data transmitted or stored in the cloud is protected from interception and unauthorized access.

In addition to access control and encryption, firewalls are also an essential security control in IoT security. Firewalls are used to filter network traffic between devices and networks to prevent unauthorized access. A firewall can be used to block unauthorized incoming traffic while allowing authorized traffic to pass through. Firewalls are important because they help prevent unauthorized access to IoT devices and networks, reducing the risk of data breaches or device compromise.

Finally, regular software updates and patching are also critical security controls in IoT security. Software updates and patching ensure that IoT devices and software are up to date and have the latest security features and patches. Regular updates help prevent security vulnerabilities that can be exploited by attackers to gain unauthorized access to IoT devices or data.

IR

IR is a crucial component of risk management for IoT security. Despite all the precautions, an incident may occur, and it is necessary to be prepared to respond quickly and effectively. IR is a well-defined process for responding to security breaches and incidents, aimed at minimizing the damage and reducing recovery time.

Here are some key steps to include in an **IR plan (IRP)** for IoT security:

1. **Identify the incident**: The first step is to recognize that an incident has occurred. This can be done through the monitoring of devices, networks, and logs, which should be done in real time.

2. **Contain the incident**: Once an incident has been identified, the next step is to contain it to prevent it from spreading. This may involve isolating affected devices, networks, or systems.

3. **Assess the damage**: After containing the incident, assess the damage caused by the incident. This will help in determining the severity of the incident and the required response.

4. **Notify appropriate parties**: Notify appropriate parties, such as internal IT staff, external vendors, and legal and regulatory authorities. The notification should include a description of the incident, the damage caused, and the steps taken to contain it.

5. **Investigate the incident**: Conduct a thorough investigation to determine the cause of the incident, the extent of the damage, and the vulnerabilities that were exploited.

6. **Remediate the incident**: Take necessary steps to remediate the incident and prevent it from occurring again in the future. This may involve patching systems, updating security policies, or modifying configurations.

7. **Monitor the system**: After an incident has been remediated, continue to monitor the system to ensure that the incident does not reoccur. This may involve monitoring logs, devices, networks, and systems for any unusual activity.

With that, we've gained a much better understanding of risk management within the cloud. Now, we can have a look at privacy and compliance within IoT networks.

Privacy and compliance within IoT networks

Privacy and compliance are critical concerns within IoT networks. As IoT devices collect and share sensitive data, protecting the privacy of individuals becomes a significant challenge. Additionally, various regulations require companies to comply with specific privacy and security standards to ensure that they handle sensitive data properly.

One significant challenge of IoT privacy is the collection and storage of personal information, such as biometric data or location information, which can be used to identify individuals. Companies must have strong data governance policies in place to ensure that personal data is only collected and used, when necessary, with consent and explicit permission from users.

Another critical aspect of privacy and compliance in IoT networks is the need to comply with regulations such as the **General Data Protection Regulation (GDPR)**, which applies to companies that collect and process personal data of EU citizens, regardless of the location of the company. Other regulations, such as the **California Consumer Privacy Act (CCPA)** and the **Health Insurance Portability and Accountability Act (HIPAA)**, also require companies to adhere to strict privacy and security standards.

To comply with these regulations, companies must ensure that they have implemented adequate security measures such as encryption, access controls, and audit logs to protect sensitive data from unauthorized access or data breaches. Furthermore, companies should conduct regular risk assessments to identify and address vulnerabilities and implement security best practices, such as the use of secure communication protocols and the regular updating of software and firmware.

In conclusion, privacy and compliance are significant concerns in IoT networks. Companies must have strong data governance policies in place, comply with relevant regulations, and implement robust security measures to protect sensitive data and ensure the privacy of individuals. By prioritizing privacy and compliance, companies can build trust with their customers and stakeholders, protect their brand reputation, and avoid potential legal and financial repercussions.

We have now obtained a better understanding of privacy and compliance considerations and controls. We can next look at cryptography controls for the IoT landscape.

Cryptography controls for the IoT landscape

Cryptography is a crucial security control in the IoT landscape. It is the practice of protecting information by converting it into an unreadable format, using mathematical algorithms, and then converting it back to its original form by authorized individuals. Cryptography controls are used to safeguard IoT networks from unauthorized access, data theft, and cyberattacks.

One essential cryptography control is encryption. Encryption is the process of converting plain text into cipher text, which can only be deciphered using a key. Data encryption is crucial for IoT devices since data transmitted from these devices over the network can be intercepted by unauthorized individuals. End-to-end encryption ensures that the data is encrypted before it is transmitted and can only be decrypted by the intended recipient. Implementing encryption controls ensures that the data stored and transmitted in the IoT network is secure and can only be accessed by authorized individuals.

Another important cryptography control is digital signatures. Digital signatures ensure that the sender of the data is authentic and that the data has not been tampered with. Digital signatures are based on public-key cryptography, which uses two different keys for encryption and decryption. The sender uses a private key to sign the data, while the recipient uses the sender's public key to verify the digital signature. Digital signatures prevent unauthorized modification of data, ensuring that the data received is authentic and has not been tampered with.

Finally, key management is another essential cryptography control. In IoT networks, keys are used for encryption and decryption of data. These keys must be kept confidential and secure. Key management includes key generation, key distribution, key storage, and key revocation. IoT networks must have robust key management policies and procedures in place to ensure that keys are kept secure and are only accessible to authorized individuals.

In conclusion, cryptography controls are essential for ensuring the security of IoT networks. Encryption, digital signatures, and key management are critical cryptography controls that must be implemented in IoT networks to protect data from unauthorized access and cyberattacks. Cryptography controls should be implemented as part of a comprehensive security strategy to ensure the confidentiality, integrity, and availability of data in the IoT landscape.

With that, we have a foundational understanding of cryptography controls within the IoT landscape. We can look at one such implementation through a case study.

Schneider Electric's implementation of an IoT solution security architecture

Schneider Electric is a global leader in energy management and automation, with a presence in over 100 countries. The company offers a wide range of products and services, including IoT solutions, that help customers manage energy more efficiently and sustainably.

To ensure the security of its IoT solutions, Schneider Electric implemented a comprehensive security architecture that includes several layers of protection. One of the key components of this architecture is a secure boot process, which ensures that the device's firmware and software are genuine and have not been tampered with. This is accomplished by using secure boot technology to verify the authenticity of the firmware and software during the boot process.

Another important aspect of Schneider Electric's security architecture is its use of encryption to protect data in transit and at rest. All data transmitted between the IoT device and the cloud is encrypted using industry-standard protocols, such as SSL/TLS, to prevent unauthorized access. Additionally, all data stored on the device and in the cloud is encrypted using strong encryption algorithms to prevent data breaches.

To further enhance the security of its IoT solutions, Schneider Electric also implements secure communication protocols, such as MQTT and CoAP, which are designed specifically for IoT devices. These protocols provide a lightweight and secure means of transmitting data between the device and the cloud.

In addition to these technical measures, Schneider Electric also implements robust policies and procedures to ensure the security of its IoT solutions. This includes regular vulnerability assessments and penetration testing to identify and address potential security weaknesses, as well as employee training and awareness programs to promote good security practices.

Practical – Creating a secure smart lock system

In this practical, we will create a secure smart lock system using an Arduino board, an **Radio-Frequency Identification (RFID)** reader, and an electronic lock. The focus will be on implementing security best practices and risk management principles to ensure the privacy and safety of the system.

Materials

We can start off by taking a look at the following hardware and software required for this practical:

- Keyestudio Arduino Super Starter Kit
- MFRC522 RFID reader module
- Electronic lock or solenoid
- Jumper wires
- AWS account

Part 1 – Setting up the Arduino board and RFID reader

We can now look at setting up our hardware to be then loaded with the software.

1. Connect the Arduino board to your computer using a USB cable.

2. Connect the MFRC522 RFID reader module to the Arduino board using the following wiring:

   - SDA to pin 10
   - SCK to pin 13
   - MOSI to pin 11
   - MISO to pin 12
   - IRQ to unconnected
   - GND to GND
   - RST to pin 9
   - 3.3V to 3.3V

3. Connect the electronic lock or solenoid to a digital pin on the Arduino board (for example, pin 2) and the other end to GND.

With the hardware set up, we can now look to creating Arduino code for the encrypted RFID communication.

Part 2 – Arduino code for encrypted RFID communication

We now need to code up the Arduino code to provide encrypted RFID communication. Follow these steps:

1. Install the MFRC522 library for the RFID reader module in the Arduino IDE by going to **Sketch > Include Library > Manage Libraries**, then search for **MFRC522** and install the library by Miguel Balboa.

2. Create a new Arduino sketch and include the necessary libraries:

```
#include <SPI.h>
#include <MFRC522.h>
```

3. Define constants and variables for the RFID reader module, the electronic lock, and the encryption key:

```
#define RST_PIN 9
#define SS_PIN 10
#define LOCK_PIN 2

MFRC522 rfid(SS_PIN, RST_PIN);
```

4. Initialize the RFID reader and set the electronic lock pin as an output in the setup() function:

```
void setup() {
  Serial.begin(9600);
  SPI.begin();
  rfid.PCD_Init();
  pinMode(LOCK_PIN, OUTPUT);
}
```

5. Implement a function to convert the RFID UID byte array to a string:

```
String getUidString(byte *buffer, byte bufferSize) {
  String uidString = "";

  for (byte i = 0; i < bufferSize; i++) {
    uidString += String(buffer[i], HEX);
  }

  return uidString;
}
```

6. Implement a simple XOR-based encryption function (for demonstration purposes only; use a proper encryption algorithm for real-world applications):

```
String encrypt(String data) {
  String encrypted = "";
  char key = 'K';

  for (int i = 0; i < data.length(); i++) {
    encrypted += data[i] ^ key;
  }

  return encrypted;
}
```

7. Implement the `loop()` function to read RFID tags, encrypt the UID, and send the encrypted UID to the server for authentication (replace the placeholder code for server communication with actual AWS IoT communication code):

```
void loop() {
  if (!rfid.PICC_IsNewCardPresent() || !rfid.PICC_
ReadCardSerial()) {
    return;
  }

  String rfidUid = getUidString(rfid.uid.uidByte, rfid.uid.
size);
  Serial.print("RFID tag detected: ");
  Serial.println(rfidUid);

  String encryptedUid = encrypt(rfidUid);
  // Send the encrypted UID to the server for authentication

  // Receive the server's response
  // (Replace this with the actual server communication code)
  bool authenticated = true; // This is just a placeholder

  if (authenticated) {
    digitalWrite(LOCK_PIN, HIGH);
    delay(5000);
    digitalWrite(LOCK_PIN, LOW);
  } else {
    Serial.println("Access denied");
  }

  rfid.PICC_HaltA();
```

```
    rfid.PCD_StopCrypto1();
}
```

With that, we've wrapped up the Arduino code we need to provide for encrypted RFID communication, Now, we can look at setting up the AWS side.

Part 3 – AWS server-side setup

We now need to set up the AWS server side to take care of the authentication requirements. Follow these steps:

1. Log in to your AWS account and navigate to **AWS IoT Core**.

2. Create a new **Thing** instance and download its certificate, private key, and Amazon Root CA certificate.

3. Set up the AWS IoT SDK for Arduino and upload the necessary certificates to the Arduino board.

4. Modify the Arduino code to use the AWS IoT SDK to send the encrypted RFID UIDs to AWS IoT Core.

5. Create a new AWS Lambda function in Python to handle the RFID authentication.

6. Add the decrypt() function to the Lambda function, using the same XOR-based decryption algorithm as in the Arduino code:

```
def decrypt(data):
    decrypted = ""
    key = 'K'

    for char in data:
        decrypted += chr(ord(char) ^ ord(key))

    return decrypted
```

7. Add the authenticate() function to the Lambda function, with a predefined list of authorized RFID UIDs:

```
AUTHORIZED_RFID_UIDS = [
    "12345678",
    "87654321",
]

def authenticate(decrypted_data):
    if decrypted_data in AUTHORIZED_RFID_UIDS:
        return True
    return False
```

8. Implement the Lambda function to decrypt the received RFID data, check whether the UID is in the authorized list, and send a response back to the Arduino board:

```
def lambda_handler(event, context):
    encrypted_data = event["encryptedUid"]
    decrypted_data = decrypt(encrypted_data)
    is_authenticated = authenticate(decrypted_data)

    # Send the authentication result back to the Arduino
    return {
        "isAuthenticated": is_authenticated
    }
```

With that, we've made the necessary configurations for the hardware and AWS server-side code. We can now configure the Lambda side.

Configuring the Lambda function to be triggered by AWS IoT Core

We need to configure the Lambda function to then be triggered by AWS IoT Core, as outlined in the next steps:

1. In the AWS Management Console, go to the **AWS IoT Core** service.

2. Click on **Act** in the left-hand menu, and then click on **Create a rule**.

3. Enter a name and description for the rule.

4. Under **Rule query statement**, enter a SQL query to filter incoming messages. For example, use this:

```
SELECT * FROM 'your/topic'
```

5. Replace `'your/topic'` with the specific MQTT topic where the Arduino board sends encrypted RFID UIDs. Under **Actions**, click on **Add action** and select **Send a message to a Lambda function**.

6. In the **Select a Lambda function** drop-down menu, choose the Lambda function you created earlier for handling RFID authentication.

7. Click **Add action** and then click **Create rule** to save the new rule.

Now, whenever a new message is received by AWS IoT Core on the specified topic, the Lambda function will be triggered to process the message. We can then look at receiving the authentication code from AWS IoT Core.

Updating the Arduino code to receive the authentication result from AWS IoT Core

To update the Arduino code to receive the authentication result, you need to subscribe to an MQTT topic where the Lambda function sends the authentication result. Let's assume the Lambda function publishes the result on a topic named `'your/response_topic'`. The following steps will guide you through updating the code accordingly:

1. First, include the required libraries for the AWS IoT SDK for Arduino:

    ```
    #include <WiFi101.h>
    #include <MQTT.h>
    ```

2. Replace `WiFi101.h` with the appropriate library if you are using a different Wi-Fi module.

3. Set up the Wi-Fi and AWS IoT MQTT client configurations:

    ```
    const char* ssid = "your_ssid";
    const char* password = "your_wifi_password";
    const char* aws_endpoint = "your_aws_endpoint";
    const char* aws_key = "your_aws_key";
    const char* aws_secret = "your_aws_secret";

    WiFiClientSecure wifiClient;
    MQTTClient mqttClient(256);
    ```

4. Connect to Wi-Fi in the `setup()` function:

    ```
    WiFi.begin(ssid, password);

    while (WiFi.status() != WL_CONNECTED) {
      delay(500);
      Serial.print(".");
    }

    Serial.println("Connected to Wi-Fi");
    ```

5. Connect to the AWS IoT MQTT broker:

    ```
    wifiClient.setCACert(aws_root_ca);
    wifiClient.setCertificate(aws_client_cert);
    wifiClient.setPrivateKey(aws_client_key);

    mqttClient.begin(aws_endpoint, 8883, wifiClient);
    mqttClient.onMessage(messageReceived);
    ```

```
while (!mqttClient.connect(aws_key, aws_secret)) {
  delay(1000);
  Serial.println("Connecting to AWS IoT Core...");
}

Serial.println("Connected to AWS IoT Core");
```

6. Add a function called `messageReceived` to handle the incoming authentication result from AWS IoT Core:

```
void messageReceived(String &topic, String &payload) {
  bool authenticated = payload == "true";

  if (authenticated) {
    digitalWrite(LOCK_PIN, HIGH);
    delay(5000);
    digitalWrite(LOCK_PIN, LOW);
  } else {
    Serial.println("Access denied");
  }
}
```

7. In the `loop()` function, after sending the encrypted UID to AWS IoT Core, subscribe to the response topic:

```
mqttClient.subscribe("your/response_topic");
```

Replace `your/response_topic` with the topic where the Lambda function publishes the authentication result.

With these changes, the Arduino code now sends the encrypted UID to AWS IoT Core.

By following these steps, you can create a secure smart lock system that integrates security best practices and risk management principles. This practical will help you gain a deeper understanding of IoT security, privacy, and risk management, providing a foundation for building more advanced secure IoT applications.

As always, feel free to look at the documentation from all the hardware and software involved in this practical. We encourage you to also explore more security options when it comes to usage of IoT on-premises and within the cloud, as it continues to be an imperative part of the diverse architectures that are present within the ecosystem.

Summary

In this chapter, we explored the current state of risk and security within the IoT landscape. We delved into the security and privacy controls within the cloud management landscape and emphasized the importance of risk management within the IoT ecosystem. The chapter highlighted the need for privacy and compliance within IoT networks and discussed the various cryptography controls that can be implemented for the IoT landscape.

In the next chapter, we will be looking at how we can work with open source in IoT and develop a project within that space.

Further reading

For more information about what was covered in this chapter, please refer to the following links:

- Explore more on how AWS IoT provides security: `https://docs.aws.amazon.com/iot/latest/developerguide/iot-security.html`

- Take a look at IoT vulnerability case studies: `https://www.ece.nus.edu.sg/stfpage/bsikdar/papers/net_mag_20.pdf`

- Explore lightweight cryptography for IoT: `https://www.nec.com/en/global/techrep/journal/g17/n01/170114.html`

- Understand more about what makes up a security framework for IoT: `https://iotsecurityfoundation.org/wp-content/uploads/2021/11/IoTSF-IoT-Security-Assurance-Framework-Release-3.0-Nov-2021-1.pdf`

12

Exploring and Innovating with Open Source IoT

Open source software is software that is freely and publicly available for anyone to use, modify, and distribute. This allows for collaboration within software development, where individuals and organizations can contribute to the software and build, improve, and maintain it. Within the field of IoT, it is becoming increasingly important as a standard because it allows for greater collaboration and innovation. Through open source software, developers get access to a myriad of tools and resources to help them develop their IoT solutions without having to be tied to a specific vendor or platform.

Through our work within IoT, we can also help advance the state of IoT and create solutions that are powerful and flexible. Even the smallest of contributions will still make a significant impact on a project. We need to learn about the best practices that we need to keep in mind while performing these contributions, why we need to contribute to open source, and understand how we can best approach working within open source **repositories (repos)**.

In this chapter, we're going to cover the following main topics:

- Understanding the current focus areas within the community for IoT
- Taking advantage of open source IoT that works for your use cases
- Learning how to create, maintain, and contribute to a repo for open source IoT

Technical requirements

This chapter will require you to have the following hardware and software installed:

- Hardware:

  - ESP32

- Software:
  - Blynk app
  - Arduino IDE

You can access the GitHub folder that contains the code that's used in this chapter at `https://github.com/PacktPublishing/IoT-Made-Easy-for-Beginners/tree/main/Chapter12/`.

Introduction to community innovations within IoT

In this section, we will discuss why open source has been a key factor in propelling IoT forward within both personal and professional settings, and how it has developed within organizations as a standard and a culture. We will also talk about the reasons why we should contribute to open source projects, the guiding principles toward it, and the structure of open source repos.

These will be useful for you to apply to your learnings as you will understand more about why you are learning about open source contributions and how you can be a more effective contributor in the meantime, all while taking inspiration for the next open source project that may strike your fancy.

Open source as a standard

Open source is becoming more of a standard within many industries as it allows for transparency and collaboration, leading to the development of more stable and secure software. It also helps reduce the reliance of users and organizations on proprietary solutions, hence allowing them to save on costs. This has been seen in many industries, where organizations and users foster their contributions as open to the public (aside from their private contributions). This is also what leads to them fostering a culture of contribution, which is what we will talk about next.

Open source as a culture

Open source as a culture is often adhered to; it is all about creating and sharing software that is freely available to use, modify, and distribute. It focuses on promoting a culture within organizations that encourages collaboration and community-driven development to ensure that high-quality, reliable software is created that can benefit a wide range of users. The culture prioritizes transparency, inclusivity, and sharing resources and knowledge. It encourages participation and contributions from every individual as there is always something that someone can contribute This way, we can achieve common goals and build better, more beneficial technology for anyone and everyone.

Why contribute to the community?

Contributing to the open source community is not just a powerful avenue for individual growth and skill enhancement. It also nurtures a collaborative ecosystem that benefits the entire tech industry. Let's delve into six pivotal components that highlight the significance of such contributions and how they collectively shape the open source landscape:

- **Innovation**: Open source projects allow developers to collaborate and have access to the latest cutting-edge work, allowing for further innovations and advancements within IoT.

- **Flexibility**: Open source projects offer much flexibility, allowing developers to tailor the code according to their use cases. This is very powerful within IoT, given that we often need to fit a myriad of use cases depending on what we are creating the solution for.

- **Cost-effectiveness**: Open source projects generally have very low or no costs that are associated with them, making them a cost-effective solution for the different users and organizations that are looking to invest in them and implement IoT solutions with them.

- **Community support**: Open source projects generally have large and active communities of developers who contribute to the project and continuously provide support to users. This is especially useful to get in-house expertise within select areas within IoT.

- **Improved security**: Given that there are contributors from varying backgrounds, more eyes are reviewing the code, ensuring that improved security is adhered to given the continuously looming threat of attackers.

- **Interoperability**: Open standards are often adhered to by open source projects, allowing the different IoT systems and devices to easily communicate with each other. Interoperability is a very important requirement in IoT. We will talk more about this in the next chapter.

With this, we can now look at what the guiding principles of open source are.

Guiding principles of open source

The ethos of open source is deeply rooted in a set of guiding principles that ensure transparency, collaboration, and community-driven development. In this section, we will explore five fundamental principles that underpin the open source movement and define its unique character in the world of software development:

- **Transparency**: Open source depends on the unlimited access to information that is required to complete a contributor's work. Through this, developers can share ideas and make decisions more efficiently and effectively while building on each other's strengths.

- **Collaboration**: Open source depends on the participation of contributors within different projects, creating the ability to modify the work of others, and opening up new opportunities. It is all about ensuring that everyone works on a problem that cannot be solved by individuals, leveraging the different perspectives that have been brought together by the different contributors who are currently present and ready to contribute to the code.

- **Release early and often**: This principle follows the agile methodology, ensuring that rapid and iterative approaches are adopted and that the freedom to experiment and change perspectives is encouraged.

- **Inclusive meritocracy**: This principle ensures that everyone is included in decision-making in open source projects, taking in good ideas and suggestions that come from anyone. It is very important as we need to build a culture where every voice matters.

- **Community**: Building as a group of like-minded individuals is important as we want to base decision-making on shared values. Additionally, we need to ensure that everyone understands that it is imperative to adhere to the big-picture goals before personal agendas to ensure that the collaboration and work on the project will be a success.

Now that we understand the guiding principles, we can start exploring the structure of an open source project.

Structure of an open source project

The success and coherence of an open source project often hinge on its underlying structure, which serves as its architectural blueprint. In this section, we will unravel five integral components that constitute the foundation of any robust open source endeavor, ensuring its sustainability and growth:

- **Author**: The author is the person(s) or organization that has created the project.

- **Owner**: The owner is the person(s) that has the appropriate administrative privileges in terms of ownership over the repo. This may or may not be the same as the original author.

- **Maintainers**: Maintainers are the contributors to the project who manage the organizational aspects of the project, and also may be the authors or owners of the project. They ensure that the vision of the project is being adhered to.

- **Contributors**: Contributors are anyone who has contributed something to the success of the project.

- **Community members**: Community members are people who have or are yet to use the project. They may choose to be active in conversations, expressing their opinions on the development of the project.

Now that we understand the structure of the project, let's look at how we can find a project to contribute to.

Finding a project to contribute to

When looking for an open source project that you'd like to contribute to, there are several factors that you need to consider. Here are five of the most important:

- **Relevance**: You need to look for a project that aligns well with your interests and expertise. This will ensure that you will enjoy working on the project while being able to make valuable contributions.

- **Community**: You then need to research the community that is behind the project. You need to keep a lookout to see if it is an active community of contributors since some projects may be left in a stale state and with not many active contributors. This will make it easier for you to reach out to them and get guidance and help where necessary.

- **Development stage**: You need to consider at which stage the development is at. Depending on your intentions and interests, you may prefer to contribute to one that is just starting compared to one that is already mature and simply being maintained without many new features being proactively rolled out to the community.

- **Licensing**: You need to pay close attention to the license as some may have certain restrictions or obligations that you may find difficult to abide by.

- **Code base**: You need to review the code base of the project. You need to see if the code is well-organized and maintained well as it will help you understand the project better and follow its style for future contributions. Often, some projects have unorganized code bases; this does not mean that you should not contribute to it. Instead, it should make you think if you can still understand it and can abide by the same formatting. This is often why it is important to discuss the standards of code formatting at the beginning of an open source project.

Once you've found an open source project that you feel fits well with you, you can start exploring the project through its documentation and the code base that it is based on. Feel free to reach out to the community around it as well for more information.

Contributing to projects

Diving into the realm of open source contributions requires a thoughtful approach, ensuring that your efforts are both impactful and harmonious with the project's objectives. In this section, we'll illuminate four key considerations that every contributor should keep in mind to make their involvement truly meaningful:

- **Provide the relevant context**: Ensure that you include the context of the contribution and how you feel that it would help the development of the project. You do not need to make this wordy, but you must make a point of how this will help the future of the repo and the overall vision of the project.

- **Understand what assistance you are asking for**: Make sure that you read the documentation and the existing issues to ensure that your concern has not already been addressed by either a contribution or an answer to an issue.

- **Be concise**: Maintainers may not have much time to answer questions since they most likely have other things to do aside from maintaining the open source project, so you need to ensure that you keep communications concise and to the point! This way, maintainers can address things quickly, be it within questions made in issues or pull request reviews.

- **Ensure you keep a respectful attitude**: Ensure that you're civilized within discussions and communications in open source projects. Respect decisions that are made as a team and ensure that you conduct yourself accordingly.

From here, we can look at how we can continue managing our contributions.

Continuing to manage contributions

Once you start contributing to projects, you need to continue managing the contributions that come through. This includes continually reviewing pull requests, making pull requests of your own, responding to issues, and more. The work for an open source repo never ends – unless it is deprecated and archived, of course! You will need to continue developing based on the vision that has been set out by the team and ensure that it is adhered to for the project to remain alive and continuously used by the community.

In this section, we learned about the essentials of open source IoT projects and how to contribute to them. Now, we can look at areas that open source contributors are focusing on in the community.

Current focus areas in the community

Within IoT, there are areas of prioritization that are focused on. These are usually areas that are either seeing wide adoption or areas that are still lacking development. In this section, we will delve into the top focus areas and walk through one such solution for one of the focus areas that is developed in the community.

Top focus areas

There are a myriad of focuses that the IoT community currently has. Here, we will discuss some of the top focus areas that are currently being looked at by the IoT community:

- **Connectivity**: This factor is all about how we enable devices and sensors to connect to the internet and communicate with the myriad of devices, gateways, and cloud platforms that they can connect to. Matter is an example of an open source standard for increased compatibility among smart home products and increased security. It aims to improve the connection between various smart home devices.

- **Device management**: Managing and maintaining the life cycle of IoT devices is a big focus area, especially in being able to better provision and monitor our devices, alongside rolling out important software updates.

- **Data processing and analytics**: Collecting, processing, and analyzing data is a crucial factor that many focus on within the community to create solutions for extracting insights and driving better decision-making.

- **Security**: With the increase in security cases spiking with the transition of many workloads to the cloud infrastructure, security has become a bigger focus within the open source community, with the need to ensure that unauthorized access and data breaches are prevented.

- **Interoperability**: This factor is all about looking into how different devices, gateways, and platforms can communicate and work together seamlessly despite not being from the same provider.

- **Edge computing**: This factor is how we decide to process data at the edge of the network, and the new technologies that could help facilitate further innovations within this area.

- **User experience and visualization**: This factor is all about how we can create more user-friendly interfaces and visualizations in interacting and making sense of IoT data.

There are still many more focus areas, but these are certainly the top ones that are being looked at. Now, we can take a look at some focus areas within open source technologies.

Open source technologies

Here are some examples:

- **Open source endpoint hardware**: This focus area concentrates on the hardware aspects of IoT devices. It involves developing and refining the physical components that are integral to IoT systems, such as sensors and actuators. The community focuses on making these hardware components not only more efficient and reliable but also open source, ensuring accessibility and customization.

- **Open source client software development kits (SDKs)**: SDKs are essential for building IoT applications. The emphasis here is on creating open source SDKs that provide developers with the tools and libraries necessary to build, test, and deploy IoT solutions efficiently.

- **Open source gateway/access point**: This focus area deals with the development of gateways or access points that facilitate communication between IoT devices and the network. By making these gateways open source, the community aims to enhance interoperability and flexibility in IoT networks.

- **Open source or free data platforms**: This area is about developing open source or free platforms for data processing and analytics. These platforms help in efficiently managing the vast amounts of data generated by IoT devices, providing insights and aiding in better decision-making.

There are still many more technology focus areas, but these are some highlights of trending areas. Now, let's take a look at a case study on an open source project.

A case study on an open source project

Many open source projects have been created by many companies and users. We are going to talk through one of them, which promotes how users can deploy a fully open source IoT edge computing solution:

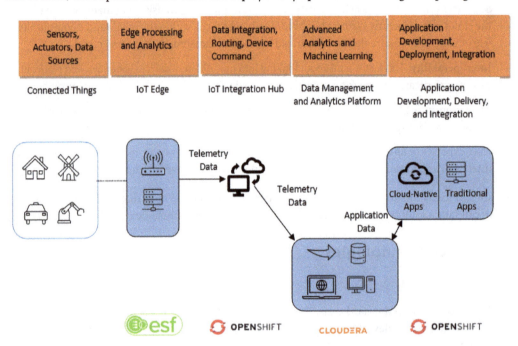

Figure 12.1 – Sample open source project by three companies

Contributors from the Eclipse IoT Foundation and the Apache Software Foundation developed this architecture. It lets users provision resources freely and later offers them the ability to commercialize using enterprise-grade solutions.

Initially, the Intelligent IoT edge stack leverages the **Eurotech Everyware Software Framework (ESF)** in tandem with the Red Hat middleware. This combination aids in data intake, smart routing, and ensuring device connectivity. Subsequently, it transitions to the IoT integration hub, powered by **Eurotech Everyware Cloud (EC)** and Red Hat Middleware operating on the OpenShift container platform. Here, it oversees the integration of connected devices, orchestrates downstream data traffic, and implements access and authentication controls. Afterward, it taps into the data management and analytics platform built on Cloudera Enterprise, streamlining data processing, ensuring lasting data storage, and facilitating analytics to glean profound business insights. Finally, it is put through the application development and delivery environment based on the Red Hat OpenShift Container Platform for development, deployment, and integration with other cloud-native applications.

With that, you now have a better view of what the open source community has been working on. Now, we can take a look at how to start building and maintaining a repo for open source IoT.

Building and maintaining a repo for open source IoT

When venturing into the dynamic landscape of IoT, building and maintaining a repo forms the cornerstone of collaborative and transparent development. A well-structured repo not only fosters inclusivity and accessibility but also ensures the security and efficiency of IoT solutions. As we delve into the intricate process of building and sustaining a repo, we will explore the nuances of version control, documentation, license compliances, and community engagement. Furthermore, we will elucidate the practices that accentuate the robustness and reliability of open source IoT projects, facilitating a breeding ground for avant-garde solutions that resonate with the ethos of community-driven development, and walk you through a practical exercise of doing so properly so that you can get familiar with the appropriate steps.

Establishing guidelines for the project

When setting up an open source project, it's crucial to lay down clear guidelines to ensure seamless collaboration and understanding among contributors:

- **LICENSE**: All open source projects need to have an open source license. It is important to note that if it does not have a license, it will not be open source.

- **README**: The README file serves as a guide that states how community members can start exploring it, while also talking about how it can be used by the community for different use cases that they need.

- **CONTRIBUTING**: Contributing documents outline how people can contribute to the project, specifying the types of contributions that are needed and how the process works.

- **CODE_OF_CONDUCT**: The code of conduct outlines the ground rules of how members within the project community should abide to ensure that the environment will be welcoming and friendly.

- **Other documentation**: There may be other types of documentation that are needed for certain projects, such as tutorials or walkthroughs.

You can find a sample structure of this, along with its contents, in this chapter's GitHub repo.

With a comprehensive understanding of project guidelines in place, it's equally vital to delve into the best practices that ensure the project's sustained success and growth.

Best practices for maintaining your open source repo

Embarking on the open source journey requires not only creating a repo but also nurturing it to ensure continued engagement and relevance. Here are some best practices to ensure that it is maintained properly:

- **Automate**: Where possible, automate dependencies within your repo. You need to ensure that you reduce your manual workloads as much as you can; you simply need to create mechanisms that can help with the development process. An example is setting up a CI/CD pipeline that can check for errors and deploy to a staging environment.

- **Address issues**: Ensure that you address issues as they emerge. People dislike repos that do not have active answers on them, so they would appreciate quick responses to issues that are raised. At the same time, this is beneficial for you as a contributor as well, as you become aware of the different new issues that may be affiliated with your project and can promptly make the necessary changes to it.

- **Spread the word**: Make sure you let everyone know about the project. As mentioned previously, getting the word out to potential contributors and the community is challenging. You need to build up a reputation as an open source contributor, and soon enough, you'll be announcing projects that many will want to jump into and contribute to.

With these best practices in hand, let's delve into the intricacies of managing your open source project.

Your open source project

Now that we've looked at best practices for contributions, let's look at the steps you can take toward starting your first open source project.

Researching and starting your project

First, you will need to perform due diligence and perform research before starting your project:

1. Identify the problem or use case that you want your open source project to address within the IoT ecosystem.

2. Research existing open source projects to see if a similar solution already exists. If so, you need to decide how the proposed project can differ from it or if you need to simply contribute to the existing project; there would not be much value within open source communities in having two projects that essentially function similarly.

3. Assemble a team of developers, engineers, and other stakeholders who have the skills and resources to contribute to the project. You can also start one yourself; you just have to ensure you have the right skill set and can get the word out well as that is one of the trickiest things about open source if you are not too familiar with it.

4. Establish clear guidelines and processes for collaboration, code review, testing, and documentation.

5. Start a repo based on a version control system such as Git to manage and track the relevant changes that will be made to the project's code base.

6. Develop the roadmap for the project and set milestones for when you would like key features and deliverables to be done.

7. Push the first pieces of code to your repo so that you have something in it to maintain.

With that, you've started your journey to open source development! Now, let's discuss how you can maintain your repo.

Maintaining your repo

Once you start the project, you need to continue maintaining your repo and ensuring the community base that uses it is happy with the current outcomes from it. Here are a few steps that you need to take to develop and maintain your first open source project:

- Regularly communicate the progress that you are making alongside updates to the community through channels such as mailing lists, forums, or social media

- Encourage the community to get involved by making the project easily accessible, ensuring that there are clear instructions on how they can get involved

- Continuously monitor the performance of the project, ensuring that adjustments are made when necessary to ensure that the project will be an ongoing success

- Ensure that you are up to date with new developments within the IoT ecosystem, and make updates to your project accordingly based on that

We'll put this theory into practice with this next practical, which will let you research for and create an open source project, ensuring that you adhere to best practices.

Practical – taking advantage of open source IoT for your use case

In this end-of-chapter practical, we are going to do a somewhat different practical than we have done previously. We want to utilize this practical as a more freeform practical that allows you to use the skills you've gained so far to build on some open source IoT based on your use case.

Required tools and technologies

You will need to utilize the following tools and technologies for this practical:

- A computer with internet access

- An Arduino UNO/ESP32/Raspberry Pi (choose this based on your familiarity and the requirements of the chosen project)

- Sensors (for example, temperature sensor, motion sensor, and so on) and actuators (for example, relay, servo motor, and so on) that are compatible with your chosen board

- Access to open source repos (such as GitHub)

- A compatible coding environment (Arduino IDE, Thonny Python IDE for Raspberry Pi, and so on)

Now that you understand the requirements, you are ready to begin developing your open source project.

Delving into open source

In the following steps, you will be guided on how to start looking into developing your open source project. This is meant to let you use your interests and the skills you have developed thus far, so be creative!

Identifying and setting up the development environment

Understanding your tools and environment is the foundational step in any project. Here, you must deeply consider the strengths and capabilities of your chosen platform, aligning them with a specific, practical use case that leverages open source IoT for a meaningful, realizable goal:

- **Identify a specific use case**: Leverage your existing knowledge of Arduino, ESP32, and Raspberry Pi platforms to identify a particular use case that suits your interests and the hardware's capabilities. Consider realms such as home automation, weather monitoring systems, or health monitoring systems. Detail the problem you wish to solve, the target audience, and why it is pertinent to address this issue. Craft a brief document highlighting your reflections and findings.

- **Refine your development environment**: Next, you will need to refine your development environment based on the hardware you are using. You will be guided through the refinement accordingly, so look for the hardware you are currently looking to have the development environment refined for:

  - **For Arduino and ESP32 users**:

    - Revisit your Arduino IDE setup to ensure it is up to date and conducive to your selected project. Ensure you have all the necessary libraries and tools installed for your chosen platform (either Arduino or ESP32).

- Take a moment to explore recent updates or plugins available in the Arduino IDE that could be beneficial for your project. Make a list of any additions you have made to your IDE during this revisitation.

- **For Raspberry Pi users**:

  - Check your Raspbian operating system to ensure it is up to date and configured correctly for your selected project.

  - Review the programming languages and tools available in your setup. If Python is your choice, confirm that you have a well-configured Python environment, including any necessary libraries or frameworks that will facilitate your project.

Now that you have refreshed and ready environment, you are ready to start exploring and analyzing open source repos that you can use.

Exploring and analyzing open source repos

Open source repos are rich hubs where you can find a plethora of resources and accumulated knowledge. Here, you'll venture into the open source ecosystem, deep-dive into various projects, and grasp their technical nuances. Your objective is to identify a project that resonates with your chosen use case and leverages the capabilities of Arduino, ESP32, or Raspberry Pi:

1. Begin your exploration by heading to GitHub. Utilize the search function to find projects that correspond with your identified use case and involve the use of Arduino, ESP32, or Raspberry Pi platforms. Aim to explore projects that have good documentation and active maintainers.

2. From the projects you find, choose three that catch your interest. Make a list that includes the following details:

    - The repo link for future reference

    - The main features of the project, highlighting what makes each stand out

3. Now, take a closer look at each of your listed projects. Dive into the available technical documentation in the respective repos to fathom the underpinnings of each project. Focus on the following aspects:

    - Understanding the hardware setup and the rationale behind the choice of components

    - The libraries that are utilized in the project and their roles in the functionality of the system

    - Gaining an overview of the code structure and familiarizing yourself with the main functions and classes, and how they interact to create the solution

4. Armed with insights from the deep dive, create a detailed technical breakdown for each project. This should entail the following:

    - A list of hardware components with a brief description of the role each plays in the project

    - Details of the necessary libraries and frameworks being utilized, accompanied by a brief note on what each facilitates in the project

    - A brief overview of the code structure while delineating main functions, classes, and their interrelationships. This will give you a sense of the project's architectural blueprint

Through doing this, you will have fostered a rich understanding of a selection of open source projects, grasping not just their functionalities but the technical intricacies that power them. This analytical endeavor prepares you to leverage existing works adeptly, with a nuanced understanding of how to select and adapt open source solutions for your prototype, propelling you a step closer to transforming your IoT concept into a tangible reality.

Prototype development

After an extensive exploration and analysis of open source projects, it's time for you to roll up your sleeves and immerse yourself in the fulfilling process of prototyping. Here, you will be practically applying the knowledge you've gathered so far, setting up the hardware meticulously, and configuring the software robustly to breathe life into your chosen IoT prototype. Here is a detailed breakdown of the steps you must follow:

1. Refer back to the technical breakdown you created earlier and procure all the necessary components. Ensure that you verify the specifications and compatibility with your Arduino, ESP32, or Raspberry Pi platform.

2. Following the guidelines stipulated in the project repo, assemble the hardware setup. Pay close attention to the connections and configurations to prevent any errors during testing. It would be beneficial to cross-verify with images or schematics available in the repo for an accurate setup.

3. Clone the repo of your chosen project into your local development environment. This will allow you to have all the project files readily accessible.

4. Set up the development environment while following the detailed instructions available in the project's documentation. Ensure all the necessary libraries and frameworks are installed correctly.

5. With everything in place, delve into the code. Start by understanding the existing code structure and functionalities. Then, modify it so that it aligns with your personalized requirements. This could involve setting different threshold values for sensors or even adding new functionalities that enhance the project's utility to suit your use case.

6. As you configure and personalize the software, ensure that you document the entire process meticulously. Highlight the modifications that were made in the code and the rationale behind them.

7. Use GitHub to manage your code efficiently. This will facilitate tracking changes and maintaining a clean code repo.

By performing these steps, you will have transformed an open source project into a customized prototype that resonates with your identified use case. You would have journeyed through procuring and setting up hardware components, configuring the software environment, and tailoring the code to your preferences, emerging with a prototype that is a testimony to your analytical and technical prowess. Remember, the prototype doesn't have to be perfect; it's a learning journey where you have the liberty to experiment, learn, and iterate.

Documentation and reflection

As you approach the end of your prototype development, it is essential to document your journey meticulously. Here, you will need to reflect on your learning and experiences:

1. Compile a comprehensive document detailing every aspect of your prototype development journey, including hardware setup details, software configurations, and testing logs.

2. Reflect on your learning journey. Identify what worked well and what was challenging and articulate how you can apply the knowledge you've gained in future projects.

By engaging with this practical, you will have cultivated a rich understanding and competence in utilizing open source repos to devise and realize a robust IoT prototype. You will have gained a hands-on understanding of harnessing the versatile functionalities of platforms such as Arduino, ESP32, or Raspberry Pi to address real-world scenarios. Engaging deeply with the specific sensors and actuators that are compatible with your chosen board has imparted knowledge about the integral components required to build an IoT solution from the ground up. Moreover, you have developed a discerning eye for identifying and selecting valuable open source projects based on their features and technical backbone, a skill that's indispensable in the ever-evolving landscape of IoT.

Beyond the technical prowess you've cultivated, this practical session has ushered you into the nitty-gritty of prototype development, including the meticulous processes of debugging and optimization to enhance system efficiency and functionality. They have honed their ability to conduct precise hardware setups and nuanced software configurations, transforming repo code into a personalized IoT solution. This journey through the iterative cycle of development, from inception to realization, has also fostered an understanding of the vital role of comprehensive documentation and reflective practices in project development. So, this exercise has crafted a well-rounded skill set in you, nurturing not only technical acumen but also a conscientious approach to development rooted in reflection and continuous learning. The optional task of setting up a GitHub repo further offers a foothold into the collaborative and contributory ethos of the open source community, opening pathways for innovation and collective growth in IoT endeavors.

Summary

In this chapter, we looked at how we can contribute to the open source community and the different principles that we must adhere to in doing so. We also learned about the components of any open source repos, saw how we can put our process of contributing into actionable steps, and put this into practice through our practical by having you find a topic that has not yet been addressed by the open source community and hence creating a repo on it.

In the next chapter, we will learn how to develop solutions for digital transformation within Industry 4.0, where we will discuss how we can tackle architecting modern workloads with best practices.

Further reading

For more information about what was covered in this chapter, please refer to the following links:

- A look into another definition of fog computing: `https://www.heavy.ai/technical-glossary/fog-computing`
- Learn more about TensorFlow from its official documentation: `https://www.tensorflow.org/learn`
- Understand why edge computing is important for the development of smart cities: `https://www.intechnologysmartcities.com/blog/why-edge-computing-is-vital-for-smart-cities/`
- Learn how AWS IoT is being used to detect cryptocurrency mining threats on edge devices: `https://aws.amazon.com/blogs/iot/detect-cryptocurrency-mining-threats-on-edge-devices-using-aws-iot/`
- Take a look at more edge computing case studies: `https://www.nec.com/en/global/techrep/journal/g17/n01/170106.html`

Part 4:
Delving into Complex Systems and the Future of IoT

In this culminating part, we venture into the intricate tapestry of advanced IoT systems and their transformative potential. Beginning with the interplay between IoT and the fourth industrial revolution, we explore how cutting-edge solutions are driving digital metamorphosis across industries. Moving forward, we grapple with the multifaceted nature of designing and structuring holistic IoT environments, understanding the complexities and uncovering methodologies to address inherent challenges. As we near our journey's end, we cast our gaze forward, envisioning the trajectory of IoT in the coming half-decade. Through this exploration, we prepare ourselves to not only adapt to but also to shape the transformative tides awaiting in the IoT landscape. This section serves as both a synthesis of our acquired knowledge and a beacon for the thrilling evolution ahead.

This part has the following chapters:

- *Chapter 13, Developing IoT Solutions for Digital Transformation within Industry 4.0*

- *Chapter 14, Architecting Complex, Holistic IoT Environments*

- *Chapter 15, Looking Ahead to the Future of IoT*

13

Developing IoT Solutions for Digital Transformation within Industry 4.0

In previous chapters, we discussed how organizations can bring IoT into their operations, build smart ecosystems for work, work with partners on IoT, and navigate the risks and opportunities of Industry 4.0. In this chapter, we will delve into the development of IoT solutions for digital transformation within Industry 4.0. As we know, Industry 4.0 has brought about a revolution in the way industries operate by enabling the integration of IoT devices, sensors, and machines to communicate with each other to make intelligent decisions. Developing IoT solutions can help businesses optimize processes, reduce costs, and improve productivity.

We will discuss the importance of IoT in Industry 4.0 and explore the steps involved in developing IoT solutions for digital transformation. We will also discuss the challenges that organizations may face when implementing IoT solutions and provide strategies for overcoming them. Moreover, this chapter will include a case study on powering healthcare within a smart city with IoT, which will demonstrate how IoT solutions can be used to create a more efficient and effective healthcare system.

In this chapter, we're going to cover the following main topics:

- Understand best practices of IoT frameworks and standards that are used when adopting IoT in the workplace

- Understand how to can build and foster a smart ecosystem at work and work with partners and other parties to establish it

- Learn how to make the case for more innovation and research into how IoT can be brought into the workplace

- Understand architecting smart cities

- Learn how to navigate the risks and opportunities within IoT's role in Industry 4.0
- Learn how to create tools for expendable smart city applications

Technical requirements

This chapter will require you to have the following hardware and software installed:

- Hardware:
  - ESP32-WROOM
  - A GPS module
  - An OLED display module
  - Jumper cables
  - A breadboard
  - A speaker (can be laptop speakers as well)
- Software:
  - The Blynk app
  - Arduino **Integrated Development Environment (IDE)**
  - An AWS account

You can access the GitHub folder for the code that is used in this chapter at `https://github.com/PacktPublishing/IoT-Made-Easy-for-Beginners/tree/main/Chapter13/`.

Bringing IoT into the organization

The **Industrial Internet of Things (IIoT)** is rapidly transforming the manufacturing industry, and it is becoming an essential component of Industry 4.0. Industry 4.0 refers to the integration of physical and digital technologies, creating a smart manufacturing environment where machines, systems, and humans can communicate and work together more effectively. As a result, the use of IIoT is becoming increasingly popular in the manufacturing industry, with a focus on data-driven decision-making, optimization, and automation.

One significant trend in bringing IIoT into organizations as a part of Industry 4.0 is the increased adoption of cloud computing and edge computing. With the vast amounts of data generated by IIoT devices, it can be challenging to store, manage, and analyze this data effectively. Cloud computing provides a scalable and flexible solution for managing data, while edge computing can help reduce latency and ensure that data processing is performed close to the source.

Another trend in bringing IIoT into organizations is the use of AI and machine learning algorithms to analyze and make sense of the data generated by IIoT devices. These algorithms can identify patterns and insights that may not be apparent to humans, helping organizations make data-driven decisions that can improve efficiency, reduce downtime, and enhance overall productivity.

Finally, there is a trend toward greater collaboration and partnerships between technology vendors, system integrators, and industrial companies to develop and implement IIoT solutions. By working together, these organizations can leverage their unique strengths and expertise to create comprehensive, integrated solutions that address the specific needs and challenges of the manufacturing industry. A great way to depict how value is created as part of addressing these needs and challenges can be seen in *Figure 13.1*.

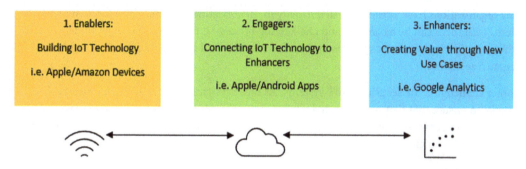

Figure 13.1 – Flow of enablers to enhancers

The figure depicts a sequential process that elaborates on the stages of IIoT deployment and utilization, which are as follows:

1. **Enablers**: This is the foundational stage where IoT technology is built. Here, devices are created to collect and transmit data. Examples provided include devices from major companies such as Apple and Amazon, indicating the development of hardware components equipped with sensors and connectivity features tailored for industrial settings.

2. **Engagers**: Upon building the IoT technology, the next step is to connect these devices to platforms or applications that can process and manage the data they collect. This stage is vital for integrating IoT technology with existing infrastructure and systems. The example given is Apple and Android applications, suggesting that these platforms play a role in interfacing with the IoT devices, managing data inflow, and potentially offering controls or insights to users.

3. **Enhancers**: The final stage emphasizes the importance of deriving value from the collected data. It's not just about collecting data but utilizing it to its full potential by analyzing it and extracting actionable insights. Tools such as Google Analytics are mentioned, which in the context of IIoT could imply advanced analytics platforms that process IoT data to produce meaningful information, which in turn can guide decision-making, optimize operations, or even open up new business avenues.

In essence, the flow represents the life cycle of IIoT, starting from device creation, progressing through data collection and management, and culminating in data analysis and value generation.

With an understanding of the essentials of IIoT, we can now look at the challenges that it has within an organizational context.

Challenges within an organizational context

Bringing IIoT into the organization as a part of Industry 4.0 comes with its own set of challenges. While it promises to bring increased productivity, efficiency, and cost savings, it also presents several challenges.

One of the main challenges is the integration of new IoT systems with existing legacy systems. Many organizations have already invested heavily in their existing systems, and integrating new IoT systems with them can be a complex and challenging process. It requires a thorough understanding of the organization's current systems and infrastructure, and how the new IoT systems can be integrated seamlessly.

Another challenge is the security of IoT systems. As these systems collect and store sensitive data, it is crucial to ensure that they are protected against cyber threats and attacks. Many IoT systems are vulnerable to cyber threats, and a security breach can cause significant damage to the organization's reputation and financial well-being.

Data privacy is another challenge that organizations must consider when bringing IoT systems into the organization. When gathering and handling personal information, organizations must adhere to privacy laws, including GDPR. Non-compliance can lead to significant penalties and potential legal consequences.

The complexity of IoT systems is also a challenge that organizations must navigate. IoT systems involve a complex network of interconnected devices, sensors, and software. Managing these systems requires specialized knowledge and expertise, which may not be readily available within the organization.

Finally, cost is another challenge that organizations must consider when bringing IoT systems into the organization. While IoT systems promise cost savings in the long run, they require significant investment upfront. Organizations must carefully consider the costs associated with implementing, integrating, and maintaining these systems.

Overcoming organizational barriers

Organizational barriers can often be overlooked when it comes to digital transformation in manufacturing. However, it is crucial to overcome these barriers to successfully manage the technological aspect of the transformation. To harness the benefits of transformation, it's essential to adopt a new work approach and develop the necessary capabilities.

Understanding the full potential of IIoT-powered advanced technologies requires a comprehensive perspective of its applications throughout the journey. This involves looking at the entire deployment process, enhancement cycles, expansion, and industrial adaptation. For success, clear goals should be set throughout the journey with efficient monitoring, reporting, and handling of discrepancies.

The initial move toward harnessing this potential involves charting a clear IIoT transformation path and setting benchmarks for each application on this journey. These benchmarks should encompass budgetary KPIs, the progress status over time, and the projected value impact of each application.

To effectively harness the benefits, it's advisable to have a specialized team in place. This team can serve as the main hub for overseeing reporting and conveying the progress status to top management and other interested parties. Their duties also involve keeping an eye on set benchmarks and taking corrective actions when goals aren't being met, such as mobilizing specialized teams to aid in deploying applications at various facilities.

This central team should employ a systematic approach to spot deviations from the planned roadmap, establish corrective actions to get application development and deployment back in line, and aid in the rollout of these corrective steps led by project heads.

Digital transformation and building a smart ecosystem for work

As more and more IoT devices are connected to the internet, cloud management has become an essential component of IoT networks. The cloud provides a scalable, flexible, and cost-effective solution for storing and processing the vast amounts of data generated by IoT devices. However, with the benefits of the cloud also come security and privacy concerns.

This section will discuss the security and privacy controls that are necessary within the cloud management landscape to ensure the safe and effective operation of IoT networks. We will explore the key security and privacy considerations in the cloud, including data encryption, identity and access management, network security, and compliance with regulatory requirements.

Framework for digital transformation

Digital transformation is a crucial aspect of any business's growth in the current technological era. Although digital transformation is heavily reliant on technology, it is the business strategy that drives the transformation. The implementation of digital transformation is an essential principle for SMEs, but it is necessary to avoid a technology-push approach due to limited resources and low fault tolerance.

In the following figure, we can see one such framework of how digital transformation can be done.

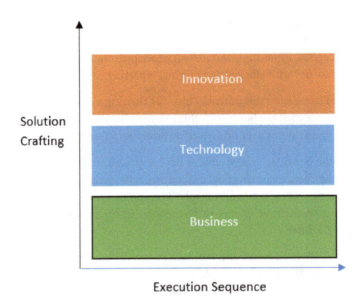

Figure 13.2 – Reference framework for SMEs to achieve digital transformation

This figure shows a suggested model for SMEs undertaking digital transformation. It recommends integrating IoT and cloud computing within the manufacturing sector. This model employs a tri-phase structure, addressing business, technology, and innovation, progressing in a bottom-up manner. The transformation journey is influenced by business needs, facilitated by technology, and directed by innovation.

The model encompasses three developmental paths: a stage-specific deployment process, a cross-stage solution design, and a business growth trajectory. The journey begins with the business phase, emphasizing the generation of new value, targeting different customer groups, fostering relationships, and developing new revenue avenues. Drawing from the primary elements of the business phase, the subsequent stage sets technical benchmarks, providing a systematic methodology to reach the desired outcomes. This allows for a flexible choice of technologies within the realms of IoT and cloud computing to meet these benchmarks.

The apex phase is centered on innovation, and the model introduces two core principles: amalgamation and segmentation. The deployment and solution design paths offer a directional framework both within and between the three phases. Repeated cycles of this tri-phase method result in the business growth dimension, marking the progression phase, with the inaugural cycle deemed as a transformative phase.

Smart ecosystem

IoT networks face numerous threats that come from various sources. Attackers could target physical devices, communication channels, or the cloud services that manage the devices. Each layer of the IoT network presents a different vulnerability, and attackers have different techniques for exploiting each layer.

Figure 13.3 shows one such smart ecosystem and its composition.

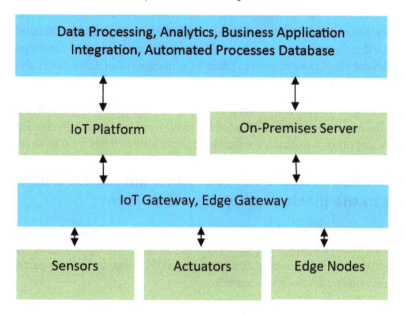

Figure 13.3 – IIoT ecosystem

Assessing an IIoT tech ecosystem is a complex process that requires careful consideration of several key factors. To ensure that the ecosystem is sustainable and capable of achieving its intended objectives, it is necessary to follow a series of steps. The steps encompass grasping the essentials of a lasting environment, selecting appropriate collaborators, and setting up business growth units to handle the intricate environment while maintaining adaptability.

Step 1 – grasping the fundamental components of a long-term environment

To assess an IIoT tech ecosystem, it is crucial to have a deep understanding of the key elements that make an ecosystem sustainable. These elements include having a clear purpose, a diverse range of stakeholders, a flexible and adaptable structure, effective governance, and the ability to create value for all stakeholders.

A clear purpose is essential to ensure that all stakeholders understand the ecosystem's objectives and are aligned in working toward achieving them. It is important to articulate the ecosystem's value proposition, the problems it is solving, and the benefits it provides to all stakeholders. A diverse range of stakeholders is crucial to ensure that the ecosystem contains the necessary skills, resources, and perspectives to create value and remain sustainable. The ecosystem should include a mix of technology providers, service providers, customers, and other stakeholders that contribute to its success.

A flexible and adaptable structure is essential to ensure that the ecosystem can evolve and adapt to changing market conditions and stakeholder needs. The ecosystem's structure should be designed to accommodate new partners, technologies, and business models as they emerge. Effective governance is critical to ensure that the ecosystem operates within a set of agreed-upon rules and regulations. The governance framework should be designed to balance the interests of all stakeholders and ensure that the ecosystem remains sustainable over the long term.

The ability to create value for all stakeholders is essential to ensure that the ecosystem remains viable and sustainable. The ecosystem should be designed to create value for customers, technology providers, service providers, and other stakeholders, ensuring that everyone benefits from its success.

Step 2 – selecting suitable collaborators, aiming for a diverse mix of partners in the platform-driven environment

Choosing the right partners is critical to the success of an IIoT tech ecosystem. It is essential to select partners that complement each other's strengths and have a vested interest in achieving the ecosystem's objectives. The partners should represent a diverse range of skills, resources, and perspectives to ensure that the ecosystem remains flexible and adaptable.

It is essential to select partners based on a set of agreed-upon criteria that align with the ecosystem's objectives. The selection process should be transparent and inclusive, ensuring that all stakeholders have a voice in the decision-making process. Partner diversity is crucial to ensure that the ecosystem can create value and remain sustainable over the long term. The ecosystem should include a mix of technology providers, service providers, customers, and other stakeholders, ensuring that it can provide a comprehensive range of solutions and services.

Step 3 – establishing business growth units to oversee the intricate environment and maintain flexibility

Implementing business development teams can help manage the complex IIoT tech ecosystem and ensure agility. The teams should comprise individuals with expertise in various areas, such as product development, marketing, and customer service. The business development teams should be responsible for managing the ecosystem's day-to-day operations, ensuring that partners are aligned with the ecosystem's objectives, and identifying new opportunities for growth and development.

The teams should also be responsible for building and maintaining relationships with partners, ensuring that they are engaged and motivated to contribute to the ecosystem's success. Agility is critical to ensure that the ecosystem can adapt to changing market conditions and stakeholder needs. The business development teams should be empowered to make decisions quickly and efficiently, ensuring that the ecosystem remains responsive to changing circumstances.

Practical exercise – GPS tracking with the ESP32

GPS is a technology that allows us to track the location of a device anywhere in the world. It works by using a network of satellites called the **Global Navigation Satellite System** (**GNSS**) to transmit signals to a GPS receiver module. This receiver module then uses the signals to calculate its location and provide us with accurate coordinates.

You will require the following components for this practical exercise:

- An ESP32 NodeMCU module
- A breadboard
- Jumper wires
- I2C OLED module
- GPS NEO-6M/L86 module
- The Blynk app

We will be building an IoT-based GPS vehicle tracking system using ESP32. We can see a visualization of how it will be wired up as follows.

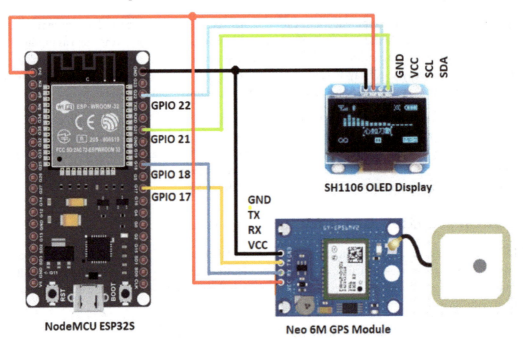

Figure 13.4 – GPS-to-ESP32 wiring diagram

This new system will allow us to display the latitude and longitude values on an OLED display as well as on the Blynk app, making it easy to monitor the location of the vehicle from anywhere in the world.

Configuring the Blynk app

After wiring up as necessary, we will need to configure the Blynk app accordingly:

1. First, go to the Google Play Store or Apple App Store and download the Blynk IoT app. Once you have the app installed, you can either create a new account or log in if you already have an account.

2. After you're logged in, you will find the Blynk dashboard. Click on the **+ New Template** button to start.

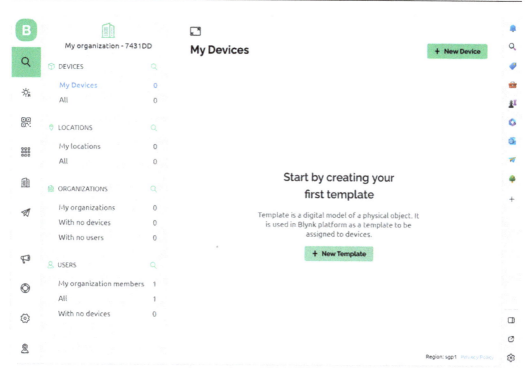

Figure 13.5 – Blynk dashboard for creating your first template

3. On the **Create New Template** window, fill in the name with `Plot Location Coordinates to Map` for this project, choose **ESP32** for the hardware, and choose **WiFi** for the connection type. If you wish, you can fill in a meaningful description. Click **Done** when you're done.

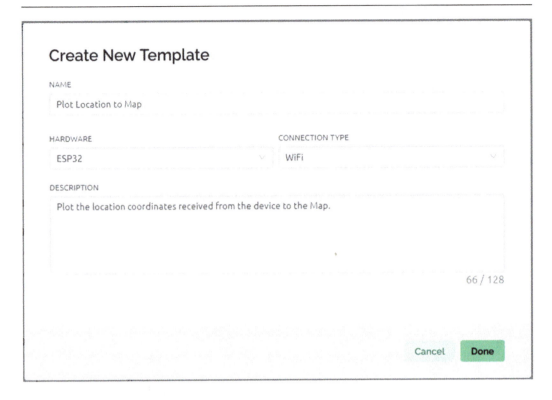

Figure 13.6 – Blynk Create New Template window

The **Plot Location to Map** window will open.

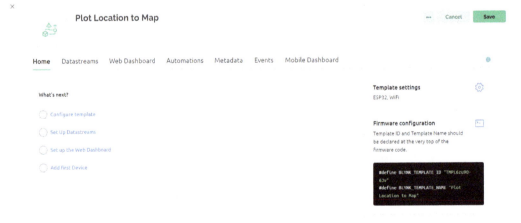

Figure 13.7 – Blynk Plot Location to Map window

4. For the template, first we click on **Configure template**. You can insert your preferred image for the template if you wish; otherwise, just leave it blank. The name, hardware, connection type, and description that you typed in previously will be shown in this window.

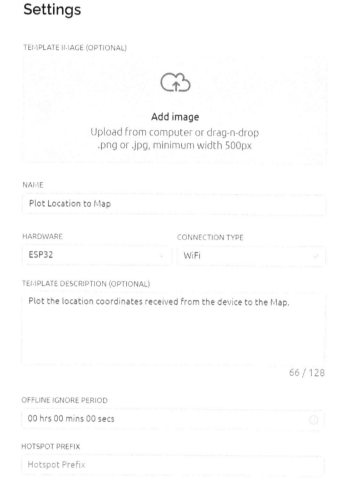

Figure 13.8 – Blynk Settings window as part of configuring the template

5. Click back to the **Plot Location to Map** window on the left to continue configuring the template. Now, click on **Set Up Datastreams** and then click on **+ New Datastream** and choose a location.

6. On the **Location Datastream** window, set the PIN to **V5**. This will automatically change the name and alias to **Location V5**. Leave the rest at the default values. Then, click **Create**.

Location Datastream

Send coordinates (longitude, latitude) in decimal degrees as two values of "double" variable type.
For example: (50.4501, 30.5234)

NAME

Location V5

ALIAS

Location V5

PIN

V5

DEFAULT COORDINATES (LON/LAT)

0   0

⊞ ADVANCED SETTINGS

Cancel   Create

Figure 13.9 – Blynk Location Datastream window

Now, on the **Plot Location to Map** window, the datastream you just created will be listed there.

Figure 13.10 – Blynk Plot Location to Map window

7. Click on the **Home** tab and then on **Set up the Web Dashboard**. In the **Widget Box** section on the left, scroll down until you find the **Map** picture. Double-click or click and drag the **Map** picture to the **Add new widget** area. Click **Save** to save the configuration.

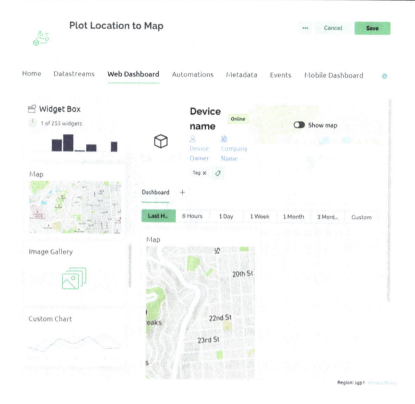

Figure 13.11 – Setting up the web dashboard on the Plot Location to Map window

8. Click back on the **Home** tab and now, click on **Add first Device**. Give the device the name `ESP32 Neo 6M GPS` and click **Create**.

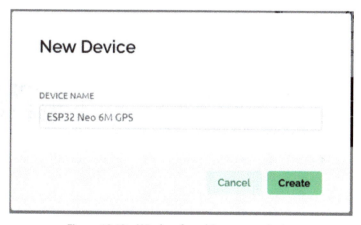

Figure 13.12 – Window for adding a new device

9. A pop-up window saying **New Device Created** will appear. You will find three `#define` `Blynk` parameters in the black area of the window. Click on the **Copy to clipboard** button to copy the parameters (`BLYNK_TEMPLATE_ID`, `BLYNK_TEMPLATE_NAME`, and `BLYNK_AUTH_TOKEN`) that will be needed when we try to connect the ESP32 to the Blynk IoT site. Paste and save it for later purposes. After you've finished, close the pop-up window.

Figure 13.13 – Pop-up window for new device created

10. We can see **ESP32 Neo 6M GPS** on the **Plot Location to Map** window. Click on the **Save** button to save all the configurations we made.

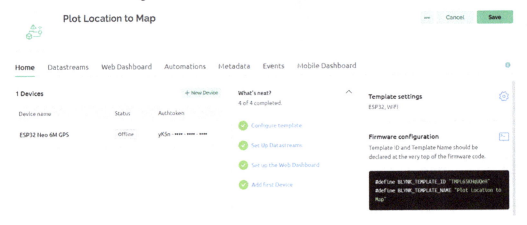

Figure 13.14 – ESP32 Neo 6M GPS shown on the Plot Location to Map window

11. We can monitor the Blynk IoT result through the Blink IoT mobile app, which supports both iOS and Android smartphones. To get the information on how to make the connection, click on the **Mobile Dashboard** tab on the preceding window, and you will find some information on how to do that.

Figure 13.15 – Getting information on how to make a connection from the Mobile Dashboard tab

12. From your mobile phone, download and install the Blynk IoT app. Open the app and log in using the same email address and password you used on the desktop version. You will find the device that you just created using your computer on the first window that opens in the app.

Figure 13.16 – Blynk IoT app showing the device created

13. Click on the 🔍 icon on the top part of the window. A **Developer Zone** window will appear and you will also find your previously created template, that is, **Plot Location to Map**, shown in the **My Templates** area. Click on that template and click on the + button to add a widget. Scroll down through the widgets until you find **Map** in the **Interface** group. Click on the **Map** icon, and the map will be added to the template window.

Figure 13.17 – Map added to the template window

14. Click on the ⬅ icon to return to the template window, and close the template window. Now, on the main window, click on the **ESP32 Neo 6M GPS** icon. A similar window to the one in the preceding figure will appear.

Now that we are all set, we can walk through the coding for the hardware.

Walk-through of the code

The following libraries are used as part of the code:

- `Wire.h`: This library enables communication with I2C/TWI devices.

- `TinyGPS++.h`: TinyGPS++ is utilized for parsing GPS sentences, which is the standard format used by GPS devices to report location, time, altitude, and so on. Download this library from `https://github.com/mikalhart/TinyGPSPlus`.

- `U8g2lib.h` and `U8x8lib`: These libraries are used to display text and graphics on a 128x64 SH1106 OLED display connected via I2C to the Arduino. You can get this library from the **Library Manager** by searching for `U8g2 by oliver`.

- `BlynkSimpleEsp32.h`: A library allowing ESP32 to interact with Blynk. This library can also be installed from **Library Manager** by searching for `Blynk by Volodymyr Shymanskyy`.

- `SH1106.h`: A library that provides functions and tools to interface with SH1106-based OLED displays, enabling the creation and manipulation of graphics and text on these screens.

To begin, make sure to include all the necessary libraries in your code. You'll need to include `SH1106.h`, which is specifically designed for ESP modules:

```
#include <Wire.h>
#include <TinyGPS++.h>
#include <WiFi.h>
#include <U8g2lib.h>
#include <U8x8lib.h>
```

Now, we define some Blynk parameters that we set during setup of the Blynk template and device. Change the `BLYNK_TEMPLATE_ID`, `BLYNK_TEMPLATE_NAME`, and `BLYNK_AUTH_TOKEN` to the values configured previously. You need to define those parameters first before including the Blynk library:

```
#define BLYNK_TEMPLATE_ID "Your Blynk Template ID"
#define BLYNK_TEMPLATE_NAME "Your Blynk Template Name"
#define BLYNK_AUTH_TOKEN "Your Blynk Auth Token"
#include <BlynkSimpleEsp32.h>
```

In the following steps, you'll need to enter your Wi-Fi name and password, along with the Blynk authorization key in your code:

```
const char *networkSSID = "YourNetworkName";
const char *networkPASS = "YourNetworkPass";
```

We create some variables to enable the interval at which to send periodic messages to Blynk:

```
unsigned long startLoopTime;
unsigned int sendPeriod = 30000;
```

Next, we define some variables to store the satellite, latitude, and longitude values:

```
double gpsLat, gpsLong;
unsigned int gpsSatNumber;
char charGPSSatNumber[4] = {0};
char charLatitude[12] = {0};
char charLongitude[12] = {0};
```

We initiate `HardwareSerial` parameters (RX and TX pins) and the TinyGPSPlus library:

```
#define RXD2 17
#define TXD2 18
HardwareSerial ser2(2);
TinyGPSPlus gps;
```

We need to set the U8G2 parameter to match the type of SH1106 I2C version of the OLED display:

```
U8G2_SH1106_128X64_NONAME_2_HW_I2C oledDisplay(U8G2_R0, /* clock=*/
SCL, /* data=*/ SDA, /* reset=*/ U8X8_PIN_NONE);
```

In `void setup()`, initialize the Serial Monitor at a baud rate of `115200` for debugging purposes and Serial variable `ser2` at `9600`. Also, initialize the Wi-Fi, OLED display, GPS module, and Blynk using the `begin()` method. We also set the `lastSentTime` variable to the current time (`millis()`). We will use this to monitor the time difference between sending data to and receiving data in Blynk:

```
void setup() {
  Serial.begin(115200); // Start serial communication at 115200 baud
rate
  ser2.begin(9600, SERIAL_8N1, RXD2, TXD2);
  WiFi.begin(networkSSID, networkPASS); // Initiate WiFi connection

  while (WiFi.status() != WL_CONNECTED) {
    delay(500); // Wait for connection
  }

  Serial.println(F("Connected to WiFi"));

  oledDisplay.begin();

  Blynk.begin(BLYNK_AUTH_TOKEN, networkSSID, networkPASS);
  Blynk.virtualWrite(V5, "clr");
  lastSentTime = millis();
}
```

Inside the `loop()` function, the code checks whether there is new, incoming data from the GPS module.

If there is data available, the code checks whether the GPS location data is valid or not, and if it is valid, then it will print the data to the console (using the `printToConsole` function) and the OLED display (using the `printTo OledDisplay` function) and finally, send the data to Blynk (by using the `sendToBlynk` function).

If there is data available, the code encodes the data and checks whether it is valid or not. If it's valid, the code further calculates the GPS coordinates to transform the NMEA data into understandable data:

```
void loop()
{
  boolean newData = false;
  boolean newData = false;
  for (unsigned long start = millis(); millis() - start < 1000;)
  {
    while (ser2.available())
    {
      if (gps.encode(ser2.read()))
      {
        newData = true;
      }
    }
  }

  if(newData == true){
    newData = false;
    Serial.println("New Data");
    gpsSatNumber = gps.satellites.value();
    dtostrf(gpsSatNumber, 3, 0, charGPSSatNumber);
    Serial.println(gpsSatNumber);
    if (gps.location.isValid() == 1){
      gpsLat = gps.location.lat();
      dtostrf(gpsLat,10,6,charLatitude);
      gpsLon = gps.location.lng();
      dtostrf(gpsLon,10,6,charLongitude);

      printToConsole();
      printToOledDisplay();
      sendToBlynk();
    }
    else {
      Serial.println("Finding satellites ... ");
    }
  }
  else
  {
    Serial.println("No Data");
  }
  delay(5000);
}
```

Next, we need to write down the two functions that print the GPS location data to the console and OLED display, and the function that sends the data to Blynk:

```
void printToConsole()
{
  Serial.print("Detected Satellites:");
  Serial.println(gpsSatNumber);
  Serial.print("Lat: ");
  Serial.print(gpsLat, 6);
  Serial.print(", Lon: ");
  Serial.println(gpsLon, 6);
}
```

```
void printToOledDisplay()
{
  oledDisplay.firstPage();
  do
  {
    oledDisplay.clearBuffer();                       // clear the
internal memory
    oledDisplay.drawRFrame(0, 0, 127, 63, 3);
    oledDisplay.drawLine(0, 20, 127, 20);
    oledDisplay.setFont(u8g2_font_8x13_tr);
    oledDisplay.drawStr(15,15, "GPS Sat :");
    oledDisplay.drawStr(88, 15, charGPSSatNumber);
    oledDisplay.drawStr(4, 37, "Lat:");
    oledDisplay.drawStr(42,37, charLatitude);
    oledDisplay.drawStr(4, 55, "Lng:");
    oledDisplay.drawStr(42, 55, charLongitude);
    oledDisplay.sendBuffer();                        // transfer internal
memory to the display
  } while ( oledDisplay.nextPage() );
}
```

```
void sendToBlynk()
{
  if(millis() - lastSentTime > sendPeriod){
    Serial.print("Data sent to Blynk!");
    Blynk.virtualWrite(V5, gps.location.lng(), gps.location.lat());
    lastSentTime = millis();
  }
}
```

Please note that in the sendToBlynk function, we check first whether current time (millis()) is more than the sendPeriod time from the last time we sent the message (store the current time in the variable lastSentTime).

After setting up the hardware and programming the ESP32 board, you will need to upload the GPS tracking program to the board using the Arduino IDE. To do this, connect the ESP32 board to your laptop using a micro USB cable and then click the **Upload** button in the IDE. Once the code is uploaded, the latitude and longitude values will be displayed on the OLED.

When the code is running, you will need to wait for a while for the NEO-6M GPS module to find the GPS satellites. You may need to bring the device outdoors so it can get better at receiving the satellite signals. If the GPS module is already receiving satellite signals, you may find a blinking LED inside the module. You'll also receive information in the Serial Monitor regarding the number of satellite signals received by the module and the latitude and longitude location position. Please notice that once every 30 seconds, a message will appear in the console notifying that data was sent to Blynk. You can change the interval at which this message appears by changing the value of the sendPeriod variable.

```
17:16:23.996 -> New Data
17:16:23.996 -> 8
17:16:23.996 -> Detected Satellites:8
17:16:23.996 -> Lat: -6.186587, Lon: 106.762547
17:16:30.055 -> New Data
17:16:30.055 -> 8
17:16:30.055 -> Detected Satellites:8
17:16:30.055 -> Lat: -6.186585, Lon: 106.762545
17:16:36.134 -> New Data
17:16:36.134 -> 8
17:16:36.134 -> Detected Satellites:8
17:16:36.134 -> Lat: -6.186581, Lon: 106.762543
17:16:36.166 -> Data sent to Blynk!New Data
17:16:42.195 -> 8
17:16:42.195 -> Detected Satellites:8
17:16:42.195 -> Lat: -6.186577, Lon: 106.762540
```

Figure 13.18 – Output shown on the Arduino IDE Serial Monitor

You will also can see the location coordinates and the number of GPS satellites read by the GPS module.

Figure 13.19 – Coordinates shown on the GPS module

Additionally, the Blynk app will show the location of the device on a map, as in the following example, showing the GPS in Melbourne, Victoria, and Australia.

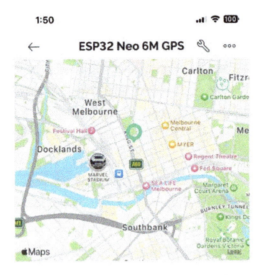

Figure 13.20 – Blynk app showing the device's location

From the Blunk Dashboard on a Windows computer, we can also view the map by clicking on the ESP32 NEO-6M GPS device.

With that, we've managed to implement GPS tracking by utilizing the ESP32! Now, we can move on to looking at how we can work with industrial partners to ensure the success of our IIoT projects.

Working with partners on IIoT

Working with industry partners is critical to the success of IIoT projects. Partnering with the right organizations can bring complementary skills, technology, and expertise to the table, helping to accelerate development and implementation while minimizing risk.

To effectively work with industry partners on IIoT, it is important to identify the right partners. The best partners are those whose capabilities complement and enhance the project. For example, if an IIoT project involves developing a new sensor-based technology, a partner with expertise in wireless communication may be beneficial. On the other hand, if the project is focused on developing a new software application, a partner with expertise in software development may be more appropriate.

Selecting partners

Selecting the right partners to work with on IIoT projects is a crucial aspect of Industry 4.0 implementation. As IIoT projects can be complex and involve multiple components and technologies, working with partners that have complementary skills and expertise can help ensure successful project delivery.

One trend in selecting IIoT partners is the rise of strategic partnerships and collaborations between companies. By forming strategic partnerships, companies can leverage each other's strengths and resources, share knowledge and expertise, and work toward common goals. For example, a company that specializes in IoT sensors and a company that specializes in data analytics may form a partnership to deliver a comprehensive IIoT solution.

Another trend is the increasing importance of selecting partners that have experience in the specific industry or application area. IIoT solutions are highly customized to the needs of specific industries and use cases, so working with partners that have experience in the target industry can help ensure that the solution is tailored to the specific needs of that industry. For example, a company that specializes in IIoT solutions for the manufacturing industry may be a better partner for a manufacturing company than a company that has experience in healthcare.

It is also important to select partners that have a solid understanding of security and data privacy, as IIoT solutions involve the collection and transmission of sensitive data. Partners that have experience in securing IIoT solutions and implementing best practices for data privacy can help ensure that the solution is secure and compliant with relevant regulations.

Finally, it is important to select partners that have a culture of innovation and are willing to work collaboratively to drive innovation in IIoT solutions. As IIoT is a rapidly evolving field, working with partners who are committed to innovation and continuously improving their solutions can help ensure that the IIoT solution is cutting-edge and able to keep pace with future advancements.

In summary, selecting the right partners is a key consideration in the success of IIoT projects. The trends in selecting partners include forming strategic partnerships, selecting partners with industry-specific experience, selecting partners with a focus on security and data privacy, and selecting partners with a culture of innovation.

Maintaining partnerships

It is important to establish mutually beneficial relationships with partners. This can be achieved through sharing knowledge and resources, collaborating on joint projects, or providing opportunities for both parties to grow and benefit from the partnership. Working with industry partners can bring significant benefits to IIoT projects, including complementary skills and expertise, accelerated development, and risk minimization. To work effectively with industry partners, it is essential to identify the right partners, ensure alignment with the project's goals and values, establish clear communication and collaboration frameworks, and establish mutually beneficial relationships.

Navigating Industry 4.0 risks and opportunities

Industry 4.0, also known as the Fourth Industrial Revolution, has brought about significant changes to the manufacturing industry. The integration of IIoT technology has created both risks and opportunities for manufacturers looking to stay competitive in the digital age.

Risks

One of the main risks of adopting IIoT technology is cybersecurity. With the increased connectivity of devices and systems, the risk of cyberattacks and data breaches also increases. Manufacturers must take proactive steps to protect their networks, devices, and data by implementing robust cybersecurity measures.

Another risk is the potential for job loss as automation increases. With the use of IIoT technology, many routine tasks can be automated, reducing the need for human labor in certain areas. While this can lead to increased efficiency and productivity, it can also result in job displacement for some workers. Manufacturers must navigate this risk by finding ways to reskill and retrain their workforce for new roles that align with the needs of the digital age.

Opportunities

Despite these risks, IIoT technology also presents many opportunities for manufacturers. With the increased connectivity and data collection capabilities of IIoT, manufacturers can gain deeper insights into their operations, optimize production processes, and reduce waste. Predictive maintenance, enabled by IIoT, can also help manufacturers reduce downtime, extend equipment life, and save costs on repairs.

Another opportunity is the ability to create new revenue streams through innovative business models, such as servitization. By using IIoT technology to monitor equipment performance, manufacturers can offer maintenance and repair services as a subscription-based model, creating a new source of recurring revenue.

In navigating the risks and opportunities of Industry 4.0 with IIoT, manufacturers must approach the adoption of technology strategically. They must assess their current capabilities and gaps in technology, understand the needs and expectations of their customers, and identify the specific areas where IIoT can create the most value. Additionally, manufacturers must invest in their workforce, providing training and reskilling opportunities to ensure they are equipped to work with the new technology.

Now that we understand navigating the risks and opportunities, we can look at getting started with digital transformation with IoT.

A few best practices for a digital transformation within IoT

To ensure a successful transformation journey toward IoT, organizations must consider specific elements that will help them bridge the gap between their current state and the first step of the transformation process. Five practical recommendations for achieving IoT success are as follows:

- Develop and articulate a coherent vision, communicating the anticipated advantages of the new operational framework to stakeholders
- Identify and promptly validate the efficacy of 8 to 10 impactful use cases

- Engineer a flexible IT architecture and foster partnerships with technology providers to swiftly scale up use cases

- Recognize the imperative for unconventional talent, and undertake recruitment or capacity building as necessary

- Understand that success in IoT is not solely predicated on technology; it significantly depends on the transformation of processes, organizational structure, and capabilities

Adopting a holistic approach to IoT adoption is crucial to manufacturers in overcoming the challenges that come with scaling up from pilot projects to company-wide rollout. Success in digital transformation can bring substantial value, but it requires an appropriate approach that considers not only technology-related factors but also the fundamentals of the organization and business. Several real-world cases have shown the potential for significant value creation through digital transformation when approached correctly.

A case of digital transformation of healthcare within a smart city

Barcelona stands as a beacon of success in the smart city landscape, having utilized IoT technologies to revolutionize urban systems and improve quality of life. Following the 2008 recession, the city established the Smart City Barcelona team to consolidate existing projects and identify new opportunities. The extensive fiber optic network laid decades ago facilitated the city's transformation by enabling citywide Wi-Fi access and serving as the backbone for integrated city systems. The IoT technologies deployed across various sectors, from transportation to waste management, have contributed to substantial cost savings, new job creation, and improved energy efficiency.

The Sentilo platform was developed to manage the vast amount of data generated from 18,000 active sensors in the city. These sensors monitor various aspects, such as weather, electricity, water supply, and air quality, allowing for efficient management of urban systems. Moreover, open data projects such as the City Operating System were adopted, promoting the growth of various smart city applications and services. However, the digital transformation journey presents its own set of challenges, including security risks, energy consumption, and e-waste. To address these challenges, Barcelona invested in renewable energy, implemented recycling programs, and enforced strict data protection measures.

Additionally, Barcelona undertook a remarkable initiative to enhance healthcare services for its citizens using IoT technology. A pilot project was developed in collaboration with technology companies to monitor the health of vulnerable individuals, such as the elderly and those with chronic illnesses, using wearable devices. These devices tracked vital signs in real time and transmitted the data to healthcare providers, enabling remote monitoring of patients' conditions.

We can look at how this functioned systematically in *Figure 13.6*.

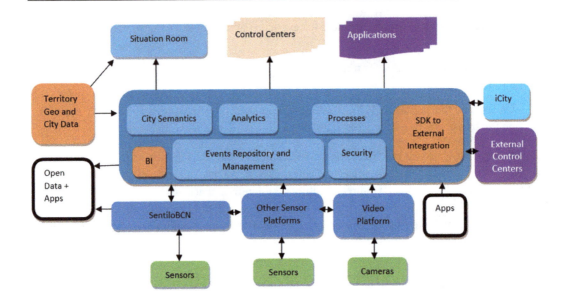

Figure 13.21 – System diagram of the Barcelona smart city solution

The system diagram illustrates the Barcelona smart city solution's multifaceted architecture, integrating various data sources and platforms to facilitate urban management. At its foundation, the city utilizes a broad spectrum of sensors, ranging from geographical and city-specific data collectors to video platforms. This raw data is funneled into specialized platforms, such as SentiloBCN, which subsequently channel the data to analytical components such as **business intelligence** (**BI**) tools and specific city semantics modules.

In parallel, there's an emphasis on openness, with modules dedicated to open data and applications that can be leveraged by developers and stakeholders. Key features such as **events repository and management** underscore the city's focus on real-time event monitoring, while components such as **security** and **processes** ensure the safe and streamlined operation of the entire ecosystem. Complementing the setup are control centers, situation rooms, and external integration points, ensuring comprehensive oversight and seamless coordination between Barcelona's smart city infrastructure and external entities.

Now, let's look at the case of implementing security measures in IIoT.

A case of implementing security measures in IIoT

Schneider Electric is a global leader in energy management and automation, with a presence in over 100 countries. The company offers a wide range of products and services, including IoT solutions, that help customers manage energy more efficiently and sustainably.

To ensure the security of its IoT solutions, Schneider Electric implemented a comprehensive security architecture that includes several layers of protection. One of the key components of this architecture is a secure boot process, which ensures that the device's firmware and software are genuine and have not been tampered with. This is accomplished by using secure boot technology to verify the authenticity of the firmware and software during the boot process.

Another important aspect of Schneider Electric's security architecture is its use of encryption to protect data in transit and at rest. All data transmitted between the IoT device and the cloud is encrypted using industry-standard protocols, such as SSL/TLS, to prevent unauthorized access. Additionally, all data stored on the device and in the cloud is encrypted using strong encryption algorithms to prevent data breaches.

To further enhance the security of its IoT solutions, Schneider Electric also implements secure communication protocols, such as MQTT and CoAP, which are designed specifically for IoT devices. These protocols provide a lightweight and secure means of transmitting data between the device and the cloud.

In addition to these technical measures, Schneider Electric also implements robust policies and procedures to ensure the security of its IoT solutions. This includes regular vulnerability assessments and penetration testing to identify and address potential security weaknesses, as well as employee training and awareness programs to promote good security practices.

Benefits

The benefits of this case study are numerous and significant. Firstly, the project demonstrates the enormous potential of IoT and smart city technologies to transform healthcare services in urban areas. By leveraging these technologies, cities can improve the quality of care and access to healthcare services, while also reducing costs and improving efficiency. This can have a profound impact on the health and well-being of citizens, especially those in underserved or marginalized communities who may face barriers to accessing healthcare services.

Secondly, the case study highlights the importance of collaboration and partnerships between stakeholders in the healthcare and technology sectors. The project involved a wide range of stakeholders, including hospitals, universities, government agencies, and technology companies, all working together toward a common goal. This collaborative approach not only helped to ensure the success of the project but also fostered a culture of innovation and knowledge sharing that can benefit other organizations and initiatives in the future.

Thirdly, the case study provides a valuable model and roadmap for other cities and healthcare providers looking to implement smart city healthcare projects. By outlining the key steps and considerations involved in the project, including stakeholder engagement, technology selection, data management, and evaluation, the case study can help other organizations navigate the complex and rapidly evolving landscape of smart city and IoT initiatives.

Furthermore, the project has the potential to generate significant economic benefits, including job creation and economic growth, as well as cost savings for healthcare providers and patients. For example, the use of telemedicine and remote monitoring technologies can help to reduce the need for costly in-person visits and hospitalizations, while also improving the overall quality of care.

Finally, the project has broader implications for the future of healthcare and urban planning. As cities continue to grow and face increasing challenges related to healthcare, mobility, and sustainability, the integration of IoT and smart city technologies will become increasingly important. The case study offers important insights and lessons that can inform future initiatives and help shape the direction of smart city development in the years to come.

Learnings

The case study demonstrated how IoT technology can improve patient care by enabling real-time monitoring of patients and their health status. This data can be used to provide alerts to healthcare providers when interventions are needed and can facilitate more efficient and coordinated care. For example, remote monitoring of patients with chronic diseases can help prevent complications and reduce hospitalizations.

A smart city approach involves the integration of various systems and services to optimize resource allocation and improve overall city sustainability. In the context of healthcare, this can mean integrating healthcare facilities, transportation, and emergency services to ensure the timely and efficient delivery of care. The case study highlighted how the smart city approach can enable healthcare providers to better serve their patients and contribute to overall city sustainability.

The case study demonstrated the importance of partnerships and collaboration among stakeholders, including healthcare providers, city officials, and technology providers. The successful implementation of IoT technology in healthcare facilities requires input and cooperation from various stakeholders. Healthcare providers can provide insights into the needs of patients, city officials can ensure the infrastructure is in place to support the technology, and technology providers can ensure that the technology is reliable and secure.

IoT devices generate vast amounts of data that need to be managed and secured to protect patient privacy and ensure the reliability and accuracy of the data. The case study highlighted the importance of effective data management and security measures, including data encryption, access controls, and network segmentation. These measures can ensure the privacy of patient data and the reliability and accuracy of the data collected through IoT devices.

Now, we can apply all the learnings so far to designing and implementing a smart plant monitoring system.

Practical – smart garden system with open source IoT

By the end of this section, you will have designed and implemented a smart plant monitoring and care system. The project will explore IoT integration, sensor data processing, and automated plant care actions.

Required tools and technologies

The following are the hardware and software that will be required for this practical exercise:

- ESP32S NodeMCU
- Four-port 3.3V relay module
- One-port 3.3V relay module
- Four-unit 12V solenoid water valve
- Four-unit capacitive soil moisture sensor
- 12V mini water pump with 5 mm inlet/outlet hose connector
- SH1106 1.3" I2C OLED display
- Silicon hose: 7 mm outer diameter, 5 mm inner diameter
- A 12V 2A DC power supply, or you can use a 12V car/motorcycle battery
- A 5V micro USB power supply for ESP32
- Breadboard, jumper wires, and other necessary accessories

With that, we can now start setting up the hardware.

Setting up the hardware for the project

To start off with, we can wire up the hardware for the project:

1. Wire up the necessary hardware according to *Figure 13.22*.

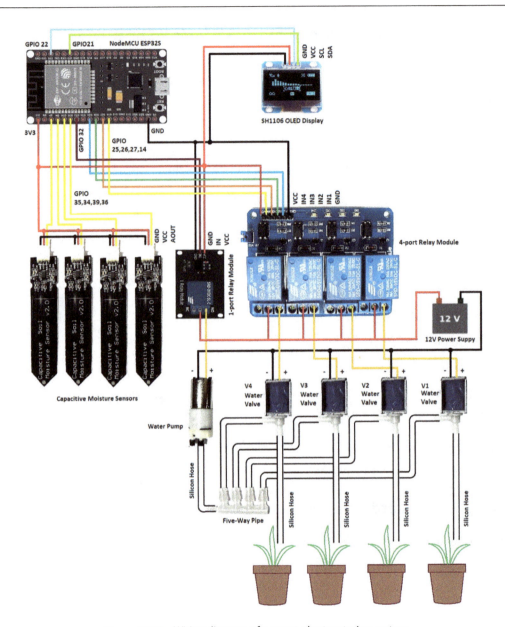

Figure 13.22 – Wiring diagram of a smart plant watering system

2. Connect the VCC and GND of the first capacitive soil moisture sensor to the 3V3 and GND pin of the ESP32. Connect the AUOT/Data pin of the sensor to the sensor1 pin of the ESP32S, that is, GPIO 36 (G36). Connect the other capacitive soil moisture sensors' (sensor2, sensor3, and sensor4) VCCs and GNDs to the 3V3 and GND pins of the ESP32. Connect the AUOT/ Data pins of the sensors to the G39 pin for sensor2, G34 for sensor3, and G35 for sensor4.

3. Connect the VCC and GND of the inputs of the four-port relay module to the 3V3 and GND of the ESP32. Connect pins IN1, IN2, IN3, and IN4 to pins G26, G27, G14, and G13, respectively.

4. Connect all the COM pins (the center pin of each relay output) to the +12V power supply. Connect the **NO** (which stands for **Normally Open**) pin of relay1 connected to the red wire of water valve 1, the NO pin of relay2 to the red wire of water valve 2, the NO pin of relay3 to the red wire of water valve 3, and the NO pin of relay4 to the red wire of water valve 4.

5. Connect the VCC and GND of the inputs of the one-port relay module to the 3V3 and GND of the ESP32. Connect the IN1 ping to the pump_relay pin (G32). Connect the COM port of the output of the one-port relay to the +12V power supply, and connect the NO port of the output of the one-port relay to the red cable (+) of the water pump. Next, connect the black cable (-) of the water pump to the (-)/ GND pin of the 12V power supply.

6. Using the silicon hose, connect one end to the intake outlet of the water pump (on the side), and put the other end into a bucket filled with water. Connect the outtake outlet (the middle one) to the input of the four-way splitter connector.

7. To each output of the four-port splitter connector, connect to the water intake of a solenoid water valve, while the outtake of the water valve goes to a plant pot through another piece of hose. You can adjust the length of each hose according to your needs.

With that, we have finished wiring up the hardware and can move on to setting up the necessary software.

Setting up the software for the project

Now, we can set up the software part using the Arduino IDE:

1. In the Arduino IDE, search for and install the U8g2 library by **oliver**.

2. In the ketch window, include the following libraries:

```
#include <Wire.h>
#include <U8g2lib.h>
#include <U8x8lib.h>
```

3. Initialize the U8g2 library for the SH1106 OLED display using I2C communication:

```
U8g2_SH1106_128X64_NONAME_2_HW_I2C u8g2(U8G2_R0, /* clock=*/
SCL, /* data=*/ SDA, /* reset=*/ U8X8_PIN_NONE);
```

4. Initialize some of the available ESP32 analog input pins for the soil moisture sensor and digital pins for relays:

```
// set all moisture sensors PIN ID
int sensor1 = 36;   // ADC1 CH0
int sensor2 = 39;   // ADC1 CH3
int sensor3 = 34;   // ADC1 CH6
```

```
int sensor4 = 35;   // ADC1 CH7

// set ESP32 pins for relays
const int relay1 = 26;
const int relay2 = 27;
const int relay3 = 14;
const int relay4 = 13;
const int pump_relay = 32;
```

5.   Initialize variables to store sensor results. We need to declare the moisture values. We will also declare the moisture level to switch on or off for the plant watering. Additionally, we can also set the minimum and maximum values of the sensor reading, which we can adjust based on the sensor we use. The analog read value will be displayed in the Arduino serial port after reading the value. Try using a wet cloth covering the sensor to get the minimum value, and wipe the sensor until dry to get the maximum value:

```
int moisture1_value = 0;
int moisture2_value = 0;
int moisture3_value = 0;
int moisture4_value = 0;

const int low_trigger_level = 30;
const int high_trigger_level = 55;
const int sensor_min_value = 1200;
const int sensor_max_value = 3800;
const int no_sensor_value = 800;
bool relay_on = LOW;
bool relay_off = HIGH;
int button = 33;
int pump_state = 0;
int relay1_state = 0;
int relay2_state = 0;
int relay3_state = 0;
int relay4_state = 0;
```

6.   Now, we initialize some functions and pins in void setup():

```
void setup()
{
Wire.begin();
Serial.begin(115200);
  u8g2.begin();
  pinMode(relay1, OUTPUT);
  pinMode(relay2, OUTPUT);
```

```
        pinMode(relay3, OUTPUT);
        pinMode(relay4, OUTPUT);
        pinMode(pump_relay, OUTPUT);
    }
```

Finally, in the `void loop()` function, we insert some commands:

```
void loop()
{
read_sensor_value();
plant_watering();

    u8g2.firstPage();
    do
    {
        drawMoisture();
        drawPlant();
    } while ( u8g2.nextPage() );
    delay (5000);
}
```

7. We need to add several functions that we called in the `void loop()` function. Place these functions after `void loop()`.

This `void` function is to read the soil moisture sensors and map the result value within the range of 0-99. If no sensor is present, the result value will be set to 999:

```
void read_sensor_value()
{
    float value1 = analogRead(sensor1);
    if(value1 < no_sensor_value)
        moisture1_value = 999;
    else if(value1 < sensor_min_value)
        moisture1_value = 99;
    else if(value1 > sensor_max_value)
        moisture1_value = 0;
    else
        moisture1_value = map(value1, 1200, 3800, 99, 0);
    Serial.println("");
    Serial.print("S1 = "); Serial.print(value1); Serial.print(" -
"); Serial.print(moisture1_value);
```

We will apply this to three other moisture values accordingly. You will be able to see the full code for this function in the GitHub repository for this exercise.

Here is the `void` function that decides whether to start or stop the relay that controls the solenoid water valve and the water pump:

```
void plant_watering()
{
  if (moisture1_value < low_trigger_level)
  {
    digitalWrite(relay1, relay_on);
    relay1_state = 1;
    delay(20);
    if (pump_state == 0)
    {
      digitalWrite(pump_relay, relay_on);
      pump_state = 1;
      delay(20);
    }
  }
  else if (moisture1_value > high_trigger_level)
  {
    digitalWrite(relay1, relay_off);
    relay1_state = 0;
    delay(20);
    if ((relay1_state == 0) && (relay2_state == 0) && (relay3_
state == 0) && (relay4_state == 0))
    {
      digitalWrite(pump_relay, relay_off);
      pump_state = 0;
      delay(20);
    }
  }

}
```

We will apply this conditional to the three other values as well. This `void` function is to draw bad plants or good plants on the top part of the OLED display. If no sensor is detected, it will not draw anything:

```
static const unsigned char bitmap_good_plant[] U8X8_PROGMEM = {
  0x00, 0x42, 0x4C, 0x00, 0x00, 0xE6, 0x6E, 0x00, 0x00, 0xAE,
0x7B, 0x00, 0x00, 0x3A, 0x51, 0x00,
  0x00, 0x12, 0x40, 0x00, 0x00, 0x02, 0x40, 0x00, 0x00, 0x06,
0x40, 0x00, 0x00, 0x06, 0x40, 0x00,
  0x00, 0x04, 0x60, 0x00, 0x00, 0x0C, 0x20, 0x00, 0x00, 0x08,
0x30, 0x00, 0x00, 0x18, 0x18, 0x00,
  0x00, 0xE0, 0x0F, 0x00, 0x00, 0x80, 0x01, 0x00, 0x00, 0x00,
0x01, 0x00, 0x00, 0x00, 0x01, 0x00,
```

```
  0x00, 0x00, 0x01, 0x00, 0x00, 0x00, 0x01, 0x00, 0x00, 0x02,
0xC1, 0x00, 0x00, 0x0E, 0x61, 0x00,
  0x00, 0x1C, 0x79, 0x00, 0x00, 0x34, 0x29, 0x00, 0x00, 0x28,
0x35, 0x00, 0x00, 0x48, 0x17, 0x00,
  0x00, 0xD8, 0x1B, 0x00, 0x00, 0x90, 0x1B, 0x00, 0x00, 0xB0,
0x09, 0x00, 0x00, 0xA0, 0x05, 0x00,
  0x00, 0xE0, 0x07, 0x00, 0x00, 0xC0, 0x03, 0x00
};


static const unsigned char bitmap_bad_plant[] U8X8_PROGMEM = {
  0x00, 0x80, 0x00, 0x00, 0x00, 0xC0, 0x00, 0x00, 0x00, 0xE0,
0x0D, 0x00, 0x00, 0xA0, 0x0F, 0x00,
  0x00, 0x20, 0x69, 0x00, 0x00, 0x10, 0x78, 0x02, 0x00, 0x10,
0xC0, 0x03, 0x00, 0x10, 0xC0, 0x03,
  0x00, 0x10, 0x00, 0x01, 0x00, 0x10, 0x80, 0x00, 0x00, 0x10,
0xC0, 0x00, 0x00, 0x30, 0x60, 0x00,
  0x00, 0x60, 0x30, 0x00, 0x00, 0xC0, 0x1F, 0x00, 0x00, 0x60,
0x07, 0x00, 0x00, 0x60, 0x00, 0x00,
  0x00, 0x60, 0x00, 0x00, 0x00, 0x40, 0x00, 0x00, 0x00, 0xC0,
0x00, 0x00, 0x00, 0x00, 0x01, 0x00,
  0x00, 0x00, 0x01, 0x00, 0x00, 0x00, 0x01, 0x00, 0x00, 0x80,
0x00, 0x00, 0x00, 0xC7, 0x1C, 0x00,
  0x80, 0x68, 0x66, 0x00, 0xC0, 0x33, 0x7B, 0x00, 0x40, 0xB6,
0x4D, 0x00, 0x00, 0xE8, 0x06, 0x00,
  0x00, 0xF0, 0x03, 0x00, 0x00, 0xE0, 0x00, 0x00
};
```

We can then create a void function to draw the plant value in the OLED display. If no sensor is present, it will display nothing, but we account for the three different options of having a sensor value larger than the low trigger level, having it smaller than the low trigger level, and having no sensor value:

```
void drawPlant(void)
{
  if (moisture1_value < low_trigger_level)
  {
    u8g2.drawXBMP(0, 0, 32, 30, bitmap_bad_plant);
  }
  else
  {
    if(moisture1_value != 999)
      u8g2.drawXBMP(0, 0, 32, 30, bitmap_good_plant);
  }
}
```

Similarly, we do the same for the other three moisture values. This can be seen in the code in the repository.

This is the `void` function to draw the moisture value in the OLED display. If no sensor is present, it will display nothing:

```
void drawMoisture(void)
{
  int A = 0;
  int B = 0;
  int C = 64;
  int D = 96;
  char moisture1_temp[5] = {0};
  char moisture2_temp[5] = {0};
  char moisture3_temp[5] = {0};
  char moisture4_temp[5] = {0};
  read_sensor_value();
  if(moisture1_value != 999)
    itoa(moisture1_value, moisture1_temp, 10);
  u8g2.setFont(u8g2_font_8x13_tr);
  u8g2.setCursor(9, 60);
  u8g2.print("S1  S2  S3  S4");
  if (moisture1_value < 10)
  {
    u8g2.drawStr(A + 14, 45, moisture1_temp);
  }
  else if (moisture1_value < 100)
  {
    u8g2.drawStr(A + 6, 45, moisture1_temp);
  }
  else
  {
    u8g2.drawStr(A + 2, 45, moisture1_temp);
  }
  if(moisture1_value != 999){
    u8g2.setCursor(A + 23, 45 );
    u8g2.print("%");
  }
}
```

We do a similar thing for the other three moisture values, which can also be referenced from the GitHub repository.

8. After finishing writing the sketch, compile and download the code to the ESP32 by clicking on the ⟳ button on the Arduino IDE. Open the Serial Monitor to see the console where you can monitor the printed result. You will see something like this on your console:

```
Output    Serial Monitor  ×

Message (Enter to send message to 'Node32s' on 'COM3')

00:41:14.628 -> S1 = 3286.00 - 20, S2 = 3280.00 - 20, S3 = 226.00 - 999, S4 = 1904.00 - 73
00:41:14.628 ->
00:41:14.628 -> S1 = 3302.00 - 19, S2 = 3280.00 - 20, S3 = 273.00 - 999, S4 = 1904.00 - 73
00:41:19.615 ->
00:41:19.615 -> S1 = 3302.00 - 19, S2 = 3295.00 - 20, S3 = 140.00 - 999, S4 = 1936.00 - 71
00:41:19.741 ->
00:41:19.741 -> S1 = 3313.00 - 19, S2 = 3280.00 - 20, S3 = 93.00 - 999, S4 = 1919.00 - 72
00:41:19.741 ->
00:41:19.741 -> S1 = 3311.00 - 19, S2 = 3293.00 - 20, S3 = 202.00 - 999, S4 = 1909.00 - 73
00:41:19.785 ->
00:41:19.785 -> S1 = 3303.00 - 19, S2 = 3271.00 - 21, S3 = 202.00 - 999, S4 = 1926.00 - 72
00:41:19.785 ->
00:41:19.785 -> S1 = 3311.00 - 19, S2 = 3286.00 - 20, S3 = 272.00 - 999, S4 = 1901.00 - 73
```

Figure 13.23 – Sample output from Serial Monitor

Each sensor will display two values: the raw analog read value and the mapped value (between 0 and 99). If a sensor is not present, the analog read will provide quite a small value (<800), which will be assigned a value of 999 to easily identify as no sensor is present or the sensor is broken. In the preceding result, we only connect three moisture sensors (S1, S2, and S3), of which sensor S3 is not attached. We can see that the S3 raw value is quite small and translated to 999, which means no sensor is attached or the sensor is damaged. Sensors S1 and S2 are left dry, while sensor S4 is covered with a damp cloth. We can see that the raw values of S1 and S2 are very high (>3,000) and the mapped moisture values are low, that is, near 20%, which is below the low trigger level, so the S1 and S2 relays should be switched on. This will trigger the solenoid water valve; the water pump will turn on and the water will flow to the destination plant pots. The raw value of sensor S4 is low (around 1,900), and the mapped value is high (more than 70%). Since this value is higher than the high trigger level (65%), the appropriate relay for S4 should be switched off. This condition can be seen in the LED representation on the four-port relay module, where only IN1 and IN2 are turned on, while IN3 and IN4 both are turned off.

Figure 13.24 – LED status of the four-port relay module

The OLED display will show something like this:

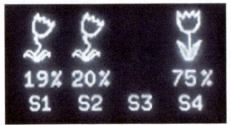

Figure 13.25 – OLED display sample of the four sensors

As the mapped values of sensors S1 and S2 are considered dry, the bitmap picture will display a bad plant picture, while for sensor S4, since the moisture level is high, it will display a good plant picture. Since sensor S3 is not present or is malfunctioning, no picture and no value will be displayed.

And that's it; you've made your smart garden system!

By undertaking this exercise, you have acquired the knowledge and skills to design and implement a smart garden system. You have learned the importance of various sensors, as well as actuators such as submersible water pumps and relay modules, in maintaining optimal plant growth conditions.

Furthermore, this practical exercise has helped you to develop your programming skills, enabling you to implement custom logic for analyzing sensor data and controlling the relay module according to the plant's needs. Optionally, you will have had the opportunity to learn how to store sensor data in a database and create a web-based dashboard for real-time data visualization and system monitoring. The hands-on experience with open source IoT tools and platforms has given you a foundation for understanding the potential of IoT technologies, promoting innovation and practical applications in various fields.

Summary

In this chapter, we have delved into the development of IoT solutions for digital transformation within Industry 4.0, which has revolutionized the way industries operate. We have highlighted the importance of IoT to Industry 4.0 and explained the steps involved in developing IoT solutions to optimize processes, reduce costs, and improve productivity in organizations.

However, the implementation of IoT solutions can be challenging due to various factors, such as selecting the right IoT devices and sensors, data security, and training employees. To overcome these challenges, we have provided strategies for effective IoT implementation. In addition, we have included a case study on the use of IoT solutions in healthcare within a smart city. This case study demonstrated the potential of IoT solutions to create a more efficient and effective healthcare system. You have then been able to implement a plant monitoring system to put into practice the concepts that you have learned.

Overall, this chapter aimed to provide you with an understanding of how IoT can be used to transform industries and drive digital transformation within organizations. By adopting the strategies outlined in this chapter, organizations can leverage the power of IoT to stay ahead in the rapidly evolving technological landscape. In the next chapter, we will build on this through seeing how we can build complex, holistic IoT environments with multi-cloud architectures and navigating complexities with other techniques.

Further reading

For more information about what was covered in this chapter, please refer to the following links:

- Look at more use cases of Industrial IoT: `https://www.iotworldtoday.com/iiot/the-top-20-industrial-iot-applications`

- Read use cases of Industrial IoT solutions on AWS: `https://aws.amazon.com/iot/solutions/industrial-iot/`

- Take a look at core challenges that make Industrial IoT hard to implement in organizations: `https://www.worldscientific.com/doi/abs/10.1142/S0219877023500414` Read more on digital transformation taking place with IoT: `https://magazine.wharton.upenn.edu/digital/internet-of-things-the-key-to-digital-transformation/`

- A look at Blynk used for the industrial context: `https://blynk.io/clients/seametrics-water-level-sensors-iot-software`

14
Architecting Complex, Holistic IoT Environments

As IoT technology advances, it has become increasingly complex and sophisticated when deployed in growing architectures, and businesses and organizations are seeking ways to leverage its power to improve efficiency, reduce costs, and enhance customer experiences. However, developing and deploying complex, holistic IoT environments presents significant challenges, including navigating hybrid deployments, managing risks and threats, and ensuring seamless integration with existing IT infrastructure.

One of the key challenges of developing IoT environments is navigating complex hybrid deployments and trying to avoid complexity as the architecture grows. As IoT solutions often involve multiple devices and systems, integrating them into an existing IT infrastructure can be a significant undertaking. This requires a deep understanding of the various components involved, including sensors, gateways, cloud platforms, and other systems, as well as the ability to integrate them into a cohesive whole.

In this chapter, we will explore key challenges within this area in detail and provide practical guidance for developing complex, holistic IoT environments. We will examine strategies for navigating complex hybrid deployments, managing threats and risks, and leveraging multi-cloud architecture to support IoT environments. By understanding these challenges and developing effective solutions, organizations can unlock the full potential of IoT technology and drive real business value.

In this chapter, we're going to cover the following main topics:

- Understanding how complex some environments can be, and the considerations that must be taken when building on them

- Understanding the threats and risks within complex environments for IoT and planning accordingly

- Understanding how to navigate building a multi-cloud architecture

Technical requirements

This chapter will require you to have the following hardware and software installed:

- Hardware:

  - ESP32-Wroom

  - GPS module

  - OLED display module

  - Jumper cables

  - Breadboard

  - NodeMCU ESP32S microcontroller

  - Bosch Sensortech BME680 module

  - Speaker (these can be laptop speakers if necessary)

- Software:

  - Microsoft Azure account

  - Raspberry Pi

  - AWS account

You can access the GitHub folder that contains the code that will be used in this chapter at `https://github.com/PacktPublishing/IoT-Made-Easy-for-Beginners/tree/main/Chapter14/`.

Navigating complex hybrid deployments for IoT

IoT deployments are complex, and **hybrid deployments** add an additional layer of complexity. Hybrid deployments are those that use both on-premises infrastructure and cloud services. The reason for using a hybrid approach is that it allows organizations to leverage their existing infrastructure while also taking advantage of the scalability and flexibility of the cloud.

However, managing hybrid IoT deployments comes with its own set of challenges. The primary challenge is managing the complexity of the system. In a hybrid environment, data must flow between the on-premises infrastructure and the cloud seamlessly. This requires a high degree of integration between the different components of the system. Additionally, organizations must manage the security of the system and ensure that data is always protected.

To navigate these challenges, organizations should take a holistic approach to managing their hybrid IoT deployments. This includes having a clear understanding of the system architecture and how data flows between the different components. Organizations should also prioritize security and implement measures such as encryption and access controls to protect data.

The following figure shows a high-level representation of a connection diagram of a hybrid cloud deployment:

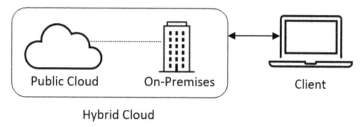

Figure 14.1 – A connection diagram of a hybrid cloud deployment

The public cloud and on-premises will have their own security and architectural components to consider while the client communicates with that network. The public cloud and on-premises will be able to communicate with each other through an encrypted network.

Now, we can take a look at a new platform we can add as part of our hybrid deployment: Microsoft Azure.

Introduction to Microsoft Azure

Microsoft Azure, developed by Microsoft, is an extensive cloud computing platform that enables creating, testing, deploying, and managing applications and services within Microsoft-controlled data centers. This platform offers a variety of cloud-based services such as computing, analytics, storage, and networking. Users have the flexibility to select from these offerings to build and expand new applications or migrate existing ones to the public cloud. Azure is compatible with a wide range of programming languages, tools, and frameworks, including Microsoft's products and those from other vendors.

Regarding **Internet of Things (IoT)** applications, Azure provides a comprehensive IoT suite that aids in gathering, monitoring, and analyzing data from IoT devices. This scalable Azure IoT platform supports a broad spectrum of devices and delivers immediate insights, which is crucial for enhancing operational efficiency, improving decision-making processes, and discovering new commercial opportunities. Employing Azure in conjunction with other cloud services such as AWS allows companies to diversify their cloud solutions, reducing reliance on a single provider and taking advantage of distinct services offered by different clouds. This strategy results in more robust and adaptable architectures, allowing workload distribution to the most suitable cloud service based on performance or cost. For IoT systems, this approach means broader global reach and advanced analytics capabilities, all while leveraging the strengths of various cloud environments.

Now, let's look at how we can start architecting for a hybrid deployment.

Architecting for a hybrid deployment

Designing the architecture for deploying a hybrid cloud model on AWS requires careful planning and consideration of the organization's needs and objectives. Note that this is beyond the scope of what you are expected to put into practice, but this will be useful when you look at how it is done in industrial contexts. Let's walk through the steps:

1. **Determine your hybrid cloud strategy**: Before you begin designing your hybrid cloud architecture on AWS, you must define your hybrid cloud strategy. This involves identifying which workloads will be deployed in the public cloud and which will remain on-premises, as well as the data and application integration requirements.

2. **Choose the right AWS services**: AWS offers a wide range of services that can be used in hybrid cloud environments. It's important to choose the right services that fit your specific use case and can seamlessly integrate with your on-premises infrastructure.

3. **Build a secure network architecture**: A secure network architecture is critical to ensuring the protection of your data and applications in a hybrid cloud environment. This involves configuring your **virtual private cloud** (**VPC**) and subnets, establishing secure connectivity between your on-premises environment and AWS, and implementing appropriate security controls.

4. **Define your data storage strategy**: Data storage is a key component of any hybrid cloud architecture. You need to decide how your data will be stored, where it will be stored, and how it will be accessed. This may involve leveraging AWS storage services such as Amazon S3, Glacier, or EBS, as well as on-premises storage solutions.

5. **Ensure high availability and disaster recovery**: Hybrid cloud architectures must be designed to ensure high availability and disaster recovery. This involves leveraging AWS services such as Elastic Load Balancing, Auto Scaling, and Route 53 to distribute traffic across multiple instances and regions, as well as implementing backup and recovery solutions.

6. **Implement monitoring and management tools**: To effectively manage your hybrid cloud environment, you need to implement monitoring and management tools that can provide visibility into your on-premises and AWS resources. This may involve using AWS CloudTrail, CloudWatch, and other third-party tools.

By following these steps, organizations can design a hybrid cloud architecture on AWS that meets their specific needs and provides the flexibility, scalability, and cost-efficiency of cloud computing, while also maintaining control over their sensitive data and applications.

The following figure shows an AWS architecture for a hybrid deployment:

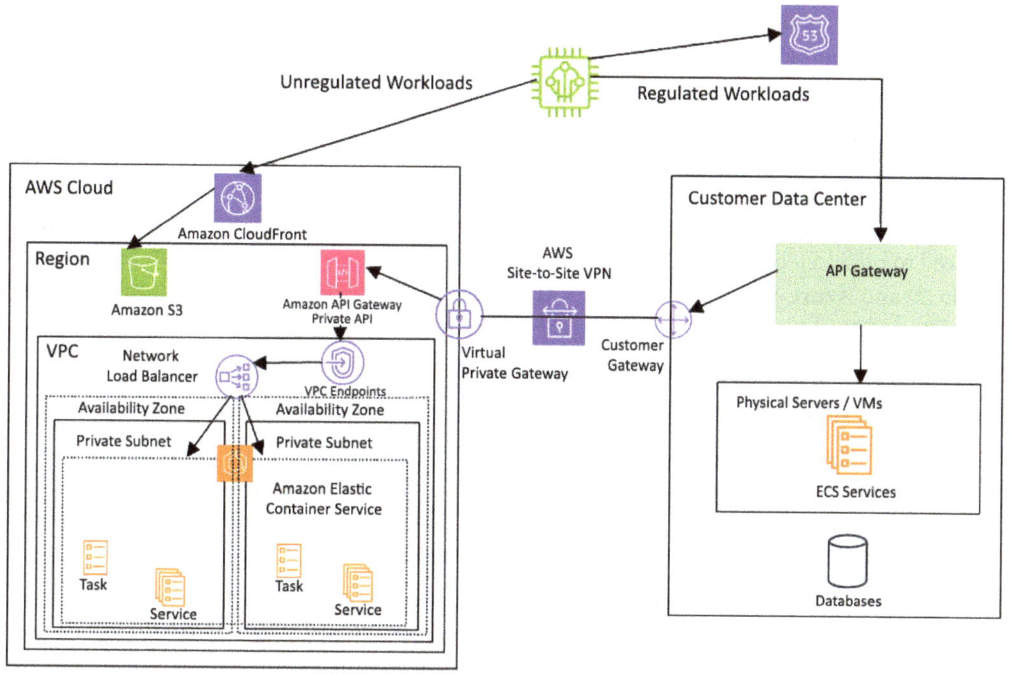

Figure 14.2 – AWS architecture for a hybrid environment

The environment is well-integrated and is where AWS services are leveraged alongside an on-premises data center. The infrastructure is designed for resilience and is spread across multiple Availability Zones, with a clear distinction between handling regulated and unregulated workloads, suggesting a setup that is both compliant and performance-optimized.

Secure connectivity between the cloud and on-premises components is established via a site-to-site VPN, with the API gateway serving as a critical point of management and access control for APIs. This enables a seamless and secure interaction between cloud-hosted services and on-premises resources, allowing for a centralized approach to managing application interfaces.

Finally, the use of ECS in both the cloud and on-premises indicates a containerized approach to application deployment, providing the flexibility to run workloads where they are most appropriate, whether it's for compliance, performance, or other operational efficiencies. This duality in container services underscores the architecture's readiness for a dynamic and scalable application landscape that's well-suited for modern enterprise needs.

Next, we'll look at how we can approach a multi-cloud hybrid deployment.

Architecting for a multi-cloud hybrid deployment

Designing the architecture for deploying a hybrid multi-cloud model that spans AWS and Azure requires careful planning and consideration. The following are some steps that need to be taken:

1. **Identify the requirements**: The first step is to identify the business requirements, such as scalability, high availability, and disaster recovery. It is also important to identify the security and compliance requirements.

2. **Select the necessary cloud services**: Based on the requirements, the appropriate cloud services need to be selected from both AWS and Azure. For example, AWS **Elastic Compute Cloud (EC2)** and **Azure Virtual Machines (VMs)** can be used for compute, AWS **Simple Storage Service (S3)** and Azure Blob Storage can be used for storage, and so on.

3. **Choose the right connectivity option**: A reliable and secure connectivity option is essential for a multi-cloud architecture. AWS Direct Connect and Azure ExpressRoute can be used to establish a private and dedicated network connection between AWS and Azure.

4. **Implement a load balancer**: A load balancer can be implemented to distribute traffic between the instances running in both AWS and Azure. AWS **Elastic Load Balancing (ELB)** and Azure Load Balancer are the respective load balancers for each cloud platform.

5. **Implement monitoring and logging**: Monitoring and logging are essential to ensure the smooth functioning of a multi-cloud architecture. AWS CloudWatch and Azure Monitor can be used to monitor the performance and health of the services running in both clouds.

6. **Implement security and compliance**: Security and compliance are critical for any architecture. AWS **Identity and Access Management (IAM)** and **Microsoft Entra ID** can be used for IAM. AWS Security Hub and Azure Security Center can be used for security and compliance management.

7. **Test and validate**: Once the architecture has been designed and implemented, it is important to test and validate it thoroughly to ensure that it meets the business and technical requirements.

Designing a multi-cloud architecture on AWS and Azure requires expertise in both cloud platforms and the ability to seamlessly integrate them. By following these steps, businesses can design a reliable, scalable, and secure multi-cloud architecture that meets their requirements.

The following figure shows a sample migration that can be performed as part of moving to a multi-cloud model:

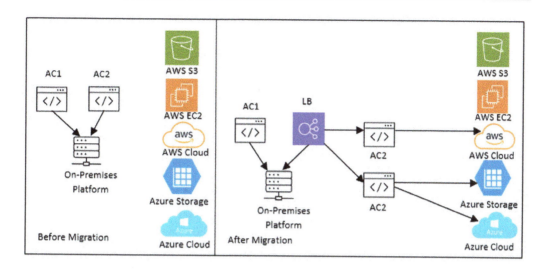

Figure 14.3 – Multi-cloud rebinding

This diagram illustrates the evolution of an IT infrastructure from a single-cloud setup to a multi-cloud hybrid model. Before migration, we see a traditional on-premises platform with application components, AC1 and AC2, directly interacting with AWS services, including S3 for storage and EC2 for compute. Azure's cloud storage is also in use, indicating a nascent hybrid state, but without a sophisticated integration between the clouds.

Post-migration, the architecture transforms into a more complex multi-cloud environment. A load balancer has been introduced on-premises, signifying an upgrade in traffic management and distribution. This suggests a move to a more resilient and scalable system as the load balance can dynamically distribute workloads not just between on-premises servers but also across cloud providers.

The application components are now configured to interact with both AWS and Azure, showcasing a true hybrid cloud scenario where services from both providers are utilized in tandem. This kind of setup allows for flexibility in resource utilization and can be a strategic move to optimize costs, enhance disaster recovery capabilities, and ensure regional compliance by leveraging the geographical spread of both AWS and Azure. It epitomizes a modern enterprise architecture that is agile, resilient, and designed for optimal performance across multiple cloud environments.

Now that we have obtained a good understanding of migrating to a multi-cloud hybrid deployment, we can look at moving data from IoT Core to S3, which will be important to know as part of creating hybrid cloud models.

Threats and risks to complex IoT environments

Hybrid and multi-cloud models are increasingly being used in complex IoT environments and provide many benefits in terms of scalability, agility, and cost-efficiency. However, they also introduce several security risks and threats that must be managed carefully.

Threats and risks

One of the biggest risks of hybrid and multi-cloud environments is the potential for data breaches. With data being transferred between different cloud providers and on-premises systems, it becomes more challenging to secure data in transit and at rest. This creates a larger attack surface for hackers and malicious actors to exploit and makes it more difficult to ensure data privacy and confidentiality.

Another threat is the risk of vendor lock-in, which can occur when a company becomes too reliant on a particular cloud provider or technology stack. This can make it difficult to migrate data and applications to other platforms or to take advantage of new technologies and services. Companies must carefully evaluate their cloud provider options and select a mix of providers that can meet their business needs while minimizing the risk of vendor lock-in.

The complexity of hybrid and multi-cloud environments also makes it more difficult to ensure compliance with regulations such as the **General Data Protection Regulation (GDPR)** and the **Health Insurance Portability and Accountability Act (HIPAA)**. The GDPR is a regulatory standard that governs the handling of personal data in the European Union, while HIPAA is a US law aimed at protecting the privacy and security of individual medical information. Companies must ensure that they have a clear understanding of data residency and protection requirements and that their cloud providers can comply with these requirements.

Finally, managing security across multiple cloud environments can be challenging as each provider may have different security controls and tools. Companies must develop a comprehensive security strategy that addresses the unique security risks of each cloud provider and ensures that they have the resources and expertise to manage security effectively.

Managing threats and risks

To effectively safeguard hybrid and multi-cloud environments, businesses must engage in both risk and threat management through a proactive and holistic security strategy. This strategy should include the implementation of stringent security protocols and the use of cutting-edge encryption and authentication methods. Conducting thorough vulnerability checks and penetration tests is critical to identify potential system weaknesses. It's also imperative to define and communicate clear security responsibilities within the organization, ensuring that every member understands their role in maintaining a secure environment.

A key aspect of this approach is regularly updating all devices and systems with the latest security patches and updates. Given the complexity and scale of the systems involved, utilizing automated tools for patch and configuration management can help maintain consistent security standards across the board. Moreover, incorporating advanced threat detection and response technologies, powered by artificial intelligence and machine learning, enables the organization to detect and respond to potential threats promptly.

The human factor in security is also crucial. Educating employees about identifying and reporting potential security issues, particularly prevalent cyber threats such as phishing and social engineering, is essential in minimizing human error-related security breaches. Regular threat analysis sessions are necessary to stay ahead of new and emerging threats, ensuring that the organization's security strategy remains relevant and effective in the face of an evolving cyber threat landscape.

Furthermore, collaborating with external security specialists and industry colleagues to share insights on new threats and effective practices can significantly enhance security measures. This collaborative approach forms a stronger collective defense, making it more challenging for cyber threats to penetrate multiple systems.

Lastly, it is critical to have a comprehensive plan for incident response. This plan should outline clear procedures for addressing a security incident, including immediate notification processes, containment strategies, and data and system recovery methods. Such a plan helps in minimizing the impact of security incidents and enables a quick recovery to normal operations. By continually adapting and updating their security practices, businesses can navigate the complexities of managing risks and threats in hybrid and multi-cloud environments effectively.

With these key points in mind, we can now look at a case study of how a multi-cloud architecture supports Volkswagen's IoT operations.

Case study – a multi-cloud architecture supporting Volkswagen's IoT operations

Volkswagen is a German multinational automotive manufacturing company. It is one of the world's largest automakers and is known for producing some of the most popular car models in the world, including the Volkswagen Golf and the Volkswagen Beetle.

Volkswagen wanted to utilize IoT technology to improve its manufacturing processes and create more efficient supply chains. However, implementing IoT at such a large scale requires significant cloud computing power and storage capacity. Volkswagen needed a solution that could handle the large amounts of data generated by IoT devices and provide real-time insights.

Volkswagen opted for a multi-cloud approach to support its IoT initiatives. It partnered with several cloud providers, including AWS, Microsoft Azure, and **Google Cloud Platform (GCP)**. By utilizing multiple cloud platforms, Volkswagen was able to distribute its workloads across different cloud providers, avoiding any potential downtime or performance issues.

This multi-cloud architecture also allowed Volkswagen to take advantage of the unique features and services offered by each cloud provider. For example, Volkswagen used AWS IoT Core to connect and manage its IoT devices, Azure IoT Hub for device management and data ingestion, and GCP for real-time analytics.

To ensure seamless integration and communication between the different cloud providers, Volkswagen used Kubernetes, an open source container orchestration platform. Kubernetes allowed Volkswagen to easily manage and scale its containerized workloads across different clouds.

Volkswagen's multi-cloud architecture has allowed the company to scale its IoT initiatives and achieve real-time insights into its manufacturing processes. By utilizing AWS, Azure, and GCP, Volkswagen has been able to take advantage of the unique features and services offered by each cloud provider. The company has been able to improve its supply chain and logistics processes, reduce maintenance costs, and enhance the overall quality of its products.

Overall, Volkswagen's multi-cloud architecture has been critical to its success in IoT. The company's ability to distribute workloads across multiple cloud providers has ensured high availability, improved performance, and enhanced security. As a result, Volkswagen has been able to stay at the forefront of innovation in the automotive industry and continue to produce some of the most popular car models in the world.

With that, we can now look at our practical exercise for this chapter, which will involve building a smart inventory management system with multi-cloud architecture.

Practical – building a smart inventory management system with multi-cloud architecture

In this practical, you will learn how to build a smart inventory management system with multi-cloud architecture using an ESP32 microcontroller, a BME680 sensor, AWS IoT Core, and Azure IoT Central. This unique end-of-chapter exercise is designed to help you apply the concepts you've learned in this chapter on developing complex, holistic IoT environments. This practical focuses on navigating complex hybrid deployments for IoT, understanding threats and risks within complex environments, and building multi-cloud architectures with AWS and Azure. By following the step-by-step instructions, even those unfamiliar with the topic will be able to create a functioning smart inventory management system that leverages the power of multiple cloud platforms.

Materials required

The following hardware and software are required as part of this practical:

- NodeMCU ESP32S microcontroller
- Bosch Sensortech BME680 module

- AWS account

- Azure account

Now, we can move on to setting up our ESP32 and BME680.

Setting up ESP32 and BME680

Follow these steps to set up ESP32 and BME680:

1. Connect the ESP32 board to your computer using a USB cable.

2. Connect the BME680 sensor module to the ESP32 using the following wiring:

    I.   SDA to pin G22

    II.   SCL to pin G21

    III. VCC to pin 3V3

    IV.   GND to pin GND:

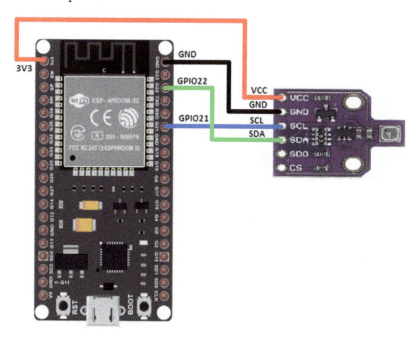

Figure 14.4 – Connection diagram for ESP32 to BME680

Next, we'll set up the Arduino IDE to put through the code needed for ESP32.

Setting up the Arduino IDE

Follow these steps to set up the Arduino IDE with the necessary libraries and code:

1. Install the Arduino IDE on your computer by going to the official website: `https://www.arduino.cc/en/software`.

2. Connect ESP32 to your computer using a micro USB cable.

3. In the Arduino IDE, navigate to **Sketch | Include Library | Manage Libraries**.

   Install the necessary libraries for the project. For the first library, you will need to use the GitHub link provided, but for the rest, you can just search for them on **Manage Libraries**:

   - BME680, by `https://github.com/SV-Zanshin`

   - AWS-SDK-ESP8266, by Ronan Schmitz (support ESP32 as well)

   - Azure SDK for C

   - PubSubClient, by Nick O'Leary

Now that our libraries are ready, we can set up IoT Core for usage.

Setting up AWS IoT Core for usage

We need to create an AWS IoT Core *thing* and obtain its MQTT endpoint. The following steps will guide you on this:

1. Log into the AWS Management Console and navigate to the IoT Core service.

2. Click on **Manage** in the left sidebar, then click **Things**.

3. Click **Create a single thing** and follow the prompts to create a new thing.

4. Once created, click on the thing and navigate to **Interact**. Take note of the **Rest API Endpoint** value (`your_mqtt_server_address`) so that you can use it in your Arduino code.

Now, we can take a look at setting up the Azure IoT Central account.

Setting up Azure IoT Central for usage

Follow these steps to set up Azure IoT Central:

1. Go to Azure IoT Central (`https://apps.azureiotcentral.com`) and create a new IoT Central application by clicking on **Build app**:

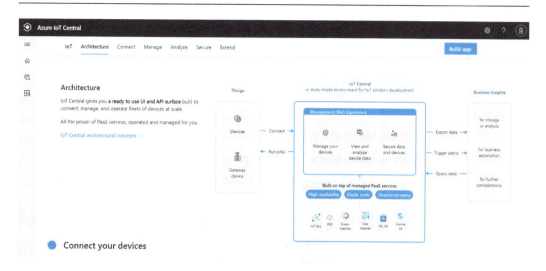

Figure 14.5 – Azure IoT Central landing page

2. Click on **Create app** inside **Custom app**:

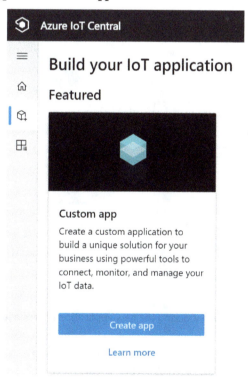

Figure 14.6 – Clicking on Create app inside Custom app

3. A new application window will appear. Fill in the form as follows.

    - **Application name**: `ESP32-BME680`

    - **URL**: `esp32-bme680`

    - **Application template**: `Custom application`

    - **Pricing plan**: Click **Standard 0** if you would prefer to have a free plan

    In the **Billing info** section, choose the following options.

    - **Directory**: Choose the account directory that you created previously (normally, it will appear as *yourname.onmicrosoft.com*).

    - **Azure subscription**: For the Azure subscription, you need to create a subscription first. Please choose the free tier if you wish to have a free plan. After that, choose the subscription name that you just created – for instance, `Azure subscription 1`.

    The location will be chosen automatically according to the Azure subscription you created previously.

    Once you're finished, click **Create**:

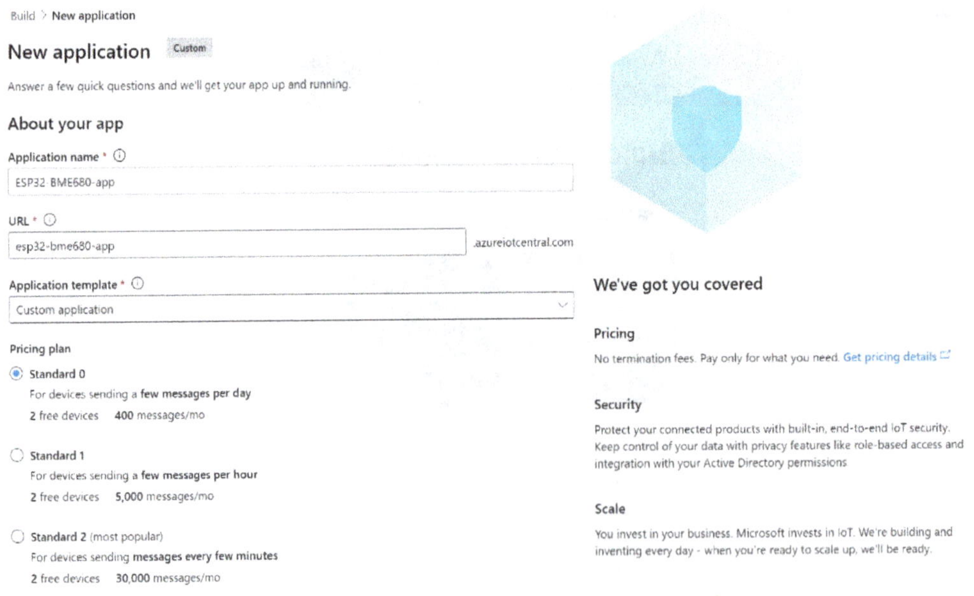

Build > New application

New application Custom

Answer a few quick questions and we'll get your app up and running.

About your app

Application name * ⓘ

    ESP32-BME680-app

URL * ⓘ

    esp32-bme680-app   .azureiotcentral.com

Application template * ⓘ

    Custom application   ⌄

Pricing plan

◉ Standard 0
  For devices sending a **few messages per day**
  2 free devices   **400** messages/mo

◯ Standard 1
  For devices sending a **few messages per hour**
  2 free devices   **5,000** messages/mo

◯ Standard 2 (most popular)
  For devices sending **messages every few minutes**
  2 free devices   **30,000** messages/mo

We've got you covered

Pricing

No termination fees. Pay only for what you need. Get pricing details ↗

Security

Protect your connected products with built-in, end-to-end IoT security. Keep control of your data with privacy features like role-based access and integration with your Active Directory permissions

Scale

You invest in your business. Microsoft invests in IoT. We're building and inventing every day - when you're ready to scale up, we'll be ready.

Figure 14.7 – Configuring the new application appropriately

4. You will be redirected to `esp32-bme680.azureiotcentral.com/devices`. The **Devices** window will be open; here you can create device(s).

5. Now, we are ready to create a device. Go to the **Device** menu by clicking on the device icon in the left pane.

Click + **New** to create a new device:

Figure 14.8 – Creating a new device in Azure IoT Central

6. The **Create a new device** window will pop up. Here, you need to fill in the form, as follows:

- **Device name**: ESP32-BME680-001

- **Device ID**: ESP32-BME680-001-DeviceID

For **Device template**, leave it as-is.

7. Click **Create** to create the device. Now, in the **Devices** window, you will see the newly created device appear in the **All devices** list:

Figure 14.9 – Navigating to the All devices window

8. Click on **ESP32-BME680-001**; you will see a new window, as shown here:

Figure 14.10 – New window after clicking on the device

9. Click on the **Connect** icon at the top left of the window; the **Device connection groups** window will appear. Save or copy the **ID scope**, **Device ID**, **Authentication type**, **Primary key**, and **Secondary key** values to a file since we will use this information to connect to Azure IoT Central later:

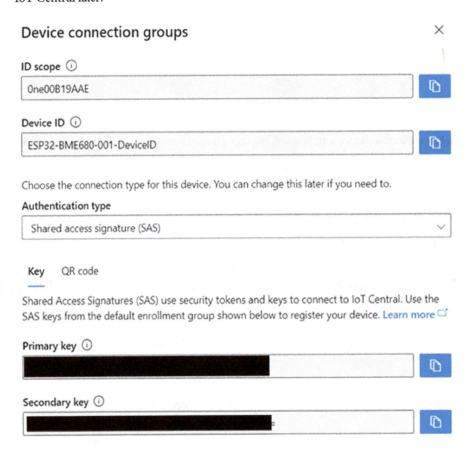

Figure 14.11 – The configuration sample for Device connection groups

10. Go to the **Devices** page and click **Connect**. Get the **ID scope** and **Device ID** values. Set **Authentication type** to **Shared access signature (SAS)**. Finally, get the **Primary key** value. We will use these in *step 3* of the next section.

With that, you've set up Azure IoT Central for use. Now, we can upload the Arduino sketch and run ESP32 for inventory management.

Building the inventory management system

With the libraries ready, we can start building the implementation of the inventory management system:

1. First, we must write the Arduino code to read distance measurements from the ultrasonic sensor and transmit the data via MQTT. The code is based on the example of Azure SDK for C with some modifications and combined with AWS SDK codes. Open this chapter's GitHub repository and locate this practical to get through this section easily.

2. To start, we need to open the Azure SDK for C example file in the Arduino IDE by going to **File | Examples | Azure SDK for C | Azure_IoT_Central_ESP32**. Once the code has loaded, we need to save the sketch under another name so that we can modify it. Click on **File | Save As** and name it ESP32_Azure_AWS_BME680:

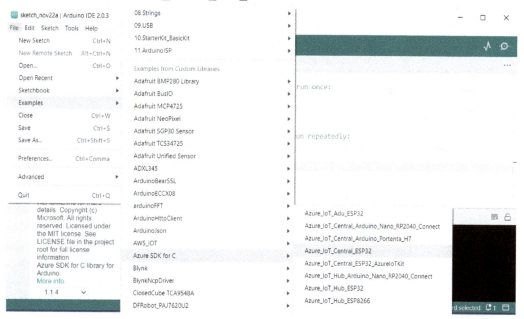

Figure 14.12 – Opening the Azure SDK for C sample code

3. The connection parameter settings are located in the iot_configs.h tab, so we need to click on this tab. In this example, we will not use the X509 Certificate option; instead, we will use DEVICE_KEY. To enable a connection to Azure IoT Central, we need to change the contents of iot_configs.h. You need to replace IOT_CONFIG_WIFI_SSID and IOT_CONFIG_WIFI_PASSWORD with your Wi-Fi credentials, and DPS_ID_SCOPE, IOT_CONFIG_DEVICE_ID, and IOT_CONFIG_DEVICE_KEY with the values you saved when you configured Azure IoT Central.

Look for the following lines and replace them in the file accordingly:

```
// Wifi
#define IOT_CONFIG_WIFI_SSID              "YOUR_WIFI_SSID"
#define IOT_CONFIG_WIFI_PASSWORD          "YOUR_WIFI_PASSWORD"


// Azure IoT Central
#define DPS_ID_SCOPE                      "YOUR_DPS_ID_SCOPE"
#define IOT_CONFIG_DEVICE_ID              "YOUR_DEVICE_ID"
#define IOT_CONFIG_DEVICE_KEY             "YOUR IOT_CONFIG_
DEVICE_KEY "
```

4. Click on the main tab – that is, **ESP32_Azure_AWS_BME680**. We also need to change the code here. Source this code directly from the project code in this book's GitHub repository. You may delete the whole code first for easier programming.

    Write or copy these codes accordingly, as per the project code.

5. Since we moved the sensor reading to the main program and to accommodate sensor measurement parameters, we need to modify `Azure_IoT_PnP_Template.cpp`. Again, we can source the code from the project repository on GitHub.

    We need to add a new tab to store the AWS certificates. Create a new tab by clicking on the ⋯ button near the top right of the window and clicking the **New Tab** option. Name the tab `certificates.h`. Change THINGNAME (if you're using another name) and AWS_IOT_ENDPOINT and insert the appropriate three certificates that you saved when you created your thing via AWS IoT between BEGIN and END:

```
#include <pgmspace.h>

#define CERTIFICATES
#define THINGNAME "ESP32_DHT"
const char AWS_IOT_ENDPOINT[] = "YOUR_AWS_IOT_ENDPOINT";

// Amazon Root CA 1
static const char AWS_CERT_CA[] PROGMEM = R"EOF(
-----BEGIN CERTIFICATE-----
-----END CERTIFICATE-----
)EOF";

// Device Certificate
static const char AWS_CERT_CRT[] PROGMEM = R"KEY(
-----BEGIN CERTIFICATE-----
-----END CERTIFICATE-----
)KEY";
```

```
// Device Private Key
static const char AWS_CERT_PRIVATE[] PROGMEM = R"KEY(
-----BEGIN RSA PRIVATE KEY-----
-----END RSA PRIVATE KEY-----
)KEY";
```

Now, we can look at testing our implementation.

Uploading the Arduino sketch and running ESP32

With everything set up, we can upload the Arduino sketch and run ESP32:

1. Upload the Arduino sketch we created. After uploading the code to ESP32, it will restart, start connecting to our Wi-Fi, and try to make a connection to Azure IoT Central and AWS IoT Hub. It will read the BME sensor data and send it to both AWS IoT and Azure IoT Central. If we look at the Serial Monitor, we will find a message similar to the following:

```
22:56:24.781 -> AWS IoT Connected!
22:56:24.781 -> 2023/11/7 15:54:09 [INFO] MQTT client target uri set to 'mqtts://global.azure-devices-provisioning.net'
22:56:24.781 -> 2023/11/7 15:54:09 [INFO] MQTT client connecting.
22:56:26.356 -> 2023/11/7 15:54:11 [INFO] MQTT client connected (session_present=0).
22:56:26.356 -> 2023/11/7 15:54:11 [INFO] MQTT client subscribing to '$dps/registrations/res/#'
22:56:26.396 -> 2023/11/7 15:54:11 [INFO] MQTT topic subscribed (message id=14143).
22:56:26.396 -> 2023/11/7 15:54:11 [INFO] MQTT client publishing to '$dps/registrations/PUT/iotdps-register/?$rid=1'
22:56:26.522 -> 2023/11/7 15:54:11 [INFO] MQTT message received.
22:56:26.522 -> 2023/11/7 15:54:11 [INFO] MQTT client publishing to '$dps/registrations/GET/iotdps-get-operationstatus/?$rid=1&operationId=5.84c2c92c2f224ee7.5d61324d-
22:56:26.554 -> 2023/11/7 15:54:11 [INFO] MQTT message received.
22:56:29.024 -> 2023/11/7 15:54:14 [INFO] MQTT client publishing to '$dps/registrations/GET/iotdps-get-operationstatus/?$rid=1&operationId=5.84c2c92c2f224ee7.5d61324d-
22:56:29.097 -> 2023/11/7 15:54:14 [INFO] MQTT message received.
22:56:29.097 -> 2023/11/7 15:54:14 [INFO] MQTT client being disconnected.
22:56:29.097 -> 2023/11/7 15:54:14 [INFO] MQTT client target uri set to 'mqtts://iotc-57e3c03e-ea54-437e-a61b-90ce2f76a4c8.azure-devices.net'
22:56:29.132 -> 2023/11/7 15:54:14 [INFO] MQTT client connecting.
22:56:30.410 -> 2023/11/7 15:54:15 [INFO] MQTT client connected (session_present=0).
22:56:30.410 -> 2023/11/7 15:54:15 [INFO] MQTT client subscribing to '$iothub/methods/POST/#'
22:56:30.442 -> 2023/11/7 15:54:15 [INFO] MQTT topic subscribed (message id=13302).
22:56:30.442 -> 2023/11/7 15:54:15 [INFO] MQTT client subscribing to '$iothub/twin/res/#'
22:56:30.442 -> 2023/11/7 15:54:15 [INFO] MQTT topic subscribed (message id=60044).
22:56:30.442 -> 2023/11/7 15:54:15 [INFO] MQTT client subscribing to '$iothub/twin/PATCH/properties/desired/#'
22:56:30.473 -> 2023/11/7 15:54:15 [INFO] MQTT topic subscribed (message id=28662).
22:56:30.473 -> 2023/11/7 15:54:15 [INFO] MQTT client publishing to '$iothub/twin/PATCH/properties/reported/?$rid=0'
22:56:30.508 -> BME680 results = 33.32, 36.74, 1010.35, 1576.15, 24.17
22:56:30.508 -> Publish Message to AWS IoT!
22:56:30.508 -> 2023/11/7 15:54:15 [INFO] MQTT client publishing to 'devices/ESP32-BME690-001-DeviceID/messages/events/'
22:56:30.694 -> 2023/11/7 15:54:15 [INFO] MQTT message received.
22:56:30.694 -> 2023/11/7 15:54:15 [INFO] Properties update request completed (id=0, status=204)
22:57:00.513 -> BME680 results = 33.23, 36.32, 1010.35, 1526.58, 24.17
22:57:00.513 -> Publish Message to AWS IoT!
```

Figure 14.13 – Output from the Serial Monitor

2. Once ESP32 is connected to Azure IoT Central, you will find that a device template called **Espressif ESP32 Azure IoT Kit** is automatically generated in the Azure IoT Central portal.

3. Next, you need to modify the data model. In the **Device Template** menu, select **Model** | **{} Edit DTDL**. Copy and paste the content of `Azure_IoT_Central\Device_Template\Model\Espressif ESP32 Azure IoT Kit.json` and click **Save**. Then, click **Publish** at the top.

4. Once the updated template has been published, navigate to **Devices | Espressif ESP32 Azure IoT Kit | Adafruit Feature ESP32**, then the device you created. You should see its **Status** change to **Connected**. Click on the **Raw data** tab; you will see the data with the latest data model uploaded from the device.

By following the preceding steps, you will have built a smart inventory management system with multi-cloud architecture using ESP32, AWS IoT Core, and Azure IoT Hub.

And that's it! By following these step-by-step instructions, you have successfully navigated the complexities of a hybrid IoT deployment, assessed the potential threats and risks in the environment, and leveraged the benefits of multi-cloud architecture.

This hands-on experience has provided you with a deeper understanding of the concepts covered in the chapter on developing complex, holistic IoT environments. As you continue to explore IoT and multi-cloud technologies, you can expand upon this practical to develop more advanced and sophisticated applications tailored to your specific needs. With the foundation laid out by this exercise, you are now well-equipped to tackle the challenges of building complex IoT environments in the real world.

Summary

In this chapter, we delved into the development of IoT solutions for digital transformation within Industry 4.0, which has revolutionized the way industries operate. We have highlighted the importance of IoT in Industry 4.0 and explained the steps involved in developing IoT solutions to optimize processes, reduce costs, and improve productivity in organizations.

However, the implementation of IoT solutions can be challenging due to various factors, such as selecting the right IoT devices and sensors, data security, and training employees. To overcome these challenges, we have provided strategies for effective IoT implementation. In addition, we have included a case study on the use of IoT solutions in healthcare within a smart city. This case study demonstrated the potential of IoT solutions to create a more efficient and effective healthcare system.

Overall, this chapter aimed to provide you with an understanding of how IoT can be used to transform industries and drive digital transformation within organizations. By adopting the strategies outlined in this chapter, organizations can leverage the power of IoT to stay ahead in the rapidly evolving technological landscape.

Further reading

For more information about what was covered in this chapter, please refer to the following links:

- Take a look at multi-cloud deployments: `https://www.techrepublic.com/article/multi-cloud-deployment/`

- Understand how hybrid cloud models look like in AWS: `https://aws.amazon.com/hybrid-multicloud/`

- Learn how to utilize Microsoft Azure for your own use cases through the official documentation: `https://azure.microsoft.com/en-au`

- Get insights for multi-cloud architectures: `https://www.synopsys.com/cloud/insights/multi-cloud-architecture.html`

- Understand the challenges and novel architectural models of multi-cloud native applications: `https://journalofcloudcomputing.springeropen.com/articles/10.1186/s13677-022-00367-6`

15

Looking Ahead into the Future of IoT

The **Internet of Things (IoT)** has come a long way since its inception and has transformed how we interact with our environment. The proliferation of smart devices and connected technology has made it possible to automate and optimize a wide range of processes, from home automation to industrial manufacturing. As we look ahead to the future of IoT, we can see a world where smart devices are even more integrated into our daily lives, and the potential for this technology seems limitless.

This chapter will explore the next 5 years of IoT and what we can expect to see in terms of advancements and innovation. We will discuss the future of smart businesses with IoT, and how companies can leverage this technology to improve their operations and create new revenue streams. Additionally, we will examine threats and challenges posed by the continuing trend of big data and how businesses can mitigate risks while taking advantage of its benefits. Furthermore, we will provide best practices and the dos and don'ts of IoT, highlighting key considerations that businesses and individuals need to keep in mind when implementing and using IoT devices. Finally, we will address the topic of IoT sustainability and the importance of responsible design and usage to ensure the longevity of this technology and its positive impact on society and the environment.

You will gain valuable insights into the future of IoT, learning to navigate emerging trends and mitigate associated risks. The chapter offers practical guidance for managing IoT projects and emphasizes sustainable and responsible technology usage in the future, making it an essential resource for anyone looking to see how to continuously deploy IoT effectively in their personal or professional endeavors.

In this chapter, we're going to cover the following main topics:

- Understanding more about the trends of IoT that are likely to shape the future within the next 5 years and being prepared to respond accordingly based on businesses' own use cases
- Understanding more about the threats and challenges that come along with current and future trends, helping businesses plan further for possible risks

- Learning best practices in managing IoT projects and how to ensure that they can be sustainable in the long run
- Learn to create an IoT-integrated Amazon Bedrock RAG web application

Technical requirements

This chapter will require you to have the following hardware and software installed:

- Hardware:
  - Raspberry Pi
  - A computer with internet access
- Software:
  - Python IDE
  - **Amazon Web Services (AWS)** account

We will be running our programs on Python and have a slight bit of SQL syntax that we need to use as part of querying data in this chapter. Again, don't worry if you don't understand some of the code; we will walk you through it and get you down to understanding how each part of the code works in no time.

You can access the GitHub folder for the code that is used in this chapter at `https://github.com/PacktPublishing/IoT-Made-Easy-for-Beginners/tree/main/Chapter15/`.

The next 5 years of IoT – what next?

Data analysis is often done at scale to analyze large sets of data using the capabilities of cloud computing services such as AWS. Designing a workflow for the data analysis workflow to follow is the pivotal starting point for this to be performed. This will follow five main categories: collection, storage, processing, visualization, and data security.

In this section, we will be introducing you to data analysis on AWS, discussing which services we can use as part of AWS to perform the data analytics workloads we need it to, and talking through best practices that are part of this. We will understand how to design and incorporate workflows into the current IoT network that we currently have and work with it to better power our capabilities.

Common trends and challenges

There are five key main trends and challenges that are on the horizon for the future of IoT:

- **Increased adoption and integration**: According to Ericsson's *IoT connections outlook* report (`https://www.ericsson.com/en/reports-and-papers/mobility-report/dataforecasts/iot-connections-outlook`), the number of IoT connections between connected devices is expected to reach 34.7 billion by 2028, and this growth will come from both consumer and **industrial IoT (IIoT)** applications. We can expect to see greater integration between IoT devices and other technologies, such as AI, blockchain, and edge computing.

- **Focus on security and privacy**: As the number of connected devices grows, so does the potential for security breaches and privacy violations. We can expect to see an increased focus on security and privacy, with companies investing more in secure design, encryption, and authentication protocols.

- **Standards and regulations**: As IoT continues to grow, there will be a greater need for standards and regulations to ensure interoperability and security. We can expect to see continued efforts to establish standards and regulations, both at the national and international levels.

- **Edge computing**: Edge computing, which involves processing data closer to where it is generated, is becoming increasingly important in the IoT space. We can expect to see greater adoption of edge computing in the coming years, as it enables faster processing, lower latency, and reduced data transmission costs.

- **Sustainability and energy efficiency**: IoT has the potential to help address some of the world's most pressing challenges, including sustainability and energy efficiency. We can expect to see greater emphasis on IoT applications that promote sustainability and reduce energy consumption, such as **smart buildings and cities**, **precision agriculture**, and **renewable energy monitoring**.

With those key trends explored, we have gained some great insights into the main key trends that will be impacting IoT. Now, we can look at how the future of smart businesses will be with IoT.

The future of smart businesses with IoT

Businesses will certainly progress quickly with IoT. This section will discuss key areas where businesses are expected to progress with IoT and take you through a case study with Amazon as to how this future is unfolding.

Key areas of the future of smart businesses

The future of smart businesses with IoT is promising, as more and more companies are discovering the potential benefits of this technology. With IoT, businesses can streamline their operations, improve customer experiences, and gain valuable insights into their products and services.

One area where IoT is expected to have a significant impact is in the retail industry. According to the *IoT in Retail Market Size Report, 2030* by *Grand View Research* (https://www.grandviewresearch.com/industry-analysis/internet-of-things-iot-retail-market), the market for IoT in retail, which had a value of USD42.38 billion in 2022, is projected to expand at a compound annual growth rate of 28.4% from 2023 to 2030. With IoT sensors and beacons, retailers can track customer behavior in stores and use this data to optimize store layouts and product placement. They can also use this data to offer personalized recommendations and promotions to customers based on their shopping habits.

Another area where IoT is expected to make a big impact is in the transportation industry. The IoT in transportation market, which was worth USD 83.25 billion in 2020, is forecasted to grow to USD 495.57 billion by 2030, with an expected compound annual growth rate of 19.9%, as outlined in the *IoT in Transportation Market in 2022* report by *Allied Market Research* (https://www.alliedmarketresearch.com/IoT-in-transportation-market). With IoT sensors on vehicles, companies can track their fleet in real time and optimize routes to reduce fuel consumption and improve efficiency. IoT can also be used to improve safety by providing alerts when a vehicle is being driven in an unsafe manner or when maintenance is required.

In the manufacturing industry, IoT is already being used to optimize production lines and improve efficiency. The market, with a valuation of USD202 billion in 2022, is anticipated to experience a compound annual growth rate of 24.7% from 2023 to 2032, according to *Precedence Research*'s *IoT in Manufacturing Market* report for 2022 (https://www.precedenceresearch.com/iot-in-manufacturing-market). With sensors on machines and equipment, manufacturers can monitor their operations in real time and make adjustments to improve productivity. They can also use IoT to predict when maintenance is required, reducing downtime and improving overall efficiency.

Finally, in the healthcare industry, IoT is expected to have a significant impact on patient care. Outlined by *Grand View Research*'s *Internet of Things in Healthcare Market Size Report, 2030* (https://www.grandviewresearch.com/industry-analysis/internet-of-things-iot-healthcare-market), in 2022, the market size for IoT in healthcare stood at USD252.1 billion and is projected to expand with a compound annual growth rate of 16.8% from 2023 through 2030. With IoT devices such as wearables and remote monitoring systems, healthcare providers can monitor patient health in real time and intervene when necessary. This can lead to better outcomes for patients and reduce healthcare costs in the long run.

Case study of Amazon

One real business that is leading the charge in the future of smart businesses with IoT is Amazon. Amazon has been using IoT technologies to revolutionize the e-commerce industry with its smart warehouses, delivery drones, and Alexa-enabled devices.

One of the key ways Amazon is using IoT in its warehouses is through the use of robotics. Amazon uses autonomous robots to transport items around its warehouses, which has increased efficiency and reduced errors. These robots are equipped with sensors that allow them to navigate around obstacles and avoid collisions, making them highly effective in large warehouses with complex layouts.

Amazon has also been using IoT technologies in its delivery process through the use of delivery drones. These drones are equipped with cameras, GPS sensors, and obstacle detection technology, allowing them to safely navigate to a delivery location and deliver a package with precision. By using drones for delivery, Amazon is able to reduce delivery times and increase efficiency.

Finally, Amazon has been using IoT to improve the customer experience through its Alexa-enabled devices. Alexa is Amazon's voice-controlled virtual assistant that can be used to control smart home devices, order products, and even play music. By integrating Alexa with IoT devices, Amazon is able to provide a seamless experience for its customers and make their lives easier.

Smart businesses clearly have a lot of potential moving forward to make the most out of IoT. However, there are numerous threats and challenges that also will play hand in hand with them, as we will discuss next.

Challenges in the continued big data trend

The continued trend of big data is a significant challenge for the future of IoT. The exponential increase in the number of connected devices, combined with their ability to collect and transmit large amounts of data, presents both opportunities and challenges. The sheer volume and complexity of this data have the potential to unlock valuable insights and drive innovation in fields such as healthcare, transportation, and energy. However, the challenge of effectively analyzing and utilizing this data cannot be underestimated.

One of the biggest threats associated with big data is privacy. With so much data being collected, it is essential to ensure that sensitive information is protected and data is used only for its intended purposes. This requires careful attention to data governance and security protocols, as well as robust data protection measures. Furthermore, with the increasing number of connected devices, there is a greater risk of cyberattacks, and it is essential to build security into IoT systems from the outset and continually monitor and update security measures to address new threats and vulnerabilities.

Another significant challenge associated with big data is the need for effective data management and analysis. With such a vast amount of data being generated, it can be challenging to store, organize, and analyze this data effectively. This requires advanced data analytics tools and technologies, as well as skilled professionals who can manage and analyze this data. Additionally, the need for interoperability and standardization of data formats and protocols is critical to ensure that data can be shared and analyzed across different platforms and systems.

Another potential challenge is the energy consumption associated with IoT devices and the transmission of data. As the number of connected devices continues to increase, there is a need to develop more energy-efficient devices and networks to reduce the impact on the environment.

Furthermore, the issue of data ownership and control is also a potential challenge. With so many entities involved in the collection, storage, and analysis of data, questions arise as to who owns the data and who has control over its use. Ensuring transparency and clarity around data ownership and control will be essential in building trust and maintaining the security and privacy of sensitive information.

With that, we've gained some insights into different threats and challenges that will come into play when we consider IoT and its role in big data. Now, we can look at some best practices moving forward in utilizing IoT.

IoT best practices – dos and don'ts

As IoT continues to evolve and expand, it is important to follow best practices for the dos and don'ts of IoT to ensure the security, privacy, and functionality of IoT systems. IoT holds the capability to radically transform various industries and alter our day-to-day lives, work, and interactions with our surroundings. However, as with any new technology, there are risks and challenges associated with IoT that must be addressed to maximize its benefits and minimize its negative impact. In this section, we will discuss some best practices for the dos and don'ts of IoT toward the future of IoT, including guidelines for security, privacy, testing, and standards compliance. By following these best practices, we can ensure the safe and effective deployment of IoT systems and unlock the full potential of this transformative technology.

Dos

The following are some dos as part of the best practices we need to consider with IoT:

- **Secure IoT devices**: Security is one of the most important aspects of IoT, and it is important to ensure that all IoT devices are secured against potential threats. This can include implementing strong passwords, keeping software up to date, and using encryption.

- **Protect privacy**: IoT devices often collect and transmit personal data, so it is important to protect users' privacy by implementing privacy policies, obtaining consent for data collection and use, and providing transparency around how data is being used.

- **Test thoroughly**: IoT devices and systems should be tested thoroughly to identify potential issues and vulnerabilities before deployment. This can include testing for interoperability, scalability, and security.

- **Follow industry standards**: There are a number of industry standards and best practices for IoT that can be followed to ensure the security and functionality of IoT systems. These can include standards such as the **IoT Security Foundation's (IoTSF's) Best Practice Guidelines (BPGs)** and the **Industrial Internet Consortium's (IIC's) Industrial Internet Security Framework (IISF)**.

With that, we've gained a great understanding of the dos as part of the best practices needed. Now, let's look at some of the don'ts.

Don'ts

Now, we can take a look at some of the don'ts we need to consider with IoT:

- **Neglect security**: Security should never be an afterthought when it comes to IoT. Neglecting security can leave devices and systems vulnerable to attack and compromise.

- **Collect unnecessary data**: Collecting unnecessary data may not only pose a risk to privacy but can also increase the risk of data breaches and make systems more vulnerable to attack.

- **Assume interoperability**: Not all IoT devices and systems are interoperable, and assuming interoperability can lead to compatibility issues and vulnerabilities.

- **Ignore end-of-life (EOL) considerations**: IoT devices often have a limited lifespan, and ignoring EOL considerations can lead to issues with disposal and recycling. It is important to design IoT devices with EOL considerations in mind, such as using recyclable materials and designing devices that can be easily disassembled and recycled.

By following these best practices for the dos and don'ts of IoT, we can ensure the security, privacy, and functionality of IoT systems as we move toward the future of IoT.

IoT sustainability

Sustainability is a big goal that many companies and individuals are moving toward. In this section, we will explore guidelines for being able to achieve better United Nations sustainability goals and understand how to better IoT sustainability.

Aligning IoT practices with sustainable development goals

Architecting for IoT sustainability involves designing IoT systems with a holistic approach that considers the environmental, social, and economic impacts of IoT devices. This aligns with several of the United Nations' **sustainable development goals (SDGs)**:

Figure 15.1 – IoT for SDGs

These goals include the following:

- **SDG 7**: Ensure access to affordable, reliable, sustainable, and modern energy for all. To align with this goal, IoT systems should be designed to reduce energy consumption by using low-power communication protocols and energy-efficient hardware.

- **SDG 9**: Build resilient infrastructure, promote sustainable industrialization, and foster innovation. To align with this goal, IoT systems should be designed to promote sustainable industrialization by using recyclable materials and designing devices that can be easily disassembled and recycled.

- **SDG 11**: Make cities and human settlements inclusive, safe, resilient, and sustainable. To align with this goal, IoT systems should be designed to promote sustainable urbanization by reducing energy consumption and designing for EOL considerations.

- **SDG 12**: Ensure sustainable consumption and production patterns. To align with this goal, IoT systems should be designed to promote sustainable consumption by designing devices with EOL considerations in mind and by implementing circular economy models around IoT devices.

With the preceding list, we have obtained a better understanding of the SDGs relevant to IoT. Now, we can take a look at what we can do for further IoT sustainability.

What to do for IoT sustainability?

IoT sustainability is a growing concern as the number of connected devices continues to increase. As we integrate more devices into our lives and businesses, we need to ensure that we're doing so in a way that is environmentally responsible and sustainable.

One of the main ways to promote IoT sustainability is by reducing the energy consumption of IoT devices. This can be achieved using low-power communication protocols and energy-efficient hardware. For example, using protocols such as **LoRaWAN** and **NB-IoT**, **LTE-M**, **BLE**, **BLE-LR**, and **Wi-Fi HaLow** can significantly reduce the power consumption of IoT devices compared to traditional Wi-Fi and cellular networks.

Another way to promote IoT sustainability is by designing devices with EOL considerations in mind. This includes using recyclable materials and designing devices that can be easily disassembled and recycled. This not only reduces the environmental impact of IoT devices but can also create new opportunities for businesses to develop circular economies around IoT devices.

New wireless technologies, coupled with the development of low-cost IoT chipsets, are significantly making an impact as well. These advancements are enabling a vast expansion in the deployment of IoT devices, as lower costs and improved wireless capabilities make them more accessible and versatile. This proliferation is particularly beneficial for environmental monitoring, energy management, and resource conservation. For instance, IoT devices can now more effectively monitor environmental conditions, optimize energy use in smart buildings, and streamline waste management, all of which contribute to reduced carbon footprints and enhanced resource efficiency. The integration of these technologies is not only making IoT devices more affordable and efficient but also driving innovation toward a more sustainable and technologically advanced society.

In addition to reducing energy consumption and designing for EOL considerations, IoT sustainability also involves addressing issues such as data privacy and security. As IoT devices collect and transmit sensitive data, it's important to implement strong security measures to protect that data from being compromised. This includes using encryption, implementing secure communication protocols, and regularly updating device firmware to address any known vulnerabilities.

To effectively promote IoT sustainability, it's essential to adopt a comprehensive approach that considers the environmental, social, and economic effects of IoT devices. By considering the entire life cycle of IoT devices and designing for sustainability, we can ensure that IoT continues to benefit society while minimizing its impact on the environment.

With that, we have taken a good look at what sustainability means for IoT, including how it stands with SDGs. We can now take a look at our final practical for the book: creating an IoT-integrated Amazon Bedrock **Retrieval Augmented Generation** (**RAG**) web application.

Practical – Creating an IoT-integrated Amazon Bedrock RAG web application

The convergence of IoT and advanced data processing opens a realm of possibilities for innovation. In this practical exercise, we explore how to deploy a RAG model on an IoT device, specifically a Raspberry Pi, using Flask as our web server framework. By setting up a Flask server on a Raspberry Pi, we demonstrate a lightweight yet powerful approach to integrating AI capabilities into IoT devices. This exercise provides a hands-on experience in deploying AI models to edge devices, highlighting the potential of IoT systems to not only collect data but to host services that can interpret and provide intelligence.

RAG combines the retrieval of informational documents with the generation of responses, enabling the system to provide informative, contextually relevant answers to user queries. We will be accomplishing this by using one of the newer emerging technologies for generative AI: **Amazon Bedrock**. Amazon Bedrock is a service that offers advanced AI tools to businesses, enabling them to create interactive, intelligent applications. One of these tools is called **Claude**, a smart program that can understand and generate human-like text. Claude can read through large documents and help with tasks such as answering customer questions, managing emails, or even coding. It's designed to be very safe and reliable, aiming to communicate effectively and without causing any misunderstandings or issues. This makes Claude an efficient assistant in various fields, including customer service, office administration, and legal work.

The goal is straightforward: to empower your IoT device with the ability to process queries and return informed responses, showcasing the integration of **machine learning** (**ML**) models within an IoT architecture. This serves as a practical step into the future of IoT, where devices are not mere data collectors but knowledge providers.

Setup for the working directory

We will start out by making sure that we have the right dependencies for the project:

1. If you have not yet done so, boot up your Raspberry Pi.

2. Create a new directory on your Raspberry Pi for where you want your project files to be located.

3. Create a `requirements.txt` file. Inside it, put the following code:

```
Flask
numpy
boto3
langchain
```

4. Run the following command:

```
$ pip install -r requirements.txt
```

After executing this command, you should see the dependencies installed accordingly.

With that, we are set up for development! Now, we will begin creating the code for the HTML landing page.

Coding up the HTML landing page

The first component of the coding starts with setting up the HTML landing page for us to be able to submit queries:

1. We first need to create the HTML code that will be used for the landing page. Create a `Templates` folder in the working directory.

2. Change directory into `Templates` and create a file named `query_form.html`.

3. Insert the following code into the file:

```html
<!DOCTYPE html>
<html lang="en">
<head>
    <meta charset="UTF-8">
    <title>Query Form</title>
</head>
<body>
    <form action="/query" method="post">
        <input type="text" name="query" placeholder="Enter your
query here" required>
        <input type="submit" value="Submit">
    </form>
</body>
</html>
```

The code defines a simple web page with a form intended for user interaction. The language is set to English. The form comprises a single text input field where users can type a query. The text field is labeled **Enter your query here**, which serves as a placeholder inside the box, and it is a required field, meaning the form cannot be submitted without filling it out. There is also a submit button labeled **Submit**. When the form is submitted, it sends a POST request to the `/query` URL, which is typically handled by a server-side script to process the query. The form's functionality is often used for search operations or data retrieval requests on a website.

With that, we have been able to create the landing page for the site. We can now move on to creating the RAG component of the site.

Coding up the RAG capability of the site

We now want to create a RAG capability. As part of this, we will look at defining the appropriate routes for the Flask app while powering the site with the RAG capability:

1. Create a new file called `app.py`. This will be where we put our main code.

2. Import the dependencies needed as follows:

```
import boto3
import json
import os
import sys
import numpy as np
from urllib.request import urlretrieve
import ssl
from langchain.text_splitter import CharacterTextSplitter,
RecursiveCharacterTextSplitter
from langchain.document_loaders import PyPDFLoader,
PyPDFDirectoryLoader
from langchain.embeddings import BedrockEmbeddings
from langchain.llms.bedrock import Bedrock
from langchain.chains.question_answering import load_qa_chain
from langchain.vectorstores import FAISS
from langchain.indexes import VectorstoreIndexCreator
from langchain.indexes.vectorstore import
VectorStoreIndexWrapper
```

The following are descriptions of what each dependency does:

- `boto3`: This is the AWS SDK for Python. It allows Python developers to write software that makes use of services such as **Amazon Simple Storage Service** (**Amazon S3**) and **Amazon Elastic Compute Cloud** (**Amazon EC2**). In the context of your application, it's used to interact with the AWS services, possibly for storing data or utilizing AWS AI/ML services.

- `os`: The os module, part of the standard library, offers a user-friendly method to perform operating system-specific tasks such as file reading/writing, path management, and environment variable access across different systems.

- `sys`: The sys module, also included in the standard library, allows users to access certain variables that the Python interpreter uses or maintains, as well as functions that have a significant interaction with the interpreter. This module is commonly utilized for adjusting the Python runtime environment.

- `numpy`: numpy, which stands for **Numerical Python**, is a Python library designed to enhance the language by adding support for extensive, multi-dimensional arrays and matrices. Additionally, it provides a wide range of advanced mathematical functions to work with these arrays.

- `urllib.request`: This module is used to open and read URLs. `urlretrieve` is a function within this module that is used to download a file from a remote URL to a local file path.

- `ssl`: The `ssl` module offers tools for implementing **Transport Layer Security (TLS)** encryption and verifying the identities of peers in network connections, applicable to both client and server sides. It's useful for safeguarding communication between a client and a server.

- `langchain.text_splitter`: `CharacterTextSplitter` and `RecursiveCharacterTextSplitter` are classes within the `langchain` package used for splitting text into manageable pieces for further processing or analysis.

- `langchain.document_loaders`: This module contains utilities for loading and reading documents. The `PyPDFLoader` and `PyPDFDirectoryLoader` are classes used to load PDF files or directories containing PDF files into Python objects for manipulation or data extraction.

- `langchain.embeddings`: This module deals with generating embeddings for text. `BedrockEmbeddings` is a class that interacts with the Bedrock API to create numerical representations of text that capture semantic meaning.

- `langchain.llms.bedrock`: This module is a part of the `langchain` library that likely interfaces with the Bedrock language learning models. The `Bedrock` class is used to interact with a specific language model provided by Bedrock.

- `langchain.chains.question_answering`: This is a module within `langchain` dedicated to **question-answering (QA)** functionality. `load_qa_chain` is a function or method for loading a QA process chain, possibly setting up a series of steps for processing and answering questions.

- `langchain.vectorstores`: This module handles the storage and retrieval of vectors, which are the result of converting text into numerical embeddings. **Facebook AI Similarity Search (FAISS)** is a class or interface for working with the `FAISS` library, which is a library for efficient similarity search and clustering of dense vectors.

- `langchain.indexes`: These classes (`VectorstoreIndexCreator` and `VectorStoreIndexWrapper`) are for the indexing of vectors for efficient retrieval during operations such as similarity search or document retrieval in the context of the RAG system. Indexing is essential for scaling up to large datasets where quick retrieval is necessary.

3. We can then initialize the Flask application with the following line of code:

```
app = Flask(__name__)
```

4.   We can then initialize the Amazon Bedrock client through the following code. Replace the values for `aws_access_key_id` and `aws_secret_access_key` with your account's values:

```
print("Initializing Boto3 client...")
bedrock_runtime = boto3.client(
    service_name='bedrock-runtime',
    aws_access_key_id= '<YOUR_AWS_ACCESS_KEY_ID_HERE>',
    aws_secret_access_key= '<YOUR_AWS_SECRET_ACCESS_KEY_HERE>',
    region_name='us-west-2'
)
print("Boto3 client has been initialized.")
```

5.   We can then move ahead and initialize the embeddings and language model:

```
llm = Bedrock(model_id="anthropic.claude-v2", client=bedrock_
runtime, model_kwargs={'max_tokens_to_sample':200})
bedrock_embeddings = BedrockEmbeddings(model_id="amazon.titan-
embed-text-v1", client=bedrock_runtime)
```

With this, we create an instance of a **large language model** (**LLM**) using Anthropic's `claude-v2` model. This model is designed for tasks that require an understanding of human language, such as conversation, content generation, reasoning, and coding. The `max_tokens_to_sample` parameter is configuring the model to generate responses with a maximum length; in this case, `200` tokens.

We then create an instance for generating text embeddings using Amazon's `titan-embed-text-v1` model. Text embeddings are vectorized representations of text that can be used for a variety of **natural language processing** (**NLP**) tasks, such as similarity search or classification.

6.   We then load and preprocess the documents:

```
print("Preprocessing your files...")
ssl._create_default_https_context = ssl._create_unverified_
context
os.makedirs("data", exist_ok=True)
files = [
"https://www.cisa.gov/sites/default/files/publications/Federal_
Government_Cybersecurity_Incident_and_Vulnerability_Response_
Playbooks_508C.pdf",
"https://www.cisa.gov/sites/default/files/2023-10/
StopRansomware-Guide-508C-v3_1.pdf",
]

for file in files:
    file_path = os.path.join("data", url.rpartition("/")[2])
    urlretrieve(url, file_path)
print("Files preprocessed.")
```

We download files from the internet using HTTPS. We have the code print a message indicating the start of the download process. Then, it modifies the SSL context to create an unverified context, which means it will not verify SSL certificates. This is typically not recommended due to security concerns but may be necessary in certain environments where the SSL certificate cannot be verified. The script then ensures that a directory named data exists, creating it if it does not. After that, it defines a list of file URLs. Finally, we have the code print a message stating that the files have been downloaded.

7. We then need to perform embedding on the files:

```
loader = PyPDFDirectoryLoader("./data/")
documents = loader.load()
text_splitter = RecursiveCharacterTextSplitter(chunk_size=1000,
chunk_overlap=100)
text_to_process = text_splitter.split_documents(documents)
vectorstore_faiss = FAISS.from_documents(text_to_process,
bedrock_embeddings)
```

We then process the PDF documents for text analysis. It begins by establishing a loader that targets a directory where PDFs are stored and then loads these documents into a format suitable for analysis. The documents are then segmented into smaller sections of text, a common practice in NLP to make handling large documents more efficient. Finally, the segments are indexed using an advanced library designed for fast retrieval, setting the stage for sophisticated operations such as searching for information within the documents based on query inputs. This setup is foundational for systems that aim to extract and utilize knowledge from extensive textual data efficiently.

8. We then start initializing the landing page of the Flask app:

```
@app.route('/', methods=['GET'])
def home():
    return render_template('query_form.html')
```

The @app.route decorator registers the URL path (/, the root of the website) with the home function, which is defined immediately below it. When a user navigates to the root URL of the web application using a web browser (which sends a GET request), the home function will be invoked. This function responds by rendering and returning the query_form.html HTML template we created.

9. We now define a route to handle the queries that we will make:

```
@app.route('/', methods=['GET'])
def home():
    return render_template('query_form.html')
```

We define an endpoint in a Flask web application that responds to POST requests at the /query URL path. When this endpoint is hit, typically by a user submitting a form on a web page, it attempts to process the input named query. This input is then transformed into an embedding—a numerical representation used for ML tasks—by the FAISS library, which is optimized for efficient similarity search.

The application then performs a search to find documents that are like the query embedding. The matched documents are collated into a response object, which is returned as JSON to the requester. If an error occurs during this process, it catches the exception and returns an error message, also in JSON format, with an appropriate HTTP status code. This setup allows for the creation of a web-based interface where users can search through indexed documents by submitting queries and receiving relevant document content as a response.

10. Finally, we set up the host and port for the Flask application to run on when it is started:

```
if __name__ == '__main__':
    app.run(host='0.0.0.0', port=5000)
```

With this, you've coded up the appropriate RAG capability that is needed for the site. Now, we can move ahead and test that the application is working without any issues.

Testing the application

We can now test our application. As part of this, we will need to spin up the Flask app and access it from our computer:

1. On your Raspberry Pi terminal, run the following command on the working directory you have created:

```
$ python app.py
```

This may take a few minutes to properly spin up, as the downloading and embedding process takes a while. You then should see that your Flask application is running.

2. Take note of the IP address of your Raspberry Pi.

3. Into your web browser on your computer, type the following link: http://<raspberry_pi_ip>:5000.

4. You should now be able to see a textbox being rendered on the local site. You can then start to try to query, by typing in queries such as the following: Could you tell me more about what to do if I found out that I got a Ransomware?

You will then see that the appropriate section of the document is returned.

With that, you've managed to create your first RAG web application! This is a great step forward to exploring one of the most in-demand use cases of **generative AI (GenAI)** and is set to play a big role in the future of IoT in building smarter devices.

To dive deeper into the integration of IoT and AI technologies, you can build upon the IoT-integrated RAG web app project and expand your knowledge by exploring the following areas:

- **Voice recognition and text to speech (TTS)**: Add a voice recognition module and a TTS module to the existing project. This way, users can interact with the RAG application using spoken language, and the assistant can provide spoken responses, creating a more natural and intuitive user experience.

- **Custom Amazon Bedrock foundational models**: Train a custom Amazon Bedrock model to answer domain-specific questions and provide expert insights relevant to your industry or application. This could include creating a model for answering questions about IoT security, energy efficiency, or specific IoT use cases. For this, you will have to explore more with the Amazon Bedrock documentation.

This practical project demonstrates how IoT and AI can work together to provide results based on specific bodies of knowledge. It shows the potential of integrating IoT devices with advanced AI capabilities such as Amazon Bedrock's foundational models in the context of smart businesses and future IoT applications. By adjusting the prompt variable, you can explore various aspects of IoT, including challenges, best practices, and sustainability. Additionally, you can use the project as a starting point for creating more advanced IoT solutions that integrate AI services such as Amazon Bedrock or ChatGPT to provide valuable information and services to users.

Summary

As we come to the end of this book, it's important to look ahead of IoT and understand its potential for innovation and growth. In this final chapter, we have explored the next 5 years of IoT, the future of smart businesses with IoT, challenges associated with big data, and best practices for implementing and managing IoT devices.

The chapter highlights the increasing importance of IoT in businesses and industries, offering numerous opportunities for optimization, automation, and enhanced decision-making. However, as we continue to generate large amounts of data from IoT devices, there are potential threats to privacy and security, emphasizing the need for proper data management practices. Moreover, this chapter emphasizes the dos and don'ts of IoT, promoting the need for proper security measures, device management, and interoperability between IoT devices. Additionally, the chapter emphasizes the importance of sustainability in IoT, promoting the use of renewable energy sources and eco-friendly practices.

Overall, this book has provided a comprehensive introduction to IoT, covering the basics of IoT architecture, devices, communication protocols, and security measures. It has also explored the applications of IoT in various industries, such as healthcare, agriculture, and smart cities, offering insights into the potential of IoT for innovation and growth. As we look ahead to IoT, it's essential to continue learning and adapting to the ever-changing landscape of IoT. By implementing best practices, promoting sustainability, and maintaining proper security measures, we can unlock the full potential of IoT and build a more connected and efficient world.

Further reading

For more information about what was covered in this chapter, please refer to the following links:

- Learn more about best security practices for building with AWS for IoT architectures: `https://pages.awscloud.com/rs/112-TZM-766/images/IoT_Security_Best_Practices_Guide_design_v3.1.pdf`

- Learn more about the significance of big data analytics for IoT in industrial governance and sustainability: `https://www.sciencedirect.com/science/article/pii/S2666603020300294`

- Leverage Amazon Bedrock in multiple ways through the official workshops from AWS: `https://workshops.aws/categories/Amazon%20Bedrock`

- Understand more about how to use Amazon Bedrock through the official AWS documentation: `https://docs.aws.amazon.com/bedrock/`

- Look at a framework of evaluating IoT deloyments against the UN sustainable development goals: `https://widgets.weforum.org/iot4d/index.html`

Index

Other Books You May Enjoy

If you enjoyed this book, you may be interested in these other books by Packt:

Developing IoT Projects with ESP32

Vedat Ozan Oner

ISBN: 978-1-80323-768-8

- Explore ESP32 with IDE and debugging tools for effective IoT creation
- Drive GPIO, I2C, multimedia, and storage for seamless integration of external devices
- Utilize handy IoT libraries to enhance your ESP32 projects
- Manage WiFi like a pro with STA & AP modes, provisioning, and ESP Rainmaker framework features
- Ensure robust IoT security with secure boot and OTA firmware updates
- Harness AWS IoT for data handling and achieve stunning visualization using Grafana
- Enhance your projects with voice capabilities using ESP AFE and Speech Recognition
- Innovate with tinyML on ESP32-S3 and the Edge Impulse platform

Architectural Patterns and Techniques for Developing IoT Solutions

Jasbir Singh Dhaliwal

ISBN: 978-1-80324-549-2

- Get to grips with the essentials of different architectural patterns and anti-patterns
- Discover the underlying commonalities in diverse IoT applications
- Combine patterns from physical and virtual realms to develop innovative applications
- Choose the right set of sensors and actuators for your solution
- Explore analytics-related tools and techniques such as TinyML and sensor fusion
- Overcome the challenges faced in securing IoT systems
- Leverage use cases based on edge computing and emerging technologies such as 3D printing, 5G, generative AI, and LLMs

Packt is searching for authors like you

If you're interested in becoming an author for Packt, please visit `authors.packtpub.com` and apply today. We have worked with thousands of developers and tech professionals, just like you, to help them share their insight with the global tech community. You can make a general application, apply for a specific hot topic that we are recruiting an author for, or submit your own idea.

Share Your Thoughts

Now you've finished *Internet of Things from Scratch*, we'd love to hear your thoughts! Scan the QR code below to go straight to the Amazon review page for this book and share your feedback or leave a review on the site that you purchased it from.

`https://packt.link/r/1837638543`

Your review is important to us and the tech community and will help us make sure we're delivering excellent quality content.

Download a free PDF copy of this book

Thanks for purchasing this book!

Do you like to read on the go but are unable to carry your print books everywhere?

Is your eBook purchase not compatible with the device of your choice?

Don't worry, now with every Packt book you get a DRM-free PDF version of that book at no cost.

Read anywhere, any place, on any device. Search, copy, and paste code from your favorite technical books directly into your application.

The perks don't stop there, you can get exclusive access to discounts, newsletters, and great free content in your inbox daily

Follow these simple steps to get the benefits:

1. Scan the QR code or visit the link below

https://packt.link/free-ebook/9781837638543

2. Submit your proof of purchase
3. That's it! We'll send your free PDF and other benefits to your email directly

www.ingramcontent.com/pod-product-compliance
Lightning Source LLC
Chambersburg PA
CBHW060647060326
40690CB00020B/4549